MARIO LANZA
An American
Tragedy

by

Armando Cesari

Discography by Armando Cesari with Bill Park

Compact disc compiled and edited by Armando Cesari,
and mastered by José Feghali, Vince Di Placido,
and Derek McGovern.

Notes on the CD by Derek McGovern

Foreword by Lindsay Perigo
Preface by Plácido Domingo

GREAT VOICES

7

BASKERVILLE
PUBLISHERS

Copyright 2004 by Armando Cesari

Baskerville Publishers, Inc.
2455 Halloran
Fort Worth, Texas 76107

Library of Congress Cataloging-in-Publication Data

Cesari, Armando, 1941-
  Mario Lanza : an American tragedy / by Armando Cesari ;
discography by
Armando Cesari with Bill Park.— 1st American hardcover ed.
      p. cm. — (Great voices ; 7)
Includes discography (p.   ).
  ISBN 1-880909-66-9 (alk. paper)
  1. Lanza, Mario, 1921-1959. 2. Tenors (Singers)—United
States—Biography. I. Title. II. Series.

ML420.L24C48 2004
782.1'092—dc22

                                  2003019092

Manufactured in the United States of America
Second Printing, 2008

ACKNOWLEDGEMENTS

THIS BOOK has had an unusually long gestation. The seed was planted in 1975 by a newly acquired friend, Lindsay Perigo, who at the time was both young and impressionable enough to believe that I was equal to the challenge of writing a biography of Mario Lanza. 28 years of research and countless interviews later, I trust that Lindsay's faith in me has finally been rewarded.

"Why Mario Lanza?" one may reasonably ask. Quite simply because I have always been enthralled by great voices—one of the important reasons I studied with A.C. Bartleman, a baritone of some renown who had sung with the legendary Melba. My studies with Bartleman only confirmed what I had always known instinctively: that Mario Lanza was the possessor of a voice and technique far greater than was commonly acknowledged at the time.

My interest in Lanza dates back many years. In 1962 I had exchanged correspondence with the tenor's mother, Maria Lanza Cocozza, a remarkable woman by all accounts, though I never met her. "Writing about my son makes me feel as though he is still around," she revealed to me. "Yes, he [lives through] his records and movies but, my, how I miss my boy. My heart aches when I think of how short a life he had. My only consolation is that I have his four children and in each one I see a little of my lovely boy."

In 1972 I visited Lanza's father, Antonio Cocozza, at his Los Angeles home. Antonio was a gentle, affable man who patiently answered my questions and related many valuable anecdotes on the life and career of his son.

Four years later, prompted by Lindsay Perigo's exhortation that Lanza's life was indeed a story worth telling, I began my research in earnest. Numerous trips to the United States, Italy, and England followed, and I soon realized the enormity of the task I had set myself. At the same time, I was becoming increasingly aware that few publishers were interested in a book that dealt with the singer's life in an objective and musical fashion. Again and again I was told: "There's no market for *that* kind of biography."

Baskerville Publishers were of a different mind. In this company I was fortunate enough to find two gifted, musical individuals who accepted my manuscript with gratifying alacrity. To the owner of the company, Ron Moore—accomplished pianist, composer and opera lover, and to Senior Editor, Jeff Putnam—distinguished baritone and novelist—I offer my heartfelt thanks for their support and integrity.

Of course in a project as lengthy as this there are many people who have contributed to its development, and to whom I shall always feel extremely grateful. If I have accidentally omitted any names, I offer my sincere apologies.

First and foremost I am indebted to Derek McGovern for his invaluable assistance and useful suggestions regarding various aspects of the manuscript. Derek's support and unfailing enthusiasm for the project has never wavered. He believed in it from the start and for that alone I am eternally grateful to him.

I must also thank Judith Cesari for typing the initial manuscript. The task for the following drafts was then taken up by Kaye Marion Colombo, to whom I also extend my heartfelt thanks. Considerable work in printing various chapters of the manuscript was also undertaken by my daughter Dee. Thank you, my darling.

I am also indebted to the late Colleen Lanza, who was immensely helpful in putting at my disposal her father's photographs, clippings, letters and documents, as well as supplying many of the recordings that were used for the enclosed CD. I also thank Peter Cesari and Roberto Scandurra for their initial work on this disc, and José Feghali, Vince Di Placido, and Derek McGovern for their substantial efforts in creating the CD.

My sincere thanks go to Clyde Smith and Michael Panico for the RCA discography; the late George Stoll for the MGM recordings; the late Ray Heindorf for the *Serenade* recordings; Damon Lanza and Bob Dolfi for the Radio Program Selections and for the use of some of their photographs and selected material; Elsie Sword, the late Pauline Franklin, and the late Mildred Fisher for supplying many valuable articles, documents clippings and photographs; John Goldsmith and Amanda Seaborne for restoring some of the photographs and John and Robert Bogotto for solving countless computer problems. Lastly I would like to thank my darling Carmel, who has not only supported and believed in me throughout this project, but for the last 18 months has had to endure a lounge room filled with wall-to-wall documents, photos and sundry other material.

Among those interviewed, and who are listed below in alphabetical order, I must single out the late Barry Nelson, whose outstanding contribution was invaluable in understanding the human side of Lanza. Another precious testimony was provided by the late Samuel Steinman, whose patient and informative recollections have contributed significantly to this biography.

Acknowledgements: Licia Albanese, Robert Allman, Carlo Bergonzi, Curtis Bernhardt, Henry Blanke, Richard Bonynge, Umberto Borsò, Constantine Callinicos, José Carreras, Antonio Cocozza, Stefano Colombo, Rossella Como, Fiorenza Cossotto, Costa Di Angelo, Giuseppe di Stefano, Plácido Domingo, Vincent Edwards, Pablo Elvira, Otello Fava, Antonio Fabianelli, Franco Ferrara, Giulio Ferrari, Nicola Filacuridi, Zsa Zsa Gabor, Pat Gordon, Vivian Gordon, Stewart Granger, Ivan Goff, Kathryn Grayson, John Green, Ray Heindorf, Rita Hunter, Luigi Infantino, José Iturbi, Dorothy Kirsten, Marc Lanza, George London, Eddy Lovaglio, Antonio Moretti Pananti, Ann Myers, Edmond O'Brien, Joe Pasternak, Dorothy Pasternak, Luciano Pavarotti, Lindsay Perigo, Afro Poli, Cavill Armstrong Poli, Vincent Price, Edmund Purdom, Bill Quirk, Renato Rascel, Judith Raskin, Ben Roberts, Terry Robinson, Roy Rowland, Mario Salinelli, Giuditta Saltarini, Carlo Savina, Roberto Scandurra, Alessandro Scardovi, Maurizio Scardovi, John Shaw, Ray Sinatra, Andrew Solt, Jerry Steinberg, Ron Stevens, George Stoll, Giancarlo Stopponi, Dr. Giuseppe Stradone, Ferruccio Tagliavini, Al Teitelbaum, Vito Torelli, Ivo Vinco, Riccardo Vitale, Giovanni Viglione, Sam Weiler, Keenan Wynn, Sharly Wynn, Franco Zauli.

FOREWORD

It gives me enormous gratification to be writing a foreword to this book, "Mario Lanza: An American Tragedy," if for no other reason than that it was *I* who pestered its author into writing it, way back in the mid-seventies. Nearly thirty years later, lo!—it has come to pass! A classic case of, "better late than never."

The perception of Mario Lanza has changed significantly during that period, in such a way as to make the late arrival of this biography in actual fact timely!

At the time of Armando's and my first meeting, Lanza's admirers still had to contend with the sneering dismissiveness of those who considered themselves arbiters of good taste. These latter seized on this or that rough edge, mis-pitch or misjudgment, and claimed vindication for their view that the name "Mario Lanza" did not belong in the hallowed precincts of Great Singers, that he was a second-rate Hollywood singer who owed his popularity to the ignorance of the masses who adored him.

Now, as tenor Richard Leech has proclaimed publicly, it's "cool" to like Lanza again.

One reason for this is that precisely such respectable figures as Mr. Leech—and the biggest possible names such as Pavarotti, Domingo and Carreras—have made no bones about the fact that it was Mario Lanza who inspired *them* to become opera singers. Maestro Domingo has graciously written the Preface to this very book! Maestro Carreras has recorded and toured with "A Tribute to Mario Lanza." And so it goes. What can the critics say to *that*?

A second reason for Lanza's posthumous rehabilitation is that, in an era awash in "Super-Stars" it has dawned on serious observers that there's no necessary *dis*connection between greatness and popularity; that being popular doesn't automatically disqualify one from greatness. There were legitimate *reasons* for Mario's popularity—his looks, his charisma, his beguiling combination of intelligence with naiveté—that were part of a package that spelled "greatness" and could not be dismissed with a mere sneer.

But the most obvious and inescapable reason for the upgrading of Lanza's status is, of course, the voice. All that's necessary to know that one is in the presence of greatness is to listen to it! The greatest voice ever bestowed on a human being, said his colleague George London. The voice, and—I would add—the way he used it. Yes, there were rough edges from time to time. But in a contest between a note-perfect performance devoid of feeling and a note-*im*perfect performance that brings you to the edge of your seat with pulse racing, spine tingling and hair standing on end, the latter is always going to win out. It is not *just* his godly voice that has rekindled the Lanza flame; it is also the super-human *passion* with which he delivered it. In Mario's own words, "I sing each word as though it were my last on earth."

Armando Cesari's biography is a fitting tribute to a beautiful voice and a beautiful soul. It explains the tragedies that stilled his talent far too prematurely. It is meticulously researched and scrupulously fair. I salute its author and its publishers on its timely release.

Lindsay Perigo
Wellington
New Zealand
June, 2003

NOTES ON THE COMPACT DISK
THE STUFF OF LEGEND

In October 1959 the English critic Leslie Mallory argued that, "From any musical standpoint, Mario Lanza never sang—he shouted. Everything was fortissimo, and so was his life." Gleefully predicting that, "The music world will little note nor long remember Mario Lanza's contribution to vocal splendor," Mallory was by no means alone in his scorn.

And yet the tenor had not always been so vilified. A decade before Mallory's pronouncement, Lanza's rendition of *Che gelida manina* was voted Operatic Recording of the Year by the National Record Critics Association—a remarkable honor for a man with only four appearances in opera to his name. Meanwhile his concerts and recitals were receiving near-unanimous acclaim. By 1952 even the conservative *Gramophone* Magazine had capitulated, acknowledging that the tenor was indeed "an artist worthy of serious consideration."

Lanza's subsequent fall from critical grace was as swift as it was undeserved. Denounced as *vulgar* because of his commercial success, and his every stylistic lapse now mercilessly dissected, the embattled tenor took the criticisms painfully to heart. Had he been a less sensitive individual, he might have found comfort in the words of Giuseppe Verdi, who was himself no stranger to adversity. Ignore the critics, Verdi told his admirers. "The day of justice will come, and it is a great pleasure for the artist—a supreme pleasure—to be able to say: 'Imbeciles, you were wrong!'"

For Mario Lanza that day is fast approaching.

Helping the tenor's cause is the enclosed CD, which should severely undermine the efforts of those who still scoff at this "movie singer." Comprising live performances and other rarities recorded between 1945 and 1958, this collection offers proof not only of

Lanza's vocal prowess and versatility, but also ample evidence that the tenor was not the stylistic ruffian Mr. Mallory and his followers would have us believe. Indeed, the only *shouting* to be found here is that of the singer's adoring public.

The CD begins with three selections from the radio program *Great Moments in Music*. Just 24 when he began his four-month stint as a temporary replacement for Metropolitan star Jan Peerce, the tenor sounds surprisingly assured for a man who had not yet mastered his technique. The natural beauty of the voice is unmistakable, and Lanza's singing abounds in the warmth and vitality that would later become his trademarks. Above all these recordings illustrate the tenor's *instinctive* gifts, qualities that the critic Claudia Cassidy would soon identify in his singing. "Though a multitude of fine points evade him," she wrote in 1947, "[Lanza] knows the accent that makes a lyric line reach its audience, and he knows why opera is music drama."

These attributes are immediately apparent in the first selection, the demanding *Già nella notte densa* from Act I of Verdi's *Otello*. Marred by the appalling singing of soprano Jean Tennyson, the duet conjures up images of Otello singing with his bride's *grandmother*, rather than the youthful Desdemona that Verdi had envisioned. While some listeners will be tempted to skip to the next track to avoid Miss Tennyson, the duet is worth staying with for the commitment and musicality of Lanza's delivery. He pushes a little at times—and there are other wayward moments here and there—but overall this is an astonishing performance from a mere stripling. Ten years later Lanza would return to *Otello*, this time with a soprano worthy of his talent. In the meantime the hapless Miss Tennyson must have provided the tenor with ample fodder for indulging in his well-known gift of mimicry.

Irving Berlin's *A Pretty Girl Is Like A Melody* follows. One of the earliest examples of Lanza's versatility, this attractive ditty is a foretaste of romantic offerings to come. Singing with a good deal of lyric bloom to his voice, the tenor is clearly enjoying himself.

Golden Days from Romberg's *The Student Prince* completes the trio of early radio performances. Sung here in its original form as a duet between tenor and baritone, *Golden Days* features Lanza's friend and occasional teacher, the Metropolitan singer Robert Weede. Although the tenor sounds slightly tentative, his voice blends beautifully with that of the impressive baritone. Six years later Lanza would return to Romberg's score, recording memorable renditions of *Golden Days* and other songs for the film version of *The Student Prince*.

Although only 16 months separate the previous tracks from the 1947 Hollywood Bowl concert that follows, the improvement in Lanza's vocal production and musicianship is remarkable. Under the guidance of the celebrated Enrico Rosati, the tenor had acquired a solid technique, enabling him to support the voice correctly and sing with greater freedom, an improved sense of line and outstanding breath control.

The five selections here represent most of Lanza's contribution to the concert, which also featured the tenor's regular singing partner, soprano Frances Yeend, and orchestral solos under the baton of conductor Eugene Ormandy. This was the event that introduced the 26-year-old tenor to Louis B. Mayer, and one can readily imagine the impact of Lanza's singing on the MGM mogul. Displaying a ravishing tone of pure legato, the tenor is in magnificent form, switching seamlessly between *spinto* and lyric repertoire, and singing two splendid high Cs in the process.

Both the *Improvviso* from *Andrea Chénier* and *E lucevan le stelle* from *Tosca* reveal elements of the complete identification Lanza would soon achieve in the recording studio with these arias. The opening phrases of the *Tosca* aria are particularly affecting, with Lanza imbuing the words with a poignancy that underscores his respect for the composer's wishes. "What a Chénier and Cavaradossi he would have been!" enthused the critic James Miller 33 years later, adding that for all the talk of Lanza's unfulfilled potential, the tenor "could scarcely *get* any better" than he does here.

Outstanding are the duets with Frances Yeend that follow. The difficult *Parigi, O cara* from *La traviata* comes first, and offers immediate proof of Lanza's newly acquired technical expertise. As Armando Cesari rightly observes, the tenor's controlled sense of line and impressive use of *mezza voce* and *diminuendo* are a revelation here, especially in a singer so young and more dramatically inclined. The encore *O soave fanciulla* from *La Bohème* is equally well sung, with Lanza displaying considerably more finesse than on his somewhat graceless soundtrack recording of eight years later.

But for many listeners, the highlight of the concert will be the preceding track – *Vogliatemi bene* from *Madama Butterfly* – a performance that underscores the very qualities for which the tenor would soon become famous. Magnificently sung, Lanza's rendition here provides a tantalizing hint of how he must have sounded in his acclaimed role of Pinkerton just eight months later. Dreamily caressing the one moment ("*Guarda dorme ogni cosa...*"), as his voice floats off into the night, and exultant the next, the tenor's ardor is irresistible. Lanza has "a crescendo to set susceptible folks shouting," Claudia Cassidy had written a month before, and here that assessment is equally true. The climax, when it finally happens, is wonderfully realized, with both singers ending on a sustained and thrilling high C.

Three selections from Lanza's 1948 Toronto concert follow. From a stylistic standpoint, these recordings rank among the tenor's finest performances, with some hauntingly beautiful touches in the *Lamento di Federico*, and a restrained but moving *Vesti la giubba*, which is all the more poignant for Lanza's eschewal of histrionics. His singing is controlled and musical, and it is fascinating to hear Lanza performing arias that would later become closely associated with him. He forgets the words in the first stanza of *La donna è mobile*, but redeems himself with a considerably more stylish rendition of the aria than his overblown commercial version. His memory also falters momentarily on the *Lamento*, a lapse that he skillfully conceals. Modulating his coloring effortlessly from the lyric demands of the *Lamento* to the more dramatic requirements of *Vesti la giubba*, Lanza also copes impressively with conductor Paul Scherman's slow tempo on the latter, displaying excellent breath control on the long phrases of the aria.

Slow tempi again feature on the next two selections from Lanza's 1948 Hollywood Bowl appearance. Bizet's *Agnus Dei* and Puccini's *Nessun dorma* are thrillingly rendered, with the tenor's upper register on full display in the latter as he soars to a spectacular high B natural on the final "*Vincerò!*" Transcending the poor sound quality as effortlessly as he outshines Miklos Rosza's indifferent conducting, Lanza's rendition of *Nessun dorma* surpasses his more familiar soundtrack recording.

Next is the tenor's third and final appearance at the Hollywood Bowl on August 15, 1949. Together with soprano Mary Jane Smith, Lanza sings the duet *È il sol dell'anima* from *Rigoletto*, followed by the *Addio, addio*. I say *duet* with some hesitation here, for Miss Smith's contribution is negligible. But with Lanza in such exceptional form, I doubt that anyone will care. Singing with great sensitivity and beauty of tone in the duet, he makes a superb Duke. The *Addio, addio* that follows is a vocal *tour de force*, with Lanza ending on an exciting (albeit slightly off-key) high D flat that all but drowns out the unfortunate Miss Smith.

Three home recordings from 1952 are next, and these are arguably the most fascinating items on the entire disc. Unrestrained by the meddling of sound engineers, mediocre conductors and other irritations, the tenor is vividly captured as he rehearses two arias and a song. Peter Herman Adler once observed that Lanza possessed a voice seemingly "without limitation," and these recordings do nothing to discourage that assessment.

Un tal gioco from *Pagliacci* comes first, and here the tenor's performance is, if anything, more operatic and assured than on his memorable radio show recording of the same year. Displaying the full power of his voice to devastating effect, the sudden fury he unleashes on "*altramente finirebbe la storia, com'è ver che vi parlo!*" is a potent reminder of the Canio he could have been on the stage.

Lanza is equally compelling in the *Improvviso* from *Andrea Chénier*. His voice noticeably more *spinto* than on the Hollywood Bowl rendition of five years earlier, the tenor was by now ideally suited to the role of the romantic poet. In 1950 he had recorded what the critic Delcie C. Howard later described as "a well-nigh model account" of this daunting aria, and here Lanza's affinity for Giordano's music remains as convincing as ever. Listening to this rendition, it is easy to understand why La Scala's Victor De Sabata was desperate to secure Lanza for the role of Chénier. Everything is right about his singing here: the phrasing, the breath control, the effortless upper register.

But more than that, Lanza is clearly living the part. Whether sweetly extolling the beauty of his country (*"veniva una carezza viva"*)—or denouncing the aristocracy with bone-chilling hatred—Lanza makes the idealistic poet come dazzlingly to life. Who can resist *this* Chénier's heartfelt plea (*"d'un poeta non disprezzate il detto"*)—or the ecstatic belief in love that concludes the aria? No matter that he sings "T'amo" instead of "Amor" at the climactic moment; to borrow the words of José Carreras, this is *singing from the soul*.

Vittorio Giannini's *Tell Me, Oh Blue Blue Sky* concludes the trio of 1952 home rehearsals. Although a staple of Lanza's recital repertoire, the song was never recorded commercially by the tenor, and, indeed, his only other surviving rendition is that of his first Albert Hall recital. While both performances are memorable for the aria-like intensity with which Lanza reinvigorates the slightly dated lament, this home recording is noteworthy for the tenor's use of light and shade, coupled with an often-exquisite sense of poetry.

Concluding the CD is another staple from the tenor's recital program. Victor Herbert's *I'm Falling In Love With Someone* was one of three songs that Lanza sang on his final British television appearance on January 18, 1958. Two days earlier he had performed the same number to great acclaim at the Royal Albert Hall, and here his audience is no less enthusiastic. Singing with greater sensitivity than on the previous occasion, the tenor is alternately playful and romantic, ending the song—and this CD—on a thrilling note of Lanzarian bravado.

* * * * *

It's no secret that stylistic subtlety and musical perfection often eluded Mario Lanza. But as the critic James Miller observes, "there is little point in belittling [the tenor] just because he wasn't Dietrich Fischer-Dieskau." Nor, for that matter, would Lanza have wanted to be. He *knew* that he was different. What he lacked in sheer finesse, he compensated for in other more important ways, including an innate sense of phrasing that enabled him to reach the deepest emotions of the listener. As Claudia Cassidy once wrote, Lanza "possesses the things almost impossible to learn."

These qualities alone would set him apart from most other singers. When combined with a vocal gift that can only be described as a phenomenon, the result—as this CD compellingly demonstrates—is the stuff of legend.

Derek McGovern

PUBLISHER'S NOTE: Recording engineer José Feghali (the noted pianist who won the gold medal at the Cliburn international competition) would like it noted that this CD derives from acetate disks, and though typical of "live" transcriptions, the sound is not always up to the "professional" recording standards of the day. Occasional surface noise will be encountered.

SELECTIONS ON THE CD

1/ Già nella Notte Densa from *Otello* (Verdi) [8:59]
with Jean Tennyson, soprano.
Live radio broadcast, November 7, 1945: George Sebastian, conductor.
2/ A Pretty Girl is Like a Melody (Berlin) [3:00]
Live radio broadcast, January 23, 1946: Sylvan Levin, conductor.
3/ Golden Days from *The Student Prince* (Romberg) [3:48]
with Robert Weede, baritone.
Live radio broadcast, February 6, 1946: Sylvan Levin, conductor.
4/ Un Dì all'Azzurro Spazio (Improvviso) from *Andrea Chénier* (Giordano) [4:50]
Hollywood Bowl concert, August 28, 1947: Eugene Ormandy, conductor.
5/ E Lucevan le Stelle from *Tosca* (Puccini) [3:23]
Hollywood Bowl concert, August 28, 1947: Eugene Ormandy, conductor.
6/ Parigi, O Cara from *La Traviata* (Verdi) [5:18]
with Frances Yeend, soprano.
Hollywood Bowl concert, August 28, 1947: Eugene Ormandy, conductor.
7/ Vogliatemi Bene from *Madama Butterfly* (Puccini) [6:24]
with Frances Yeend, soprano.
Hollywood Bowl concert, August 28, 1947: Eugene Ormandy, conductor.
8/ O Soave Fanciulla from *La Bohème* (Puccini) [3:48]
with Frances Yeend, soprano.
Hollywood Bowl concert, August 28, 1947: Eugene Ormandy, conductor.
9/ La Donna è Mobile from *Rigoletto* (Verdi) [2:11]
Massey Hall concert, Toronto, March 5, 1948: Paul Scherman, conductor.
10/ È la Solita Storia (Lamento di Federico) from *L'Arlesiana* (Cilea) [4:21]
Massey Hall concert, Toronto, March 5, 1948: Paul Scherman, conductor.
11/ Vesti la Giubba from *Pagliacci* (Leoncavallo) [3:13]
Massey Hall concert, Toronto, March 5, 1948: Paul Scherman, conductor.

12/ Agnus Dei (Bizet) [4:08]
Hollywood Bowl concert, July 24, 1948: Miklos Rozsa, conductor.
13/ Nessun Dorma from *Turandot* (Puccini) [3:48]
Hollywood Bowl concert, July 24, 1948: Miklos Rozsa, conductor.
14/ È il Sol dell'Anima...Addio! Addio! from *Rigoletto* (Verdi)
[4:25] with Mary Jane Smith, soprano.
Hollywood Bowl concert, August 16, 1949: John Green, conductor.
15/ Un Tal Gioco from *Pagliacci* (Leoncavallo) [2:30]
Home recording, Hollywood, 1952: Constantine Callinicos, pianist.
16/ Un Dì all'Azzurro Spazio (Improvviso) from *Andrea
Chénier* (Giordano) [4:52]
Home recording, Hollywood, 1952: Constantine Callinicos, pianist.
17/ Tell Me, Oh Blue Blue Sky (Giannini) [2:40]
Home recording, Hollywood, 1952: Constantine Callinicos, pianist.
18/ I'm Falling in Love With Someone (Herbert) [2:33]
Live television performance, London, January 18, 1958:
Constantine Callinicos, pianist.

Play time: 74:31

**Compact disc compiled by Armando Cesari, and mastered
by José Feghali, Vince Di Placido, and Derek McGovern.**

PREFACE

Any book that sheds light on the phenomenon named Mario Lanza is of importance. I call Mario Lanza a phenomenon advisedly, because his place in music history has always been controversial. Let us ignore the typical Hollywood hype which was inflicted on any star performer under the old studio system. What remains to this day as the essence of his persona is, to my mind, one of the truly great natural tenor voices of the past century—a voice of beauty, passion and power! The voice communicated to millions all over the world and I venture to say that his films did more to lure the general public to the art form of operatic singing than the voice of almost any other performer before his time. Of course the cinematic medium was a prime factor in this achievement, because a film reaches so many millions. BUT, and I spell this "but" with capital letters, that is no guarantee that the public will be spellbound, because there are film performers whom the public simply ignores. There was a visceral quality to the Lanza voice which even to this day—on reviewing the old films or relistening to the old recordings—grabs one with astonishing force.

Many people in the classical music world refused to recognize him and actually belittled not only his impact on the public but his God-given voice. As I write this, I have before me the 1980 edition of Grove's Dictionary of Music and Musicians. There are 5 entries under the name of "Lanza"—Francesco Giuseppe Lanza, a composer and singing teacher who lived from 1750 to 1812, and three of his sons, all of them composers and teachers; the fifth entry is Alcides Lanza, Argentinian composer, conductor and pianist who was born in 1928. This is merely one example of him being dismissed by the musicological fraternity. Several years ago I was interviewed on a television program that dealt with Lanza. Afterward I received letters from a number of well-meaning musicologists who took me to task for "defending Mario Lanza." What these people didn't recognize, or didn't want to recognize, is that I made no references to his personal life, his behaviour or his troubles, but purely to his voice—a voice which, incidentally, not only made an impact on me, but also on many of my tenor colleagues, like Luciano Pavarotti and José Carreras.

Why was there this antagonism? Was it because some people felt that success had come too easily to him—that he hadn't "suffered" for his art—or was it jealousy that someone who wasn't very sophisticated, academically speaking, could become such an effective "pied piper" for leading the uninitiated to the allure of the operatic voice?

As so often happens with time, attitudes change. The fact that we are still interested in his movies and recordings and that this book has been written proves that the persona of Mario Lanza has survived the test of time and that his voice remains a force of nature to this day.

Plácido Domingo

To Derek.
For Carmel, Dee, Lisa, and Peter, and
in memory of my mother.

MARIO LANZA

An American
Tragedy

"I sing with all my heart and soul. Each word is important. I sing as though my life depends on it. If ever I stop doing this, then I will certainly stop living."
Mario Lanza

INTRODUCTION

ANY ATTEMPT to write a biography of Mario Lanza must begin by dispensing with certain legends and myths that have lingered years after his untimely death. During his brief, highly successful and controversial career, Mario Lanza was the target of more publicity and criticism than almost any other singer of acknowledged operatic capabilities before or since. Many statements about him have often been completely unfounded or grossly distorted and exaggerated. Much of what has been written has either been incomplete, inaccurate, self-serving, sensational, or a combination of all four. Unfortunately, when discussing Lanza's career, this mixture of fiction and sensationalism is often quoted as fact, even by music critics who have no excuse for their ignorance. Moreover, Lanza's biographers—with the sole exception of Constantine Callinicos—have lacked the requisite musical competence to do justice to their subject.

The truth about the artist and the man is far less sensational, but by no means less interesting and a great deal more tragic than one might suspect. To begin with, there is no doubt that in terms of quality, timbre, color and range, Lanza possessed an outstanding tenor voice—a gift that lacked only the proper channelling, nurture and guidance to fulfill its promise.

Clearly, this was a voice that belonged in opera. Initially, at least, this was Lanza's one clear objective: a career on the operatic stage. Yet Lanza's resounding success in films, and the mass publicity comparing him prematurely to Caruso, were two important factors contributing to his lack of acceptance by most music critics and so-called operatic experts. They would ask: how can a tenor—no matter how famous or successful—who performs in films, rather than opera, be regarded as a serious artist? It would be convenient to dismiss Lanza as just another film singer. Indeed, there are many cases of successful film singers who either failed dismally on the operatic stage, or—at best—managed a career in opera without attaining any real distinction.

For example, Hollywood soprano Jeanette MacDonald and tenors Alan Jones, James Melton, Nino Martini and Gino Mattera had voices that sounded acceptable in films or radio, but could barely be heard in the larger opera houses such as the Metropolitan, La Scala or the War Memorial Opera House in San Francisco.

Melton's voice, in his debut season in 1942/43 at the Metropolitan, was described as being of "agreeable quality but gravely limited in size."[1] Nine years earlier, Martini's voice had been described as "thin and pallid...pleasant enough when it could be heard"[2] after a performance at the Metropolitan. To be fair, the aforementioned had pleasant voices combined with good musicality and were competent singers—regardless of the size of their voices. But while they sounded adequate when amplified in a cinema, it was a different story in the operatic theater.

Even the voice of the Italian tenor Ferruccio Tagliavini, who had an illustrious career in both Europe and America, was said to be of "agreeable but certainly limited sound"[3] when he sang at the old 3615-seat Metropolitan in New York. It is not altogether surprising then that Lanza was labelled by those who had never heard him sing "live" as being another amplified "Film Singer," whose voice was strictly the product of the MGM and RCA sound engineers. Furthermore, it was not only the size of his voice that was questioned. Since he was active primarily in films and in the recording studios, rumors began to circulate that he could neither sing nor sustain an entire opera and that he was, in fact, incapable of learning a complete role. Yet there is ample evidence that Mario Lanza not only possessed a voice of more than adequate size, combined with the ability to sustain the most rigorous of singing schedules, but that he also had the intelligence, instinctive musicality, and artistic temperament necessary for a successful operatic career.

It will suffice for the moment to quote conductor Richard Bonynge, a renowned expert on voices and a vocal historian, who—together with his wife, the celebrated soprano Joan

Sutherland—heard Lanza sing at the Albert Hall, London, in 1958. "We were both surprised by the size of the voice," said Bonynge. "Frankly, we expected it to be smaller. After all, one hears how film singers' voices are amplified." Bonynge further commented: "We were also impressed by Lanza's innate musicality. No doubt he could have had an outstanding operatic career."[4]

Lanza may well have lacked the polish that results from years of singing in opera. No doubt he developed some obvious mannerisms and lapses in style during his Hollywood years. However, similar comments were being made about no less a singer than Enrico Caruso after eleven years on the operatic stage.

Others started off even less impressively. Tenor Mario Del Monaco's debut at the Metropolitan in 1950 was dismissed by music critic Douglas Watt in *The Daily News* with a simple "We can forget him."[5]

Two years later, Del Monaco's critical appraisal had not improved. His Otello was described as being "screamed rather than sung, ranted rather than acted."[6]

Del Monaco was not exactly noted for his modesty. He not only ignored the critics, but went on to proclaim—somewhat implausibly—that he was the greatest tenor of all time, with possibly only Caruso as his equal—whereupon he continued to sing for another 25 years.

Had Lanza been an established opera singer before he went into films, he would not have been the exception to the rule. Instead, he would be remembered as one of the many opera singers who benefited from the large sums of money and huge popularity that the cinema can offer. Caruso starred in two silent films, and many other opera singers were lured before the cameras. Beniamino Gigli, for example, starred in sixteen sound features. Tito Schipa and Jan Kiepura appeared in ten. John McCormack, Lily Pons, Rise Stevens, Tito Gobbi, Giacomo Lauri Volpi, Richard Tauber, Gino Bechi, Ferruccio Tagliavini, Lawrence Tibbett, Ezio Pinza, Jussi Björling, Lauritz Melchior, Alfredo Kraus, Giuseppe Di Stefano, Mario Del Monaco, Luciano Pavarotti, José Carreras—and many more—all made films.

Of them all, only Grace Moore would realize anything remotely resembling the success that Lanza achieved in his ten-year film career. While it is true that Nelson Eddy, a former opera singer with considerable stage experience, was also a notable success in films, his stardom was not achieved solo but in partnership with soprano Jeanette MacDonald.

But let us return for the moment to Lanza, at precisely the beginning of a career that promised to be nothing short of sensational. All through his vocal studies, Lanza had experienced none of the problems that afflict many tenors—namely those of conquering the notes in the upper register of the voice. He never had to struggle in order to extend the compass of his voice, as even two giants such as Caruso and Domingo had to do. It took Corelli six years before he could sing a high C and a full nine years to finally place the voice correctly. Lanza had a splendid natural voice with a compass equivalent to almost two and a half octaves: from low A to D above high C.

His vocal studies, particularly with Gigli's teacher Enrico Rosati, supplied him with a solid technique that enabled him to sing with ease for hours without tiring. At the start of his career in 1947, the 26 year-old tenor was singing impressively in concerts throughout the United States as part of the "Bel Canto Trio", together with bass-baritone George London and soprano Frances Yeend. Lanza, in particular, received rave reviews for his efforts.

At this point, Lanza was heading only in one direction: the operatic stage. He could already count on the support of some famous names in the music world: conductors Serge Koussevitzky and Peter Herman Adler, tenor Tito Schipa and Edward Johnson, General Manager of the Metropolitan Opera.

To these would be added in subsequent years the no less illustrious names of Victor De Sabata, Conductor and Artistic Director of La Scala, and Gaetano Merola, Principal Conductor and Musical Director of the San Francisco Opera. But an operatic career was not to be. Lanza was destined to sing in only four full operatic performances: twice as Fenton in *The Merry Wives of Windsor* in Tanglewood, Massachusetts; and two more as Pinkerton in *Madama Butterfly* in New Orleans.

Instead of Italy and La Scala, or New York and the Metropolitan, Lanza went to California and Hollywood. In the celluloid capital he became an instant success, an overnight sensation. He was labelled the *New Caruso*.

4

Yet despite the fame, success and mass adulation, Lanza never felt secure in Hollywood. He knew that his rise to stardom had been too fast and that it had been attained, not on the operatic stage, but in motion pictures. He also knew that he lacked the stage experience to be regarded as a full-fledged opera star.

More than anything, Lanza wanted to be accepted as a serious artist. But because of his involvement with Hollywood and the resulting loss of confidence in himself—coupled with a desire to keep earning the astronomical sums of money that the film world could provide—all attempts to lure him back to the operatic stage failed. Lanza kept refusing offers to sing at the San Francisco Opera; La Scala; the Rome Opera and Covent Garden, among others. He procrastinated by saying: "I'm young, I have time." But time was running out.

Finally, Lanza went to Italy. Offers from the most respected theaters continued to arrive, but it was already too late. Plagued by ill health and more insecure than ever, had he lived it is unlikely he could have fulfilled his lifelong dream of appearing in an opera in a major theater.

In assessing Mario Lanza, the fact that his career took place mainly at MGM, instead of the Metropolitan, should not be the issue. On the contrary, he should be judged purely on the evidence he left behind, which contains many recorded performances that will stand comparison with—and often surpass—those of more fortunate singers whose careers have been almost entirely devoted to opera.

To this day there are still those who refuse to accept Lanza as a legitimate artist. A number of music critics and musical snobs have never accepted him, and never will, regardless of the recorded evidence.

Lanza is not listed in the Grove Dictionary of Music, for example, although his name has recently been added to the Oxford Dictionary of Music. It's extremely difficult to overcome prejudice.

Sadly, subterfuge is often the best way to validate Lanza's claim to legitimacy as a singer. I once played a selection of arias for a cultured friend of mine who is very musical, plays the piano, and sang in his youth. He had started off as a Lanza admirer but soon realized that the small circle of musical snobs to which he belonged were laughing at him. There would be no more Lanza for him. Knowing this, I played aria after aria for him without revealing the identity of the singer. All the while he raved about the beauty of the voice, the brilliant phrasing, the pathos, the incredible diction, the phenomenal interpretation and so on.

Naturally he kept asking who the singer was. I told him it was a young Spanish singer. "What's his name?" The first thing that came to mind was Garcia. "Manuel Garcia," I told him. "Wonderful! Wonderful! Where can I buy the record?" "You can't," I replied. "Why not?" he asked. "Because if you do your snobbish friends will crucify you." "What do you mean?" "I mean that you have been raving on about Lanza for the past forty-five minutes." "Impossible. It can't be him."

I rest my case.

The aim of this book is to give a factual and objective account of the life and career of Mario Lanza by finally divorcing truth from fiction. Mario Lanza had a great tenor voice and a larger than life personality. He was also a basically simple, generous, warm and extremely sensitive human being who found himself suddenly trapped by success and notoriety in a world in which he did not belong and whose life, because of it, ended tragically.

1—THE EARLY YEARS

THERE WAS NOTHING particularly exceptional to distinguish the arrival of Alfred Arnold Cocozza, later to be known professionally as Mario Lanza, on that cold winter's day in 1921. The birthplace was a small bedroom above a grocery store owned and operated by his maternal grandfather, Salvatore Lanza, and located at 636 Christian Street in the heart of South Philadelphia's Little Italy, where it still stands today.

Above the store were the living quarters accommodating Salvatore, his wife Elisena (known as Ellisa), their daughter Maria, and her husband Antonio. Originally from the town of Tocco da Casauria, in the northern part of Central Italy's Abruzzi region, Salvatore had set out for America in 1902 in search of a better life. He was joined in May of the following year by his 28-year-old wife and their 11-month-old daughter, Maria.

The unification of Italy in 1861 had done nothing to improve conditions among the poor. If anything, tax increases—combined with the economic depression that hit Europe towards the end of the 19th century—had caused an economic crisis in Italy with devastating effect upon the country's poorest. The result of such poverty was massive emigration. From 1876 onwards, hundreds of thousands of Italians began leaving their country and migrating to the United States and South America, as well as Germany, Belgium, and France. Between 1880 and 1929, 4 million Italians emigrated to the United States alone.

Salvatore chose America. Settling in Philadelphia, he initially found work on the docks and later sold fruit and vegetables door to door, eventually saving enough money to open a grocery store.

Maria was the eldest of his eight children. Not yet eighteen years old when she began helping her father in his store, Maria

7

secretly yearned for a singing career. An attractive, vivacious young woman with a beautiful coloratura soprano voice, she confided to her mother that she aspired to something more than working in a grocery store.

Ellisa Lanza was a caring and loving mother but—like all good Italian wives—would not have dreamt of contradicting her husband's wishes. She knew that for Salvatore, the mere thought of his daughter appearing on the stage was anathema. No daughter of his would cheapen herself in such a way. "The stage is no place for a respectable woman!" fumed Salvatore.[1]

Salvation from working in her father's grocery store came for Maria in the form of a handsome soldier. Antonio Cocozza had recently returned home after having fought in World War I as a member of the 37th Division, 145th Infantry, in the battle of the Meuse-Argonne. He had been severely wounded, cited for bravery, and granted a disability pension for the rest of his life. Born in 1894, he had migrated to America with his parents in June 1905, when he was eleven years old. Antonio's family, consisting of his father Pompilio, mother Carmela, two older sisters, Pasqua and Michela, and younger siblings Vincenzo and Maria, had come from Filignano, a little village situated in the southern part of the Molise region, which borders Campania. Prior to fighting in World War I, Antonio had been a renowned cyclist who excelled in six-day races. Ironically, his first job had been a short stint as a French polisher (shellacking cabinets) working for the Victor Talking Machine Company.

Years later the same company—renamed RCA—would sign his son to an exclusive contract.

One day in 1920, Antonio visited the Lanza store to purchase some groceries. Maria was serving in the shop that day, and after she had finished wrapping the various items, the young man lingered for some time talking to the attractive brunette. His conversation must have charmed the young woman more than eight years his junior, for less than two months later they were married.

Alfred was born on the 31st of January 1921. To his family and friends he would always be known as Freddie, even in later years when the world was acclaiming him as Mario Lanza.

The Cocozzas were not rich. Antonio's pension, coupled with

some of the proceeds from the grocery store that grandfather Salvatore generously gave them, was not sufficient to sustain a comfortable life, so Maria began to sew and embroider to earn extra money. Initially, she worked at home so that she could look after little Freddie.

The one thing not lacking in their household was music. Maria would play the pianola and sing to Freddie in her beautiful soprano voice, while her husband would occasionally accompany her on the French horn he played moderately well. The music consisted mainly of Antonio's large collection of operatic recordings, which were played virtually day and night on the old Victrola in the small dining room. Many were by his favorite singer, Enrico Caruso.

Antonio, who had heard Caruso sing four times, ate, drank and breathed opera. Little Freddie was constantly surrounded by music and would listen attentively to his mother's singing and to the recordings spinning on the Victrola. "My father was a great opera enthusiast and had a large collection of records of his favorite singers," recalled Lanza of his childhood. "I heard these [records] from the time I could first hear a clock tick."[2]

Growing up in such an environment, it is hardly surprising that Freddie became immersed in music. By the age of five, Freddie was so infatuated with the old Victrola that he would sit and listen for hours to the operatic greats as though in a trance. Sometimes Antonio and Maria would invite their friends to dinner. Many, such as Earl Denny and Johnny Varello, were professional musicians and invariably the evening would finish with music, singing, and record-playing. Wide-eyed Freddie would listen and absorb it all until bedtime.

Then one day when he was seven, he told his father, "I want to play records." Antonio was thrilled, albeit a little bemused. "You want to play records? Instead of going outside to play?" he asked in astonishment. "Show me how, Pop," was the little boy's reply. Murmuring an Italian blessing, his father patiently showed his son how to use the Victrola. "You must wind this handle. It's hard." "I can do it Pop," replied a confident Freddie.[3]

That day marked the start of countless sessions between Freddie and the Victrola. At times he would play the same record over and over again. Once his parents and grandmother heard him play Caruso's recording of *Cielo e mar* twenty-seven consecutive times. Antonio was beside himself with joy. When they went up to kiss their son good-night he whispered to his wife: "I should kiss him twenty-seven times."[4]

Whether Freddie's constant record-playing was merely imitating his father, or whether Caruso's voice was the reason for the repeated playing, is open to speculation. What is clear, however, is that music had already become an important part of his young life. All he knew at this stage was that the music excited him. It gave him "*la pelle d'oca*" (Italian for "goosebumps").[5] He preferred to be alone when he played the records. There, in the solitude of the room, he could drink in every tone and inflection and lose himself in the radiant maze of sound.

School was a different story. Although a bright child, Freddie was by no means a good student. As he would later say: "My school marks at the public school and at South Philadelphia High School were average but not brilliant."[6] In fact, by the time he attended high school, the only time Freddie showed any interest was when someone mentioned music or sport.

It was while in high school that he was first exposed to music theory. "I learned something of musical notation from the school's musical supervisor, Jay Speck,"[7] Lanza was to recall years later. The young Freddie would also develop a fondness for animals. His love of horses, in particular, would stay with him for the rest of his life. As a boy he would cut out every picture he could find in magazines and newspapers, eventually filling a number of boxes which he kept under his bed.

At his grandparents' home, where they lived until he was nine, Grandfather Salvatore was something of an autocrat. In addition to their first-born Maria, Salvatore and his wife had seven other children; two boys, Arnold and Robert, and five girls, Lucy, Giulia, Agnes, Hilda and Ann. When their father spoke, his children jumped. But not Freddie. While he could be respectful when it mattered, he was not above arguing over things that were important to him. Grandfather was not accustomed to having his word questioned. "Maria," he would call out, "this boy!" But Maria stood her ground: "Papa," she would plead, "you brought me up your way; we bring this boy up our way. We want him to be our friend, not to be afraid."[8] But Maria need not have worried. Behind the stern façade, Salvatore adored his little grandson and was proud of the way the boy stood up to him and engaged him in long conversations and debates.

There is no doubt that the center of Maria and Antonio's lives was their only child. Freddie grew up in warm and loving surroundings. From his parents and grandparents he learned the meaning of giving rather than taking, and he learned the meaning of the word generosity. It was a trait that would remain with him for the rest of his life and which would make him an easy target for a number of sycophants and opportunists.[9]

As Freddie was growing up, his two great loves continued to be music and sport. He showed a natural ability for sport and excelled in football and baseball. He went to see baseball games as often as he could afford it. His heroes were Ted Williams and Joe DiMaggio. He also enjoyed boxing. At one stage, he informed his parents that he would like to play professional football, much to the consternation of his mother, who visualized her Freddie with broken limbs and bones. She consequently did everything in her power to discourage him, urging him to concentrate on music instead.

To this end, they bought Freddie a violin with the $75 they had managed to save and sent him to the Settlement Music School. But young Freddie's vitality, energy and zest for life did not find the proper outlet in violin lessons. "Somehow I did not take to the drudgery of early violin study," Lanza would recall in later years. "When the teacher discovered that I was playing by ear, instead of by note, that was the end of that."[10] Piano lessons at the same school followed and were only slightly more successful. One positive aspect was that although Freddie did not learn to read music and continued to play by ear, the piano lessons provided him with a basic grounding in music. They would prove invaluable in later years, allowing him to run through his vocal exercises by playing the scales on his grand piano in the absence of a coach or accompanist.

In the meantime, Freddie's knowledge of opera continued to widen. By the time he was ten, he had already learned the plots and principal arias of some fifty operas. He was twelve when his parents took him to see his first opera, *Aida*. The young boy sitting entranced in the darkened theater, listening to one of Verdi's masterpieces, had no doubts. This was his world. Nothing surpassed its beauty and excitement, he would later recall.[11]

His immersion was such that by the age of fifteen, he was able to discuss competently the merits and demerits of all the most important operatic works, as well as some of the more obscure ones.

By now the Cocozzas had moved out of Salvatore Lanza's home and were renting a two-storey red brick house—six small rooms and a bath—which they would eventually purchase, at 2040 Mercy Street in an Italian neighborhood.

After attending St. Mary Magdalen De Pazzi school, where he had performed a stint as an altar boy, Freddie moved on to Edgar Allan Poe Elementary School, subsequently attending Vare Junior High School and later Southern High.

Freddie's warmth and bubbling personality made him popular among his numerous friends. He loved life and having fun, and was always entertaining his friends with his uncanny impersonations of various singers and actors. "He had a great sensitivity to people," recalled Philip Sciscione, one of his closest boyhood friends, in 1977. "You just liked to be with him, because he felt for people, he really felt for people."[12]

Although most of his friends knew little or nothing about opera, Freddie was adept at finding companions who shared his love for this music to accompany him to performances at the Philadelphia Academy of Music.

The main source of musical inspiration for Freddie, however, continued to be the records in his father's collection. Antonio bought them all from the local Victor dealer, a colorful character known to everyone as "Pop" Ianarelli. "Pop" had placed a speaker in front of his store, and when he put on a record the whole neighborhood turned into an opera house. One could hear the sound all year long from three blocks away, but from all accounts nobody ever complained. "Pop" took a great interest in Freddie who, in turn, found the old man a continuous source of inspiration as well as information. "Pop" kept him up to date with the latest releases of his favorite singers, as well as reissues of those of his idol, Caruso. For the young man it was akin to growing up on the stage of an opera house. Occasionally, Freddie would sing a snatch from an aria or let out a high note, but until he was sixteen, nobody really knew he had a voice. There's no question however that his dream was to become a singer one day.

On the score of *Lucia di Lamermoor* which his parents had given him while he was still in high school he substituted the names of the original cast with the ones he felt would do real justice to Donizetti's masterpiece. Lord Enrico Ashton became Titta Ruffo, Lucia: Luisa Tetrazzini, Edgardo: Enrico Caruso, Arturo: Tito Schipa, Raimondo: Ezio Pinza, Alisa: Ernestine Schumann-Heink and next to Normanno he wrote his own name.

Naturally, the Cocozzas had high expectations of their only child's career ambitions. Maria Cocozza, in common with many Italian mothers of the time, hoped he would become either a doctor or a lawyer. The first idea had to be abandoned when it became apparent that he was not remotely interested in pursuing a medical career. Not only was Freddie academically disinclined, but the sight of blood made him ill. His parents then suggested a legal career, reasoning that his ability to win arguments with his grandfather displayed a budding lawyer. As far as they were concerned, the matter was settled. But Freddie had other ideas. Sensing that his destiny lay elsewhere, he pleaded with them to reconsider. "Give me a little time to feel my way," he asked. "I'll finish high school but forget college, I know what I want." His ambition was clear, he told his startled parents. "I want to be a singer." [13]

This statement must have flabbergasted the elder Cocozzas, who up to then had never heard their son sing. Freddie had always been careful to ensure his parents were not at home when he occasionally sang along with a record of his idol, Enrico Caruso. When the Cocozzas finally heard their son sing, the impact on them was overwhelming. Antonio Cocozza was reduced to tears. "My boy," he sobbed, "you have a truly magnificent voice." [14] For her part, Maria, dumbstruck by the raw beauty of her son's tenor, abandoned all notions of Freddie becoming a lawyer and joined her husband in encouraging their son to become a singer.

First, however, they decided to seek the opinion of an expert. Antonio Scarduzzo was a retired baritone who earned his living by coaching promising young singers. Scarduzzo was greatly impressed by what he heard, but at the same time cautioned

Freddie's parents against rushing their son into singing lessons at this early stage. There was ample time for that, he declared, recommending that actual singing lessons be delayed for two years.[15] In fact, the old teacher was merely repeating what Freddie himself had told his parents prior to the audition. Freddie's knowledge not only of opera, but of anything pertaining to vocal matters, was already quite extensive. Before the audition he had told his parents, "At sixteen the male voice isn't mature enough to work on it. A girl yes, but not a boy."[16]

Scarduzzo suggested that instead of singing lessons the boy should study solfeggio (sight-reading), languages, and maintain his piano work. Money, however, was a big obstacle for the Cocozzas. It fell upon Maria to provide the solution.

She would resume her work as a seamstress at the Philadelphia Quartermaster Depot, where she had worked briefly when Freddie was six years old, and would supplement that income by taking a second job as a waitress. Convinced that Freddie possessed the necessary mental and physical equipment for an operatic career, Maria was determined that her son would be given the chance that had been denied to her by her strict father.[17]

Shortly after, Freddie began weekly lessons in both solfeggio and Italian. He loved studying Italian with Mario Pelizzon, a friend of the family, but hated the sight-reading sessions with Giovanni De Sabato, whom Maria had engaged for the task. Although De Sabato was by all accounts a delightful man, his advanced years made scaling the stairs to the Cocozza's second-floor quarters an immense challenge.

If teaching Freddie solfeggio was an effort for the old man, it was doubly so for his student, whose complete lack of aptitude for sight-reading soon resulted in the project being abandoned.[18] Studying Italian was an entirely different matter and essential for a budding opera singer. At home the Cocozzas, like most Italians, spoke their native dialect. Theirs was the dialect of the Abruzzi region, which differs considerably from standard Italian. Although Freddie displayed an early aptitude for languages, he never quite mastered Italian until he moved to Italy many years later. In the predominantly Italian neighborhood where they were living he did, however, manage to pick up several Italian dialects; his knowledge of Neapolitan would prove particularly useful in his subsequent career. Ultimately, he would also manage to learn enough Spanish and French to make himself understood.

In the meantime, Freddie continued to listen to his records. At times the glorious sounds of Caruso, Ruffo, Gigli and Ponselle, among others, would move him to tears. He continued to accompany the records, letting his voice ring out with those of his idols. As always, Caruso reigned supreme.

Freddie was becoming strong and muscular as he grew into adulthood, but a tendency to gain weight was also becoming apparent. Determined to tone his body, the young man turned his bedroom into a gymnasium of sorts, with weights, pulleys and a stationary bicycle. Downstairs his parents would often feel the entire ceiling shake. Fearing it might cave in at any moment, they would call out to their son, who would immediately reassure them by bursting into one of his favorite arias. Listening to the unschooled but glorious sounds emanating from their son's throat would soon make them forget all about the ceiling.[19]

As with most parents, the Cocozzas wanted Freddie to mix with the right kind of people. One of his closest friends was Eddie Durso, who became a guardian angel of sorts to Freddie. "Eddie, come and get me, " young Cocozza would plead. "My old man won't let me out!" The Cocozzas approved of Eddie and would frequently ask him to watch over their lively son.[20] "He was as colorful a character as I've ever known," Durso recalled, adding "I will never forget his prophetic words: 'Eddie, I'm going to be the greatest dramatic tenor that ever lived.'"[21]

Summers were usually spent at Grandfather Salvatore's holiday home in the resort center of Wildwood. With its wide sandy beach, situated on a little island at the extreme southern tip of New Jersey, Freddie would frequently invite his friends to holiday with him there. This was a carefree time for them. Away from the city, school, homework, and most of all their parents, it was a time almost exclusively dedicated to discovering girls.[22] Although Grandfather did his best to keep a watchful eye on the youngsters, Freddie was frequently in trouble with his "Nonno," as he called him, for coming home in the early hours of the morning after spending time on the beach with his latest conquest. Regardless of such teenage escapades, however, music still came first.

Back in Philadelphia the word had begun to spread about Freddie's phenomenal voice, eventually coming to the attention of Rodolfo Pili, a dignified gentleman responsible for the musical curriculum of the YMCA Opera Company. Pili began coaching "Alfredo"—he refused to call him Freddie—and eventually cast him in a number of opera productions. They included the part of Contino Del Fiore in *Crispino e la Comare*, the best of the operas written by the Neapolitan brothers Federico and Luigi Ricci, and first performed in Venice in 1850. History has not recorded the other operas Pili staged, in which "Alfredo" sang. We do know, however, that those who heard him remembered the young tenor's "overpowering voice."[23] A number of private recordings that the budding tenor made in 1940 have survived and, thanks to these, we have a clear indication of what he sounded like at the very beginning, prior to working with a coach. What emerges from the very first two records, a verse of the Neapolitan song *Pecche'* and the aria *E lucevan le stelle* recorded in April 1940—both dedicated to his father on the occasion of his birthday—is a surprisingly mature voice. The voice is round and rich throughout its range, revealing a true spinto sound, and the style, particularly in the operatic aria, is impressive for a 19-year-old.

It was just as well that Freddie had decided on a singing career. Shortly before graduation from Southern High, the Cocozza household was shaken by an unexpected and upsetting event: Freddie was expelled from the school. The reason given was "Misconduct." It seems that one of his teachers had slurred the Italian people by referring to them as "dagos." Freddie's immediate reaction was a punch that almost broke the teacher's jaw. In his defense years later, Lanza said: "He called us dagos. Now, if one of my friends—or even an enemy of my own age—had called me that, I would have laughed in his face. It was the fact that a teacher had said it."[24]

Although upset by this unexpected event, his parents had by now fully realized that the only thing of interest to their son was his dream of becoming an opera singer. They had little alternative but to forgive and forget their son's misdemeanor. For his part, Freddie was now ready for serious study.

2—FIRST SUCCESS

IN THE SUMMER OF 1940, when he was nineteen, Freddie decided that it was time to start working on his voice. He sought the help of Irene Williams, a former soprano who had sung with Nelson Eddy, among others, in his pre-Hollywood days. Miss Williams agreed to coach Freddie on alternate days at the rate of $5 per lesson. It was not to be voice study as such, since she was not teaching voice production or technique, but repertoire. In typical fashion with anything that he liked or was interested in, Freddie was both passionate and enthusiastic about his vocal work with Miss Williams. He was so completely immersed in what he was doing that his progress was extraordinary.[1]

During the year and a half he studied with Miss Williams, he learned two operatic roles and twenty songs. Miss Williams was well aware that Freddie was considerably more talented than her other students. It also become increasingly evident to her that he needed more than she was able to provide as a teacher.[2]

Up to that time, she had arranged for Freddie to sing at student concerts, which were sometimes held in John Wanamaker's great court in the famous department store in Philadelphia. At other times, Freddie would sing in the homes of some of the prominent figures of Philadelphia and New York's society. Among the latter was a wealthy Manhattan society hostess he called the countess who, two years later, would go so far as to write a letter to the White House to prevent the Army from recruiting her young tenor.

Back in Philadelphia on Christmas morning, 1940, parishioners heard Lanza for the first time in a moving rendition of the Bach-Gounod "Ave Maria" at his old church, St. Mary Magdalen De Pazzi, where he had served as an altar boy.[3]

Even at this early stage Freddie was convinced of his destiny. Fully confident that one day he would become a great opera singer, he believed utterly in his voice and displayed none of the doubts and insecurities that would plague him in later years as a consequence of his Hollywood experience. When asked about his career plans, he would answer simply: "Don't worry, you'll hear about me!"[4]

Two years earlier, at 17, Freddie displayed unbelievable confidence, as well as incredible audacity, in managing to enter the dressing room of tenor Giovanni Martinelli following a performance of *Otello*, with Lawrence Tibbet as Iago, at the Philadelphia Academy of Music. After congratulating Martinelli on his performance, he startled the 52-year-old tenor by telling him that, as good as he was, there existed a young man who was even better than he. Naturally, Martinelli wanted to know more about his young rival, but the mischievous Freddie answered simply: "Don't worry about it now, but his name is Mario Lanza and you will hear about him!"[5]

Miss Williams knew that Freddie had a voice of rare quality and beauty and was determined to do the very best she could for him. She knew a great deal of people and her circle of friends included most of the music lovers in Philadelphia.

One of the most influential was William K. Huff, 1919 Harvard cum laude and author, who happened to be not only one of the great patrons of music of the city, but also Executive Secretary of the Philadelphia Concerts Forum. Because of his great respect for Irene Williams's musical judgment, Huff agreed to hear her pupil sing.

A private audition was arranged which made a strong impression on the seasoned concert executive. Referring to the 21-year-old tenor's incredible voice, Huff commented enthusiastically: "I did not believe there was anything like it in this country," going so far as to prophesy: "He will replace Caruso!"[6]

Amid the generally favorable consensus regarding Freddie's total involvement with his singing studies, however, there was at least one dissenting voice. Grandfather Salvatore had been complaining unsuccessfully to his daughter and son-in-law for months that his grandson should find some form of alternative employment, and could no longer contain himself. Claiming that Freddie was a scandal, he stormed: "What is this talk of singing? The boy must have a useful occupation. He can at least sit on a grocery truck and help the driver with the deliveries for five hours a day!"[7]

A family conference followed. Both Antonio and Maria were determined that nothing should interfere with their son's singing studies, but Freddie sympathized with his grandfather's view and convinced his parents that he could do both: work for grandfather and keep up his singing studies. "Mom, Pop, I'll help delivering groceries for a while and make him happy. It won't interfere with the singing, I promise you."[8] Reluctantly his parents agreed, but the future Mario Lanza's only non-singing job was destined to last a mere ten days and end with an audition before the great conductor of the Boston Symphony, Serge Koussevitzky.

William K. Huff's parting words to Freddie had been: "We shall have to do something about you."[9] Two months had now passed since he had stood in Miss Williams' studio and listened to the glorious tenor sound emerging from the throat of a slightly overweight but charming young man. Now he saw an opportunity to fulfill his promise.

Koussevitzky was scheduled to give a concert at the Academy of Music, and Huff saw this as an excellent opportunity for the maestro to hear his "uncut diamond"[10,] as he called Freddie. Huff informed Miss Williams that he had arranged for Koussevitzky to hear her star pupil after the maestro finished a rehearsal for the concert at the Philadelphia Academy of Music. "I knew that if Dr. Koussevitzky heard Mario, it would be the start of his professional career," Miss Williams recalled in a subsequent interview, adding that she felt "he had a great talent and it had to be nurtured by the best people I knew."[11]

Arriving punctually at the Academy of Music on the day of the audition, Freddie was met by William K. Huff, who accompanied him backstage to meet the legendary Russian conductor. Dr Koussevitzky, who had just finished rehearsing for the upcoming concert, was stripped to the waist and about to be given an alcohol massage. After the appropriate introductions, the maestro told Freddie that an accompanist was waiting in a rehearsal room directly across the hall, and that he should select a number to sing. Sensing the significance of the moment, and feeling nervous but confident, Freddie told the pianist that he would sing "*Vesti la giubba*," Canio's famous arioso from Act 1 of Leoncavallo's *Pagliacci*.[12]

After the first few bars, Koussevitzky, wearing only pyjama pants and holding a small towel in his hands, entered the rehearsal room. He stood close to Freddie and listened reflectively as he dabbed his face with his towel. As Canio's lament came to an end there was a moment of silence. Then Koussevitzky embraced him, kissed him on both cheeks, and almost in a reverie said: "You have a truly great voice. You will come with me to the Berkshire."[13] This amounted to an invitation to the Berkshire Music Center in Tanglewood, Massachusetts, to study on a full scholarship.

Candor being one of his charms, Lanza would later confess that he had never heard of the Berkshire, but at the time he had enough sense to reply, "Yes, I will come." Koussevitzky's reputation for helping gifted young artists was well-known. His protégés included, among others, conductor Leonard Bernstein and the brilliant American soprano Dorothy Maynor.

Soon, Koussevitzky would deliver an even more impressive verdict to his latest protégé: "Yours is a voice such as is heard only once in a hundred years"[14,] he told the tenor at age 21, when he was already known as Mario Lanza.

Meanwhile, Irene Williams was not about to wish her star pupil a mere "Good luck!" as Lanza prepared to leave for the Berkshires. Certain that the young tenor was heading for stardom, she accompanied him to the railway station and persuaded him to sign a contract stipulating that he would pay her 5% of his singing income in excess of $5,000 a year, and 10% if earnings exceeded $7,500 per year. Williams would subsequently sue Lanza for breach of contract in 1948 and the suit was eventually settled in May 1952 with Lanza agreeing to pay his former teacher $10,000.[15]

In his court hearing, Lanza told Judge Stanley N. Barnes that he had never seen the agreement until thirty minutes before his train departed. Stating that he had signed the contract without reading it, he had believed Miss Williams' assurances, he said, that the agreement would protect him from unscrupulous agents who might defraud him if his appearances at Tanglewood proved successful.

As for the change of name to Mario Lanza, "Alfred Cocozza" had always been problematic. Since his high school days, possibly sensing that one day he would become famous, he had been experimenting with alternatives, many of which can be seen today in one of the surviving exercise books of the time.

He wrote down a succession of possible alternatives such as Al Cocozza, Al Lanza, and Fred Lanza, finally settling for the masculine version of his mother's maiden name, Maria Lanza. Koussevitzky wholeheartedly supported the name change, but the new Mario Lanza felt uneasy about dropping his father's surname. "Are you sure you don't mind too much, Pop?" he asked his father, who answered bravely: "Sing! What difference is the name?"[16] On July 5, 1942, four months after his impromptu audition before Koussevitzky, Mario Lanza reported for work at the Berkshire Music Center.

For Koussevitzky the Music Center represented the fulfillment of a lifelong dream. Although Dr. Henry Hadley had founded the actual Berkshire Festival in 1934, it was not until 1936, when Koussevitzky entered the American musical scene, that the festival achieved national importance.

Then, in 1940, the Music Center was opened at Tanglewood. Situated in the beautiful Berkshire hills of Western Massachusetts, the Center provided a means for students, teachers and professional musicians to benefit from the stimulating exchange of experiences and ideas. During the first summer in 1940, three hundred students from every part of the country attended the Center.[17]

By 1942, Tanglewood had become a national institution and it was here, for the first time in his life, that Lanza was exposed to serious, basic musical training. Lanza recalled: "When I arrived in Tanglewood, Dr. Koussevitzky placed me under the direction of strict taskmasters such as conductors Leonard Bernstein, Lukas Foss and Boris Goldovsky, with whom I worked eight to ten hours a day."[18] The strain was immense, and Lanza relieved it by falling in love with a soprano and a contralto—both in the first week—and forgetting them by the second.[19]

Clearly, someone as extroverted, dynamic and non-conformist as Lanza, who could be quite overbearing at times, was not going to be universally liked. Boris Goldovsky disliked him intensely. Koussevitzky had given Goldovsky the task of teaching Lanza the tenor part in Beethoven's Ninth Symphony, which the former had scheduled for the season. Goldovsky would later claim that Lanza's lack of musical ability made learning this part an impossibility, and that he had been obliged to teach Lanza the role of Fenton in *The Merry Wives of Windsor* instead.[20] This is clearly an absurd statement. The tenor solo in the symphony consists of less than one minute of not particularly difficult singing, together with a few bars in ensemble. By contrast, the role of Fenton, though not very long, is much more complex. In Act I, Fenton has a recitative with Page and a solo totalling approximately five minutes. In the Second Act, the tenor has considerably more singing to do.

He has to sing the Serenade, the demanding duet with Ann, and the difficult quartet with Ann, Cajus and Slender – in all at least twelve minutes. Goldovsky had claimed that he was unable to teach Lanza the part in the Ninth Symphony in the allotted time of five weeks, yet at the same time he managed to teach him Fenton in six weeks.

Goldovsky further claimed that he had been obliged to shorten the role of Fenton as much as possible. However, closer examination of the score does not bear this out. The only possible omission would have been cutting the solo in Act One, a mere two minutes of singing. If further proof that he sang the entire role is needed, one has only to refer to *The New York Times* critic Noel Straus, who among other things wrote, "Practically all the numbers allotted Fenton and Anne Pave proved bereft of musical interest."[21] And this from opera director Herbert Graf, writing in *Opera News*: "The choice of Nicolai's *Merry Wives of Windsor*, as the one opera given in its entirety, proved a happy one."[22] One can only infer, then, that Goldovsky was overstating his own importance. Interestingly, when this author spoke to the Metropolitan Opera soprano Dorothy Kirsten, who was herself extremely critical of Lanza, her response on learning that Goldovsky had conducted the tenor's operatic debut was a dismissive "Oh, him."[23]

Equally ridiculous is the statement made by one of Lanza's biographers that it would have been extremely difficult for the tenor to learn a piece as "complex" as the Ninth Symphony in German.[24] As already stated, the tenor solo is less than a minute long and involves exactly twenty words.

In any event, Lanza would learn the part of Fenton in little more than a month. This role was not the only task assigned to him, however. On July 26, 1942 – less than three weeks after arriving at Tanglewood – he took part in a performance that included a number of scenes from various operas. As Rodolfo, he sang the third act of Puccini's *La Bohème* with Irma Gonzales as Mimi, James Pease as Marcello, and Laura Castellano as Musetta. Jay C. Rosenfeld of *The New York Times* reported that, "Miss Gonzales as Mimi and Mario Lanza as Rodolfo were conspicuous by the beauty of their voices and the vividness of their characterizations."[25]

Twelve days later, Lanza was considered sufficiently advanced to make his operatic debut. On August 7, 1942, he sang Fenton in Otto Nicolai's opera *The Merry Wives of Windsor*.

Singing opposite Lanza, in the role of Ford, was the baritone Mack Harrell. He stared at Lanza and said: "Aren't you the Cocozza boy who studied violin with me in Philadelphia?"[26] It was true; the former violin student-turned-singer was teamed in the opera with his own former violin teacher, who had also become a singer. The two laughed uproariously at this strange trick of destiny.

Nicolai's last and most important opera had been first performed in Berlin in 1849. At Tanglewood it was staged by the renowned Metropolitan opera director Herbert Graf, and performed in English in three acts and seven scenes, with Boris Goldovsky conducting an orchestra of 37 students from the Center. Others in the cast that night were James Pease as Falstaff and Christine Johnson as Mrs. Page. Writing in *The New York Times*, music critic Noel Straus first praised the Ford of Mack Harrell, then went on to report:

> Second honors went to the Fenton of the cast, Mario Lanza, 21 year old tenor, an extremely talented, if as yet not completely routined student, whose superb natural voice has few equals among tenors of the day in quality, warmth and power.[27]

Straus's sharp ear also detected something else for which

Lanza was to become renowned: "His English diction was first rate," wrote the critic.

The enthusiasm of *The New York Times* was shared by the music critic of *The New York Herald Tribune* who wrote:

> Another outstanding member of the cast was a young tenor, Mario Lanza...If Lanza's natural abilities are developed in the proper direction, he will own a splendid dramatic voice. At present he needs more fundamental training and the rudiments of style. Yet even now he offers good musicality and diction.[28]

For the young tenor the reviews were more than encouraging, and Lanza was thrilled. In the *Opera News* of October 5, 1942, Herbert Graf wrote of the tenor: "A real find of the season was Mario Lanza [...] He would have no difficulty one day being asked to join the Metropolitan Opera."[29]

It was on the strength of the critical consensus about these performances that Lanza was heard for the first time by opera and concert manager Arthur Judson, head of the giant Columbia Artists Management. Judson and his assistant William M. Judd had already heard about Lanza's impressive audition with Koussevitzky. Wasting no time, they auditioned Lanza and, although an actual contract would not be negotiated until 3 years later, they took the young tenor under their wing in order to ensure that their new potential star kept working.

The task was given to baritone Robert Weede. Like those before him, he was bowled over by the magnitude of Lanza's voice. The 39-year-old Weede, who had studied with Oscar Anselmi in Milan, was a well-established singer who had already enjoyed a considerable career. It had included five seasons with the Metropolitan Opera, where he had made his debut in 1937 as Tonio in *Pagliacci*. After a further five seasons, Weede would go on to become one of the stars of San Francisco Opera, where he sang for more than twenty seasons. He would later score a big hit on Broadway in the 1950s with the musical *The Most Happy Fella*.

Weede and Lanza became instant friends. The older singer was greatly impressed by the young tenor's voice, was protective of him and thought that he possessed all the requisites for a major operatic career.[30] While In New York and working with

Robert Weede, Lanza auditioned for opera and concert promoter Michael De Pace. De Pace, whose clients included Giovanni Martinelli and Robert Weede, signed the young tenor immediately.

Through De Pace Lanza also met Maria Margelli, secretary to basso Ezio Pinza of the Metropolitan Opera. The 42-year-old Margelli had considerable clout in the music world, and liked Lanza' s extroverted personality. Her reaction to his singing was decisive. "Yours is the greatest voice I've ever heard and I've heard them all," she exclaimed to the young tenor.[31] Margelli would become a patron of sorts to Lanza, championing his career and introducing him to a number of influential people. In the occasional concerts that he sang Lanza never failed to impress. The verdict after his appearance in Union City, New Jersey at the end of November 1942 was typical: "From a tremendous frame and chest a tremendous dramatic voice came forth, belying his youth in the tragic arias *Ch'ella mi creda, E lucevan le stelle* and *Un di all'azzurro spazio*."[32]

If events were turning out extremely well for the young singer, they were about to change quite drastically. Lanza had become so involved in his new-found musical world that he had almost forgotten the outside world. His memory was soon put to the test when his mother phoned him from Philadelphia with some startling news. "Fred," she said, "there's a funny letter for you here. It says 'Greetings'."[33]

The greetings were from the United States Government or, more precisely, from the Philadelphia Draft Board, requesting that he report for his medical examination for induction into the Army.

Lanza was convinced that the Army would reject him due to his defective vision. As a baby, he had suffered a convulsion which had left him partially blind in his left eye.

He reassured his mother that the Army could get by without him; he had, after all, more important things to do. Lanza's agent Michael De Pace was also convinced the Army could wait and in December 1942 promptly wrote a letter to the Local Draft Board in which he stated:

Mr Giovanni Martinelli, noted tenor of the Metroplitan Opera, has heard Mr. Lanza and has taken a great interest in him. He has urged Mr. Lanza to study certain operatic roles. Mr. Fausto Cleva, well-known operatic conductor, is also interested in Mr. Lanza and has agreed to coach him. We seriously believe that intense study during the next few months is very necessary for Mr. Lanza in order that he may be able to start the fine career he has in store.[34]

At the same time the countess, Lanza's admirer and society hostess, wrote a letter to an assistant of President Roosevelt which included the following:

I feel that if there is anything in your power that you can do to help Mr. Lanza to be free to complete his studies you will not fail to try. Because of the account of the faulty condition of his left eye [I am] led to believe that this particular un- usual case could be submitted to his Excellency the President or the Draft Board in Philadelphia. Everyone that hears Mario Lanza sing with his beautiful, glorious, rich, voluminous, unlimited voice truly believes that Mario could do duty to his country by giving delight and morale uplift to the army and civilians as well.....Just now Mario Lanza has the whole of New York to back him financially.[35]

Unfortunately for Lanza, regardless of his bad eye or De Pace's and the countess's pleas the Army thought otherwise and sent him off first to Miami for basic training, and from there to the hot and dusty air base of Marfa, Texas.

3—SPECIAL SERVICES

THE IDEA OF BECOMING A SOLDIER did not appeal to the recently acclaimed young tenor. The world may have been at war, but Lanza was unable to imagine of what possible use he could be to the Army. More importantly, he resented the sudden interruption of what had constituted an excellent start at Tanglewood, and the postponement of the intensive vocal training that he knew he still needed.[1]

His frame of mind at this time is evident in a letter he wrote in March 1943 to his agent Michael De Pace:

> This place is second only to the kingdom of Mefistofele....in fact it's worse than Hell. We are living here on a vast desert. We breathe nothing but dust and believe me my voice has not benefited from it.[2]

In a similar depressed fashion he wrote the following month to his friend and patron Maria Margelli.

> I am living in one of the strangest places in the United States because we are at an altitude of five thousand feet, yet in a valley surrounded by much higher mountains. However this valley is not fertile, nor beautiful but simply a huge desert with nothing but cactus plants, dust, snakes, terrific heat and continuous dust storms.[3]

After mentioning that he was now undergoing throat treatments twice a day because of the dust, he reminisces about happier times.

> How I miss those happy days back in New York. How well I remember those nights when I used to get on the 7th Avenue bus and go right down to the Metropolitan Opera House and see all the operas I love. There are many nights I spend out here just lying on my bed reliving the many beautiful

27

and touching scenes from *La Bohème*. I sing all the arias to myself and as I do this I am for the time being away from this boring army life and back to grand opera where I really belong.

The solution to the misery of army life, and what was to become a standard procedure in future moments of crisis and depression, was to overeat. And overeat he did. Huge amounts of army food were consumed until he weighed in the vicinity of 260 pounds (118 kg).

This out-of-shape and depressed character was just what Corporal Johnny Silver, a diminutive burlesque comic assigned to the Special Services, was looking for. Silver's task was to find suitable talent among the soldiers for the staging of shows designed to entertain the Armed Forces. Going through the soldiers' service records one day, he came across Private Cocozza's file, which listed the tenor's recent accomplishments at Tanglewood. Silver wasted no time in summoning the burly military policeman to his office. Lanza was a sight to behold. "His shirt was open, he didn't have a hat, no laces on his shoes," recalled Silver. But regardless of his appearance, the charm and personality of the young private worked its magic, and the pair would soon become close friends. "There was something about Mario I liked instantly," said Silver. "Sure he was heavy and out of shape, but he had a fantastic personality, a great deal of charm, and eyes that sort of gleamed when he talked." Silver was also swept away by the beauty of the young tenor's voice.[4]

Lanza's morale showed a marked improvement after he met Silver. His next break came with the announcement that Sergeant Peter Lind Hayes was putting together a show and would be coming to Marfa to search for appropriate talent. Hayes, an entertainer and comedian, had collaborated in writing the play *On The Beam* with Frank Loesser for the Army Air Force show. Loesser would later gain fame with the memorable Broadway musical *Guys and Dolls*. At first, however, Lanza's prospects of escaping the dreary air base seemed slim. Hayes had already given Silver a part in the show, and despite the latter's best efforts to secure a role for Lanza, Hayes was far from convinced that he needed a tenor. But Silver was persistent. Finally Hayes relented and agreed to hear Lanza.[5]

Then as a foretaste of the problems that would plague him more than a decade later, Lanza announced that he was unable to sing. He told Silver that the climate in Texas, combined with the dust at the army base, had resulted in a throat inflammation. Possibly suspecting that Lanza's condition was psychosomatic, the ever-resourceful Silver again refused to give in to Hayes's indifference. He came up with a home-made recording of Metropolitan tenor Frederick Jagel singing *"E lucevan le stelle"* from Puccini's *Tosca*, pasted a label over the record with the words, "Mario Lanza with the Boston Symphony Orchestra," and persuaded Hayes that this was indeed a recording of Lanza singing under the baton of Serge Koussevitzky. The deception worked, and an impressed Hayes invited Lanza to join the company of *On The Beam.*[6]

A week later the company left Marfa and moved to Phoenix, Arizona, where Lanza and the rest of the cast found themselves occupying the luxurious Westward Ho! Hotel. Lanza had a claustrophobic hatred of small rooms and loved his new surroundings. Whether it was the comfortable new environment or the agreeable climate in Phoenix, his voice soon recovered its brilliant luster.

And this was just as well. Many associated with the show, including Captain Fred Brisson (son of singer-actor Carl Brisson and actress Rosalind Russell's husband), who was in charge of the production, were convinced that Lanza was a fake and unable to sing a note. By the time they reached Phoenix the pressure on Lanza was mounting: sing or else. With typical chutzpah, Lanza chose to sing the *Tosca* aria that he and Silver had played for Hayes on the falsified Jagel recording. Confident of his newly-restored voice, Lanza gave a thrilling performance of *"E lucevan le stelle."* While Brisson was more than impressed by the young GI's golden sound, Hayes commented in disbelief: "You sound even better in person than you did on the record!"[7]

On The Beam proved a big hit and for a year the company toured the various Army service bases. It was also an ideal outlet for Lanza and his outgoing personality. Consisting of a variety of acts, the show revolved around the considerable talents of actor-comedian Peter Lind Hayes, doing both straight parts and impersonations; dancer Ray McDonald; and harmonica player

Jerry Adler (brother of the more famous Larry). Lanza would sing well-known arias such as "*E lucevan le stelle*" and "*Vesti la giubba*," and also joined the rest of the cast in comedy sketches for which he proved himself particularly adept. It was a happy time for Lanza and his military audience. For their part, the GIs responded to his singing with thunderous applause and roared with laughter at his comedy antics.[8]

As the run of *On the Beam* was coming to an end Lanza was assigned to a new play, Moss Hart's *Winged Victory*. The noted playwright and director had achieved fame through his collaboration with the playwright-director George S. Kaufman in hit plays such as *The Man Who Came To Dinner*.

Winged Victory opened in New York's 44th Street Theater on November 20, 1943 after a tryout in Boston. A tribute to the Air Force, it told the stories of six air cadets from different parts of America who leave behind their wives, sweethearts and families to join the Air Force and fight for their country. In the play Lanza had a small non-singing part but was relegated to virtual obscurity as part of a fifty-man chorus under the direction of Lieutenant Leonard de Paur.

The talented cast reads like a show business directory: Don Taylor, Karl Malden, Red Buttons, Gary Merrill, Kevin McCarthy, Alan Baxter, George Reeves, and Ray Middleton. The cast included three other actors who would become close to Lanza: Barry Nelson, Edmond O'Brien and Bert Hicks.

The four became virtually inseparable. Bert Hicks, who was originally from Chicago, had moved to Los Angeles with his wife Harriet and their young daughter Dolores to pursue an acting career. In the late1950s and early 1960s, Dolores would begin a promising career as an actress in a number of Hollywood films under the screen name Dolores Hart before retiring to become a Benedictine nun in 1963.

Bert Hicks, a tall, good-looking young man sporting a Robert Taylor moustache, had found work as a supporting actor, then relatively easy to find in Hollywood.

His sister Betty had also left Chicago for Los Angeles, where she lived with her brother and his family. Betty worked in the Educational Department at the Douglas Aircraft Plant.

From time to time Bert would tease Lanza with a photo of a

pretty girl perched on the fender of a car, shapely legs crossed, smiling with her friendly dark eyes and generous warm curves of the mouth. "Hey, who's that?" Lanza would ask Hicks, who merely responded with a smile. Eventually giving in to Lanza's persistence, Hicks admitted that the smiling brunette was his sister Betty.[9]

Romance, let alone marriage, was the farthest thing in Lanza's mind at this stage. "Before I met Betty I always knew my interest in women was merely interest. I never told one of them it was love," he said. "No girl had ever touched me deeply and so I decided that I would never get married. It was brief fun just to feel romantic about a lot of girls."[10]

Prior to joining the Army, Bert had become close friends with Barry Nelson, a young actor under contract to MGM. Nelson had made his film debut in *Shadow Of The Thin Man* in 1941 and had been receiving good notices for his work in mediocre films such as *A Yank On The Burma Road*. A much-admired actor, Nelson would continue to alternate between film and a more impressive stage career in New York, where he would star in the Broadway productions of *The Moon Is Blue*, *The Rat Race* and *Cactus Flower* among others. A television career also followed with lead roles in *My Favorite Husband* and *Hudson Bay*.

Through his friendship with Bert Hicks, Barry Nelson became Lanza's close friend. At the time Lanza was dating Teresa Celli, an attractive young Italian, while Barry Nelson was seeing Bert's sister Betty.

Lanza would later marry Betty, while Nelson married Teresa Celli, who had operatic aspirations, and would feature briefly in some of the musical sequences in Lanza's biggest film success, *The Great Caruso*, less than a decade later.

"Mario was in the chorus, which is very ironic," recalled Nelson of the *Winged Victory* period. "There he was, one of many and larger than most. He became increasingly heavy because army life was awful and Mario took it particularly hard. He was a great big boy who enjoyed life to the hilt; he just loved living life and getting away from anything that might be dull, and the Army was dull!"[11]

In addition to singing in the chorus, Lanza was assigned as Barry Nelson's dresser. Nelson, together with Edmond O'Brien, was among the six leads in the show and each of them had been given a dresser to help with the fast changes that took place between scenes. Consequently Lanza and Nelson spent a great deal of time together and became close friends.

Nelson remembers the period fondly.

> He was an interesting fellow to be with because of his tremendous vitality. It was unmistakable and it's not something that one runs into all the time. It bubbled over. So it was never dull in a time in one's life when so much could be dull. The whole army routine, even if you were in a show, was still filled with routine.[12]

For someone with the vitality and zest for living that Lanza possessed, the Army was not only dull but thoroughly depressing. At one stage during the run of *Winged Victory*, Lanza put on so much weight through sheer despondency that he became an embarrassment to Colonel Durham, the Texan organist in charge of the cast and the staging of the show. "Send that man to hospital!" shouted the Colonel. "I won't have him in the company!"[13]

Consequently, Lanza was sent to Mitchell Fields Hospital in New York, where coincidentally his friend Barry Nelson had also been sent to recover from a virus. Since Lanza was not confined to bed he was assigned a number of duties by the hospital staff. These consisted mainly of bringing trays of food to bed-ridden patients such as Nelson. Here Lanza once again displayed his flair for escaping humdrum tasks, and for finding novel ways to indulge his prodigious appetite.

When it came time for assigning duties Lanza would simply disappear. As Nelson later recalled, Lanza would evade the hospital staff by hiding in one of the phone booths. His technique involved sinking down below the upper glass section of the booth where he could just sit there—hiding—until it was all over. The staff would never think of looking in the phone booths and so for that day he was spared the task of serving the trays.[14]

Now and then, however, someone would be using the phone or he would get caught before he had the opportunity to hide. On those days he would be forced to serve the meals to the sick. "He would start down the hall in line with the others carrying the trays of food," recalled Nelson, "and then he'd move out of line and go down the left side of the hall.

Everybody else is going on a straight line with these trays to serve and Mario just careens off and he's eating the food! He became a legend there because people saw him eat up to two and a half chickens by himself! Well you had to like him you know. I hated the Army so much myself. I had to applaud him even though I might be the one that had to go without [food] that day waiting for Mario. He became what you might call a '*cause célèbre*.'"[15]

Overall *Winged Victory* proved a positive experience for Lanza. Finding himself surrounded by an astonishing array of talent, he was also exposed to an atmosphere conducive to wild living, thus relieving the boredom of army life.[16]

Although overweight, Lanza was very muscular. According to George London, "His fat was hard and his grip was like steel. He was one of the most powerful men I have ever known."[17] And the out of shape soldier was not without his fair share of young women willing to surrender to his undeniable charms. His sexual escapades were facilitated considerably by the help that he was unwittingly getting from none other than the company doctor, Bill Cahan. After the war Cahan would become an eminent cancer specialist.

A music lover, Cahan would give Lanza excuses to evade tedious hospital duties. "He'd say Mario wasn't well, and then let him slip off so that he could go to the opera," recalled actor Edmond O'Brien.

"Sometimes Mario would go to the opera and sometime he would go and make love to a girl he had previously arranged to meet."[18] The result of these frequent clandestine encounters was that word began to spread of Lanza's sexual prowess, causing a certain amount of friction between him and some of the GIs who were jealous of his exploits.[19]

O'Brien, a New Yorker of Anglo-Irish ancestry, was already a well-established actor when he became close friends with Lanza. He had made his film debut in the 1939 version of *The Hunchback Of Notre Dame* with Charles Laughton and Maureen O'Hara, and in 1954 would win the Oscar for Best Supporting Actor for his performance in *The Barefoot Contessa*.

Together, O'Brien and Lanza were quite a team. Not only would they discuss their latest conquests and compare notes, but at times they would even exchange girlfriends. Word began to spread that Lanza was well-endowed. For whatever reason, O'Brien would not hesitate to recommend his younger friend to women. "I used to tell the ones I introduced him to: 'If you want the real thing, there it is!'"[20]

The older O'Brien became very fond of Lanza and took an almost paternal interest in him. While in New York, O'Brien would often visit his mother at her home in Scarsdale and on these occasions would take Lanza along to have dinner with them. "I found him so kind, to me, my wife, my mother," recalled O'Brien. "He sang 'Danny Boy' for my mother and I didn't ask him to. He said, 'I've got a surprise for your mother' and Mario with that incredible voice... if he liked you, the warmth flooded all over the place.

> Other times we'd go to Tony's Restaurant in New York. Tony, the proprietor, loved music but couldn't sing. Whenever we went there, Tony always ended up singing some aria for us. He had no idea who Mario was and eventually he asked him to sing a song. Mario, who loved practical jokes, at first pretended he couldn't sing, but finally he relented. He stood up and imitated Tony by singing just as flat.
>
> When he finished singing, Tony came over and told him it was best to forget it, that he had no future as a singer, no talent whatsoever. He had hardly finished handing down his harsh verdict when Mario began to sing. Well, you should have seen the stunned look on Tony's face. It was a mixture of amazement and embarrassment....then Mario grabbed Tony and gave him a great big hug and the two of them roared with laughter.[21]

After six months and 212 performances playing to capacity audiences on Broadway, the entire *Winged Victory* Company moved to Los Angeles. Following the success of the play, 20th Century Fox had acquired the rights to it and was now ready to start filming with George Cukor as director. Work on the production started in June 1944. Limited to singing in the chorus and appearing as an extra, Lanza now found himself with some unexpected free time to visit Hollywood record shops, searching for rare records of lesser-known tenors such as Alessandro Valente, or simply listening to those he knew of Caruso, Pertile,

Gigli, Martinelli and others.[22]

His favorite was the Rhapsody Record Shop on North Highland Avenue. He had become friendly with the owner, Doris Nelson, and would often sing along with the recordings much to the astonishment of the customers and passers-by who would gather around and listen to the soldier with the beautiful voice.

On Friday nights Lanza would usually sing without payment at the exclusive Masquer's Club in Hollywood, where the audience consisted mainly of members of the film colony: producers, directors, writers, actors and their respective guests.[23]

As a result of his limited work in *Winged Victory* and his appearances at the Masquer's Club, word soon spread throughout the movie colony about Lanza's extraordinary tenor voice. Invitations to parties and functions began to come in from all directions. Lanza did not have to be begged. He loved to sing and often accepted the invitations. Wherever he sang, he never failed to impress. Frank Sinatra and Walter Pidgeon were only two of the celebrities who became staunch Lanza supporters after they heard him sing. Sinatra commented: "The kid knocked a hole through me. Talk about people swooning when I sing, the tables were turned when I heard Lanza."[24]

Actor Walter Pidgeon, a classically trained singer who began his career as a baritone in several stage musicals before going to Hollywood, was captivated by the young soldier's voice. Pidgeon first heard Lanza sing at singer's Irene Manning's home in Hollywood. Manning, who had a brief career as a musical comedy star under contract to Warner Brothers in the forties, was giving a party to celebrate her departure for overseas. Lanza was one of her guests and sang to the piano accompaniment of Walter Pidgeon for most of the evening.

Pidgeon was overwhelmed: "The voice was so magnificent, so beyond anything I'd heard in years. I did know from my own experience as a singer that here was a voice in a million."[25] He rushed to columnist Hedda Hopper with his news. "The most beautiful voice I've heard," was his verdict. "That dark, velvety lusciousness, that terrific color. Mark my words Hedda, there goes the great tenor of the century."[26]

After hearing Lanza sing at a party at screenwriter Frances Marion's home, Hedda Hopper did not require any convincing and foresaw what would come to pass six years later. In her syndicated column on October 20, 1944, she wrote: "We finally found a man who, if he can act, could do Caruso's life. How he can sing!"[27]

The evening spent at Irene Manning's party was to prove instrumental in opening another door for Lanza. Art Rush was an agent whose clients included baritones Nelson Eddy and the Metropolitan Opera's John Charles Thomas. Rush was also the West Coast representative for RCA Victor classical record division. After hearing Lanza at Manning's party, Rush arranged for the young tenor to see him the following day.

The result of the meeting was that the two parties entered into a preliminary agreement. Furthermore, in an unprecedented move, RCA Victor stipulated that they would pay the then-unknown Lanza a 3000-dollar bonus upon the signing of a five-year contract that would ensure he would record exclusively for Victor.[28]

In fact RCA had just managed to get in ahead of Columbia Records who, at Frank Sinatra's urging, were contemplating signing Lanza themselves. After hearing the young tenor, Sinatra had told Columbia: "I've just heard a voice like you'll never hear again. Nail this guy before somebody else hooks him."[29]

In the meantime, Maria Margelli, Lanza's friend and patron from his New York days, had moved to Los Angeles and was now working for Jack Warner, head of the huge Burbank studio. She arranged an audition for her protégé and Lanza promptly arrived at the Warner mansion together with a pianist. Warner disapproved at first, deeming him too heavy for screen stardom . "But when he started to sing an aria from *Rigoletto,*" Warner recalled, "I could feel the chills run down my spine. The voice was so full and powerful that his high notes literally shook the chandelier, and I'm sure he could have been heard at the Beverly Hills Hotel five blocks away. I was tempted, yes. But I couldn't see him as another Nelson Eddy. Not with that excess poundage."[30]

Thanks to a number of private recordings of operatic arias which Lanza made upon Margelli's insistence, we have a clear idea of what the 23-year old tenor sounded like at the time. While concessions need to be made for the primitive quality of the recordings, they are nevertheless a testament to the sound the young Lanza was producing. The arias, ranging from the Improvviso from *Andrea Chénier* to the perennial *"Vesti la giubba"* from *Pagliacci*, reveal a voice that is amazingly dark, rich and even throughout its registers.

In between appearing as an extra in the film version of *Winged Victory*, serenading the film colony and having fun with both old and new friends—one of the latter being the bass-baritone George London—Lanza also managed to fall in love. The object of his affection was the girl in Bert Hick's photo.

Lanza met his future wife soon after filming started on *Winged Victory*. One of the first things Bert Hicks did when the cast of *Winged Victory* arrived in Los Angeles in June 1944 was to take Lanza home to meet his family. It was a classic case of love at first sight. Lanza took one look at Betty, who was wearing red slacks and an off-the-shoulder blouse, and knew she was the woman for him.

Betty recalled that first meeting:

> My brother Bert walked in with a big man with a big smile, a mass of dark curly hair, tanned skin, white, even teeth and the blackest and liveliest pair of eyes I'd ever seen. It was Mario. My throat became dry and I could feel a slow blaze creeping up my neck. Then Bert announced: 'Family, this is Mario Lanza!' The whole room lit up as I've seen so many rooms do since. I mumbled 'How do you do?' inadequately. Then, with a gesture which took in Bert's wife Harriet, our mother and me, Mario impulsively threw an arm around my shoulder. "I have known you for a long time Betty,' he said.[31]

She then recalled Bert's explanation of how he had shown the photo of his sister to his friend, how much Lanza had admired her and how he kept asking him what she was doing and whether she had written.

All through dinner Betty was unable to take her eyes off Lanza. "After dinner," she recalled, "my mother, who had come over from Chicago to visit us, sat down on the sofa with Mario on her right and me on her left. We kept playing hide and seek around my mother's head snatching glimpses of each other and he'd say, 'Mrs. Hicks, make your daughter stop looking at me!'

"I fell in love with him before I ever heard him sing," continued Betty. "I knew nothing then of the public Mario Lanza, who two years before had been hailed as a great discovery by Koussevitzky and had made an impressive debut at Tanglewood, but I knew Mario and loved him. All of us in that room did, and that quickly."[32]

Over the next fifteen years Betty would share with him not only happiness and fame, but also heartbreak and despair, ultimately joining him in death a mere five months after his own tragic demise.

But back in the summer of 1944 they were just another couple in love and by the end of August, a mere three months after their first meeting, they had become unofficially engaged. At twenty-two Betty, who was born in October 1922, was nearly two years younger than Lanza and had never been in love before. It was several weeks after that first meeting, and many family gatherings later, that Betty first heard her Mario sing. A lover of good food and a gourmet, Lanza had discovered Romeo's Chianti, an Italian restaurant that not only served excellent food but whose owner, Romeo, was also an opera lover with an extensive collection of records which he would play for his customers.

With Bert Hicks' birthday approaching, Lanza decided to organize a birthday party at Chianti's for his future brother-in-law, who was about to be shipped overseas. After a lavish dinner, he took the entire party—including the owner of the restaurant—to downtown Los Angeles to see a performance of Gounod's *Faust* by a visiting opera company.[33] After the performance, which ended very late, they all returned to the restaurant, where Lanza had arranged for a supper to be served. Romeo, who had had been thrilled by Lanza's singing on previous occasions, asked him to sing. "Come on Mario," he prodded him. "Sing with the records." At first Lanza demurred, but when Romeo put on "*Vesti la giubba,*" he could no longer contain himself.

Betty had been told many times what a wonderful voice Lanza possessed, but she could not have possibly imagined what she was now experiencing.

"I listened and my heart burst," she recalled. As the aria ended Lanza's audience closed around him and embraced him. Then Betty flung her arms around him and kissed him.[34]

On the 29th of August, 1944, Betty and Mario returned to

Romeo's Chianti. This time they were alone. The music was playing softly in the background as Lanza, speaking in a subdued voice and looking deeply into her eyes, asked her to marry him. At first she did not reply, but then reaching across the table she slipped her hand into his and softly said, "You know I will."[35]

4—MARRIAGE

MARIO AND BETTY RESOLVED not to tell anyone of their plans, but to wait instead until the war was over.[1] The weeks that followed were idyllic for the young couple, but came to an abrupt end with Lanza's sudden transfer to the military base of Walla Walla, Washington. For a sensitive, impulsive young man such as Lanza, the enforced separation must have been devastating. He found solace in telephone calls and in the occasional letter. Lanza, already a compulsive telephone user, would call Betty almost every day, cheerfully oblivious to the mounting cost.[2] Betty who wrote to him constantly was upset by his infrequent correspondence so she sent him a two–page letter on which she wrote only "Dear Honey, Love you today, tomorrow and forever." On the reverse she added "This is more than I receive from you!"[3]

The couple would not see each other again until January, 1945. Granted a medical discharge on the basis of an ear infection and postnasal drip, Lanza immediately headed for Los Angeles to see Betty. By now he was certain: Betty was the only woman for him, and marriage had become his immediate goal.[4]

As much as she also wanted to marry her Mario, Betty suggested that he should first go to Philadelphia to visit his parents, who had not seen him in almost three years. This, she reasoned, would give him the opportunity to tell them who she was, and explain that they were planning to marry.[5]

At first Lanza refused to leave without her. Then, to complicate matters further, he was summoned to New York by RCA, who were eager to begin making test recordings of his voice.[6] Betty succeeded in convincing him to go first to Philadelphia to see his parents, and then proceed to New York. She would join him later. The matter appeared to be settled, but just before he was due to leave, Lanza changed his mind. He wasn't going anywhere without her, he declared, and he would never leave Los Angeles if she did not marry him immediately. "There was no time to reason with him or hold out for the kind of wedding I'd always wanted," recalled Betty.[7] And so on Friday, April 13, 1945—with blissful disregard for superstition—they were married in a civil ceremony in Judge Charles Griffin's chambers at the City Hall in Beverly Hills. Betty's mother was present and the Best Man was Bert Hicks.

Cash was an immediate problem for the newlyweds.[8] Neither was employed, and their sole income was provided by RCA Victor, who were paying Lanza the arranged $3000 bonus in 12 monthly instalments of $250. Paid on the 15th of each month, Lanza had already received the first two installments. These should have been sufficient to tide him over, but with his taste for luxurious accommodation, fine clothing, and the best food available, the money had soon vanished, leaving him with a mere $6.95 for the wedding ring.[9] For Betty, however, the ring was unique. Years later, when Lanza was making millions and could have bought her the most expensive ring she desired, Betty never allowed him to replace it. She was still wearing it on the day she died.[10] "I would have married him if he'd been a ditch digger," Betty remarked seven years later, and added, "I married him for his love. Everything else, his voice, his career, his success—all that has been an unexpected surprise."[11]

After the wedding the couple headed east. They decided that Betty would spend a few days with her family in Chicago, while Lanza would go directly to New York to look for suitable living quarters, and summon the courage to break the news of his marriage to his parents. The couple had settled on New York as their base, not only because of the recording commitments with RCA Victor and impending contract with Columbia Artists Management, but also because the city offered a good selection of singing teachers.[12] Regardless of the flattering comments and sincere admiration he had been receiving for his voice, Lanza was acutely aware that he needed more work before he could confidently tackle the concert and operatic stage.[13] Almost three years had passed since the concentrated study of his scholarship days in Tanglewood, and while the army shows had been fun, they had contributed nothing to his musical development.

But first he had to break the news of his marriage to Maria and Antonio. Too daunted to tell his parents over the telephone, he called Betty in Chicago for support. Feeling he would be more successful in breaking the news with Betty's help, he told her: "You better come over. If they see you, I won't have to explain. They'll know it's wonderful."[14]

Meanwhile Lanza had booked a suite at New York's lavish Park Central Hotel. He justified the expense by telling a surprised Betty that this was, in effect, their honeymoon and that they should celebrate it in style.[15] He then telephoned his parents in Philadelphia, asking them to come to New York as soon as possible for some very important news.

Anticipating Antonio and Maria's arrival, the newlyweds became increasingly nervous. Reasoning now that it would be better if she were absent when Lanza broke the news to his parents, Betty decided to see a movie. This would give them ample time to recover from the shock.[16] It was an apprehensive Betty who returned to the hotel after the movie. In her anxiety she telephoned her husband from the hotel lobby. Her fears were unfounded. A jubilant Lanza announced that he had told his parents he had married "the most wonderful girl in the world" and to "hurry right up" because they were dying to meet her. Betty rushed back to their suite and, in a typically warm, effusive, Italian way, was quickly submerged in hugs and kisses by Lanza's parents. A short time later, on a rainy July afternoon, they were again married in a religious ceremony in the little chapel of St. Columba's Church in Manhattan. This time both families were present.[17]

5—A MENTOR

HAVING SETTLED COMFORTABLY with his new bride into their suite at the Park Central Hotel for what was supposedly a short honeymoon, Lanza was in his element. In typical fashion, he decided to extend their stay, blithely disregarding their lack of funds. There was no question, as far as he was concerned, of moving to a standard room or living more modestly. Quite apart from enjoying the luxury and comfort provided by the Park Central Hotel, Lanza's claustrophobia may have been a factor in considering less spacious accommodations.[1]

Meanwhile their financial situation continued to deteriorate. At a precarious moment in their fortunes, unexpected help came from Lanza's old friend, baritone Robert Weede. Learning of their predicament, Weede suggested that they take over the city apartment he was renting. He, in turn, would move to the peace and quiet of his farm in Nyack, twenty-seven miles from New York City. Although reluctant to leave the Park Central, Lanza acknowledged that their financial situation was dire, and expressed his gratitude to Weede for coming to the rescue.[2]

The apartment was modest and comfortable. Consisting of four furnished rooms, it was located on the fourth floor of one of the buildings in Rockefeller Center at 8 West, 49th Street, overlooking the Center's ice skating rink. The Lanzas affectionately named it the "Bohemian Garret."[3] At $75 a month, the rent may have been reasonable and the apartment unpretentious, but there was nothing modest about Lanza's lifestyle. He continued to live life with complete disregard for any notions of saving or budgeting.[4]

To Lanza, money was meant for spending. He enjoyed living life to the hilt and sharing his *joie de vivre* with old friends Weede and bass-baritone George London, as well as newer acquaintances such as baritone Robert Merrill, who—like Lanza—had been signed to a recording contract by RCA. Lanza's lifestyle consisted of eating the best food in the best restaurants, drinking the most expensive wines and champagnes and wearing the best clothes. On top of this, he was generous to a fault and would think nothing of buying a newspaper and leaving a ten-dollar tip. In short, Lanza had no difficulty in following his father's guiding philosophy: "Think of art and to hell with money."⁵

Betty, while acknowledging their financial difficulties, was very much in love and dependent on her husband to the extent that she was both unwilling to restrain him, and incapable of doing so. Actor Barry Nelson recalled: "Betty was a nice person, a good person, but she was not strong and, in any case, it would have taken an exceptionally strong person to be around someone as dynamic as Mario twenty-four hours a day."⁶

Betty's brother John Hicks, who was a baritone intent on pursuing a singing career, came to New York around this time and moved in with his sister and brother-in-law while he was attending the American Academy of Dramatic Arts. He recalled those post-war months:

> He was really quite a charming guy and had the most beautiful voice of anybody I ever heard. Gorgeous, just gorgeous. He wasn't the easiest guy either. Flamboyant, wildly generous, irritable, temperamental, a ballbuster, all nerves. And nerves can kill you. There was something different about him though. It's too bad he had to go so soon.
>
> Mario was a big tipper, even then. He didn't have any money but he was putting up a big front. He knew he was gonna make it, before he made it. The first night I came to New York, he and Betty took me out to dinner at Toots Shor's. I'm from the Midwest, Chicago, and in those days we hardly knew what tipping was. Everything on the menu, of course, was a la carte and I was insisting on paying my own way. When the tab came my end was about $10 and I could hardly believe it—here I was in town on the G.I.Bill and the prices were killing me the first night. Then came the topper—Mario added $25 tip and I was shocked. I'm still shocked to this day. He was generous, overly generous. The four or five

months I spent with them I really enjoyed.[7]

Regardless of his lifestyle, singing was still paramount in Lanza's mind. Since arriving in New York, he had been working on voice technique with Robert Weede – together with another baritone, Grant Garnell (whose real name was Giuseppe Gentile) – but there was also the question of learning a repertoire for both his future concert and operatic career. For this he would require a vocal coach. It was Weede who suggested that he should work with Maestro Renato Bellini on the operatic repertoire and with Miss Debarau Robinson, a coach better known as Polly to both her friends and pupils, on the songs.[8]

More importantly, Lanza had also started to work with Peter Herman Adler, Conductor and Musical Director for the newly formed Columbia Artists Management Touring Opera Company. Adler had been assigned to work with Lanza by Arthur Judson, the head of Columbia Artists, who had now signed the tenor to a contract.

Czechoslovakian-born Adler had made his conducting debut with the opera *Lohengrin* in Jablonec at the age of 22. In 1939 Adler had come to America, where he conducted the New York Philharmonic Symphony Ochestra and appeared as guest conductor with a number of leading orchestras. In 1942 he was appointed joint musical director with Fritz Busch of the New Company in New York City Opera, and in 1949 he was made Artistic and Musical Director of the NBC-TV Opera Department.[9]

Patient and understanding with young talent, Adler was the ideal man for the musically unschooled Lanza, who established an instant rapport with the conductor.[10] Adler's task was to make the tenor musically secure, and in Lanza he found an enthusiastic and talented pupil. The conductor, who was not reticent in giving praise when it was due, was unstinting in his opinion of his young charge. He would soon tell Lanza's mentor and manager Sam Weiler: "I think this boy has the greatest inherent, instinctive musicality I have ever seen. He's not only a great singing prospect, but he has usually behaved wonderfully with me."[11]

In the meantime, Lanza continued to work with coach Polly Robinson at her studio in the Carnegie Hall building. In particular, Robinson helped him with the music for a new radio engagement he had secured. Temporary relief for his floundering finances had come in the form of a tenor spot on *Great Moments in Music*, a weekly radio program for CBS. Lanza was to replace the regular tenor, the well-established Metropolitan opera singer, Jan Peerce, for a number of weeks while Peerce was away fulfilling other engagements.

Robert Weede had been the instigator. Immediately upon learning that Peerce was going on leave, Weede went to soprano Jean Tennyson, a featured singer on the show and the person responsible for the hiring of singers. Weede told her he had a friend with a wonderful tenor voice who would be the perfect substitute for Peerce.[12] Tennyson agreed to hear Lanza, but only as part of a general audition she was holding for a number of other budding tenors who were also applying for the position. No sooner had the auditions begun than it became evident to everyone present that Lanza was the only choice. Impressed, Tennyson signed the 24-year-old immediately.[13]

However, the assignment would prove challenging. Lanza later recalled: "I was required to sing things that were so difficult that I needed years of experience before tackling them. *Otello*, for example. After six programs I knew I couldn't go on."[14]

The broadcasts included highlights from such diverse operas as *Tosca* and *Otello*, Liza Lehmann's song cycle *In A Persian Garden*, the operetta *The Student Prince,* and songs of Irving Berlin. Lanza cancelled three appearances, withdrawing at the last moment from his first program, the Johann Strauss operetta *Die Fledermaus*, and also cancelling his second appearance in Thomas's *Mignon*. Of the nine programs he was scheduled to sing between October 1945 and February 1946, Lanza would sing in only six.[15]

In view of the path his career subsequently took, it is interesting to speculate whether Lanza was already setting a pattern. While he had a legitimate reason for the last cancellation, which was a broadcast of *La Traviata*[†] his motives in cancelling the first two are difficult to fathom.

Whatever the reason, it bears repeating that Lanza was unhappy at having accepted the assignment on *Great Moments In*

[†]He was leaving to start serious singing study.

Music. At a fee that ranged from $300 to $400 per program, money was certainly not an issue, but Lanza's lack of vocal training, and his belief that his voice was not yet ready for such a challenge, must have weighed heavily on his mind. The only work he had undertaken on vocal technique had been limited to what his friend Robert Weede had taught him. Yet judging from his singing of the Love Duet from Act 1 of *Otello*, he was already doing amazingly well.

Due almost entirely to its natural placement the voice is already correctly produced, while Lanza's feeling and understanding of the music is evident in his phrasing. The fact that it was not an Otello voice at this early stage of his career is not significant.

Although written by Verdi for a dramatic tenor (Tamagno), the role also contains many lyric passages such as the exquisite Love Duet in the first act of the opera. Unfortunately, the beautiful duet "*Già nella notte densa,*"in which Desdemona and Otello reaffirm their love for each other, is ruined by the atrocious singing of the very person responsible for having hired him (Tennyson).[†]

Lanza's tackling of Verdi's masterpiece, on the other hand, reveals a vocal assurance and a command of the music that is truly remarkable for a 24-year-old. Listening to the recording today, it is difficult to gauge why Lanza still felt insecure about his singing. Yet there is no question that he took his performing very seriously. While his volatility may have caused him difficulties in applying himself at times, he had great respect for the music he was singing and wanted to perform it at his best.

Unless he was fully prepared, vocally and musically, he would become both edgy and negative.[16]

What he badly required now—and would need even more later in his career—was someone who could guide him; in short,

---

[†]Jean Tennyson was a 40-year-old soprano with experience in Italy, and both the Chicago and San Francisco opera companies. Despite her considerable experience on stage and as a veteran radio performer, her appearances with Lanza left a great deal to be desired. Singing with Lanza in the *Otello* duet, and later in an ill-judged abridged version of the Act 1 duet from *Tosca*, Tennyson's singing resembles an impersonation of the infamous Florence Foster Jenkins.

a Svengali-like figure. Someone who could, at least in part, control him and whose interests would not be motivated by financial gain.[17] He required both personal and artistic guidance. He needed a Meneghini, a Serafin, or a Bonynge.

Notwithstanding her considerable talent, how would someone as insecure as Maria Callas have survived without the support of her wealthy husband Meneghini and the help of the great conductor Tullio Serafin? How would Joan Sutherland have fared without the intelligence, determination and vocal knowledge of her husband Richard Bonynge?

Tenors are no exception. The acclaimed Franco Corelli, an exact contemporary of Lanza's, required the constant reassurance and determination of his wife, the former soprano Loretta Di Lelio, as well as support from his mentor, tenor Giacomo Lauri-Volpi. Without their assistance, Corelli would not have had a career.[†]

Betty Lanza was not in this category. Although she loved her husband dearly, she was ill equipped to provide Lanza with the support he desperately needed. Never the dominant partner in their relationship, she was not in a position to advise him in either musical matters or those involving career decisions.[18]

For a time, however, it appeared that Lanza had indeed found his mentor in a wealthy realtor named Sam Weiler, whom Lanza met at Polly Robinson's studio. Weiler was an opera lover with a limited lyric tenor voice who longed for an operatic career. Like Lanza, he was also taking coaching lessons from Polly Robinson, but given the limitations of his voice, any thought of Weiler singing professionally was out of the question.[19]

Then one day in August 1945, Weiler's singing lessons came to an abrupt end. By chance Lanza had arrived early for his lesson and had walked in while Weiler was still there. An enthusiastic Miss Robinson turned to the wealthy businessman and asked him if he would like to hear a "really outstanding voice."[20]

Although momentarily shaken by the implied lack of confidence in his own vocal talent, Weiler nodded in assent. A smiling Lanza obliged, launching immediately into Leoncavallo's

[†]Even then, the constant nervous strain would see Corelli cut short his career at age 55, with his voice still virtually intact.

"Mattinata."

The effect of the young tenor's voice on Weiler was overwhelming. The quality, size and power of it completely astounded him. At the end of the performance Weiler knew that he would never again sing another note. "I have never in my life heard anything so naturally brilliant," he said. "I knew there and then that I had just heard the greatest voice in the world."[21] Weiler went home to his wife full of praise for Lanza, and was irrepressible on the subject for weeks afterward. He also listened to Lanza sing in *Great Moments In Music*, investigated his background and found that his extraordinary voice was largely untrained.[22]

Several weeks after their first meeting in Polly Robinson's studio, Lanza and Weiler went to a coffee shop and had their first good talk. As they spoke, Weiler learned that Lanza was an insecure young man, conscious of his lack of training, and aware that he was not yet ready to perform in public. Weiler also discovered that Lanza's instincts towards what he should be doing and singing were entirely correct. "He was fastidiously serious as far as music was concerned," Weiler later recalled. "He was aware of the handicaps under which he was working."[23]

Perhaps sensing that Weiler was the mentor he was looking for, Lanza poured his heart out to the wealthy businessman, revealing not only his dream of becoming a great opera singer, but also his taste for luxurious living, his debts, and his total inability to save money. Fifteen cups of coffee later, Weiler had reached a decision. Henceforth he would act as Lanza's sponsor and advisor.[24]

Weiler was thirty-one years old at the time. His successful business career included selling and refinancing buildings in partnership with his brother Jack, and operating the Fairmont and St. Francis hotels in San Francisco. Weiler had heard most of the finest singers currently performing and was convinced that Lanza had the greatest voice and potential of them all. It was only a question of proper training, he felt. He told Lanza that they should begin by finding the best voice teacher available.[25]

Lanza suggested that they seek the advice of Peter Herman Adler. For his part, Adler was unequivocal. The greatest voice teacher was Enrico Rosati, he told Weiler, who had a studio in New York.[26]

Rosati was indeed a prestigious name in the music world. Prior to settling in New York he had taught voice production at the Academy of Santa Cecilia in Rome, where his pupils had included the renowned tenors Beniamino Gigli and Giacomo Lauri-Volpi. Since coming to America he had taught tenor James Melton, among others, and would soon be teaching Lanza's old army friend, bass-baritone George London. A few days after the conversation with Adler, Lanza and Weiler entered Rosati's studio on West 57th Street.

The white-haired, bespectacled maestro greeted the two men briefly, mentioning in passing that he had heard Lanza on the *Great Moments In Music* radio broadcasts. He then sat down at the piano and asked Lanza to sing.[27]

When Lanza finished, Rosati arose without making a comment and opened the studio door. Calling his wife and his secretary to "Come and listen to something," he asked Lanza to sing again. As the last notes filled the air the maestro, head bowed, fingers still on the keyboard, spoke as though to himself: "For 34 years, since Gigli, I wait for this voice."[28] Lanza had found his singing teacher.

6—ROSATI

ROSATI HAD INDEED FOUND a voice of exceptional color, with a timbre that was fuller, darker and more ringing than Gigli's.

Having settled the important question of finding the best teacher available, Weiler turned his attention to organizing Lanza's finances. This was no simple task, as he had to begin by paying off $11,000 of accumulated debt. Weiler also agreed with Lanza that he should not sing another note in public until he had received the vocal training he needed. This entailed cancelling all of Lanza's current commitments, including the *Great Moments in Music* broadcasts, and a number of concert engagements already booked by Columbia Artists Management.[1]

Weiler would pay for the tuition with Rosati, as well as providing Lanza with a weekly allowance of $70 to cover his day-to-day expenses. Further amounts would be allocated to cover other expenses such as clothing and holidays as well as providing a small allowance for the tenor's parents. Ultimately, Weiler claimed that he had invested almost $60,000 in Lanza.[2] This might have been an exaggeration, but whatever the specifics, his support clearly indicated his complete faith, not only in Lanza's voice but also in the singer's career possibilities.[3]

On February 1, 1946, a contract was drawn in which Lanza agreed to pay Weiler 5% of all his eventual gross income. This would later be changed to 10% and 20% in subsequent contracts.[4]

With the financial considerations taken care of, Lanza was ready to begin working on his vocal technique with Rosati. Their lessons together would last for the next fifteen months.

With such vocal equipment at his disposal, Rosati found it comparatively easy to teach Lanza. The voice was complete through its almost two and a half octave range and there were traces of a basic technique, which the singer had acquired principally from working with his friend Robert Weede.[5]

Discovering that Lanza's voice was already perfectly placed, Rosati concentrated on strengthening the tenor's diaphragmatic support and breath control, and helping him to relax his throat and facial muscles. Before long Lanza, who was immensely strong to begin with, was able to sing for very long periods in the most natural way possible without tiring.[6]

Speaking of the time he spent with Rosati, Lanza said: "Slowly, carefully, he took me laboriously through exercises. At first pianissimo through the entire gamut of my voice, so that now I can sing for hours without becoming tired."[7]

George London later recalled that when he first met Lanza, "The voice was unschooled but of incredible beauty, with ringing, fearless high notes...Rosati directed him to singing more lyrically, with less pressure, to good advantage."[8]

During the time spent studying with Rosati, Lanza made an effort to find the discipline he knew he lacked. He had immense respect for the maestro and was determined to live up to the great expectations that Rosati had of him. It proved an almost impossible task. He was under strong pressure from all directions. The giant Columbia Artists Management, who represented him, were well aware that they had a major talent on their hands, and were eager to book him for a series of regular concerts. They failed to understand why it was not possible for him to continue singing concerts and study at the same time.[9]

With the help of his singing teacher, Lanza was able—for a time, at least—to resist the efforts of those who wanted him to perform before he felt he was ready. Rosati was well aware of the number of people anxious to speed up Lanza's career. These included Sam Weiler, who was eager to see a return on his investment. Rosati was determined to keep them from exploiting his star pupil before he was ready. He once told a group of people who had come to his studio in order to convince him that Lanza was ready: "You have the goose that can lay the golden egg and you want to kill him."[10]

However, the maestro encouraged his pupil to sing in occasional concerts, which he felt would benefit Lanza by giving him poise and confidence in front of an audience. Lanza sang in

Toronto, Ottawa and St. Louis, making a powerful impression on his audiences and receiving excellent reviews. The concert he sang in Toronto on July 2, 1946 took place a mere five months after he had begun studying with Rosati. The Toronto *Daily Star* reported that "Mario Lanza, tenor, a handsome black-haired young man with a flashing smile won the hearts of his audience...Together with the Finnish-born conductor Tauno Hannikainen [Lanza] made it a most enjoyable concert. He sang with spirit and revealed a thrilling tenor voice singing arias from *La Gioconda, Tosca* and the lovely *"M'appari"* from *Marta*.

Later he did a group with Leo Barkin at the piano and wound up with a couple of encores including 'Softly As In A Morning Sunrise.' His diction was remarkably good and his boyish mannerisms tickled the crowd."[11]

Even Claudia Cassidy, the respected but notoriously caustic critic of the *Chicago Tribune*, was captivated by Lanza. On July 7, following the first of two concerts with Frances Yeend at Grant Park before an estimated audience of 25,000, she wrote:

> Mr. Lanza came first. A handsome dark-haired boy with wide shoulders and a disarmingly modest presence. With the two *Tosca* arias he left no doubt that he has a true Italian tenor, beautiful, ardent and exciting. How big it is without that microphone, I don't know, but it has superb range and a crescendo to set susceptible folks shouting. In "Cielo E Mar" from *La Gioconda,* Mr. Lanza took the soaring climax like a veteran. If he keeps on like this, he may soon be filling the stratospheric regions of the opera house.[12] †

Pleased with the outcome of the concerts Lanza sent his teacher a postcard:

> Dear Maestro, Had wonderful success and am sending you reviews ...... Singing again on the 17th. Easy – only 4 numbers. Take care of yourself. Love, Mario and Betty.[13]

After his concert in Ottawa, in November 1946, *The Ottawa Journal* reported: "The appearance of the young tenor, Mario

---

†The last Sunday in December 1946, Claudia Cassidy devoted her column in the Chicago Tribune to what she considered the musical highlights in Chicago during the year. Listed among the 17 selections was the Love Duet from *Madama Butterfly* sung by Lanza and Yeend.

Lanza, was indeed close to the advertised 'sensational.' Mr. Lanza has a voice of beauty and power. Enunciation in his native Italian was perfect and intonation excellent."[14]

Writing in *The Ottawa Citizen*, music critic Lauretta Thistle stated: "Lanza has that golden quality to his voice, which is given to few tenors and he sings with ease and a welcome lack of affectation. Melodiousness and purity of tone are the most obvious qualities of his singing, but he has great reserves of power as well, and his range was indicated by the ringing high C that he produced."[15]

The high C that the critic was referring to was the climax to the aria *"Che gelida manina"* from Puccini's *La Bohème*, which Lanza had sung in the original key. The approach to the high C in the Puccini aria is particularly difficult and transposing it down a half-tone is common practice in a live performance. He may still have had doubts, but he was certainly gaining assurance.

A letter from the Ottawa concert manager W. Kilpatrick Jr. to Columbia Concerts Management representative in New York, Mrs. Ada G. Cooper, is worth quoting in full:

> Just a few lines to let you know what a tremendous impression Mr. Lanza made on our audience last night. They screamed and stamped and cheered. It was impossible for him to leave. He was even forced to repeat one of his encores.
>
> From both an artistic and personal point of view I don't think it will ever be possible for me to get such a thrill from presenting any artist.
>
> The privilege of having Mr. Lanza with us is definitely the high point of my career as a promoter. I doubt it will ever be equalled. Dr. De Ridder, our conductor, said that in his experience he had never had a soloist who was so wonderful to work with.[†]
>
> I know this local management to New York office letter has got to be more or less routine in the business. But please for

---

[†]Dutch born De Ridder was a composer and violist as well as conductor. He formed the Allard de Ridder Chamber music quartet in 1933, conducted the Vancouver Symphony Orchestra from 1930-41 and founded the Ottawa Philharmonic Orchestra in 1944. He retired in 1952.

once don't chalk this up as the same old baloney. This is the real thing and we hope we'll have the thrill of presenting Mr. Lanza many many times down through the years.[16]

It was obvious that after only nine months work with Rosati, Lanza was making excellent progress. The tenor had also come to the attention of Edward Johnson, then General Manager of the Metropolitan Opera.

A Canadian by birth, Johnson had been a successful tenor himself, studying in Italy with Vincenzo Lombardi, the maestro and conductor who had taught Caruso early in his career, and singing extensively in Italy under the name of Edoardo Di Giovanni. He was a leading tenor at the Metropolitan in New York from 1922 to 1935, and was appointed General Manager upon Gatti-Casazza's retirement.

Johnson was a respected authority on voices, and after hearing Lanza sing at a private gathering organized by Rosati, he made the tenor an offer to join the company.[17] Johnson would repeat the invitation during the remaining four years of his tenure at the Metropolitan. Lanza steadfastly declined the offers, feeling he was not yet ready.[18]

Lanza's debt and gratitude towards his teacher are clearly indicated by the inscription on the photo that he gave to Rosati at the end of his studies with him:

To Maestro Enrico Rosati—any success I am having or will have in the future I owe 100% to you, the greatest undisputed voice teacher in the world, past, present and future. I love you and you will always be close to me wherever I am or in whatever I do. Especially on the stage, however, you will always be there with the third register.

All my love for you, Maestro.

Mario Lanza.[19]

7—THE BEL CANTO TRIO

DESPITE ROSATI'S EFFORTS to prevent his star pupil from being prematurely exploited, by early 1947 Columbia Artists Management had booked a number of concerts for the tenor.[1] These would be Lanza's first regular appearances after the fifteen months of study with the maestro. It was on one of his first dates, at a concert in the small town of Shippensburg, Pennsylvania, on April 14, 1947, that Lanza met the man destined to become his principal conductor and accompanist for most of the remaining twelve years of his life.

Constantine Callinicos was a native New Yorker of Greek parentage, who had studied at the Juilliard School of Music in New York, and in Athens. Although the 28 year-old Callinicos had already worked with several famous singers, including Lily Pons and Lauritz Melchior,[2] he was neither a seasoned accompanist nor an experienced conductor. His close association with Lanza, as we will see later, would have serious repercussions on the tenor's recording output – in particular, the operatic selections. Like Lanza he was also represented by Columbia Artists Management. When asked by company representative Zena Hanenfeld whether he would be interested in accompanying a young tenor named Mario Lanza at a concert in Shippensburg, Callinicos replied he had never heard of either Lanza or the place.[3]

Hanenfeld immediately reassured him that as far as Lanza was concerned, he would most certainly be hearing about him. She then told Callinicos that Lanza was singing for a modest fee ($250) and that he would be receiving a small cut from it. Not surprisingly the mercenary Callinicos was not impressed by the offer from Columbia Artists. "I became less interested by the second but after she hung up something prompted me to dial Lanza's number," Callinicos recalled.[4] "Mario answered the phone and began discussing the concert in his exuberant, friendly manner. I had the sudden impression that I had known him all my life." Inquiring as to when the tenor would like to rehearse, Lanza's reply stunned him. "We don't need to rehearse," he said. "I've got things to do. I have confidence in you, Constantine."[5]

This was incomprehensible to Callinicos, who had assumed that a man of Lanza's limited stage experience would see rehearsing as his top priority. Not unreasonably, he also wanted to meet and hear the singer he would be accompanying.

Callinicos would soon discover that as well as possessing an extraordinary voice, Lanza loathed conformity. On meeting the tenor—a mere two hours before the concert was due to start—Callinicos was further unnerved by Lanza's informal dress. Looking fit and relaxed, the tenor smiled as he shook the accompanist's hand, casually informing him that they would have to wear business suits instead of the standard tuxedos. Lanza had failed to bring his tuxedo with him, and announced that he hated wearing them in any event.[6]

Although baffled by the singer's behavior, Callinicos—like so many others before him—was instantly won over by Lanza's outgoing and friendly personality. Nonetheless, he was nervous as they stepped onto the stage of the State Teacher's College Auditorium in Shippensburg. Callinicos had yet to hear a single sound emerge from his soloist. An increasingly edgy Callinicos sat at the piano ready to accompany his soloist in the first selection, Stradella's *'Pieta, Signore.'*

Lanza's lack of stage experience became immediately evident. As Callinicos played the introduction, Lanza—turning his back to the audience—leaned towards his accompanist with a smile, offering him a wink of reassurance. What followed is best described in Callinicos's own words:

> Then he began singing, and I knew that the tux was unimportant, and that the offensive tradition-defying back-to-the-audience was just a neophyte's lack of stage deportment. For as the rich, glorious tones flowed effortlessly from Mario's throat, I knew I was listening to one of the greatest tenor voices since Caruso. Through Mario's vocal cords, and through those bony cavities in his throat, nose and mouth

which are called the resonators, emerged phrases of such opulence, warmth and velvety quality that I sat there feeling some incredible joke had been played on me.[7]

Each note was "round and lush, satisfying and meaningful," observed the startled accompanist, and Lanza's breath control on the long phrases was "truly amazing."

He further noted Lanza's enthusiasm for each selection, and the tenor's ability to communicate his depth of feeling for his material. "It was only a matter of minutes before he had the audience in the palm of his hand, applauding and cheering him to the echo."

After the concert, an obviously pleased Lanza turned to his dazed accompanist, assuring him that "There's a lot more to come."[8]

At this stage in the 26-year-old tenor's career, there were no apparent signs of the doubts and fears that would later plague him. If his career was off to a promising start, his private life could not have been better. After two years of marriage, he was blissfully happy with his adoring Betty, who was often present at his concerts smiling reassuringly from the wings. Indeed the only cloud in an otherwise bright sky for the couple—eager to start a family—was Betty's apparent inability to conceive.[9]

Pleased with the success of Lanza's first solo concerts, Columbia Artists decided to couple the tenor with another of their budding young singers.

Three years older than Lanza, lyric soprano Frances Yeend had already acquired a fair amount of experience. A native of Vancouver, Washington, she had made her debut as Nedda in *Pagliacci* in Spokane, and had sung in a number of operettas, and performed frequently on radio in New York. She had also performed the role of Ellen Orford in the American premiere of *Peter Grimes* at the Tanglewood Music festival in 1946.[10] Lanza and Yeend had previously met in December 1945, when they sang together in excerpts from *In A Persian Garden* on the *Great Moments in Music* radio program. Subsequently they had appeared jointly in Chicago in July 1946 and St. Louis in January 1947. According to Harry R. Burke, writing in the *St Louis Globe-Democrat*, "Mr. Lanza revealed a fine tenor, splendidly placed and used with ease."[11] By the beginning of 1947, their repeated success with audiences had encouraged Columbia to add a third singer, with the aim of forming an operatic trio that would tour extensively throughout the United States as well as Canada and Mexico.

On learning of Columbia's plans, Lanza immediately suggested they engage his old friend George London.[12] The bass-baritone had also been studying with Enrico Rosati and conductor Peter Herman Adler, and would later go on to achieve both critical and public acclaim in Europe and at the Metropolitan in New York.

A year older than Lanza, London was born in Montreal, Canada to Russian/Jewish parents, and later moved to California with his family as a teenager. Following a number of comprimario roles at Hollywood Bowl, London had recently come to New York as the second lead in a touring company production of *The Desert Song*.[13]

Agreeing to Lanza's suggestion, Columbia added London to what would become known as the Bel Canto Trio. Lanza, Yeend and London began touring in Milwaukee on July 8, 1947 and sang eighty-six concerts over the next ten months, making their final appearance in Moncton, New Brunswick, on May 27, 1948. Although all three of them received impressive reviews throughout the tour, it was invariably Lanza who received the biggest acclaim from audiences and critics alike.

Following their concert at the Emil Blatz Temple Of Music, Edward P. Halline of the *Milwaukee Sentinel* wrote: "Last night 6000 patrons heard three young American singers who are very definitely on their way up...Lanza was the most impressive of all, with just the kind of voice that is needed to get all the drama out of such emotionally charged arias as '*E lucevan le stelle*' and '*Celeste Aida*.'"[14] Richard S. Davis, reporting in the *Milwaukee Journal,* was of a similar opinion: "The favorite with the audience was the tenor, Lanza, a singer unmistakably destined to enjoy a handsome career."[15]

Anyway, at this early point in his career, it seemed Lanza could do no wrong. Not only did he possess an exceptionally beautiful voice, but the time spent studying with Rosati had given him the polish and assurance that he previously lacked, enabling him to sing with a good degree of style and musicality. He was also careful to keep the tone light and lyrical rather than use the full range of his natural voice, which was darker.[16]

Throughout the tour Lanza continued to be singled out by the critics. Following the Bel Canto Trio's concert in Beaumont, Texas, Melita Melis reported in the local paper: "Admirably produced, [Lanza's] voice possesses uncommon beauty of texture with no reaching for the top notes which were remarkably firm, free and vibrant."[17]

Back in Chicago, where they were booked for a return engagement at Grant Park, the trio performed in two concerts. After the first concert which took place on July 19 before an estimated audience of 55,000, Claudia Cassidy, who had hailed Lanza as a sensational new discovery the year before, again singled him out in an article for the *Chicago Sunday Tribune* under the heading "Lanza Born to Sing."

> Mr. Lanza sings for the indisputable reason that he was born to sing. He has a superbly natural tenor which he uses by instinct, and though a multitude of fine points evade him, he possesses the things almost impossible to learn. He knows the accent that makes a lyric line reach its audience, and he knows why opera is music drama. With a voice like that he needs work to acquire a true legato worthy of that ardent coloring, but he does amazingly well right now when he attacks a completely dramatic aria like *Celeste Aida*. He clung to the tenor custom of topping Verdi on the climatic [sic] note but he did take it as written, pianissimo with a swelling crescendo. It was beautifully done and the crowd roared while Mr. Lanza happily mopped his brow. He seemed more surprised, and just as delighted as anyone else.[18]

There was more praise from critic Charles Buckley in the Chicago *Herald American*: "Mario Lanza's easily produced tenor is used with musical intelligence and fine diction."[19]

The following night, on the strength of Claudia Cassidy's review, Lanza drew 76,000 people to the huge Grant Park stadium in spite of rain.

One interesting aspect of the Bel Canto Trio concerts was that apart from the standard operatic solos, Lanza was singing duets and trios with Yeend and London that he would never sing again. These included the Farewell Scene from Mozart's *The Magic Flute*, "*Perdon, perdon Amelia*" from Verdi's *Simon*

Boccanegra, "*Qual volutà trascorrere*" from Verdi's *I Lombardi,* "*Ecco, il magico liquore*" from Donizetti's *L'Elisir d'Amore,* the Prison Scene from Gounod's *Faust* and "Nobody Could Love You More" from the operetta *Paganini* by Lehar.

When they were not performing, Lanza and George London lived life to the hilt. "We overate, over-drank, overslept, overdid things generally," recalled London.[20]

Betty's younger sister Virginia Abbatacola (née Hicks) spoke of the time her brother in law and George London came to Chicago for the Trio's concert at Grant Park:

> They had their own shenanigans at our house. We lived in an all-Irish neighborhood and George, who was Jewish and Mario who wasn't, would shout loud abrasive ethnic slurs at each other out on our sidewalk. It was part of their sense of humor.[21]

Lanza's close friend Barry Nelson would later describe the tenor as being "a sensualist with gargantuan tastes, particularly for food and women." Certainly, there is no doubt that Lanza made use of a self-serving creed or rationalization that was widespread among young men with his ethnic and cultural background in that he had learned to divorce love from mere sex, avoiding any feelings of guilt by reasoning that sex for the sake of sex was not important. Despite tales of lurid liaisons attributed to Lanza by previous biographers—one of whom conveniently named two dead actresses—Lanza's extramarital encounters were rare. He entertained the thought of having the occasional escapade if the chance arose, but in most cases he would beat a hasty retreat. Apart from the fact that he genuinely loved his wife, and would never hurt her deliberately, he was also terrified of catching a venereal disease and passing it on to her.[22]

When it came to sex, however, as well as life in general, Lanza was without inhibitions. Barry Nelson recalled an occasion on which he met up with the tenor at a luxurious hotel suite in Manhattan, where Lanza was staying. What follows would no doubt be described as outrageous behavior on the part of the tenor by most people, but Nelson makes an interesting observation about Lanza's "vulgar side."

On this occasion, Lanza had invited a young woman whom he had just met to join him, Nelson and a few other friends in his suite. Excusing himself, he then accompanied the woman to his bedroom.

"You could hear a lot of things going on," recalled Nelson, "and then he came out and beckoned any or all of us to come in and watch.

> He was so proud of his sex exploits, you see. He thought we should all see this! But it was not a thing where you say, 'Oh isn't that bad taste.' Individuals differ. It's the manner in how they do it. If you relate this in a story instead of dialogue, it's dry. Then it looks like: 'he's an animal'. But he did it with such humor that you were laughing. He did it in innocence...kind of like, 'this is really good and by God you all ought to enjoy this!' That's a different thing and not everybody could understand that...Of course, we really didn't go in.

> After that all I can tell you is...I was there the next night and the girl knocked on the door. Couldn't have been all bad. She wasn't that outraged, and Mario must have been pretty good. He didn't call her, she came, you see. So that explains a point of view. What's animal, what's charm, what's humor, what's innocence? If you just want to explain an incident, [then] that's terribly vulgar. If you were there, you wouldn't have felt that way. You would have laughed. Nobody got hurt, certainly not the girl. She wouldn't have come back if she had been.

> We have a society that's terribly concerned with—quotation marks—"not nice": too concerned. In a way Mario was an innocent who came into a very commercial world.[23]

Regardless of these shenanigans, the time with the Bel Canto Trio represented a period of assiduous study for Lanza. London would later recall them as Lanza's "best-disciplined months."[24] Given the right artistic environment—in the company of two singers, Yeend and London, who were also intent on forging important careers for themselves—it seems clear that Lanza was able to apply himself and study.

Furthermore, he was able to benefit from working with Joseph Blatt, an excellent musician, coach, and their regular accompanist throughout most of the tour.[†] "He studied seriously with the Bel Canto Trio," added London. "We used to have passionate discussions until all hours of the night about the relative merits of the masters. He had an uncanny knack for recognizing voices and imitating them. He loved to talk about and discuss anything even remotely connected with music and singing. His enthusiasm was contagious."[25]

Lanza was paid the standard fee of $300 per concert. Though nowhere near what he would soon be earning, this was reasonable money in 1947. Although Betty would occasionally join him for a day or two, the three singers usually travelled on their own.

Lanza and London would journey together by train[††] while Frances Yeend would usually arrive ahead of them by plane.

Throughout the tour he continued to live in the style to which he had become accustomed, enjoying—as always—the very best in food, clothes and hotel suites.[26]

If Lanza's career was proceeding at a faster pace than he had envisaged, nothing could have prepared him for the event that would shortly mark the turning point in his life.

[†]The Viennese born Blatt had a distinguished background as an opera conductor. Prior to coming to America in 1937, he had been director of the opera school at the Vienna Conservatory of Music.

[††]Lanza had a fear of planes dating back to his Army days, when on a flight from Walla Walla, Washington, the plane had developed engine trouble, suddenly dropping 10,000 feet. From then on he refused to board a plane, and only in the last two years of his life, during his concert appearances in Europe, would he occasionally agree to fly.

8—ENTER HOLLYWOOD

A CANCELLATION set everything in motion: the famous Italian tenor Ferruccio Tagliavini, fresh from his triumphant Metropolitan opera debut, had cancelled a concert scheduled to take place at the Hollywood Bowl in Los Angeles. It was left to Ida Koverman, Louis B. Mayer's valued executive secretary at MGM, and a director of the board of the Hollywood Bowl, to find a worthy replacement.[1]

As it happened, Koverman had recently heard one of Lanza's test records for RCA. The man responsible for bringing it to her attention was RCA representative Art Rush, who had been instrumental in securing Lanza's recording contract two years earlier. Koverman had also shown her employer a photo of the good-looking tenor, prompting an incredulous Louis B. Mayer to ask her: "Does this voice really belong to this face?"[2]

Koverman was by all accounts an elegant and cultivated woman. She had a gift for recognizing talent, and knew a great voice when she heard one.[3] It had been Koverman, for example, who brought baritone Nelson Eddy to MGM after she heard him in a concert in Los Angeles. Similarly impressed by Lanza's recording, she was further encouraged by rave reports about him from actor Walter Pidgeon and tenor James Melton. The latter—in a remarkable absence of professional jealousy—praised Lanza's voice to anyone who cared to listen and was hailing him as a new Caruso.[4]

The Hollywood Bowl board members expressed no objections to Koverman's suggestion, and proceeded to book Lanza. On this occasion the tenor would perform only with his Bel Canto Trio partner Frances Yeend, while the third member of the trio, George London, would remain in the audience.

To Lanza it was just another concert, which is to say he approached it with the same enthusiasm he had brought to other concerts on the tour.[5]

The audience that night would total a mere 3896, considerably less than the then 20,000 capacity of the Hollywood Bowl, and a far cry from the audience he had recently faced in Chicago.[6] Betty was in the audience along with actors Edmond O'Brien and Walter Pidgeon. The latter, by now one of Lanza's staunchest supporters, had sent the tenor a telegram: "Cannot tell you how much I'm looking forward to hearing you again tonight. I know everybody there will be in for a great treat. Best of luck, Walter Pidgeon."[7]

Neither Pidgeon nor the audience would be disappointed. On the night of August 28th, 1947, with the Hollywood Bowl Orchestra under the direction of guest conductor Eugene Ormandy, Lanza sang like a man inspired.

Starting with *"Una furtiva lagrima"* from Act Two of *L'Elisir d'Amore* by Donizetti, he then gave a thrilling rendition of the Improvviso from the first act of Giordano's *Andrea Chénier*, earning himself a twelve-minute ovation—one of the longest in the Bowl's history.[8] Frances Yeend followed with her three solos and she then joined Lanza in *"Parigi o cara"* from the third act of Verdi's *La Traviata,* and the love duet from the first act of Puccini's *Madama Butterfly.* As an encore they sang *"O soave fanciulla"* from the first act of *La Bohème* by Puccini.

The entire concert, including the encore *"E lucevan le stelle"* from the last act of Puccini's *Tosca,* is now available on compact disc, and listening to it today makes one more than ever aware of the extraordinary vocal equipment that Lanza possessed.

The results of his study with Rosati, coupled with the confidence he was acquiring from his concertizing with the Bel Canto Trio, are immediately evident. Lanza's singing on this occasion ranks alongside his finest recordings. It is musical, controlled, and free of the mannerisms that would mar some of his later performances. Of particular interest is the *Traviata* duet, in which Lanza's vocal line, control and use of *mezza voce* and *diminuendo* enhance the color of the voice, which at this stage of its development is ideally suited to the romantic role of Alfredo. This is intelligent singing by any standard, and demonstrates what

Lanza was capable of achieving in the proper operatic environment.

The concert also reveals Lanza's versatility and understanding of the music, switching from the lyricism required in the *Traviata* duet to the dramatic outpouring of the *Chénier* aria. His delicate handling of the *Traviata* duet is even more remarkable if one bears in mind that Lanza's voice was by nature inclined to be more *spinto* than lyric—even at this early stage in his career.

After the concert, news of Lanza's resounding success swept Hollywood. The reviews in the Los Angeles press were unanimous: this was indeed a superb tenor voice. From the *Los Angeles Times:*

> The sort of tenor voice that nearly every operatic stage in the world has been yearning for so many lean years. Lanza's is the warm, round, typically Italian type of voice that caresses every graceful phrase and makes the listener breathe with him as it molds each curve of the melody.[9]

The Los Angeles Daily News wrote:

> [Lanza] electrified an audience that cheered for several minutes...he has a truly rare asset in a naturally beautiful voice which he already handles with intelligence and native artistry. Rightly developed it should prove to be one of the exceptional voices of the generation.[10]

From the Hollywood Citizen News:

> An answer to an opera lover's prayer and any impresario's dream, Lanza gave us tenor singing in the best Italian style with a thrilling voice, resonant and warm throughout its range, this 26-year-old is fairly bursting with song. His voice has been beautifully trained and he acquitted himself brilliantly.[11]

And lastly from Ernest Lonsdale in the *Los Angeles Examiner*:

> Mario Lanza could have taken the Bowl with him. Lanza's voice is rich, full, warm and ringing. He has expression, emotion and good pronunciation. His operatic potentialities, if he works hard for a few more years, are unmistakably great.[12]

This, then, was the Mario Lanza of 1947, unmistakably destined for a major operatic career.

However, MGM mogul Louis B. Mayer was among those present at the Hollywood Bowl concert. The head of America's most powerful movie studio had been enticed to the concert by Ida Koverman. Mayer was a flamboyant character of Russian-Jewish parentage with a knack for recognizing true talent. He knew immediately that the young tenor had important movie potential and was determined to secure him for MGM.[13]

Although Mayer had earned a reputation as something of a tyrant during his then 23-year rule at MGM, he could in fact be quite benevolent, especially with his younger players. He was also blessed with the ability to inspire his employees to give him the very best they had. Actor Robert Taylor would later recall that Mayer "was kind, understanding, fatherly and protective. Always there when I had problems."[14]

It would be the same for Lanza who soon found in Mayer a father figure that he could turn to, confide in, and who would be willing to listen to the young singer's ideas and suggestions.[15] For his part Mayer was openly admiring and supportive of his new discovery. After his first meeting with Lanza, he remarked: "I knew he was great and that we had to have him. I had seen a lot of singers, but he had everything: talent, good looks and a million dollar personality."[16]

Less than three days after the Bowl concert, work came to a halt at MGM's Culver City Studios. Mayer had summoned fifty-five of the studio's top staff, including producers, executives and directors, to the huge recording studio on Stage One.[17] Among those present was producer Joe Pasternak, who along with Arthur Freed and Jack Cummings had formed the unit responsible for the output of musicals at MGM. Pasternak had been unable to attend the Hollywood Bowl concert because his pregnant wife had felt unwell.

With his baffled audience now assembled on the giant recording stage, Mayer pointed in the direction of a curtain and then announced: "I've asked you all to come here because I want you to hear a voice." Then, from behind the curtain, a magnificent voice came surging out.[18] In his autobiography *Easy The Hard Way*, Joe Pasternak recalled:

The voice was rich, warm, sensuous, virile. It had an incredible range capable of singing the highest tenor notes and, on the other end, to be able to go down as deep as a baritone. It was an absolutely beautiful and exciting sound.[19]

The performance consisted of two numbers: "*Che gelida manina*" from Puccini's *La Bohème* and "Thine Alone" from Victor Herbert's *Eileen*. When Lanza finished singing he emerged from behind the curtain and Mayer proudly introduced the owner of the voice. Looking at Lanza, Pasternak's first impression was of a manly, bushy-haired young man of medium height, with an attractive face and dark sparkling eyes.[20]

After a brief exchange Mayer thanked Lanza for coming to MGM. Shortly afterwards the tenor departed, leaving Mayer to announce to the assembly that the studio had decided to sign the young tenor to a contract. Mayer then asked for expressions of interest from those present.[21]

As the studio's specialist in producing films containing so-called "highbrow" music—both operatic and symphonic—Pasternak was the obvious choice for transforming Lanza into a singing film star. Although he privately wondered whether Lanza's stockiness would survive the tendency of the camera lens to distort, Pasternak immediately informed Mayer that Lanza had impressed him, and that he would like to work with him.[22]

Hungarian-born Pasternak had come to America in 1918 at the age of seventeen. Starting his movie career as a dishwasher at Universal Studio, he had slowly worked his way up to assistant to directors such as Allan Dwan and Wesley Ruggles. Later influenced by French and German musicals during a spell in Europe in the early 1930s, he turned to producing on his return to Hollywood, hitting the jackpot when he launched singer Deanna Durbin in a series of films directed by Henry Koster. Pasternak had moved to MGM in 1941 and was responsible for promoting the careers of Kathryn Grayson and Jane Powell among others. As a producer, Pasternak was less noted for the artistic quality of his films than for the fact that his movies always turned a profit, a fact not lost on the commercially driven MGM studio.[23]

The Pasternak films were box office hits on the strength of a well-tried formula consisting of bringing to the masses a combination of classical and popular music combined with loads of sugar coating.

His methods had been so successful that Pasternak had enticed the Metropolitan Opera's reigning Wagnerian tenor, Lauritz Melchior, and musicians Leopold Stokowsky and José Iturbi to star in his films.

At the time, the MGM contract appeared most advantageous to both Lanza and Sam Weiler. Following the Bowl concert, Weiler—at Lanza's request—had flown to Los Angeles from New York. Apart from MGM's, there had been a number of other lucrative offers and Lanza, in desperation, had phoned Weiler for advice. "Sign nothing!" Weiler told him. "Wait till I get there!"[24]

Upon arrival in Los Angeles, Weiler advised his protégé to accept the MGM offer. For the moment it seemed as if Lanza had nothing to lose and everything to gain by signing with MGM. But one thing had to be clear. Nothing could come between Lanza and his ultimate aim of an operatic career. Although the contract was the standard seven years, MGM agreed to Lanza's request that it would be for only six months of each year, leaving him free—or so he thought—for the remaining six months to pursue an operatic career, concertize, make recordings, and generally continue to perfect himself.[25]

Upon signing the contract Lanza would be paid a $10,000 bonus. He would receive an initial salary of $750 a week for a period of 20 weeks for the first year, $1250 per week for the second year, $1500 per week for the third and so on up to $3750 per week in the seventh year.[26]

These were huge amounts in 1947 and they would have been tempting for anyone. Indeed, when interviewed by Time magazine on his arrival in America in 1948, Giuseppe Di Stefano declared, "I want to make much money, have big success and stay here for a long time." To the question, "How about Hollywood?" he grandly replied, "I am here."[27] After all Titta Ruffo did not hesitate when in 1929 MGM offered him a $350,000 contract to film some operatic excerpts. Ruffo promptly bid the Metropolitan farewell and headed for Hollywood.[28] Of Caruso it was said that he sang too often, traveled too much, and was seduced to sing in the stifling heat of Havana by fees of $10,000 per performance.[29]

For Lanza, with his taste for luxurious living, the offer was doubly enticing.[30] At the time he was earning an average of $300 per concert, which although in line with current fees being paid to solo artists, was considerably less than what MGM was offering.

Lanza's rationale must have seemed logical enough at the time. Not only could he combine a film career with an operatic one, but he could also take advantage of MGM's very attractive terms, thus enabling him to live in style while making a film a year and continuing his studies in opera.

However, Lanza and those around him were overlooking a fundamental difference. The worlds of opera and cinema are spheres apart. Far from being an artistic milieu, Hollywood is a commercially driven environment, and hardly the place for a young tenor lacking in self-discipline. To develop properly Lanza needed the strictest of artistic environments—working with the best conductors, musicians and coaches—all the while learning and perfecting his art. Hollywood could provide none of this. In the fanfare and glitter of the celluloid capital, Lanza would never be able to find the peace and solace—let alone the time required— for the study of new repertoire.

Had he already been an established opera singer, it might just have been possible to combine the two careers.

In any case, there was an unexpected complication: Lanza's instant rise to fame and his impact on both cinema audiences and the record-buying public. No one, not even Pasternak—who thought it would take at least ten films to get Lanza established— could have predicted the mass response to his first two films, climaxing with the mass adulation for his record-breaking third film, *The Great Caruso*.[31]

On the other hand, Lanza failed to realize that with Pasternak at the helm, any thought of making films of high artistic quality, or even filmed operas, was out of the question. Lanza was destined to star in a series of lightweight films, produced with an eye to the box office and designed for mass appeal. Despite their commercial success, the Pasternak films were mostly banal, poorly written stories with musical interludes designed to highlight Lanza's incredible voice. Good workmanlike directors such as Norman Taurog and Alexander Hall—who hardly possessed the gifts of a Donen, Cukor or Minnelli—were assigned to direct them. *The Great Caruso* is the one possible exception.

Arguably Lanza's best film, it did have a competent director in Richard Thorpe, along with a wonderful musical score, good supporting cast and singers, but was let down by an overly fictionalized script.

Nor were Lanza's subsequent films—with the exception of *The Student Prince*, for which he provided only his voice, and *Serenade*, a Warner Bros. production—an improvement. His final films, *Seven Hills of Rome* in particular, and *For the First Time,* are decidedly inferior productions.

In less than ten years the consequences of the MGM contract would see Lanza world famous, rich, and more confused and insecure than he had ever been. True, he had conquered Hollywood, the recording world and the concert stage, but his world fame still felt undeserved.[32] He had still to appear at La Scala, the Metropolitan or on any other renowned operatic stage. To someone as sincere and serious about his singing as Lanza was, this would indeed prove a bitter pill to swallow. Lanza may have had difficulty in applying himself, but there remains no doubt about his determination to become an acclaimed opera singer. As his friend Edmond O'Brien recalled, "Mario had guilts that he really didn't do it the right way."[33]

However, back in 1947, Lanza had every reason to feel confident about the future. Wherever he sang the response was always the same; his voice never failed to impress. MGM contract notwithstanding, Lanza was still committed to the Bel Canto Trio until May 1948. For the present Hollywood would have to wait.

9—AN OPERATIC DEBUT

THE BEL CANTO TRIO continued its successful run, with Lanza receiving the type of rave reviews that most artists can only dream about. There would be the occasional departure from the regular Bel Canto Trio schedule, such as the joint recital that Lanza gave with soprano Agnes Davis (with Joseph Blatt accompanying them at the piano) in Quebec in October 1947. These diversions gave Lanza the opportunity to vary his standard program. In Quebec, for instance, in addition to his regular arias and what was by now the almost-obligatory Love Duet from *Madama Butterfly*, he and Davis sang the duet from the first act of *Tosca*. A week later in Grinnell, Iowa, with Emanuel Balabam conducting, Lanza – in addition to singing his usual repertoire of arias – joined soprano Carolyn Long in duets from *The Student Prince* and *New Moon* as well as *La Bohème*.

By the end of the month the tenor was back with Yeend and London, with the Trio resuming its tour in Oklahoma, where Tracy Sylvester, music critic of *The Daily Oklahoman*, wrote that, "[Lanza] is definitely on the way to be the leading tenor in any opera house he sees fit to join."[1]

Interestingly, the name of his idol Caruso was being mentioned with increasing frequency. After the concert in Bowling Green, Kentucky in January 1948, W.B. Hill wrote:

> The surprise of the evening was a young tenor, Mario Lanza, who simply swept the audience off their feet. This young dramatic tenor hailed by press and public as the logical successor to Caruso fully lived up to his advance build-up...Critics have said: "Lanza was born to sing," and everyone in the near capacity audience will tell you the same thing. For Lanza did sing. He sang gloriously, he sang divinely, he sang thrill-

72

ingly. And now that we have heard him we know why the noble and heroic quality of his voice is likened to the golden tones of Caruso.[2]

The comparison with Caruso is an interesting one. Despite Lanza's essentially lyric approach to singing at this early stage in his career, his voice was seldom compared to that of a lyric tenor— such as Gigli—but to the darker and more ringing tones of Caruso. While Lanza's voice was less baritonal than his great predecessor's, it had an impressively round velvety center and a brilliant top with a ringing B and B flat, and a splendid and secure high C.

In other words, a young *lirico spinto* in the making. Furthermore, Lanza's dark middle and low voice, coupled with a wide range of vocal colors and his ability to add a variety of shades to the color of his voice, enabled him to create a different sound and mood depending on the music, dramatic context, and the character he was interpreting.

In an aria from *Rigoletto* or *La Bohème*, for example, Lanza's vocal coloring would be closer to that of a pure lyric tenor, albeit with greater roundness and darker color in the middle register. For Andrea Chénier, or Don Alvaro in *La Forza del Destino*, Lanza would darken the color even further, making the *spinto* sound required for the part.

There is no question that, vocally, Lanza knew exactly what he was doing. All that he required to complete his development was experience on the operatic stage.

Between concert engagements[†] and prior to reporting for work at MGM, Lanza made his professional operatic debut. In an event that would later attain considerable significance, he appeared with the New Orleans Opera Association in two performances as Pinkerton in Puccini's *Madama Butterfly* on April 8th and 10th, 1948.

Once firmly established as a film star, Lanza's choice of Pinkerton for his operatic debut would give rise to endless speculation as to his ability to sustain an entire opera. Many would dismiss his debut (in what is essentially a soprano's opera) as proof of his supposed inadequacy.

One must bear in mind, however, that despite Pinkerton's absence from the entire second act, the role demands a consider-

[†]These included a return engagement in Toronto.

able amount of singing in Act One. The first act is almost an hour long and includes the extended Love Duet, which lasts for 17 minutes, and the demanding "*Dovunque al mondo*" scene between Pinkerton and Sharpless. The tenor also requires sufficient voice volume in order to be heard above the often-heavy orchestration. As Plácido Domingo has said, "Vocally (Pinkerton) is a lot more difficult than people think.

> If you are not very careful, you can have more trouble with Pinkerton than you could with either Cavaradossi or Rodolfo. It has a number of B flats in act one which are difficult to tackle. The tessitura of the love duet is quite high and most of the time you have the orchestra doubling the melody. There is also a beautiful but very tough B flat in 'Addio fiorito asil' you have to climb to it while accompanied by a very strong orchestra, so you have to try and sail through the orchestration without ever pushing the voice."[3]

In reality, Lanza made his professional debut as Pinkerton for the simple reason that The New Orleans Opera Association offered him the role. At the time it must have seemed a suitable choice for a young singer making his professional debut. It could just as well have been Cavaradossi, Rodolfo, Canio, Turiddu or Andrea Chénier, which were the other roles that formed his then-limited repertoire.

Lanza had begun to study the role of Pinkerton after being discharged from the Army early in 1945. At various times it was announced that he would sing Pinkerton: in Trenton, New Jersey in late 1945 with Licia Albanese, and again in Trenton in November 1947.[4] Lanza had remained on friendly terms with Michael De Pace, who was Assistant Director of the Trenton Opera Association, so Trenton was an obvious choice. We can only speculate as to why those performances did not take place. It should be remembered that in 1945 Lanza had not yet mastered the technique of singing long phrases without tiring—subsequently achieved through his study with Rosati—and this may have prompted him to reconsider his appearances. Two years later, with a solid technique now firmly in place, he accepted the New Orleans offer and began preparations for the two performances with coach Leila Edwards.

He had met Edwards, a graduate of the Juilliard School of Music, in New York the previous year through his friend Robert Merrill. Twenty-eight-year-old Merrill had recently been awarded a contract by Edward Johnson after winning a Metropolitan Opera audition. Merrill was learning repertoire with Edwards at the time, and—hugely impressed by Lanza's voice—had made it his mission for everyone to hear the tenor.[5] He had already taken Lanza to his own singing teacher, Samuel Margolis, who had sat in stunned silence while listening to Lanza's thrilling rendition of *"Nessun dorma."* Now Merrill wanted Leila Edwards to hear him, and one afternoon he took Lanza along with him to her studio.

At first Edwards was reluctant to hear the young tenor, and reminded Merrill that they had only one hour in which to work. It was only on Merrill's insistence that she relented. Sitting down at the piano, Edwards put the tenor at ease with a smile and a wink, and asked him what he would like to sing.

The tenor suggested *"Ch'ella mi creda"* from Puccini's *La Fanciulla del West.* Edwards' eyes flashed with excitement as Lanza began to sing the aria in his rich lower register. Then, as he concluded with a ringing B flat, she jumped up and exclaimed: "What a sound! Where have you been hiding?" "He suffers from stage fright," volunteered Merrill, to which Edwards replied, "What artist doesn't?"[6]

Although Merrill's remark about Lanza's apparent stage fright is interesting, it was made while the tenor was still studying with Rosati. There is little evidence of any anxiety on Lanza's part once he had completed his vocal studies with Rosati, apart from George London's remark that "[Lanza] was unschooled musically and was thus always insecure in this area."[7]

What London was referring to was Lanza's inability to sight-read – a not-infrequent phenomenon among operatic singers, and, indeed, something that the young tenor shared with Caruso, who before attempting any new opera needed much drilling from a répétiteur (or coach), supplemented by conferences on tempo with Toscanini and other conductors.[8†] Others who were reputed to be unable sight-read or were reluctant to do so were Tetrazzini,

†Although he praised the voice and the singing, Toscanini referred to Caruso as a bad musician.

Ezio Pinza, Lauritz Melchior, Richard Tucker, Leonard Warren, Franco Corelli, Giuseppe Di Stefano, Luciano Pavarotti and Mirella Freni, to name just a few.

A great deal is made of the ability to sight-read, mainly by instrumentalists who are inclined to think that this is the most important function of musicianship. In fact, the main advantage in being able to sight-read is that it usually enables the singer to learn a part faster.

The disadvantage of learning a role by sight-reading is that it can result in the singer giving a perfunctory performance. It may be a musically correct performance, but one that is rather mechanical—and less spontaneous—than the more heartfelt rendition of a singer who has spent many hours training his ear by working on each phrase of the score with a coach.

The latter approach is what singers refer to as *getting the part into the voice.* Giuseppe Di Stefano, for example, could never be described as an outstanding musician, but with his great musicality and brilliant ear was able to learn his roles in a relatively short time and forget them just as fast.[9]

The operatic composer Giuseppe Verdi once discussed the importance of interpretation versus sight-reading. In a letter to his friend Vincenzo Luccardi, Verdi wrote: "It's true that in *La Forza del Destino* the singers don't have to know how to do *solfeggi*, but they must have soul, and understand the words and express their meaning."[10] Many years later, the celebrated American soprano Geraldine Farrar would share a similar view. Speaking about her early studies in Paris, Farrar said: "I was even then aware of the monotony of beautiful even tones, when all dramatic expression was sacrificed to sound only."[11]

In discussing Lanza's musical insecurity, George London was also quick to point out that the tenor had "a wonderful natural sense of phrasing, and if he was well and carefully coached, his work was very respectable."[12]

Of course, a great deal depends on the conductor with whom the singer is working. If the conductor is patient, understanding and cooperative, the singer's task—provided he or she is well-prepared—is made much easier. On the other hand, if the conductor is a pompous, irascible tyrant, he can badly undermine a singer's confidence, as we shall see later during Lanza's first recording session.

By 1947 Lanza had already worked with a number of conductors without experiencing notable difficulties. In the fall of that year, Lanza worked on the interpretative aspects of the Pinkerton role with stage director Armando Agnini, who would be directing the New Orleans production. Agnini was an experienced opera director who, in addition to the New Orleans Opera, also worked with a number of other opera companies, including the San Francisco Opera. It was Agnini who engaged Leila Edwards to coach Lanza for the part of Pinkerton. Lanza had already begun work on the role with Agnini's regular pianist, Rudolph Scharr, but when the Viennese coach started criticizing the tiniest details of Lanza's reading of the score, the tenor predictably exploded and told him to get out. The substitute coach, Leila Edwards, had enthusiastically taken on the role at minimal remuneration on learning that the tenor was the same young man who had thrilled her the previous year.[13]

Lanza had initially learned the role by listening to the 1939 Gigli recording of the opera. At his first session with Edwards, he sang through the entire score, prompting an amused Edwards to comment: "You learned it from the Gigli recording!" A surprised Lanza asked her how she had guessed. "Because you're making the same mistakes Gigli made!" was Edwards' laughing reply.[14]

Edwards was a great répétiteur and for the next four months she worked with Lanza on the role of Pinkerton. As is usually done with a singer who does not sight-read, she patiently went through the score singing each phrase to the tenor who in turn would sing it back to her. Edwards remarked that Lanza had a very good, retentive ear and he would unfailingly repeat the phrases back to her correctly. "His phrasing was instinctive," Edwards later recalled.[15]

In the New Orleans *Madama Butterfly* performances, Lanza sang opposite soprano Tomiko Kanazawa in the title role and baritone Jess Walters in the role of Sharpless. Years later, Walters observed that Lanza was a wonderful Pinkerton:

> The Puccini scores are deceptive. Even the supposedly lyric ones have heavy orchestrations to the extent that a singer needs a certain amount of *squillo* in the voice in order to be

heard above the orchestra. 'Squillo' is the ringing quality that enables a single voice on a stage to carry over and above the sound of a pit full of musicians playing together to a theater full of listeners. Mario had it.[16]

He certainly needed *squillo* for the *Madama Butterfly* performances. The 2710-seat New Orleans Municipal Auditorium was not only a dismal venue in which to stage opera, but its acoustics were far from satisfactory.

The conductor for the occasion was German-born Walter Herbert, who had been appointed General Director of the New Orleans Opera in 1943. It was Herbert who had been responsible for signing Lanza to sing Pinkerton. His choice of tenor was soon rewarded in the unanimous praise that Lanza received for his performances.

"The choice of Mario Lanza as Pinkerton was admirable," wrote Walter S. Jenkins in the *Times-Picayune*. "His diction was excellent...[and] the quality of his voice was a delight to hear."[17] Laurence Odel, writing in the *St. Louis News*, went further:

> Mario Lanza performed his duties as Lieut. Pinkerton with considerable verve and dash. Rarely have we seen a more superbly romantic leading tenor. His exceptionally beautiful voice helps immeasurably...The combination of good looks and vocal ability should prove most helpful to Mr. Lanza in any of his more earnest undertakings.[18]

Lanza was scheduled to sing Alfredo in Verdi's *La Traviata* with Eleanor Steber the following year, but by 1949 he was already deeply engulfed in the Hollywood machinery and consequently never learned the role. Indeed, his venture into films would forever put the seal on his future in opera. The two performances as Pinkerton were destined to be the last that Lanza would make in a complete opera.

One can speculate endlessly as to why Lanza did not return for the *Traviata* performances. Given the success of his Pinkerton, the reason is unlikely to have been insecurity or stage fright. Insufficient time is the more probable explanation. *La Traviata* was not the only operatic casualty arising from Lanza's increased workload in Hollywood. He was also scheduled to sing Rodolfo in *La Bohème* for the premiere season of Opera in English on NBC-TV, but only made it as far as the important audition for

NBC Chief David Sarnoff.On June 18, 1948, together with his Bel Canto Trio colleagues George London and Frances Yeend, and with Peter Herman Adler conducting, Lanza sang part of the 4th act of the opera before a small assembly of musicians and music lovers that included Artur Rubinstein and Jascha Heifetz. The project was approved, but by the time it got underway, two years later, Lanza was already in Hollywood working on his second film.

Lanza also believed that at the age of 27, his relative youth would allow him numerous opportunities in the future to return to opera. "As an opera singer I'm still a baby," he stated in 1948, adding confidently: "Give me eight more years. Then we shall see what we shall see."[19]

At the time he also explained his reasons for accepting the MGM contract. "Metro offered me a wonderful contract. By its provisions I am committed to the studio only six months a year. The rest of the time is my own. I can study or give concerts as I please without worrying about [making] a living. And that's the reason I signed a movie contract instead of sticking strictly to grand opera."[20]

10—COMMERCIAL SUCCESS

IN LATE JUNE 1948, his commitments with the Bel Canto Trio completed, Lanza moved to Los Angeles and settled with his wife in a small rented house in the San Fernando Valley before reporting for work at the giant MGM studios in Culver City. Production on his first film, initially titled *This Summer is Yours* and later changed to *That Midnight Kiss*, had to be postponed, however, when co-star Kathryn Grayson became pregnant. Consequently, over the weeks and months that followed, Lanza would spend a great deal of time with producer Joe Pasternak.[1]

While he was confident that he had in Lanza a potential star and box office draw, neither Pasternak, nor anyone else at Metro, for that matter, had any idea of the impact the singer would make on the public with his first film.[2] For his part, Lanza remained starry-eyed, not quite able to believe that he was on a studio lot surrounded by some of the top names in show business. Lanza was a regular moviegoer. He particularly liked John Garfield, Tyrone Power and Lana Turner. His favorite singers included Al Jolson, Lena Horne, Tony Martin and Toni Arden. He was drawn primarily to singers who gave emphasis to the lyrics and felt the meaning of a song. On more than one occasion he said, "I like a singer who gives."[3] This could easily have been said of his own singing style, or of another contemporary he greatly admired, Giuseppe Di Stefano.

Lanza was excited at the prospect of working in a film. In preparing for his first cinematic experience, he was eager to know what type of films Pasternak had in mind for him and what parts he would be playing. Pasternak himself was unsure about the nature of their collaboration. What it would *not* be, he told Lanza, was an opera staged in front of the cameras.[4]

Pasternak wanted to gauge public reaction to his new find,

and chose a cautious approach for Lanza's film debut. Opera was restricted to "*Celeste Aida*" and the second half of "*Una furtiva lagrima*," and Pasternak added his customary amount of sugar-coating to make the finished product more palatable to the masses. What the producer concocted was a package combining liberal helpings of Tchaikovsky, an approach that never failed with the cinema-going public, and a number of lighter songs, including the beautiful "They Didn't Believe Me" by Jerome Kern. He also surrounded Lanza with such established stars as MGM's resident soprano Kathryn Grayson, veteran actress Ethel Barrymore, pianist conductor José Iturbi and experienced supporting players like Keenan Wynn, J. Carrol Naish and Thomas Gomez. Norman Taurog was chosen to direct. A competent director known for his comedic touch, Taurog had worked with a number of musical stars including Deanna Durbin at Universal and Judy Garland at MGM.

The screenplay by Bruce Manning and Tamara Hovey was loosely based on Lanza's own life. It also drew on the embellished official biography of the tenor put out by the Metro Publicity Department, which stated that Lanza had been discovered while delivering a piano at the Academy of Music in Philadelphia.[5] In the film the locale has been changed to Kathryn Grayson's home, where Lanza has just delivered a new piano. Grayson is seen walking into her living room, as the camera moves in slowly behind a man singing at the piano. Then a closeup of Lanza gives cinema audiences their first glimpse of him. Thus the legend of Lanza the piano mover and truck driver was born.

While Lanza was excited at the prospect of starring in a film made by a major studio, his arrival in Hollywood also meant the start of countless and extremely dangerous battles to lose weight for the cameras. At the time of his arrival in the film capital Lanza weighed a solid 200 pounds (90. 7kg), which for his height of 5 feet 7½ inches (172 cm)[†] and constitution was an ideal singing weight.

He was therefore understandably reluctant when told that because the camera lens added additional poundage to the sub-

---

[†]Like most actors under five feet, ten inches tall Lanza wore two-inch lifts in his custom-made shoes but was not the least self-conscious about them.

ject, he would have to take off approximately 30 pounds (13.6 kg) prior to the start of filming. "You need that poundage to be in best voice," he said, pointing to his diaphragm. "You sing from way down there. That's where the sounding board is and it should be well-padded."[6] Well-padded or not, the studio was adamant he would have to reduce. To assist him with the task they assigned a physical trainer, Terry Robinson, to work with him. With the help of Robinson, who would spend the next nine years as a sort of factotum for Lanza, serving as a trainer, chauffeur, occasional stand-in and general helper,[†] the tenor lost 31 pounds (14 kg).[7] By the beginning of November, he was ready to face the cameras for the start of filming on *That Midnight Kiss*.

First, however, there was the standard screen test required of every newcomer. The result of Lanza's was so bad that it almost ended his film career before it had begun. According to co-star Kathryn Grayson, the color test "didn't give Mario a chance"[8] and was hopelessly rushed by the studio, who had failed to groom and dress Lanza to the best advantage. He appeared stocky and badly in need of a good hairstyle. Many of the studio executives thought the entire thing rather humorous and were convinced that L. B. Mayer's judgment had failed him for once.[9]

Pasternak, however, persisted with Lanza, and regardless of the failure of the test was convinced that he had finally found the voice with the face. He hastily organized a second test, this time taking the precaution of grooming the tenor. He had Lanza's hair, which was very curly, straightened, re-styled and lightened from his almost natural black to reddish-brown and dressed the tenor in clothes that made him look taller and more slender.

"He was everything I'd dreamed about," recalled Pasternak. "The voice with the face. He was handsome, he was virile and charming. He looked so great that he didn't need a voice."[10]

However, another hurdle remained. Apart from the coaching he had received from Herbert Graf for the 1942 performance of *The Merry Wives Of Windsor* at Tanglewood, and from Armando Agnini for the New Orleans *Madama Butterfly*, Lanza knew nothing about acting. The studio's dramatic coach, Lillian Burns, was consequently engaged to work with him prior to the start of pro-

---

[†]Robinson was listed as "valet" on Lanza's payroll.

duction. Many thought that Burns's only qualification for the job was that she was married to director George Sidney, who happened to be the son of L. K. Sidney, one of MGM's top executives and L. B. Mayer's right-hand man. Keenan Wynn's opinion of Miss Burns was that "She couldn't direct you to the men's room." Others found her charming, capable and particularly caring with promising newcomers being groomed for stardom by the studio. Lanza found her helpful in teaching him the very basics of acting for the cameras. For her part, Miss Burns felt that given time Lanza could become a good actor.

Although he knew nothing about the technique of acting, she noticed immediately that he had the right instinctive feeling and the warmth required for it.[11] Lanza also spent time with diction coach Gertrude Fogler, a diminutive lady approaching her eighties, who spoke with a most beautiful voice. She taught deep diaphragmatic breathing and had a relatively easy task with Lanza, who—unlike most tenors—had a beautifully rounded and resonant speaking voice and was already familiar with such techniques through his singing.

Studio vocal coaches Arthur Rosenstein and Nat Stuart initially worked with Lanza on his musical numbers for the film. Within weeks, however, the studio—realizing that they had a big talent on their hands—assigned operatic coach Giacomo Spadoni to work with their new find.

The 66-year-old Spadoni had left his native Imola in Italy (Reggio Emilia) in his early twenties when he was offered a post as répétiteur with the Chicago Opera, where he was to stay for the next 30 years. Among the many singers he had coached during his tenure in Chicago was Enrico Caruso, who between 1905 and 1910 appeared there regularly as guest singer in a variety of roles. In 1935 Spadoni accepted the post of chorus master at the Metropolitan opera where he stayed for the next 10 years. After his retirement he moved to Los Angeles where he worked as technical advisor and coach on a number of films, occasionally appearing in small parts such as Ezio Pinza's valet in the ghastly *Mr. Imperium* and as a conductor in Danny Kaye's *Knock on Wood*. Spadoni was greatly impressed by Lanza. "God has put into this boy everything that is required of a great singer. Intelligence, voice, memory, personality," he remarked shortly after he began working with the young tenor.[12]

The two men became very close in the months that followed. The maestro and his wife Helen would often dine at the Lanza home and the friendship extended to Lanza's parents, who were frequent visitors. Spadoni continued to work on and off with Lanza up to the time of the singer's departure for Italy in 1957, a collaboration of almost eight and a half years. The Spadonis remained friends with Lanza's parents after the deaths of Lanza and Betty.[†]

During his initial period in Hollywood, Lanza was kept busy with acting lessons, voice coaching, daily vocal and breathing exercises and the physical training routine ordered by the studio to keep in shape. His only public appearance during his first six months in the film capital took place on July 24, 1948, when an MGM night was held at the Hollywood Bowl. With celebrated film score composer Miklos Rosza conducting the Bowl Orchestra, Lanza sang stunning renditions of Bizet's "*Agnus Dei,*" and "*Nessun dorma*" from *Turandot*, both of which were made doubly difficult by Rosza's unconscionably slow tempi. The ease with which Lanza tackles these two difficult numbers, together with his phrasing and the way in which the voice soars towards the upper spheres for the notes above the treble staff—while Rosza merely drags the orchestra along—is tenor singing in a class of its own. He followed the arias with two duets with Kathryn Grayson: "*O soave fanciulla*" from *La Bohème*, and "Thine Alone" from *Eileen*. The ending of the last number is completely ruined by a ghastly off-the-note screech from Grayson.

Ernest Lonsdale, reviewing the concert in the *Los Angeles Examiner*, wrote:

> The sound-man appeared puzzled by their (Lanza and Grayson's) respective volumes. Lanza's opening 'Agnus Dei' was under-amplified. Truthfully, I am not sure the microphone was on. In contrast, Miss Grayson's initial solo, the 'Shadow Song' from *Dinorah*, sounded over-amplified. Their duet '*O soave fanciulla*' from *La Bohème* gave the impression that the sound-man was alternately raising and lowering the volume.

[†]The maestro would survive Betty by only five months, succumbing to a heart attack in August 1960 at the age of 77.

Lonsdale concluded by stating that "Lanza, as he did at the Bowl last year, displayed fine natural gifts including a stirring high C."[13]

In November 1948, with the birth of their first baby only a matter of days away, and feeling financially more secure in light of the MGM contract, the Lanzas began renting a two-storey Colonial-style mansion at 236½ South Spalding Drive, Beverly Hills.

Meanwhile, back at the studio pre-recording sessions for *That Midnight Kiss* had begun under the direction of Charles Previn and José Iturbi. Lanza was in the midst of recording "*Celeste Aida*" when the Cedars of Lebanon Hospital—to which Betty had been admitted the previous day—phoned MGM to notify him he had become a father. The call was held until Lanza had finished the recording. After the last note, he rushed to the phone, reacting with joy when told that Betty had given birth to a baby girl.[14] The Lanzas would name her Colleen, honoring Betty's Irish ancestry.

The pregnancy had not been an easy one. For a time it seemed that Betty would be unable to have children. Upset about her suspected infertility, Betty had consulted a number of doctors in New York. "I knew that if I couldn't have children, it would kill me and Mario," she remarked years later.[15]

Eventually Betty underwent an operation which was successfully performed in late 1947. However, Betty's problems were only beginning. After the birth of Colleen she developed ovarian cysts, which caused her sheer agony prior to menstruation. Refusing at first to have another operation, she began taking medications that had been prescribed to ease her pain. Over the years, Betty would become increasingly reliant on these prescriptions until she reached a state of near-addiction, and would swallow whatever pills she could find, sometimes spending entire days confined to her room.[16]

Initially no one—not even Lanza himself—realized what was happening, but in later years when the extent of her dependency became evident, Lanza would agonize whenever he had to leave for a concert tour or location work on a film. Before departing he would always ensure that there was someone reliable to look after Betty and the children during his absence.[17]

Meanwhile, with filming on *That Midnight Kiss* due to begin, Lanza was more than a little confused. He had been working on his scenes with Lillian Burns and was finding it difficult to follow director Norman Taurog's instructions. Actor Keenan Wynn, who played Lanza's buddy in the movie, recalled: "Whenever Taurog directed Mario to play a scene in a certain way, a puzzled Mario would stare at Taurog and say, 'But Miss Burns told me to do it this way.' Taurog put up with this for a while, but eventually lost his patience and told Mario, 'I don't give a shit about Miss Burns. I'm directing this picture.'"[18]

There were other aspects of the movie-making business that the newcomer found difficult to fathom. To his bewilderment, Lanza found that he was being given directions by just about everyone on the set. The volatile Lanza was not one for mincing words. Again Keenan Wynn recalled: "Mario exploded. 'Will somebody tell me who the boss is? I cannot listen to five different people. Who is the boss? Is it so and so, so and so, or is it the director of the picture, Norman Taurog?' And Taurog, much to his credit, said 'I am the boss; listen to me and forget everyone else.'" From then on filming proceeded without further incident.[19]

Lanza was surrounded by people experienced in the business of making films, and all did their best to help him, making him feel as though he was one of them and not a mere beginner.[20] Lanza's warmth and bubbling personality made it easy for him to communicate with his fellow workers, who in turn found the unassuming young man immensely charming and fun to work with. While they liked him as a person, they were no less impressed by his voice.[21]

The fiery Spanish conductor-pianist José Iturbi made no secret of his admiration for the young tenor, whom he felt had "the voice, temperament and flair of a supreme singing actor."[22]

Another member of the cast, veteran stage and screen actress Ethel Barrymore, had known Caruso and had heard him sing.[†] Describing Lanza's voice as "absolutely beautiful," she went on to say, "He has the added advantage of combining a splendid voice with good looks and a captivating personality."[23]

[†]Her own daughter, Ethel Barrymore Colt, was a soprano singing at various times either under the name of Louisa Kinlock, or Ethel Colt.

Lanza discovered, much to his delight, that he had a number of things in common with the great actress.

They were both from Philadelphia and Barrymore, who played a leading role in the film, was not only knowledgeable in musical matters but was, as he was himself, a keen follower of baseball. Consequently the two of them spent as much time as possible during breaks in filming discussing everything from baseball, to theater, to opera.[24]

Lanza relished working on the film with Barrymore and Iturbi and such gifted character actors as J. Carrol Naish, Keenan Wynn and Marjorie Reynolds. The film was a box office success and Lanza an instant hit with cinema audiences. MGM, delighted with their discovery, paid him an additional $10,000 on top of the original $15,000 stipulated by his contract.[25]

The music of *That Midnight Kiss* was a mixed bag designed to appeal to a mass audience. Lanza's numbers consisted of the Neapolitan song "*Mamma mia, che vo' sape*"; "I Know, I Know, I Know," a new song by Polish-born Bronislaw Kaper, one of MGM's resident composers; Jerome Kern's beautiful "They Didn't Believe Me," sung in duet with Kathryn Grayson and—again with Grayson—adaptations by Charles Previn and his nephew Andre of the fourth movement of Tchaikovsky's Fifth Symphony, and the Piano Concerto No. 1 in B flat Minor (the latter cut from the final print), with added English lyrics written by William Katz. The Fifth Symphony adaptation was used as the film's closing sequence in which Lanza and Grayson appear in a fictitious opera called *The Princess*.[†] Ironically, in view of Pasternak's nervousness about the operatic selections, it was Lanza's delivery of the aria "*Celeste Aida*" that made the greatest impact on cinema audiences worldwide when the film was released in late 1949.[26]

The cinema-going public, accustomed to the archetypal portly tenor (caricatured in *That Midnight Kiss* in an amusing performance by actor Thomas Gomez), had never witnessed the combination of an extremely beautiful tenor voice emerging from a handsome face and winning personality. At a mere 169 lb (76.6 kg), Lanza had never looked better.

†The ending doesn't make much sense but, apparently, it mattered little to MGM that all through the film the singers had been rehearsing Donizetti's *Lucia di Lamermoor* and singing it in Italian.

He looked so good, in fact, that for the first time in motion picture history, the cameras had stayed on the close-up of a classical singer for the full length of an aria while Lanza sang "*Celeste Aida.*"

With the release of *That Midnight Kiss* the die was cast. There would be no turning back for Lanza. He had unwittingly taken the first step on the path that would ultimately lead to heartbreak, despair and tragedy.

For the present, however, all was rosy. "Mario, my boy, I'm going to make you a singing Clark Gable,"[27] remarked the paternal Mayer, while Pasternak added: "This is the first time I'll be able to let an operatic tenor sing and know that the audience out front isn't closing its eyes and visualizing Van Johnson."[28]

The film critics, although not particularly impressed by the film itself, were unanimous in their praise of Lanza. In his review in *The New York Times*, Bosley Crowther wrote: "As for the budding Mr. Lanza, the opinion rendered of him by the sanguine Mr. Iturbi is good enough for us. 'His voice,' says Mr. Iturbi, 'has quality and warmth and he has a very nice personality.' Check."[29]

Musical America magazine reported along the same lines. "Mario Lanza emerges from the stereotype with considerable impact...Mr. Lanza reveals a command of style and a voice that is sweet and flexible. His personality is pleasant and ingratiating."[30] And from *Newsweek*:

> Aside from José Iturbi's music, virtually the only excuse for this one is Mario Lanza, a singer whose talents would be conspicuous even outside a film devoted to opera. He can act as well as sing. But his efforts in both directions are hampered by an inconsequential story which enmeshes him with Kathryn Grayson—a girl who neither sings nor acts in his league.[31]

If professionally things were going well for Lanza, his home life was as ideal as he could possibly wish. His marriage was a good one, a love match with solid foundations. The bonding was further strengthened by the arrival of their first child, Colleen. This was possibly the happiest and most carefree time in his life so far. Betty's younger sister Virginia Abbatacola and her husband John lived with the Lanzas for about a year around this time.

Virginia recalled: "Mario was really a fun-loving person. He and my husband used to play 'cops and robbers' in the house—like kids. Mario even had a special name for John, an affectionate nickname. He slurred 'John Abbatacola into the Italian Giovanni Abbataculo which translated† means 'a crack in the ass.'"[32]

†In fact, literally translated, but with a double t in 'abbatta,' it means 'demolish ass.'

11—CONCERTS AND RECORDINGS

In early 1949, with *That Midnight Kiss* completed, Lanza set out with his accompanist Constantine Callinicos on a concert tour that had been booked by Columbia Artists Management prior to the tenor settling in the film capital. Lanza had not worked with Callinicos since their first meeting in 1947, when the tenor was still a virtual unknown. Now, a mere two years later—with a Hollywood contract in his pocket and both his first film and recordings soon to be released—Lanza was on the threshold of fame.

The concert tour, consisting of a total of 27 dates, was scheduled to take place between March 7, and May 25, 1949. By now Lanza was being paid an average concert fee of $1200—considerably larger than he had received in his Bel Canto Trio days.[1] Yet it was still nowhere near the astronomical fees he would soon be commanding after the movies had made him famous and his million-selling "Be My Love" was resounding throughout the juke-boxes of America. With his first film completed, Lanza must have sensed that he was on the verge of something bigger.

Throughout the concert tour Lanza objected to the fee Columbia Artists was paying him for each performance. According to Callinicos, Lanza reasoned that although the tour had been booked by Columbia when he was relatively unknown, he was now on the verge of stardom, and it was unfair to expect him to sing in the "tank towns" for small fees.[2] Such a stance would seem to dispel any notions of insecurity and stage fright on Lanza's part, at least at this stage of his career. If anything, the Lanza of 1949 appears to be an artist fully aware of his worth.

The tour had to be interrupted, and some of the concerts cancelled, to allow Lanza to head for New York, where his first recording session was to be held. For some time RCA had been anxious to begin making commercial recordings with their discovery. It had now been four years since the signing of Lanza's exclusive contract with RCA. Fully aware that they had an outstanding talent on their hands, RCA had been patient and for the time being had been content with making test recordings of his voice. Now with his first film about to be released, they felt it was the appropriate moment to add him to their prestigious Red Seal Label, and at the same time benefit from the MGM buildup that Lanza was receiving.[3]

The recording session was scheduled to take place in the ballroom of the Manhattan Center, the venue for many of RCA's classical recordings. RCA had selected three conductors from the Metropolitan Opera and had told Lanza he could choose whichever one he preferred to work with. Eventually Lanza settled for the French-born American resident Jean Paul Morel, who had recently been appointed to the faculty of the Juilliard School of Music.

However, as soon as the two men began to rehearse it became apparent that their collaboration was doomed to fail. As we have seen, Lanza—like many opera singers before and since—was not a trained musician. His was an instinctive talent with an inborn musicality aided by a sensational ear.

On certain musical points he would need guidance and understanding from the conductor. In short, he needed the kind of nurturing that a sympathetic conductor such as Peter Herman Adler could provide.

Morel, however, was no Adler, and at the first rehearsal things got off to a bad start. Instead of encouraging and patiently guiding the young tenor, Morel chose to lecture him, correcting him at every turn. Diplomatically handled, Lanza would usually go out of his way to please, but Morel's approach infuriated him and he stormed out.[4]

Lanza promptly informed RCA that he was unable to work with Morel, and that he would only complete the scheduled recordings with Constantine Callinicos conducting. RCA, understandably, balked at Lanza's proposal.[5] Callinicos, after all, was neither an established conductor nor had he made any previous recordings.

After prolonged discussions it became clear that nothing would change Lanza's mind. RCA reluctantly agreed to the tenor's demand on the condition that Lanza guarantee the cost of the recording session if the numbers were not recorded successfully in the allotted time.[6]

Confident that he could fulfil the assignment, Lanza accepted RCA's terms. The recording session, with Callinicos conducting the RCA Victor Orchestra,[†] went ahead as scheduled on May 5, 1949.

That Lanza chose to rely on Callinicos, who would conduct nearly all of his future operatic recordings was, in many respects, unfortunate. Lanza may have felt comfortable with someone who knew how to handle him and was a frank admirer of his voice, but Callinicos was at best a mediocre conductor and never a great accompanist. As Alfred Alexander observes in his book *Operanatomy*, "It takes 21 years of toil and study before one can call himself 'maestro.' [7] Even then, unless one is naturally gifted, he may be only a run of the mill conductor. As David Ewen, author of *Dictators of the Baton*, puts it, "A great leader can bring an orchestra to greatness; a poor one can make the very same orchestra sound much like an amateur ensemble." [8]

Although Callinicos would go on to conduct the New York City Opera for over a decade, his shortcomings are on display in virtually all the operatic recordings that he made with Lanza. A soloist – especially one as musically inexperienced as Lanza was when he began recording with Callinicos – is almost completely reliant on the conductor to interpret the composer's music, set the right tempo, and bring out every nuance in the score. Even a singer and musician of the caliber of Maria Callas relied on the conductor to set the tempi. As Nicola Rescigno recalled, "At one time I was discussing the tempi of a number of arias we were to record and asked Maria what she thought. She replied: 'You conduct and I'll sing. Your job is to conduct, mine to sing.' " [9]

Listening to Lanza's and Callinicos's combined recording output during the 1949-1951 period, it is evident that the latter's contribution was very much a hit-or-miss affair. His conducting is both vague and tentative, and the orchestra—particularly in the operatic arias—is generally lifeless under his direction, often failing to give

[†]The orchestra consisted of 45 players, made up mostly of members of the New York Philharmonic.

adequate support to the tenor. Furthermore, the tempi are often in-accurate and at times ridiculously fast as, for example, in the arias *"O tu che in seno agli angeli"* from Verdi's *La Forza del Destino,* *"Questa o quella"* and *"Parmi veder le lagrime"* from *Rigoletto* and the Flower song from *Carmen.* In arias such as *"Celeste Aida"* and *"E lucevan le stelle,"* Callinicos's conducting is dullness per-sonified.

In their first recording collaboration, Callinicos's limitations as a conductor are evident in both of the operatic arias recorded. In *"Che gelida manina,"* for example, Callinicos demonstrates that he neither understands how to conduct Puccini nor knows when to employ *rubato* appropriately.

The *rubato* has to be in relation to a certain tempo, within the boundaries of that tempo, otherwise it makes no musical sense and sounds sloppy and dragged. Whenever Callinicos attempts to use *rubato,* it becomes compounded, overdone, and therefore lacking in form. Thus in *"Che gelida manina,"* Callinicos merely drags the orchestra along, leaving Lanza to his own devices. This is a pity, for not only is Lanza in excellent voice on his first recording session, but as far as the interpretation is concerned, he understands that Rodolfo is not Radamès and sings the two arias accordingly.

It is interesting, for example, to observe the approach the tenor uses in *"Che gelida manina,"* where he keeps the tone appropriately lyrical in a beautifully convincing delivery of Rodolfo's difficult aria, topping his rendition with a splendid high C. The beauty of the voice and Lanza's expressiveness combine to make this a spine-tingling performance, regardless of the indifferent accompaniment. The con-trast is evident in *"Celeste Aida."* Lanza knows this is *spinto* terri-tory and uses a darker, more dramatic tone as Radamès, though again the orchestra under Callinicos's direction leaves the tenor in limbo. Lanza is nevertheless quite impressive in the singing of this difficult aria, the only flaw being the exaggerated parlando towards the end of the aria (*"Il tuo bel cielo vorrei ridarti le dolci brezze del patrio suol"*), which a competent conductor would have corrected. In any event, it is much more difficult to sing an aria out of context from an opera even if one has previously performed the work a number of times.

Performing an aria from an opera that one has never sung be-fore in its entirety is even more difficult because one has to capture the mood, feeling and pathos of an isolated moment from the entire work. The fact that Lanza often succeeded in doing this regardless of the fact that he was working with an undistinguished conductor makes his achievements in the recording studio even more remarkable

Callinicos's conducting is somewhat better in the two Neapolitan songs, "*Mamma mia, che vo' sape*" and "*Core 'ngrato,*" which were also part of Lanza's first recording session. The two songs are also better recorded then the operatic arias, with the tenor's voice sounding more forward, while the orchestra gives Lanza more support and he, in turn, shows great feeling for the lyrics and drama of the situation.

"*Mamma mia, che vo' sape*" is faultless, while "*Core 'ngrato*" is only marginally less so. In the latter, Lanza is splendidly effective in delivering the dramatic impact of the song—despite going sharp in his enthusiasm at the start of the reprise. Singing sharp was a problem for other great singers besides Lanza: Pertile, Björling, Corelli, Di Stefano, Callas and Olivero. At times this tendency marred some of his best performances.[†]

It is a problem that is often associated with the dramatic intensity of the singing. When a singer becomes so emotionally involved in the part, musical boundaries are momentarily forgotten. In this regard, an observation that Corelli once made about Pertile could be equally applied to Lanza: "Pertile sang with more passion and intensity than Caruso. The transport into which he fell in giving expression – that is what caused him to go sharp." [10]

Even though there should have been retakes of both "*Celeste Aida*" and "*Core 'ngrato,*" it should be noted that the four numbers scheduled for his first recording session were recorded in less than three hours, and that all were recorded in single takes. While it is not unusual for an artist to record selections in one take, the myth still persists that Lanza's recordings were a product of RCA engineers splicing together various takes. In fact it was often quite the opposite. On those occasions when Lanza had lost weight, he would often feel less strong and energetic than when he was heavier, and would consequently refuse to do more than one take.[11]

[†]Lanza was fully aware of the problem, once commenting lovingly when his first-born child, Colleen, sang a typical children's song at the age of three: "She sings sharp, just like me!"

This is a great pity, for had he taken the trouble to make a second take we would probably have better performances in many of the more than 200 commercial recordings that he made. The failure to record additional takes also applies to some of the numbers he recorded for his film soundtracks, together with the worst of his subsequent radio material.

If indeed RCA experienced any problems during the various recording sessions, these had more to do with the difficulty encountered in recording the tenor's amazing vocal range. As RCA producer C.E. Crumpacker recalled: "Without a doubt Lanza's voice was a difficult one to record. His dazzling vocal coloration, his extraordinary power and proliferation of tones severely taxed the narrow monaural technology of his time."[12] Technical difficulties and conducting inadequacies notwithstanding, the four numbers of his first recording session are among the best that he ever recorded.

Lanza's association with Callinicos would, however, have serious repercussions for the tenor's operatic recording output. Mainly as a consequence of his film career, but in part due to Callinicos's incompetence, Lanza operatic efforts would often be dismissed or ignored by most music critics. For Callinicos the opportunity of working almost exclusively with Lanza must have seemed heaven-sent, and naturally he wasted no time in seizing it. Where else could he have earned so much money? Though there can be no doubt that Callinicos sincerely admired Lanza's voice, the financial rewards were an even greater attraction. Having stumbled upon a potential goldmine in the generous tenor, Callinicos went out of his way to ensure that Lanza relied on him. He succeeded to the extent that in Lanza's eyes he became indispensable to conduct for him, accompany him and help him learn new repertoire.[13]

Given that, unlike the experienced Spadoni, Callinicos had never worked as a coach with any opera company, Lanza's erratic output is less surprising. His operatic legacy includes fine renditions of the two *Andrea Chénier* arias, "*M'appari*" from *Marta*, "*Addio alla madre*" from *Cavalleria Rusticana* and the two arias from *Tosca*—Callinicos's inferior conducting notwithstanding. In other operatic recordings such as "*Parmi veder le lagrime*" from *Rigoletto*, and "*O tu che in seno agli angeli*" from *La Forza del Destino*, Lanza sings impressively at times, but over-emphasizes the recitatives and *parlando*. Another example is the aria "*O Paradiso*" from *L'Africana*, in which he is overly emphatic on the words *"Mi batte il cor"* in the recitative, and again on *"Un nuovo mondo, tu m'appartieni"* towards the end of the aria.

This would not have been the case had he been working with a top conductor or competent coach, who would have ensured that he both learned and sang the operatic selections correctly. One has only to compare the superior 1955 recording of *"O Paradiso"* with the 1950 Callinicos version to note the difference that a capable coach can make. On the later version Lanza worked with Giacomo Spadoni.

What seems incomprehensible to this day is that RCA—with the knowledgeable Richard Mohr as recording producer and experienced conductors such as Renato Cellini, Erich Leinsdorf and Jonel Perlea at their disposal—would continue to engage Callinicos on all the tenor's operatic recordings. Presumably RCA could have insisted on another conductor. Prior to the RCA session Lanza had already worked effectively with a succession of them: Sylvan Levin, Georges Sebastian, Tauno Hannikainen, Allard De Ridder, Vladimir Golschman, Leo Kopp, Eugene Ormandy, Emanuel Balaban, Paul Scherman, Walter Herbert and Victor Alessandro.

Corelli's clashes with conductors for coming in too early or too late, scooping, and holding onto notes forever are notorious, as are Di Stefano's problems with singing both sharp and flat, as well as attacking notes from below. Yet despite their musical inadequacies, both managed considerable careers.

It was while in New York for his first recording session that Lanza met Nicholas Brodszky, a composer who would play a significant part in his future recording career. Brodszky was a Hungarian who had written a number of operettas in his native country prior to working in Britain in the late 30s and 40s, where he composed the musical scores of such films as the World War Two hit *The Way To The Stars*.

Brodszky was brought to America by producer Joe Pasternak, with the specific task of composing the songs, in collaboration with lyricist Sammy Cahn, for Lanza's follow-up film to *That Midnight Kiss*. One of the songs, "Be My Love," would become a smash hit, eventually selling nearly two million copies and providing Lanza with his first gold record.

In his autobiography, *I Should Care*, Sammy Cahn recalled his meeting with Lanza at the time of "Be My Love":

> Now if you've only heard Mr. Lanza on a record or a tape or in a movie, you've never heard him at all, because no mechnical reproduction could capture the startling brilliance of that voice. It scared the hell out of you. I believe he had a soft pedal and a loud pedal in his throat.[14]

Cahn pre-tested the lyrics of "Be My Love" on Brodszky, asking the operatically-trained composer to sing back every word. However, when the time came to perform the song for Lanza, Cahn could not resist singing it himself. "Chutzpah!" the lyricist recalled: "Cahn singing to Lanza! Happily he already knew the melody and accepted the lyrics from me."[15]

With *That Midnight Kiss* completed, MGM embarked on an intensive publicity campaign to promote their new find. Earlier, while still filming, a big party had been given at the plush Mocambo on Sunset Strip by Louis B. Mayer and Joe Pasternak to introduce Lanza to the press and the prominent figures in the movie business. Helen Rose, MGM's fashion designer for 23 years, reminisced about the evening:

> No young man ever came to this world of entertainment with more potential than Mario and few came as starry-eyed and as unassuming. I doubt if Mario knew then just how much talent he possessed. At the party Mario was like a child at his first Christmas. He shook hands with everyone and his eyes were like twin stars...I wondered if he was mentally pinching himself to find out if this was all real, or if he was just dreaming.[16]

Mid-August saw another MGM night at the Hollywood Bowl. The production was staged by director Jack Cummings with soloists including the 20-year-old Andre Previn, singing actress Jane Powell and dancer Eleanor Powell. Lanza was given the honor of closing the proceedings. With John Green conducting the Hollywood Bowl Orchestra, the tenor began with the well-tried "*Celeste Aida*". Then with Mary Jane Smith, a young coloratura soprano of no particular distinction, he delivered a most beautiful and musical account of the duet "*E il sol dell'anima*" from Verdi's *Rigoletto*, followed by the "*Addio, addio*" in which Lanza and soprano both ended on a high D flat.

That Lanza had worked on the duet with an experienced coach, Giacomo Spadoni, is again clear. His understanding of the music is also evident, as is his concept of the role of the Duke. The way in which Lanza phrases, his use of *diminuendo* coupled with a superbly beautiful voice is the type of tenor singing any opera impresario would kill for.

The premiere of *That Midnight Kiss* was scheduled for release in September 1949. Appropriately, it was held in Lanza's hometown of Philadelphia, where the film was set. MGM spared no expense in ensuring that Lanza and Betty, together with Kathryn Grayson, her then-husband Johnny Johnson, and Giacomo Spadoni and his wife Helen, travelled in comfort on their nation-wide promotional tour.[17]

On their arrival in Philadelphia they were welcomed at the railway station by Mayor Bernard Samuel. Together with Lanza's parents, they were then escorted in grand style to the tenor's old neighborhood, where a clamorous welcome awaited. The streets were strewn with "Welcome home Mario" banners. A deeply moved Lanza recalled: "I don't think that I've ever felt quite so touched in my life as at that moment."[18]

Then from the house in Mercy Street, where he had lived as a child, the entire party rode in an open car parade that took them directly through the city. With people waving and cheering, they proceeded to the Boyd Theater, where the film was premiering. There Lanza and Grayson made a personal appearance on stage. From Philadelphia it was on to New York and more interviews and appearances with Grayson at the Capitol Theater. The two were also featured on NBC's Radio Screen Guild Theater Program. Lanza sang two solos: '*Mamma mia che vo' sape*' and "I Know I Know I Know," and, in a duet with Grayson, "They Didn't Believe Me" and the first act duet from *Lucia di Lamermoor* "*Verranno a te sull'aure*," which they didn't sing in the film.[†]

Though he was basking in his newfound fame he didn't forget his teacher, to whom he sent the first of many recordings. On the album of *That Midnight Kiss* he wrote:

To Maestro Enrico Rosati,

I said it before and I'll say it again—thank you for giving me a voice.

All my love, Mario Lanza[19]

His regard for his teacher was such that he credited Rosati with

[†]Again, the end of the duet is ruined by an unwritten off-key scream from Grayson.

having given him a voice—but of course Rosati had done no such thing. What the maestro did give him, however, was a great technique and the confidence and assurance that comes with it.

With all the publicity and exposure he was now receiving in connection with his MGM contract, the release of his first film and his first recordings, Lanza was being increasingly compared with Caruso.[20] At this early stage in his career, it was an absurd comparison. Yet contrary to popular belief, Lanza did not encourage such discussion. While vocally he had nothing to envy Caruso for, his idol's operatic career was another matter entirely. Lanza was well aware of the ground he had to cover before he could begin to approach Caruso's immense achievements on the operatic stage. "I wish they (the critics) wouldn't compare me with Caruso," he pleaded at the time. "I've got a long way to go before I even rate a mention in the same breath as Caruso."[21]

The question resurfaced during an interview for *That Midnight Kiss* in New York. Again he clearly stated: "I'm humble before the memory of Caruso, and shouldn't like the public to think that I think my voice is on a par with his. Let's face it—who can be greater than the greatest."[22] One could argue that Lanza was being unduly modest. While Caruso had worked extremely hard to create his undeniably great sound, Lanza started off with far more vocal equipment than his idol had ever possessed. Lanza's voice was complete from the very beginning. The dark velvety center and fearless high notes were already in place, leaving Rosati with the sole task of turning the tenor into a more polished, finished singer.

Later, at the height of his film success in *The Great Caruso*, Lanza would be quoted as saying:

> At my age [29] Caruso was nowhere...no-how, nothing. I don't think I'm as great a singer as Caruso, because you never think you're as good as your idol, even though others might say you are, but at my age Caruso used to crack on high B flat, and I have the record to prove it, which is nothing against him of course. Sure I haven't sung at the Met yet, but the day I do, all hell will break loose the way it did in pictures.[23]

This was mere boasting of course. By 1951, after three years in the movie capital and the resultant world fame, Lanza was becoming increasingly insecure behind the bravado.

But while Lanza was being cautious in 1949, no less an authority than Arturo Toscanini was just as categorical in his positive assessment. It is uncertain whether Toscanini heard Lanza sing live or whether he heard the tenor's superb recording of "*Che gelida manina.*" Regardless, his verdict was: "This is the greatest natural tenor voice of the 20th Century."[24] When it came to the sheer quality and beauty of the voice, anyone with reasonably good hearing could have reached the same conclusion, such as Tito Schipa, a Golden Age tenor justly famed for his artistry. "Mario," he told him, "You have the greatest given throat ever heard in a young man. Take care of it."[25]

That Lanza intended to take care of his voice, and that he knew what he was doing at this stage of his career, is evident in the interview he granted to James Francis Cook for the American monthly musical publication *Etude.* Discussing prospective singers he told Cook:

> Many young folks who are unable to afford a good teacher wait around bemoaning their fate until it's too late. Get the best records of great singers and listen to them over and over again, hundreds of times. Listen to the fine, pure and relaxed production. Always sing *mezza voce* (half voice) with absolutely no strain at first...Read everything you can about the voice and then use the intelligence at your command in applying it in your own case...Many vocal aspirants do not realize how much all-important collateral information can be gained from records, books and magazines that even the best of teachers do not have time to take up in lessons.[26]

Certainly it seemed as if Tito Schipa's fears were unfounded, for here was a young man who not only possessed an outstanding tenor voice, but the intelligence and knowledge to go with it.

He was also ambitious and aiming at the top. Asked on the NBC radio network in New York what his ultimate goal was, Lanza replied: "To sing Rodolfo in *La Bohème* at the Metropolitan with Licia Albanese as Mimi, Leonard Warren as Marcello and Ezio Pinza as Colline."[27]

In common with most tenors, Rodolfo was among Lanza's favorite roles, which also included Andrea Chénier, Canio in *Pagliacci* and—above all—Otello. Lanza was well suited to the music of Puccini, and in his late 20s and early 30s would have been an ideal Rodolfo, just as two years earlier he had been an ideal Pinkerton.

12—THE TOAST OF NEW ORLEANS

FEELING CONFIDENT and elated by the success of his first film, by late October 1949 Lanza was back in Hollywood ready for a new movie and a third recording session. The latter took place at Republic Studios, where two months earlier he had worked for the first time with conductor Ray Sinatra, a cousin of the more famous Frank. Ray Sinatra was a competent conductor of popular music whose career was centered mainly in Las Vegas. He would go on to conduct a good number of Lanza's future non-operatic recordings, including many of the songs for the tenor's radio show.

The collaboration would produce many pleasing results despite a tendency on Sinatra's part for overblown arrangements and an orchestra that at times sounded more akin to a big band. One of the numbers that emerged from the second session with Sinatra is Lanza's justly famous and exciting version of "Granada". Although badly recorded, with the voice sounding distant and too bright, it is worth noting that Lanza sings it in the impossibly high key of F major instead of the standard D major. In other words, a *third* higher—with the tenor ending with a high C instead of the usual A.

This remarkable feat demonstrates Lanza's range, which enabled him to sustain the extremely high tessitura not only of "Granada," but of numerous other songs.[†]

Meanwhile at MGM, preparations were under way for Lanza's second film, which would again see him teamed with Kathryn Grayson. Encouraged by the success of their first film together, Pasternak had visions of a new MacDonald-Eddy duo. Future projects contemplated by Pasternak for his new duo included both remakes of *The Merry Widow* and *Show Boat*[1] At one point, he even considered co-starring MacDonald with Lanza, a proposal that the soprano wisely declined on the basis of the age difference between the pair.

[†]In fact, such was Lanza's ease in the high register that arrangers/orchestrators tended to do the very opposite of what is usually done, transposing songs *up* rather than down, with not always pleasing results.

The 27-year-old Grayson was a well-established performer with a dozen films to her credit since her debut in *Andy Hardy's Private Secretary* in 1940. An attractive woman with dark hair and doll-like features, Grayson had a thin, uneven coloratura soprano voice of extended range. Properly trained, it is arguable that she could have improved her vocal quality, and she could occasionally be quite good when she approached a song softly, as she does with "Time After Time" in the 1947 film *It Happened In Brooklyn.* As it turned out, Grayson would partner baritone Howard Keel in three films while Lanza would reach new heights with his next film, *The Great Caruso.*

Other projects that didn't materialize included a film based on a story by Sacha Guitry titled *Deburau* in which Ezio Pinza and Lanza would play father and son both in love with the same girl played by Ava Gardner. There was also talk of a film with Frank Sinatra, Mickey Rooney and Jimmy Durante called *They All Sing.*

Lanza was enthusiastic about *Deburau.* "In Guitry's original story they were clowns. But why would clowns be singing? So now we are opera singers and, confidentially, I win the girl at the end of the picture!" he stated in an interview.[2]

Encouraged by Lanza's impact on cinema audiences world-wide, MGM proceeded with haste to his next movie.

As designer Helen Rose recalled: "In his debut film, *That Midnight Kiss*, smart showman that Joe [Pasternak] is, he gave Mario fourth billing. The audiences made him a star."[3]

For his follow-up film, initially titled *Kiss Of Fire*, then changed to *Serenade To Suzette* and finally to *The Toast of New Orleans*, Lanza received second billing behind Kathryn Grayson and ahead of David Niven.

Filmed with the aid of 35 different sets built on the MGM backlot to recreate the New Orleans of 1905, and again under the direction of Norman Taurog, *The Toast of New Orleans* was another rags to riches story. In the screenplay, written by Sy Gomberg and George Wells, Lanza is an uninhibited fisherman whose sensational voice brings him to the attention of opera impresario Niven. The impresario, together with the help of the star soprano and romantic interest (Grayson), proceeds to change the rough fisherman into a polished and elegant gentleman, often with comic results. Lanza's character becomes stiff and unnatural, only reverting to his old self when he realizes that he must if he is to win Grayson.

This was not a significant departure from his first film, with only the period and the locale changed and the story clearly of secondary importance to Lanza's voice. Nevertheless the film was a happy experience for Lanza, who enjoyed working with co-star Niven and the Irish-American character actor J. Carrol Naish. The latter had portrayed his father in *That Midnight Kiss*, and was now playing his uncle.

At the same time, however, the first signs that Lanza was succumbing to the pressures of overnight fame would surface. While working on *The Toast of New Orleans*, he began to drink with increasing frequency. Whereas in the past he would limit his intake to a glass of red wine with his meals and the occasional beer, he was now drinking scotch. David Niven had introduced him to Chivas Regal and Lanza had taken an instant liking to it.[4]

His drinking would consequently affect his filming of the climactic scene, the Love Duet from *Madama Butterfly* with Kathryn Grayson. Lanza—high on alcohol at the time and unaware of his strength—continually grabbed Grayson's arms during filming, pulling her towards him as the script demanded. The scene required a large number of takes, resulting in the soprano's arms becoming badly bruised. A furious Grayson retaliated at the end of the duet, when the script required her to slap Lanza after he kisses her as the curtain falls. Grayson's closed fist is clearly visible as she hits Lanza with all her strength instead of merely slapping him.[5]

Third-billed David Niven, then at a low point in his career, had joined the cast merely because he needed the money.[6] Nevertheless, he liked Lanza's bubbly personality and enjoyed the time spent working with him. During breaks from filming, Niven—who was fond of opera—would often pass the time with Lanza listening to the tenor's collection of opera records.

At other times, when Lanza was skipping lunch and training with some of the weights Terry Robinson had brought over to the set, Niven, Naish and—on occasion—Grayson would join Lanza in his weight-lifting.

Another member of the cast was the talented 18-year-old

Puerto Rican dancer Rita Moreno. The charismatic Moreno thoroughly enjoyed her first experience in a film musical,[7] and would later go on to win an Academy Award for her role as Anita in *West Side Story*.

Overall the atmosphere on the set reflected the pleasant and humorous nature of the movie. Lanza would retain fond memories of the days spent on the set of *The Toast of New Orleans*, reminiscing shortly before his death that he had "never had so much fun making a movie."[8] Although Niven thought little of the film, he would remember it in his memoirs as "a success thanks only to the fact that it launched Mario Lanza's golden voice."[9]

Of course this was Lanza's *second* film, but Niven was essentially right in his assessment. Once again the producers' sole motive was to highlight the vocal talents of Metro's new discovery. Although Lanza had more to sing than in his previous movie, operatic excerpts were still being outnumbered by a variety of songs, most of them eminently forgettable. The songs were composed for the film by the newly-formed duo of Nicholas Brodszky and Sammy Cahn and ranged from the title song to "Tina Lina," "Boom Biddy Boom Boom," "The Bayou Lullaby," "I'll Never Love You," and "Be My Love." The latter would soon become Lanza's signature tune, reaching number one on the hit parade, and remaining on the best-seller charts for all of 34 weeks.

The Pasternak formula once again proved successful at the box office and Lanza's fan mail began to increase until, according to MGM, it reached the level of 500 letters a day.[10] Clearly, it was more than the Pasternak formula, however, that was working its magic on cinema audiences worldwide.

Along with his voice, Lanza also had the looks and charisma to be a matinee idol. Of course, Lanza's looks were both a blessing and a curse. As music critic James Miller aptly stated, "If he had been cross-eyed or hare-lipped or possessed of some other factor that would have disqualified him from making movies, he would have been one of the star [opera] singers of his time."[11]

None of the tenors who appeared on the screen, either before or after Lanza, effectively combined a superb voice with good looks, magnetic personality and the ability to cross over from opera to song so convincingly. Furthermore, Lanza's way with English lyrics remains unique. His diction was faultless. Admittedly he had the advantage of being born in America, but in terms of phrasing, feeling for the words and the uncanny ability to capture the mood of the situation, Lanza is without rival in many of the best songs that he recorded in English.

On the other hand, Lanza's acting has often been criticized—and indeed cruelly ridiculed at times—but he generally got by as an actor and could even be impressive on occasion. In contrast, if we examine the cinematic efforts of other tenors, we find that Gigli, for example, despite a most beautiful voice, is non-existent as an actor—and laughable as a lover—in most of the 16 films he made. In fact the Gigli films are so mediocre that they make Lanza's efforts seem like masterpieces by comparison. As an actor his contemporary, Mario Del Monaco, was even less effective both on the operatic stage and on the screen.

The same may be said of the efforts of virtually every tenor who attempted to make films: Tito Schipa, John McCormack, Giacomo Lauri-Volpi, Richard Tauber, Jussi Björling, Giuseppe Lugo, Ferruccio Tagliavini, and even Giuseppe Di Stefano. The latter started off stiffly and even though he eventually became a superb actor on stage, is decidedly uncomfortable before the cameras in his only screen appearance, the inept *Canto Per Te (I Sing For You)*. Of Caruso it was said that although he displayed a comic gift in such operas as *L'Elisir d'Amore* and *Marta* he was not handsome and was a lump as an actor.[12]

In the 1930s, tenor Nino Martini was brought to Hollywood by producer Jesse Lasky, who years later would co-produce Lanza's magnum opus, *The Great Caruso*. Martini had good looks and a small voice ideally suited for the screen, but he was a poor actor and his English was strongly accented. After three failed attempts at the box office, Lasky finally gave up. Paramount required even less incentive to drop the Polish tenor Jan Kiepura. Brought to Hollywood after a series of successful but forgettable films in England and Germany, Kiepura played a singing fisherman in *Give Us This Night* with mezzo-soprano Gladys Swarthout. Despite a score by the celebrated Austrian composer Erich Wolfgang Korngold and lyrics by Oscar Hammerstein II, the film bombed at the box office. The general critical consensus was that "Kiepura's hammy performance almost single-handedly sank the show."[13]

In more recent times there have been at least two other attempts to make film stars out of tenors. The first dates back to 1955 when Paramount, in an obvious attempt to capitalize on Lanza's self-imposed exile, enticed the Maltese tenor Oreste Kirkop from Covent Garden to star in a remake of the operetta *The Vagabond King*, a project initially intended for Lanza.

Kirkop was musical, with a pleasing, well-produced lyric tenor voice, and he possessed good looks not unlike Lanza's. Paramount spared no expense on the production, assigning veteran Michael Curtiz to direct, providing an excellent supporting cast (although he was saddled with Kathryn Grayson), and giving Kirkop the full publicity treatment. Yet the film failed dismally at the box office. Whether it was because its star lacked Lanza's charisma, or that operetta had simply had its day, Kirkop never made another film.†

The most recent attempt to turn a tenor into a movie star was MGM's in 1982 when, again with great fanfare, they labelled Luciano Pavarotti the Mario Lanza of the 1980s and starred him in the film *Yes, Giorgio*.

The film was no better and no worse than most of the vehicles Lanza had starred in. Pavarotti sang well, but that extra dimension—the magic that would bring the paying customers to the cinema—was simply lacking, and consequently MGM recouped only one of the 19 million dollars it had spent on the production.[14]‡

It is not surprising then that MGM was extremely pleased with Lanza. Not even the most optimistic of the studio's top executives had anticipated that the tenor's rise would be so rapid. Pasternak himself had predicted it would take at least ten films before Lanza would become a top star.[15] The tenor had proved them all wrong. His first film had been a hit and his second one an even bigger one.

Encouraged by the rapid ascent of their new singing sensation, MGM showed their appreciation by again paying him more

---

†*The Vagabond King* would also mark the end of Kathryn Grayson's film career.
‡Needless to say, Pavarotti has stayed well clear of the cine-cameras ever since. He did, however, appear in a filmed version of the opera *Rigoletto*.

than his contract called for. For *The Toast of New Orleans* Lanza received $50,000, which was twice the amount stipulated in his contract.[16]

The Toast of New Orleans opened at Loew's State in New York on September 29, 1950. In addition to the popular songs, Lanza sang a number of operatic excerpts including the Flower song from *Carmen*, snatches of *"M'appari"* from *Marta*, "O Paradiso" from *L'Africana*, and with Kathryn Grayson the Drinking song from Act One of *La Traviata* and the Love Duet from *Madama Butterfly*.

The latter, staged by Armando Agnini who had worked with Lanza in the New Orleans Opera performances in 1948, was the highlight of the film. Beautifully filmed by cinematographer William Snyder, it provides insight into the type of Pinkerton Lanza must have been on the operatic stage two years earlier.

Lanza received positive reviews for his performance in *The Toast of New Orleans*. Howard Thompson, film critic for the *New York Times*, wrote:

> There is no need to continue with the story, not when there is so much enjoyment to be had listening to Mr. Lanza (sic) extraordinarily gifted tenor voice...Miss Grayson and Mr. Lanza give us just enough in a duet from *Madama Butterfly* to further the wish that more of the opera had been used.[17]

The trade paper *Film Daily* reported:

> Without attempting to take anything away from the members of the cast, it must be reported that Lanza makes the picture his own. He is truly a revelation, scoring solidly both as a singer and as a laugh-inciter.[18]

With his career now full of promise, Lanza felt it was time to repay his parents for their support.

Lanza was very close to his parents and wanted them near him. After the success of his first film he had moved to yet another home—this time an even larger one complete with swimming pool—at 810 North Whittier Drive, Beverly Hills. At the same time, he persuaded his parents to move to California, where he felt his base would be for the foreseeable future. With their only son thousands of miles away, Antonio and Maria had little reason to remain in Philadelphia. Gathering a few belongings and their life savings of $7,000, they moved to Los Angeles in December, 1949, and initially lived with their son and family in Lanza's Hollywood mansion. Lanza would subsequently rent a house for them in close proximity to his own before presenting his surprised parents with a beautiful $35,000 home in exclusive Pacific Palisades a short time later.

13—DILEMMAS AND DIETS

WITH HIS SECOND FILM completed Lanza and his wife felt it was time to take a well-earned vacation. Lanza's manager, Sam Weiler, suggested they take a boat trip to Hawaii. The Lanzas, Weilers and Callinicos would be joined by two of the tenor's new friends, Tyrone Power, and his wife Linda Christian. The Powers were stopping on the islands for a week before flying on to Manila where Tyrone was to begin filming *An American Guerilla In The Philippines* for 20th Century Fox. On arrival in Honolulu the Lanza party was met by Fred Matsuo, co-promoter of the concerts, Matsuo's wife, and Joe Pasternak's wife Dorothy who had flown into town the previous Friday. Strictly speaking, it was not to be a total vacation as Sam Weiler had seized the opportunity at the last minute and booked Lanza for two concerts in Honolulu.[†]

Although he was kept busy with press interviews, attending luncheons and preparing for the concerts, Lanza enjoyed the four-day voyage on the liner Lorelei and the brief vacation in the luxurious Royal Hawaiian Hotel on Waikiki Beach. He was also pleased to be sharing the brief holiday with Tyrone Power, whom he genuinely admired (and who in turn adored Lanza's voice),[1] as well as catching up with MGM's fellow co-workers Howard Keel and Esther Williams, who were filming *Pagan Love Song* on the island of Kauai.

On one occasion they all gathered for a *luau* at the villa the Powers owned in Honolulu. After everyone had enjoyed ample portions of the succulent pig, Tyrone Power asked Lanza to sing. Lanza obliged, thrilling Power to the extent that he dived into his swimming pool, neglecting to remove his non-waterproof watch

[†]A third concert had to be hastily arranged when the first two sold out in record time

in his excitement.[2]

The three concerts Lanza sang in Honolulu consisted of his standard repertoire with one exception. The printed program included, for the first and definitely for the last time, three songs by Hugo Wolf: "The Forsaken Maiden," "Secrecy," and "Song To Spring." *Lieder* did not particularly inspire Lanza. A year earlier, during the concert tour he was then undertaking he had told Callinicos that he didn't know any *lieder* at all. He had obviously made the effort to learn at least three songs for the Honolulu concert although there is some doubt as to whether he actually sang them.[†]

Although he conceded that musically speaking *lieder* were important, he felt that they did not exploit the full range of the voice.[3] Pavarotti once expressed a similar view, bluntly opining that "a tenor will sing *lieder* because he cannot sing anything else."[4]

Perhaps a willingness to include more *lieder* in his repertory would have helped to silence critics who accused Lanza of being unable to sing anything below fortissimo. Yet there are countless examples of Lanza's ability to sing softly. The superb 1952 "Deep In My Heart" with Ann Blyth, his exquisite handling of the 1951 "All The Things You Are" or the 1955 Schubert's "Ave Maria"[‡] immediately come to mind. For sheer versatility one should also listen to the trio "*E voi ridete*" from Act 1, Scene 3, of Mozart's *Cosi fan tutte*—recorded at the Rome Opera in 1958—for further evidence of Lanza's ability to switch convincingly from the dramatic demands of Leoncavallo to the subtleties of Mozart. One would be hard pressed to name more than a handful of tenors of any era who were capable of such accomplishments.

As much as he enjoyed his success and the financial rewards that came with it, Lanza had not forsaken his ambition to become a great opera singer. In September 1949 he stated that he believed it would take him another five years of hard work be-

[†]In his third concert he did, however, sing *The Lord's Prayer*—the only known time that he sang Malotte's composition in concert.

[‡]Indeed the latter contains a central tessitura that is deceptively difficult to sing *mezza voce.*

fore he could fulfil his ambition of singing at the Metropolitan.[5] Then referring to a conversation he had had with the general manager of the Connecticut Opera Association, Lanza said: "I promised general manager Joseph Listro that I would do it [sing opera] and we shook hands on it."[6] While this project did not eventuate, it does indicate that the thought of an operatic career was constantly on his mind.

As long as he worked in Hollywood, however, Lanza would have little opportunity of fulfilling his lifelong dream. Its hectic work schedules—which frequently involved rising at 5 a.m. to be at the studio by 6, and at times not finishing work until 8 p.m.— were in sharp contrast to the routine followed by a typical opera singer. (Opera singers are often late risers who prepare throughout the day and are at their best by evening.) For Lanza making films was not only hard work, but by the time he returned home he would still need to memorize the dialogue for the next day's filming, leaving little time for anything else.

As a relatively inexperienced singer, he should have been working daily with a top coach studying new scores and their relative musical aspects. Instead he was busy learning dialogue. Working in Hollywood also meant having to contend with another problem: his weight. This never-ending battle would continue to haunt him for the rest of his life and would ultimately kill him.

His weight became increasingly difficult to control while he was making *The Toast of New Orleans*. Lanza was by nature a big man who put on weight with the greatest of ease.[7] He also had a big appetite and was destined to be on the heavy side, in common with most opera singers. A bulky tenor, however, was out of the question for the cinema. In the Hollywood of the 1950s looks were everything. One definitely had to look the part—possess the *physique du rôle*. During filming Lanza made a brave effort to control his weight by not eating lunch and exercising instead. Yet there were times when he was unable to stand it any longer. Producer Pasternak recalled:

> Once, for example, I saw a waiter head for the stage with a mountainously laden tray over his shoulder. "Where are you bringing that?" I asked him. He said J. Carrol Naish had

111

ordered lunch in his dressing room. Something made me suspicious. Lanza was then on a no-lunch kick. One meal a day was all he needed, he assured me. A round substantial dinner, nothing else. He was taking naps during the noon hour break. I followed the waiter.

He did in fact go into Carrol Naish's dressing room but when I opened the door, I found my star attacking triple helpings of potato salad, huge slabs of ham, roast beef, generously buttered rye bread, and heaven knows what else.[8]

In the long run, skipping meals and exercising would not be enough and Lanza would become increasingly reliant on crash diets, pills and injections. The drastic weight loss would in turn affect his highly volatile personality and severely damage his health. Had his career taken a different course, it would hardly have mattered what he weighed. On the operatic stage, in common with Caruso, Gigli and more recently Pavarotti, Lanza would have been the rule rather than the exception. Even in the Hollywood of today, weight would not have been the issue that it was in the 1950s, when conformity to the glamorous notion of the romantic movie hero was demanded.

14—THE GREAT CARUSO

FOR YEARS producer Jesse L. Lasky had wanted to make a film on the life of the great tenor, Enrico Caruso.[1] Lasky owned the rights to Dorothy Caruso's biography of her husband, and had known Caruso personally. Indeed, such was the popularity of the great tenor that back in 1918—nine years before the advent of sound— Lasky had produced the only two films that Caruso ever made, *My Cousin* and *The Splendid Romance*.

Despite Caruso's widespread popularity, *My Cousin* was a gigantic failure, so much so that in America, the second film was never released. Caruso was paid the huge sum of $200,000 for his efforts, admitting candidly that he had not liked himself as an actor.

Lasky's chief difficulty in bringing the life of Caruso to the screen had been the casting of the main part. Initially he had toyed with the idea of using Caruso's original acoustic record-ings and adding new orchestral accompaniments, a process RCA had already experimented with in the 1930s. Lasky had also con-templated having an unknown actor play the part, but he even-tually abandoned both ideas and the search began for a suitable tenor.

It was every tenor's dream to portray Caruso on the screen. The Italian tenor Ferruccio Tagliavini, who had made a consid-erable impression since his arrival in America in 1946, was touted for the role at one point.[†]

American star tenor Richard Tucker was another who would have been delighted to portray his great predecessor. But although his name was variously mentioned in the press as a possible con-

†The head of 20ᵗʰ Century Fox, Darryl F. Zanuck, was rumored to have been interested in filming Caruso's life.

tender for the part, at the time MGM was planning the film Tucker was not even approached.[2]

The Swedish tenor Jussi Björling went to the extent of visiting MGM, where, according to him, he was astounded to receive a request that he have his nose surgically altered to resemble Caruso's. Not surprisingly, Björling refused and that was the end of the matter.[3] However, it must be said that this is a rather unlikely story given that Björling's nose was in fact quite similar to that of Caruso. In any event, Björling – unlike Lanza – was not movie star material. If indeed MGM did ask him to have his nose altered, it may well have been merely an excuse for not considering him for the part. Furthermore, with a top box office tenor already under contract to them, it makes little sense that MGM would have risked filming the life of Caruso with someone else in the part.

Lasky was not the only one interested in filming Caruso's life, and had he not moved swiftly, the producer-director Alexander Korda might have seized the initiative. In late 1949, Korda—unbeknownst to Lasky—was not only contemplating making a film based on the life of Caruso, but also had Lanza in mind for the leading role. He had seen the tenor in his first film, and thinking him ideal for the Caruso part had approached MGM with a view to borrowing their new discovery.[4]

In the meantime Lasky was continuing his search for a tenor to portray Caruso. He had heard Lanza sing at the tenor's 1947 Hollywood Bowl concert, and considered him a strong contender for the part. Eventually Lasky decided to seek the advice of Edward Johnson, General Manager of the Metropolitan Opera.

The latter had heard Lanza sing at one of Rosati's musical soirees in 1946, and was unequivocal in his verdict. Lanza, he told Lasky, "has the voice, the looks and the artistic temperament required, and provided he is carefully handled and surrounded with the right people, he will be up to the task."[5]

It was all the reassurance Lasky needed. Seeing the tenor on the screen in *That Midnight Kiss* only reinforced his view that Lanza was the right choice to play the immortal Caruso.[6]

Lasky had a proven record as a producer. In the previous decade alone he had produced a number of successful films for various studios including *Sergeant York*, *The Adventures of Mark*

Twain, and the Gershwin biopic, *Rhapsody In Blue*.

Initially, Lasky approached MGM with the intention of borrowing Lanza, but the studio made it clear—as they had with Korda—that borrowing Lanza was out of the question. Mayer's friendship with Lasky dated back to the days of the silent era, and he decided to offer the latter a deal. Since Lasky already owned the rights to Dorothy Caruso's biography, the only way he could make the film with Lanza would be to sell the rights to Metro, who in turn would allow him to act as associate producer on the film. Lasky agreed to the deal.[7]

"Lanza has the greatest tenor voice I've ever heard. Even greater than Caruso!" enthused Mayer to all who would listen to him.[8] Yet his support for the project was not shared by the studio's top executives, who felt that an essentially operatic film was certain to fail at the box office. Although Mayer was still officially in charge of the studio, the New York office of MGM-Loew's Inc. which was headed by Nicholas Schenck—had been listening with increasing frequency to Dore Schary, Metro's vice president in charge of production. In fact Mayer and Schenck had never liked each other and relations between them had been cool at best.

Ironically, it was Mayer who had brought Schary to MGM in 1948. In many respects the two men were complete opposites. While Mayer had always stuck to big budget films that were entertaining and offered the general public escapism, the more cerebral Schary[†] was not remotely interested in romantic stories and musicals. When it came to music Schary's judgment was more than a little suspect. When Arthur Freed was casting his 1951 production of *Show Boat*, Schary thought Dinah Shore would be ideal for the role of Julie that eventually went to Ava Gardner.[9] Schary's primary concern was with so-called message pictures, low budget films that employed the services of lesser-known actors.[10] Both Schenck and Schary were opposed to the projected Caruso film. Among Schary's objections was that he considered Lanza too young for the role.[11]

This was nonsense, of course. Lanza, nearly thirty, was an

[†]Schary was a writer of screenplays, winning an Academy Award for *Boys Town* in 1938.

ideal age to play Caruso: young enough to portray the young Caruso, and with the aid of make-up, a convincing 48-year-old at the conclusion of the film.

No doubt both Schenck and Schary were influenced by other factors. In 1950 the entire film industry was in a state of panic over the advent of television, which was increasingly keeping audiences away from cinemas.

Schenck and Schary felt that an operatic film was simply not viable as a commercial proposition.[12]

Mayer held out. His faith in Lanza had been reinforced by the public response to the tenor's first two films and he was convinced that with Lanza in the starring role, the Caruso project would be a success. In the end Mayer's decision prevailed.

When informed that he would be playing Caruso, Lanza, although pleased at the prospect of playing his idol, approached the task with near-reverence. During the pre-production period, he did his own research, read and reread books and countless articles on Caruso, spoke to some of the people who had known the great tenor and generally tried to model his manner and behavior on that of his great predecessor. "All the research I did on Caruso only confirmed the admiration I have for him," he stated at the time.[13] Later he would add: "For me, the film of *The Great Caruso* was an unbelievable dream come true, but at first I didn't know if I would dare give my voice to the singer I admired above all others."[14]

Before filming could start, however, there was the inevitable weight problem to contend with. Since completing his last film, Lanza had managed to stay more or less at the same weight— approximately 195 pounds (88.4kg). However, Joe Pasternak— concerned at how the public would react if his new star looked too heavy—felt Lanza should lose an additional 25 pounds (11.3kg). Lanza demurred, reminding Pasternak that Caruso had been overweight virtually all his life, and arguing that a slight weight gain would be of little importance. Indeed, it would provide a more realistic portrayal of the great singer.[15]

Realism, however, was not a priority for Pasternak, who was more concerned with the outcome of the film at the box office. In the end Lanza managed to get his own way and began filming at 195 pounds, although he would lose approximately 20 pounds by the time the film was completed. Although better-looking than his idol, Lanza did in fact look convincing and was near perfect in the part.

Preliminary work on the film with the working title of 'The Life of Caruso' began in July 1950. The veteran Richard Thorpe was chosen to direct the picture that would soon prove the apogee of Pasternak's career. Thorpe, a former actor in vaudeville and musical comedy, had worked his way up from editor to director, joining MGM in 1935 and remaining there for the next 30 years. His numerous films included the musicals *Two Girls and A Sailor, Three Little Words* with Fred Astaire and Red Skelton, and the Elvis Presley vehicle, *Jailhouse Rock*. Thorpe had a reputation as an actor's director and as a good technician who rarely wasted film, earning him the nickname "one-take Thorpe." He was highly regarded at the studio because of his ability to finish his films on time and often under budget.[16]

At Lanza's suggestion, his old friend Peter Herman Adler was engaged to stage and conduct the operatic numbers. Dissatisfied with the second-rate singers that MGM were planning to use in the film, Adler advised Pasternak to hire a number of leading Metropolitan Opera singers in order to surround Lanza with the best available talent in the operatic sequences.[17] As a result, soprano Dorothy Kirsten, mezzo Blanche Thebom, baritone Giuseppe Valdengo, bass Nicola Moscona, together with sopranos Marina Koshetz, Olive May Beach, Teresa Celli[†] and tenor Gilbert Russell were all added to the cast.

The Czech soprano Jarmila Novotna was also engaged, although the duet "*E il sol dell'anima*" from *Rigoletto* that she recorded with Lanza was cut from the final print. Nevertheless, she appeared effectively, if briefly, as a temperamental prima donna.

With the cameras ready to roll, there were still a number of sceptics at the studio who felt that portraying Caruso would be beyond Lanza's ability as an actor.[18]

For his part, Lanza was well aware that he lacked acting experience, and he was to benefit greatly from the help given to him by the Austrian character actor Ludwig Donath, who played

---

†Lanza's girlfriend during the Army days.

his manager in the film. Lanza would often seek Donath's advice on how to play a particular scene or deliver a particular line of dialogue.

The experienced actor spent many hours working with Lanza and felt that the tenor possessed a natural instinct and flair for acting. "He had the warmth that one needs and he loved the world of make believe, but he didn't know enough about the fundamentals of acting," recalled Donath. "He never felt secure as an actor, and I guess that complemented his own hidden doubts about his talents as a singer." Donath felt that with proper training Lanza could indeed have become a fine actor. "I didn't have to teach him gestures or instinctive things about acting; he had these things."[19]

Recalling the time of filming and the obvious comparison being drawn between Lanza and Caruso, Donath added: "He never once said to me that he thought he was equal to Caruso or better, but he projected himself into the part, perhaps secretly feeling, or at least yearning, to be the rightful successor to his idol."[20]

Of course Lanza was not a movie actor in the true sense of the word. It was a role he had been obliged to assume from the moment he accepted the MGM offer, but he undoubtedly possessed the feeling and temperament that would have made him a convincing actor on the operatic stage. There is clear evidence of his acting ability in the operatic sequences in his films, particularly in his portrayal of Otello in *Serenade*, where—both with and without the aid of makeup—he shows perfect understanding and total identification with the inner struggle of the Moor.

In *The Great Caruso*, Lanza delivered a performance that was thrilling and believable both vocally and histrionically. His total commitment in portraying Caruso is evident. With its luscious coloring, darkish center and ringing top, the quality of Lanza's voice is at its brilliant best.

In a staggering total of twenty-three musical numbers, including sixteen solos, Lanza gives standout performances of "*La danza*" by Rossini, "*La donna e mobile*" and a snippet of the quartet from *Rigoletto*, "*Che gelida manina*" from *La Bohème*, the finale from *Aida* with Dorothy Kirsten, "*M'appari*" and the finale from *Marta*, "*Vesti la giubba*" from *Pagliacci*, Guy D'Hardelot's "*Because*" and the Bach-Gounod "*Ave Maria*" with soprano Jacqueline Allen dubbing for Michael Collins in a sequence featuring Lanza singing in the cathedral with the St. Paul Choristers.

Singing like a man inspired, Lanza uses his voice with appropriate warmth and feeling and delivers each phrase with impeccably clear diction. Tenor Oreste Kirkop, who a few years later would himself become a contender for Hollywood stardom, once described Lanza's singing in *The Great Caruso*.

> I always liked Lanza's vitality and temperament. To me his singing of *"Che gelida manina"* from *La Bohème*, which he sang in his excellent film *The Great Caruso*, is unmatched by any tenor. I am fascinated by the feeling he puts into it. I think Lanza, in fact, died a little every time he sang. He was so generous with his singing.[21]

Kirkop has captured the essence of Lanza's singing. Lanza lived what he sang. His involvement with the lyrics and the music was such that he was able to communicate his feelings directly to the audience, who in turn responded to his message because it believed in the singer's sincerity and total commitment.

Filming *The Great Caruso* proved to be another happy experience for Lanza. He enjoyed a warm working relationship with director Richard Thorpe, who could be extremely bad-tempered if he didn't like someone. Fortunately for all concerned Thorpe took a liking to Lanza and was both patient and understanding with his young charge.

True to his reputation, Thorpe was again on schedule and Lanza's third and most important film to date was completed in a record time of less than eight weeks.[22]

After a private screening held in Hollywood on April 11, 1951 for members of the press, *The Great Caruso* opened to overall critical and public acclaim at Radio City Music Hall in New York on May 10. It subsequently played through ten consecutive weeks, earning one and a half million at that box office alone. Gross receipts during its first year of release would total $19 million and by 1958 had reached $25 million.[23] The Hollywood Premiere on May 29 was an elaborate affair. It was held at the Egyptian Theater on Hollywood Boulevard. The theater lobby had been turned into a replica of the Old Metropolitan opera for the occasion. The walkway leading to the main lobby was covered by a

90-yard red carpet. The list of those attending reads like a Hollywood "Who's Who": After MGM's chief Louis B. Mayer and associate producer Jesse L. Lasky had arrived together with Lanza and his wife and Lanza's parents, guests included Artur Rubinstein, Clark Gable, James Stewart, Lana Turner, Elizabeth Taylor, Barbara Stanwyck, Robert Taylor, Jane Powell, Kathryn Grayson, Leslie Caron, Debbie Reynolds, Howard Keel, John Green, Pier Angeli, Deborah Kerr, Tyrone Power, Van Johnson, Dean Martin, Esther Williams, Ricardo Montalban and Robert Stack.

The film opened officially to the public the following day. Variety reported that it had grossed $10,000 for that one day alone.

Such was the anticipation for the film that even before its release, more than 100,000 copies were sold of *The Great Caruso* album, which Lanza had recorded prior to the start of production. *Time* magazine reported that Lanza was the "first operatic tenor in history to become a full blown Hollywood star."[24] The success of the film resulted not only in a renewed interest in Caruso and his recordings, but in increased sales of the recordings of practically all opera singers.[25]

Lanza succeeded not only in renewing interest in opera, but also in introducing it to countless cinema-goers who had previously been oblivious to the art form. He was also instrumental in influencing successive generations of prospective opera singers, including the famed "three tenors" of our time: Carreras, Domingo and Pavarotti.

Speaking at the time of Lanza's success in *The Great Caruso*, Peter Herman Adler had this to say:

> If opera is to survive in the United States, it must be sung by young personable singers. Artists like Mario Lanza not only have a great opportunity but also a great responsibility. They are not only stimulating to listen to, they are attractive young people who can do more for bringing worthwhile music to the greatest number of people than all the old-style, overstuffed singers put together.[26]

Caruso's son, Enrico Jr, would echo these comments almost forty years later in his biography of his father. "Mario Lanza," he wrote, "performed an invaluable service to opera. Lanza became a household name; thanks to him, opera was no longer an art form for an elite group of eggheads, but was acceptable entertainment for all."[27]

The film itself bore little resemblance to Caruso's real life, with a simplified and romanticized story which even had Ann Blyth, who played Caruso's wife Dorothy, singing "The Loveliest Night Of The Year." The real Dorothy was not particularly musical, couldn't sing a note, and had scant knowledge of opera or interest in it.[28]

In the film no mention was made of Caruso's ten-year relationship with the soprano Ada Giachetti, who bore him two sons: Rodolfo in 1898 and Enrico Jr. in 1904. The film's omission is hardly surprising given the attitudes towards *de facto* relationships at the time. In addition to the contentious issue of illegitimate children, screenwriters William Ludwig and Sonya Levien had to fashion a script that avoided issues such as libel, slander and invasion of privacy. They were also faced with the task of covering Caruso's life in a film with a running time of less than two hours, almost half of which was devoted to music.

William Ludwig later stated that "It was our intention to remain true to the mood, character and emotional content of Enrico Caruso's life and still present a dramatic and entertaining picture."[29]

Ludwig believed that audiences would respond best to a dramatic presentation that took certain liberties with fact while remaining true to character, spirit and emotion.

The success of the film proved him right and only purists were concerned with inaccuracies, of which there were many. These ranged from the depiction of Caruso working as a flour merchant[†] to his singing in the chorus and as a comprimario, to his failed debut at the Metropolitan as Radamès in *Aida*. Caruso had in fact made his debut at the Metropolitan as the Duke in *Rigoletto*.

William Ludwig would later seek to justify the substitution:

It was quite true that Caruso's debut at The Metropolitan Opera House was in *Rigoletto*, and not in *Aida* as we showed.

[†]In reality, he had worked for a time as an apprentice mechanic, a draftsman and, for two years, helped manufacture public drinking fountains.

In life these performances were over a year apart. On the screen they were less than seven hundred feet apart. It seemed to us that with so many different operatic selections to be included in the picture, this was a time to avoid statistics and not repeat in less than a reel the same opera. We, therefore, showed *Aida*, which was Mr. Caruso's second performance at the Metropolitan.[30]

Ludwig's explanation does make sense even though the failure of Caruso's first performance of *Aida* is inaccurately depicted in the movie. While it is true that Caruso did not meet with immediate overwhelming approval when he first sang at the Metropolitan, he was never a failure[†] in any of the roles he performed there.[31]

For his part Lanza delivered the performance of his life. Regardless of the film's flaws and inaccuracies, Lanza was able to capture the essence of Caruso's personality. Shortly before his death in 1987, Enrico Caruso Jr. endorsed the choice of Lanza to play his father:

> I can think of no other tenor, before or since Mario Lanza, who could have risen with comparable success to the challenge of playing Caruso in a screen biography...It was Lanza who made the film a success.

> While the crowds idolized him, the experts and purists insisted that he was a far cry from the real thing, that he had no right impersonating the great Enrico Caruso, that he was no more than a gifted amateur who never learned to sing properly. In my opinion, this was a facile and unfair dismissal.

> Mario Lanza was born with one of the dozen or so great tenor voices of the century, with a natural voice placement, an unmistakable and very pleasing timbre, and a nearly infallible musical instinct. His diction was flawless, matched only by the superb Giuseppe Di Stefano. His delivery was impassioned, his phrasing manly and his tempi instinctively right. All are qualities that few singers are born with and

[†]He did, however, encounter problems a number of times with the role of Radamès in later years.

[‡]A student of singing at one time, he had sung in a number of concerts in the 1930s.

others can never attain.[32]

Enrico Jr's endorsement is further supported by the fact that he was a tenor in his own right and knew what he was talking about.‡ Amid his reservations about the script of *The Great Caruso*, he singled out two important aspects of Lanza's singing: originality and versatility.

> Musically speaking, Lanza grew up on records, including my father's yet he imitated no one; his recordings of operatic selections are original interpretations. Let it not be forgotten that Mario Lanza excelled in both the classical and the light popular repertory, an accomplishment that was beyond even my father's exceptional talents. Lanza's acting may have been elementary, but his innate charm and sincerity compensated for any awkwardness.

> I only regret that Lanza was not given a script faithful to the facts to immortalize the Caruso story and through it his own art...Vocally and musically *The Great Caruso* is a thrilling motion picture, and it has helped many young people discover opera and even become singers themselves.[33]

The casting of Lanza was also approved by Caruso's widow Dorothy.[34] At the time of selling the rights to her book to Jesse L. Lasky in 1945, Dorothy had wanted Joan Fontaine to play her. The part was subsequently given to the petite Ann Blyth, who—in common with Joan Fontaine—bore no resemblance to the matronly Dorothy, who towered over her husband.† Nevertheless Blyth went on to give a fine performance. As for Lanza, the role of Caruso would soon hinder his career more than it benefited him.

---

†In her book Dorothy Caruso made her husband four inches taller but in reality Caruso was only five feet, five inches tall.

15—AN OPERATIC CAREER?

THE ITALIAN CRITIC PASQUALE SANTOMARTINO once wrote: "Mario Lanza's voice recalled that of the great Caruso. Lanza has Caruso's power and passionate temperament."[1] Yet as Santomartino noted, "The similarities between Lanza's art and that of Caruso were not always of benefit to the former." Precisely. In the eyes of the musical snobs Lanza had committed the ultimate sin. With virtually no operatic background he had dared to impersonate Caruso in a film. Sacrilege indeed.

Without attempting to take anything away from Caruso, one must bear in mind that at this stage Lanza was not yet thirty years old. In 1903, at the age of thirty, when Caruso was singing his first season at the Metropolitan, he often had to content himself with less than flattering reviews:

"Signor Caruso has many tiresome Italian vocal affectations, and when he neglects to cover his tone, and he always does when he becomes strenuous, his tone becomes pallid."[2]

And from W. J. Henderson in the *Sun*:

"Mr. Caruso's Cavaradossi was bourgeois. It was difficult to believe in the ardent passion of the aristocratic Tosca for this painter...his costumes were without distinction and his carriage less so."[3]

In the opinion of Gustav Kobbé of the *Morning Telegraph* Caruso was "Not a great tenor, but an eminently satisfactory one."[4] And so on. As late as 1906, Richard Aldrich of *The New York Times* was writing: "He cannot refrain from the lachrymose manifestations that usually accompany his denotements of great passion."[5] It is interesting to note the similarity of these comments with those made in *Time* magazine's cover story on Lanza of August 6, 1951: "He overworks the Caruso sob. He tends to swallow his notes. His brilliant tone is often white."[6]

While there is no denying that at times Lanza went too far in his search for dramatic effects—often resulting in his performance becoming too emphatic—for a young man with virtually no experience on the operatic stage, Mario Lanza's performance in *The Great Caruso* was remarkable indeed.

While the overall critical assessment of the film was mixed, Lanza's performance was almost universally praised. Bosley Crowther of *The New York Times*, after complaining about the contrived story line, wrote:

"Mr. Lanza has an excellent young tenor voice and he uses it in his many numbers with impressive dramatic power."[7]

Sigmund Spaeth of *Theatre Arts*: "Lanza's is by nature an overwhelming voice, with a distinctive personal quality."[8]

The New York Daily News: "Lanza emerges as a magnificent tenor and an engaging screen personality."[9]

Cue Magazine: "Lanza does very well by the script, the score and the subject."[10] *Newsweek* went further: "Lanza brings to the role not only a fine, natural and remarkably powerful voice, but a physique and personal mannerisms reminiscent of the immortal Caruso."[11]

And finally from *Variety*:

Metro has a natural in Lanza. He's handsome, personable and has a brilliant voice. He's a lyric tenor like Caruso, has his stocky build, his Italianate quality and some of his flair. His acting conveys something of the simple peasant Caruso essentially was, while his singing is easy, rich, musical and strong...Lanza's talent is obviously of high artistic caliber and quite stirring...musically he's a treat.[12]

Although pleased with the overall response to his performance in *The Great Caruso* Lanza treasured above all a letter from the great Scottish soprano Mary Garden. In it Garden told him that both his singing and acting in the film had been magnificent. She praised Lanza to the media in even more flattering terms.[13]

Jesse Lasky would later write in his autobiography *I Blow My Own Horn*: "Contrary to all rumors and reports about his behavior, Mario Lanza cooperated beautifully and enthusiastically, displaying no unusual symptoms of temperament or tantrums. I attribute the success of the picture largely to casting him in the role of Caruso."[14]

With the release of *The Great Caruso,* Mario Lanza became one of Hollywood's most valuable properties—America's most popular male singer, and world famous as well—and he had achieved this after a mere three films.[15] Despite this acclaim, or perhaps because of it, Lanza began to question the path his career was taking. The self-assurance of only two years earlier was beginning to give way to doubts that would assail him for the rest of his life. What he desired more than anything was to be accepted as a serious artist rather than as a film singer—no matter how popular or how successful. Now, with his sudden rise to fame and fortune, he felt trapped. The constant comparisons with Caruso would slowly turn into a nightmare, while the ongoing postponement of an operatic career would continue to haunt him.[16]

It is not difficult to understand Lanza's frame of mind. He was being compared with the greatest tenor of them all and while his own operatic career was virtually non-existent. Yet now that the comparison had been made, to attempt an operatic debut in a major opera house had become a frightening prospect. It would have been terrifying for any beginner, but it was much more so for Lanza. By 1951 the name Mario Lanza on a theater poster would have attracted worldwide attention. Lanza knew that performing on one of the foremost operatic stages would mean having the eyes of the entire world focused on him and his every note and movement scrutinized. Wasn't he the singer who had played Caruso on the screen? Wasn't he the one who had been acclaimed as the successor to the greatest tenor of them all? These are the thoughts that must have preyed on his mind. Hollywood had indeed become the tiger that he had to keep riding.

His dilemma was made more acute, perhaps, since the opera stars who had worked with him on *The Great Caruso*—who had been sceptical initially—thought him a magnificent tenor. Soprano Dorothy Kirsten summed up their reaction. "His was the voice we needed at the Met. Mario could have sung in any opera house in the world. The Metropolitan and San Francisco Operas were both open to him at one time and his career could have been sensational."[17] Peter Herman Adler went even further. When discussing the opera singers who appeared with Lanza in the film, he said: "In my opinion, I think Mario made mincemeat out of them."[18]

Regardless of the favorable opinions expressed by fellow singers and musicians alike, and the fact that he had outshone some of the pre-eminent figures of the Metropolitan, Lanza kept insisting that he needed more experience on the operatic stage. Again the doubts must have persisted: was he really their peer, or their superior?

In the meantime, the opera world continued to beat a path to his door. In addition to Edward Johnson's efforts to lure Lanza to the Metropolitan, Victor De Sabata the great Italian conductor and Artistic and Music Director of La Scala, Milan, had made a special trip to Los Angeles to invite Lanza to open the 1950/51 season at La Scala in *Andrea Chénier*.[19]

Gaetano Merola, Music Director and Principal Conductor of the San Francisco Opera, went to Los Angeles expressly to hear Lanza sing and was mesmerized by the young tenor.[20] Merola had heard about Lanza's extraordinary voice from a number of people who had worked with the tenor. These included John Green, who was General Music Director at MGM; baritone Robert Weede, who was singing regularly in San Francisco; and stage director Armando Agnini, who had worked with Lanza both in the New Orleans *Madama Butterfly* and, a year later, on the filmed sequence of the opera in *The Toast of New Orleans*.

Merola felt that Lanza could be the next Caruso and was determined to secure him for the San Francisco Opera. Merola spent a great deal of time in Los Angeles with Lanza and Sam Weiler discussing the upcoming San Francisco Season and, like De Sabata, offered Lanza the lead in the opera *Andrea Chénier*.[†]

Two performances were scheduled for October 1950 with the other principal roles sung by Licia Albanese and Robert Weede and with Fausto Cleva conducting.

But it was all to no avail. Pleading a lack of time and the fact that his wife was nearing the birth of their second child, Lanza declined.[21] Mario Del Monaco would subsequently sing the role in his debut season in San Francisco.

Regardless of the enthusiasm and confidence shown by

---

†In addition to *Chénier*, Lanza's repertoire at this stage consisted of *La Bohème, Madama Butterfly, Tosca, Pagliacci* and *Cavalleria Rusticana*.

Johnson, De Sabata and Merola, Lanza knew only too well that the Metropolitan, La Scala and the San Francisco Opera were outstanding opera houses. How could he possibly accept an offer to debut in one of these theaters with only two professional operatic performances behind him? It must have seemed inconceivable. Any other singer in the same situation and faced with the same predicament would almost certainly have refused.

In his autobiography, *My Life*, the great baritone Tito Gobbi writes: "Nothing is more risky for a young, rather inexperienced singer than to have to make his or her early attempts at an ambitious role in the full glare of an important opera house."[22] A case in point is that of the Romanian soprano Alma Gluck who, after singing only one season at the Metropolitan, begged General Manager Gatti-Casazza to be released from the Met for two years so she could study and gain experience by singing in small Italian opera houses. At first Gatti laughingly refused but two years later he finally became convinced that Gluck would benefit from singing in Europe and a new contract was drawn up accordingly.[23]

Lanza spoke at length of his repeated refusals to move into grand opera.

> My desire to sing in grand opera remains suppressed at my own wish...actually back in 1946 I was flabbergasted at receiving an invitation to sing at the Met. Flattered as I was, I declined. I will not be hurried or permit myself to overwork or over-sing. Mr. Edward Johnson of the Metropolitan Opera invited me to join that company, but without time for adequate preparation and repose for extensive study of the operatic roles I need to master this would be inadvisable. I do not want to be presented to the world's largest operatic audience until I have acquired an extensive repertoire of operas and the seasoned experience in interpretation that only long study and more maturity can bring.

> Before I tackle the Met I want to succeed at La Scala. The invitation to sing there is a frightening compliment. I want to go to Italy and start, not at La Scala, but in the smaller opera houses first, singing in a variety of roles to opera addicts...I should work up in opera, then I will feel qualified to say yes to the invitations from the great opera houses.[24]

Such unsparing self-criticism would seem to dispel any notions of conceit on Lanza's part. Yet for all his doubts, Lanza might well have been better off accepting the Metropolitan offer back in 1946. It would have meant starting off in secondary roles while learning repertoire and gaining poise and experience on the stage. Yet Lanza was ambitious enough to want to learn his craft in Italy, sing at La Scala and, in due course, make his Metropolitan debut as an established singer in a principal role. Accepting the offer to sing at the Metropolitan once he had attained world fame in films was therefore out of the question.

Lanza was aware that even with all the preparation imaginable, debuts in top theaters have ended the careers of many young inexperienced singers. Moreover, his decision to decline the offers from the Metropolitan was backed by the American music critic John Briggs.

> One cannot help feeling that here is an extraordinarily self-reliant young artist who is conversant with a great deal of modern operatic history. The Metropolitan is the summit of operatic achievement.
>
> After one reaches it there are no more worlds to conquer. It follows that the pressure of a Metropolitan performance is a high-tension affair with no provision made for the apprentice to learn his business. It is for finished performers only; when novices come there they usually get finished rather promptly. Mario Lanza appears to have pondered these or similar matters at some length, finally arriving at the conclusion that there is no hurry.
>
> The Metropolitan won't get away. The process is psychologically right since it is ten times easier to make a good first impression than to overcome a bad one. And once one is in the opera house he has only the alternatives of resignation or suicide to get him out of it.[25]

Briggs was right. The history of the Metropolitan Opera is full of failed singers who tried to conquer it prematurely. With very few exceptions it was the practice for young American singers at the time to go to Europe, learn their trade until they became seasoned performers and then return to America and sing at the Metropolitan. The same was true of European singers who would sing in provincial opera houses for a number of years before attempting to sing at La Scala, The Vienna State Opera, Covent Garden or any of the most respected opera houses. It had taken Gigli four years to get to La Scala, Caruso and Schipa five years, and others even longer. Lanza knew this, and prior to his involvement with Hollywood was determined to follow the same path.

Lanza was also of aware of careers that had been delayed because of insufficient psychological preparation. The great Italian soprano Renata Tebaldi had turned down an offer from the Metropolitan in 1948 when she felt she wasn't ready, despite being an established opera singer with two seasons at La Scala already to her credit.[26]

Lanza may well have felt it was too late for him to work his way up the operatic ladder. He was too famous to start at the bottom. His dilemma, then, was the need to choose between a life of fame and luxury that afforded little or no artistic fulfillment, or life as the world's most famous apprentice opera singer, risking his reputation, and having to prove himself again and again, all the more convincingly if he were to make his debut on a major operatic stage.

In view of his notoriety the latter must surely have been a particularly daunting prospect. Lanza's self-assessment and explanation for refusing various important offers to sing in opera make sense given his predicament. In fact, they reveal an intelligent and extremely serious approach to what he loved most: opera.

Had he been less self-analytical and more of an egotist, Lanza might have survived the Hollywood experience. As it was, he was doomed. Commenting on Lanza's insecurity, his contemporary the great tenor, Giuseppe Di Stefano, remarked: " I don't think he realized how good he was!"[27]

Although Lanza kept insisting that he was only 29 and had "plenty of time"[28] to devote himself to an operatic career, by 1950 his plan to sing in opera was already beginning to look less and less attainable. Lanza may have sincerely believed that eventually he would be able to combine his Hollywood career with one equally successful on the operatic stage, but it is more likely that he was procrastinating. He was well aware that as long as he continued to make films and live the hectic life of a film actor, with long hours spent on the set, it was highly unlikely, as he himself pointed out, that he could find the time and peace of mind necessary to study the roles that he would be required to sing.

To conductor Peter Herman Adler the case of Mario Lanza was a "peculiarly American tragedy."

> Opera singers are like wild animals, they must be trained, kept in strict discipline. In Italy there are a dozen opera houses for young singers to train, where they can be in the right artistic atmosphere. Where in America can a young singer go but these two opera houses in New York (The Metropolitan and The New York City Opera) to sing once or twice a week in minor roles? Mario went to Hollywood and Hollywood has become his Frankenstein. The pressure he is under is tremendous, always having to put up a front; his voice is not settled yet. He knows he has come up too fast and he feels insecure. For this he overcompensates by boasting and showing off. There is still time. Ten years with the right opera company and no one could compare with him.

> I have great hopes that aside from his film work he will go to Italy and pursue an operatic career. I have been trying to get him into touring in Italy for a year. But who can expect him, after being a star, to go back to learning? But you cannot tell.[29]

There were many who shared Adler's hope, for here was a tenor voice in a million, a tenor voice that would have made Lanza immortal in the annals of opera. As his friend George London was to remark, "If he could only have crawled out of his own skin and listened to his own voice, he might have lived his whole life differently."[30]

If Lanza was hesitant, he was not exactly being encouraged by those close to him to pursue an operatic career. Barry Nelson described the environment that Lanza was working in.

> Who around him really wanted him to do opera? Who was going to push that? It wasn't in anybody's interest. So the people he was relying on, who were thought of as giant heads of studios, friends, and managers, all of them had an axe to grind. All had vested interests.[31]

Lanza's sudden climb to fame as a film star meant big money for everyone in his circle. His income from films, concerts and recordings for 1951 alone would be in excess of $1.1 million. Even his mentor, manager and financial adviser, Sam Weiler, who believed Lanza could become the greatest opera singer of his generation, was beginning to have second thoughts.[32] Opera could wait. As George London was to say, "The continual conflict within Mario was his desire to keep on earning the unbelievable sums of money that came his way overnight in Hollywood and his need to be accepted, recognized and appreciated as the world's greatest singer, opera or otherwise."[33]

John Green, the MGM Music Director who worked with Lanza on three of his films, felt that Lanza was the embodiment of the word "conflict."

> He was in truth as insecure as it is possible for a human being to be. He knew that God had intended him to be a great operatic singer...Had he been already a leading tenor, if not the leading tenor at the Met, and come to Hollywood in between seasons to make a picture, he would have had the Met as his home.[34]

Green had mostly fond memories of his association with Lanza during that Hollywood period.

> I was convinced when I was working with Mario, and I still am, that the instrument itself, the voice itself was the voice of the next Caruso. Mario had an unusual, very unusual quality...a tenor with a baritone color in the middle and lower registers and a great feeling for the making of music. A great musicality. I found it fascinating, musically, to work with Mario. He had a sensational ear and he was bright...Mario was not stupid at all! I was very fond of him. He was capable of such warmth and he had a nice sense of humor. You could have great fun with Mario.[35]

Green also felt that for someone as undisciplined as Lanza, Hollywood was in every respect the wrong place: "It might have been possible in a different environment, because of his extraordinary basic gifts, to have moulded him in such a way that he could have handled the commercial aspects of his career."[36]

Drawing a parallel between the film capital and the giant world of manufacturing, Green remarked: "In Hollywood we made motion pictures and motion pictures are made with people. General Motors have plants where they make motor cars. Mario

Lanza was a property. An important one."[37]

As the conflict within him increased, Lanza turned for help to his former teacher Enrico Rosati. He had immense respect for Rosati and tried to convince the old man to came and live in Los Angeles, feeling that with Rosati nearby to advise and guide him, he could overcome his fears and gradually make the move to opera. Rosati was genuinely fond of his former student and would have liked to be able to help him, but at the age of 76 he had no desire to move from his settled life in New York, where he was still teaching, in order to go and live in Los Angeles.[38]

Aside from his wife, few were aware of Lanza's inner torments.[39] On the surface everything appeared to be progressing extremely well. If artistically Lanza felt partially unfulfilled, commercially he was an unqualified success on all counts. The sales of his *Great Caruso* album continued to climb.†

His new recording of "The Loveliest Night Of The Year"— an adaptation by Irving Aaronson with lyrics by Paul Francis Webster to the 19th century waltz "*Sobre las olas*" by Juventino Rosas, which Lanza didn't particularly like, again surpassed one million in sales. The new hit, together with the previous million-seller, "Be My Love," stayed in the best-seller charts for 34 consecutive weeks, the third longest period in their history.[40]

The whole of America had Lanza fever in 1951. Soon the rest of the world would follow. It seemed that practically everyone was singing or humming "Be My Love," "The Loveliest Night Of The Year," and even inconsequential but catchy tunes such as "Boom Biddy Boom Boom." While Lanza was idolized by the masses, the first murmurings were being heard from the so-called connoisseurs.

These would proceed along the following lines: "Sure he is popular, but he's become popular making films." Or: "If he is so great, why doesn't he sing in opera?" And: "His voice is too small. He can't sustain an entire opera."[41]

Interestingly, these grumblings were rarely heard from fellow singers, or from conductors, other musicians, and opera managers—that is, from the musically competent.

The well-informed knew better. On his weekly radio program

---

†It would eventually surpass the one-million mark, earning him a gold record posthumously.

"Golden Voices," Lawrence Tibbett made the following extraordinary statement: "Lanza, in spite of the longhair criticism panning him as a 'movie singer' is the greatest musical talent of America in our century. A man who is bringing great music to the kids, the farms, the ghettos and the palaces." Tibbett went on to praise Lanza's "natural zest, his unbelievable diction—unaffected yet clear and poetic," and ended by saying prophetically, "In fifty years people will recognize Lanza for the great artist he is."[42]

16—A RECORD-BREAKING TOUR

WITH *THE GREAT CARUSO* COMPLETED, Lanza took time off to be with his family and await the arrival of new baby daughter, Ellisa. His second child was born on December 3, 1950, and was named after Lanza's maternal grandmother. Once again it had been a difficult pregnancy for Betty, who was advised by her doctor not to have any further children. The Lanzas, however, were still hoping for a boy, and Betty chose to ignore the advice. This would have unfortunate consequences for her. Still plagued by ovarian cysts, she would be increasingly dependent on prescription pain-killers.[1]

By mid-January 1951, it was time for Lanza to start preparing for his forthcoming concert tour. Columbia Artists had prepared a 22-city tour schedule commencing in Scranton, Pennsylvania on February 16, and ending in Fresno, California on April 30.

Since completing *The Great Caruso*, Lanza had again gained weight. Now, with the concert tour approaching, both Sam Weiler and Constantine Callinicos were concerned by Lanza's unwillingness to submit to yet another crash diet. Not unreasonably, Lanza felt that he was a singer first and only secondarily a film star, and was uninterested in losing the 40 pounds (18kg) demanded of him. He had proved he was a success. Surely, he reasoned, the public would accept him as a concert performer whether he weighed 200 pounds (90.7kg) or 240 pounds (108.8kg). Weiler and Callinicos did not agree.

"Think of your fans! They want to see the handsome singer they see on the screen."[2] At one stage, when it looked as if Lanza would not go through with the weight loss Weiler called Callinicos and told him the tour might have to be cancelled. Callinicos immediately panicked at the prospect of losing so much income. "I was almost limp with anger,"[3] he said at the end of the conversation with Weiler. Reluctantly Lanza gave in, and in late January he and Betty—accompanied by the inevitable entourage of Weiler, Callinicos and Terry Robinson—departed for a rented ranch house in Palm Springs to begin the crash diet.

For the next three weeks Lanza lived on a diet of 500 calories per day. Subjecting himself to the strenuous training of a prize-fighter, he would arise at eight in the morning and exercise and run in the hot Californian desert wearing a heavy rubber sweat suit.[4]

Naively believing that his physique was strong enough to withstand such punishment, Lanza refused to listen to the warnings of friends about the dangers of repeated crash dieting.[5]

As well as physical training, there were daily singing sessions with Callinicos. These usually consisted of two hourly sessions, during which Lanza would warm up by vocalizing and then go over the repertoire of the forthcoming concert tour. He would spend the rest of his spare time relaxing with a book,[†] or painting the landscape. Painting was a newly-acquired passion for Lanza, who worked mainly with watercolors and, occasionally, pastels. At first he would dab awkwardly, but in time he became quite adept at capturing landscapes.[6][‡]

As the starting date for the concert tour approached, Lanza began to prepare himself psychologically for the moment when the acclaimed Hollywood film star would temporarily step aside and the concert artist would take over. This was by no means an easy transition, but one infinitely simpler than moving from an MGM soundstage to an operatic one.

The latter would have required months of preparation. Concerts, on the other hand, enabled him to sing a program based on a number of operatic arias and songs that formed part of his existing repertoire.

[†]Both Lanza and his wife liked Hemingway, while Lanza also enjoyed reading books by Damon Runyon.

[‡]In October 2002 a watercolor landcape measuring 13 x17 inches presumably painted by Lanza's hand and bearing his signature on the bottom right hand corner was offered for auction by La Scala Autographs on eBay. If it was indeed painted by the tenor it showed considerable promise.

These comprised numbers that he already knew and could sing at a moment's notice. Apart from rehearsing with his pianist, or in some cases with a conductor and orchestra, he was ready to perform.

In this sense it was much simpler than singing in an opera, but also vocally more demanding. Contrary to popular opinion, it is usually more challenging *vocally* to sing a concert than an opera. In an opera the singing is shared with the other singers, and there are long pauses and breaks. In an opera the singer has time to rest and pace himself.

There are also costumes, make-up, props and an orchestra. In contrast, the concert artist is fully exposed. He has none of the above to rely on. He faces the audience with only the accompanist assisting him. José Carreras summed it up as accurately as anyone when he stated, "In a recital you are naked, with your tails, and your piano, and your pianist."[7] Virtually all singers agree on the increased demands made on the concert singer. This is what Jussi Björling had to say on the difference between singing opera or solo recitals:

> Opera really is easier than recital work. In opera you deal with only one composer at a time, so you can have the same style of singing all night. In recital each number is by someone else and you must approach it with a different musical style. Then, too, in opera you deal with other people, so there are moments when they are singing and you can rest. Not in recital: there you are alone and must work constantly.[8]

Luciano Pavarotti has said more or less the same thing: "To sing twenty or twenty-five pieces is much more difficult than one opera; I talk about artistically vocally and physically."[9] His colleague Plácido Domingo agrees: "To go from one aria to another without the benefit of creating a character or establishing a mood like you can in an opera is extremely difficult."[10]

True enough, but for Lanza the challenge of performing in concerts must have seemed less daunting than the prospect of learning a role and facing a critical audience in a renowned opera house. Furthermore, Lanza's popularity with cinema-goers ensured a different type of audience at his concerts.

Many had only been exposed to opera through his movies. They were not there to be critical; they came to applaud and cheer their idol.

As *Time* magazine reported, "Caruso himself never commanded the adulation that swamped Lanza on his latest concert tour."[11] And adulation it most certainly was. Callinicos described the pandemonium that surrounded the tenor: "From the day the tour began, Mario was besieged by the young and the old, the shy and the bold, the diffident and the daring. They begged for autographs, peeped through the keyholes of his hotel rooms, grabbed at the scarf or tie around his neck, seized scraps of food from his mouth in public restaurants. There was a continual caterwauling and din in his ears, 'Mario we love you, you're wonderful! Let me kiss you, Mario!'"[12]

As far as the actual concerts were concerned, however, the only concession to the fans was the now obligatory "Be My Love," which inevitably brought down the house. In all other respects, Lanza sang a standard concert program that ranged from Monteverdi and Scarlatti to Verdi, Puccini, and Leoncavallo.

From a financial perspective the arrangements for the concert tour could not have been better. Lanza's contract stipulated a guarantee of $2500 per concert against 60% of the take. As it turned out, the entire tour was such a huge success that Lanza's fees far exceeded the minimum guarantee. In New Orleans, for example, where the audience—according to *Variety*—was the largest in that city's concert history, Lanza's fee was $6025. In Milwaukee he was paid $6750, with many fans travelling ninety miles from Chicago to hear him. When the 3800 seats for his concert with the Pittsburgh Symphony Orchestra conducted by Vladimir Bakaleinikoff sold out in 48 hours, the management decided to sell tickets for the afternoon rehearsal. Breaking all precedents Edward Specter, Manager of the Pittsburgh Symphony: placed a series of advertisements in the morning newspapers:

> Due to the fact that the Pittsburgh Symphony Concert on Tuesday evening, March 6 with Mario Lanza as soloist, has been completely sold out, and because of the continued and overwhelming demand for tickets, the rehearsal for this concert will be open to the public at general admission prices.[13]

Two thousand people showed up, netting Lanza an additional $1000 for his labors.

Time magazine reported on the actual concert:

Some of Pittsburgh regular concertgoers were among the 4,100 who jammed into the act on the big night. In arias from *Rigoletto* and *Pagliacci* Mario proved to the cynics' surprise that he really has a voice.[14]

In Scranton even though the concert was held in an acoustically poor gym an audience numbering 5000 sat on hard benches and chairs and another 567 stood. In his hometown of Philadelphia 400 people sat on the stage of the Academy of Music with a few more standing in the wings. In Utica the demand for tickets was so strong that the police let in groups of 25 at a time as standees in the doorway to hear a single number. In total Lanza would earn $100,245 from the 22 concerts.[15]

This was far in excess of what he would have received for an equivalent number of operatic performances at the Metropolitan, for example, where the top fee then was approximately $1,000 per performance.[16]

It should therefore not surprise us if those around him at the time were reluctant to change this winning formula. Why urge him to devote part of his time to opera? It was not in anyone's interests. Certainly Callinicos, as his regular accompanist, was earning more than he could ever have hoped from anyone else, and even the wealthy Sam Weiler was not adverse to receiving his cut, which had now risen to 20% of Lanza's gross income.[17]

Lanza's greatest earnings for the year, however, came not from his movies or his concerts, but from his recordings. Out of $1.1 million in earnings in 1951, the largest amount was represented by the royalties from his recordings. For a ten-month period RCA paid Lanza $746,000, the biggest royalty cheque ever paid to an artist up to that time.[18] Lanza celebrated the windfall by purchasing his wife an 18,000-dollar silver-blue mink coat, and his trainer Terry Robinson a Chevrolet convertible. For himself he chose a 1500-dollar watch to add to his prized collection of rare and expensive watches.

Reviews throughout the concert tour were varied. Most critics concurred that Lanza was a great operatic prospect, but pointed out that he needed more work and experience on the stage if he were to acquire the finish and polish that would indeed make him great. For once the critics were right. Artistically Lanza had not benefited from the three years spent in Hollywood. Quite the opposite, in fact. His singing was now less disciplined; the style often sloppy or inappropriate. He had begun to indulge in certain vocal exaggerations and mannerisms which were quite unnecessary, marring what would otherwise have been splendid performances—given the power, range and beauty of the voice.

Following the Chicago concert, Felix Borowsky of the *Chicago Sun Times*—while singling out Lanza's "ravishing" mezza voce in *"Gia il sole dal Gange"* and *"Pietà Signore"*—did not overlook some of the stylistic and interpretative shortcomings that were beginning to creep into Lanza's singing. Referring to the aria *"Lamento di Federico"* from *L'Arlesiana*, Borowsky noted: "This was sung throughout fortissimo and with the emotionalism which the singer evidently believed to be expected from a second Caruso." Not even Borowsky, however, could overlook the beauty of the voice. "There can be no doubt," he wrote, "about the natural magnificence of Lanza's voice."[19]

There were certainly enough attributes to satisfy the less demanding critics. Following the Richmond concert, Helen De Motte of *The News Leader* was completely won over by the tenor: "He has everything—voice, good looks, personality, dramatic flair, a natural instinct for song, fine enunciation."[20]

George Harris of *The Richmond Times Dispatch* concurred, referring to "Mr. Lanza's splendid vocal qualities" and added that in view of his reported debut in opera overseas,[†] "He has proven himself both vocally and dramatically and he should be sure of success."[21]

Overall, however, it was emerging that the three years spent in the film capital had not helped him artistically. With the exception of Peter Herman Adler, Lanza had not worked with any major conductor in Hollywood. While it is true that he worked occasionally on operatic repertoire with Giacomo Spadoni, it was primarily the less accomplished Callinicos on whom Lanza had come to rely for musical support.

Had Lanza been working regularly, as he should have been, with a great operatic coach or conductor, he would certainly have

---

[†]This was a reference to the repeated rumors that Lanza was leaving to gain experience in the opera houses of Italy.

maintained the standard of singing of his pre-Hollywood days and, as a result, would have grown artistically.

The mediocre Callinicos, on the other hand, was too compromised by his dependence on Lanza for financial reward to risk antagonizing the tenor by correcting him or even making suggestions.[22]

Nevertheless, in early 1951, life was looking positive for Lanza. He had just turned 30 and in the short span of less than two years had become RCA's top-selling classical singer. His foray into films had been equally successful, with *The Great Caruso* poised for its record-breaking release.

Overall, the latest concert tour would prove a happy experience for Lanza. The pace was hectic, the crowds often unruly and the fans demanding, but Lanza seemed to take it all in his stride.

The often-hysterical mass adulation he was receiving had previously been reserved for non-operatic phenomena such as Frank Sinatra. When detectives in Pittsburgh, where police had provided an extra squad to get him from the concert hall to his hotel, warned him that he would need protection from the fans, he replied: "Protection from what? From kissing and hugging? Hell, I love every second of it!"[23]

As he was leaving the concert hall a young woman bumped him and promptly fainted. Lanza caught her and handed her to a policeman.

Betty accompanied him throughout the tour while the children were left in the joint care of their nurse and Lanza's parents. He was particularly pleased to have his wife with him. Betty was warm, loving and attentive and she provided him with the moral support that all artists need.

Of all the cities visited on the concert tour, Lanza was particularly looking forward to singing in his hometown of Philadelphia. The venue was the 3000-seat Academy of Music—the very place where Koussevitzky had first heard him.

For its part, Philadelphia went out of its way to welcome the native son who had made good. The Chamber of Commerce sponsored a luncheon at Palumbo's Restaurant. Among the 500 guests attending were many of Lanza's relatives and friends, including his maternal grandparents Salvatore and Ellisa Lanza. In the presence of all the notable and pre-eminent figures of South Philadelphia, assistant district attorney Americo Cortese, as toastmaster, paid tribute to Lanza. Then after a speech from Judge Eugene Alessandroni, it was Lanza's turn to speak. "I'm happy to be here," an emotional Lanza told his audience.

"South Philadelphia is still the garden spot of America and even though I live in Beverly Hills, I'll always find time to come back here and meet and greet my old friends."[24]

With *The Great Caruso* recently completed and all the media exposure the film was receiving, it was inevitable that the name of Caruso would resurface time and again. In a number of interviews given to the Philadelphia press, Lanza again remarked that he preferred not to be compared with his great predecessor.

"I'm flattered of course, and it won't hurt my box office, but still I'd rather not be compared," he said, adding that "Our careers have been different, and my voice is different from Caruso's, too."[25] Again he reiterated that, although now under contract to MGM, he had not let Hollywood sidetrack his ambition to sing in opera.

Regarding the concert itself, Lanza said that he was aware that he would be facing a critical, music-loving audience at the Academy and that he wanted to show them "that what they've heard on records and soundtracks is really there."[26] This was in clear contradiction to his refusal to sing in New York. The regular omission of New York from his scheduled concert tours can only be put down to his excessive concern with the critical response he would receive in that city. When questioned he tried to justify the omission, but his reason was not entirely convincing: "I want to be heard in New York only from the stage of the Metropolitan Opera,"[27] he would explain. He had actually sung a concert in New York at the famed Waldorf Astoria but that was back in 1947, before attaining film fame.

Following the Philadelphia concert, former tenor and respected critic Max de Schauensee came as close as anyone could in accurately assessing Mario Lanza, the gifted singer caught in the web of commercial enterprise. Writing in *The Evening Bulletin*, De Schauensee stated:

> It can be immediately said that Mr. Lanza has a fine tenor voice which had no difficulty in reaching every corner of the

Academy without benefit of any amplification. The tone is straightforward and manly, resonant and of extended range. There is vitality and a disarming, uncomplicated appeal in Mr. Lanza's singing. Under normal circumstances Mr. Lanza should be singing weekly in the provincial opera houses in Italy in a succession of *Bohèmes*, *Toscas*, *Butterflys* and *Pagliaccis*, just as all the celebrated Italian operatic tenors have done since time immemorial. If this were the case, there is no reason why the young singer could not take his place on the stage of the Metropolitan Opera House with distinction to himself in a repertory for which he is only too obviously designed by nature.

But fame and fortune have dictated otherwise, and it is only to be hoped that Mr. Lanza will not allow himself to be completely swamped by commercial enterprise and will follow the pattern of the man whom he declared publicly last night he idolizes—Enrico Caruso.[28]

De Schauensee's hopes were echoed by the famous soprano Mary Garden, who after declaring that "[Lanza] has a wonderful voice – a gorgeous voice," stated, "If only he would go to Europe and study, and then come back and sing at the Metropolitan."[29] In reality, however, it was becoming increasingly unlikely that MGM would grant the tenor time off for such a pursuit. As Lanza himself observed:

So far there's been no chance to go to Italy because I am under a longterm movie contract that has kept me in Beverly Hills. I've planned for years to study opera in Italy before singing at the Met. I want to be unquestionably ready to live up to its [Metropolitan] traditions, and I feel this means more study.[30]

Meanwhile, with his activity confined primarily to the screen and the recording studio, speculation began to increase as to how good a singer Lanza really was. Did he possess the correct technique? Was his voice large enough for the operatic stage? Or was he merely the product of sound engineers who could increase the volume of a singer's voice and splice together a number of different takes into a single number?

A great deal of curiosity centered on the actual size of Lanza's voice. As a result of his non-operatic activity, the myth began to circulate that his voice was indeed small and only sounded large due to the skill of the MGM sound technicians.[31]

The last supposition is absurd, of course. No sound engineer can change the basic color of a voice and turn a light lyric tenor into a dramatic one. In other words, no tampering by sound engineers can turn the voice of a Tito Schipa or an Alfredo Kraus into that of a lirico spinto for the simple reason that the dramatic coloring and the harmonics in the voice are missing. They can make them sound louder, but they cannot change the basic color and timbre of the voice. Lanza's voice had a rich dark coloring in the center and lower registers and a brilliant ringing top which are typical of a lirico spinto. This is hardly what one would classify as a small voice.

Those who knew voices, such as the critic Max De Schauensee, or Helen Traubel (who found Lanza's voice "phenomenal"),[32] and colleagues such as bass-baritone George London and sopranos Dorothy Kirsten and Licia Albanese, all of whom worked closely with Lanza, were adamant: his voice was that of a *lirico spinto*. *Spinto* is the Italian for *pushed*, and, in operatic jargon, denotes a voice that is halfway between a lyric and a dramatic one. Among the outstanding examples of lyric tenors we have Beniamino Gigli, Giuseppe Di Stefano, Luciano Pavarotti and José Carreras. All four have also sung some spinto roles. In the cases of Di Stefano and Carreras, poor technique and the fact that they sang spinto parts too early in their careers resulted in two extremely beautiful voices being prematurely ruined. Dramatic tenors who also sang spinto and, on occasion, lyric roles include Jon Vickers, Mario Del Monaco and Ramon Vinay.

The spinto tenors include Giovanni Martinelli, Aureliano Pertile, Francesco Merli, and Franco Corelli. Jussi Björling (and to a certain extent, Giacomo Lauri-Volpi) is a case apart. Although a lyric tenor, Björling was able to sing some spinto parts such as Radamès, Canio and Manrico due to the silvery brilliance of his voice. Similarly, Plácido Domingo, who has essentially a lyric voice, but one which is rich and baritone-like in its middle register, is able to sing not only spinto parts convincingly but also the dramatic role of Otello, for which he is justly celebrated.

In a discussion with vocal historian and music critic Henry

Pleasants, bass-baritone George London, who had toured with Lanza and had subsequently sung with all the top singers of his generation, told him that in terms of natural voice endowment, Lanza had more voice than any other man he had ever known.[33]

Lanza's lack of an operatic career also gave rise to the equally mistaken notion that he could not sustain an entire opera. As we have already seen, Lanza's reasons for not singing in opera had nothing to do with either the size of his voice or his ability to sustain an entire opera but instead were paradoxically linked to his Hollywood career, his lack of experience in an opera house and the increasing insecurity that resulted from it. George London summed it up this way:

> In my opinion, Lanza, with the possible exception of Björling, had the greatest voice of his time. His singing could move people to tears and, in my presence, frequently did. His Hollywood experience undermined his inner security, which is why he avoided performing in public. I would venture that if he had not gone to Hollywood he would, at least for the beginning, have had a major operatic career.[34]

17—BECAUSE YOU'RE MINE

AFTER THE SUCCESS OF *THE GREAT CARUSO*, and Lanza's subsequent record-breaking concert tour, his contract with MGM still had three years to run. From time to time Lanza would still speak of spending six months to a year in Italy, the cradle of operatic tradition; he still voiced his wish to perform in some provincial opera houses. Then on one occasion, he said he'd like to sing Paolo in *Francesca da Rimini* at La Scala.[1]

It was an interesting and unusual choice. Composed by Riccardo Zandonai and based on the tragedy by the poet Gabriele D'Annunzio, the opera had been a success at its premiere in 1914. Initially performed quite frequently, it had become almost a rarity by the 1950s,[†] and was known mainly by operatic connoisseurs.

There's a good tenor role in the opera, and some beautiful music in the fourth act, but why choose a relatively obscure opera in which to make a major debut?

Lanza probably reasoned that if he sang a standard role such as Rodolfo, Cavaradossi, the Duke in *Rigoletto*, or Chénier, it would be easy for critics and public alike to compare his performance with those of the half dozen top tenors active at the time. Comparisons would be harder to make in the obscure *Francesca da Rimini*. Lanza's insecurity after a mere three years in Hollywood was certainly extreme enough to produce this kind of thinking.

When closely questioned about an operatic career, however, Lanza's answers were becoming increasingly evasive. Asked by *Look* magazine whether he had any plans to sing at the Metro-

---

[†]It was staged at the Metropolitan in 1984 after an absence of almost seventy years.

politan, Lanza avoided giving a direct answer. "Mr. Bing knows all about me,"[3] was his simple reply.

Yet it is difficult to imagine the autocratic Bing offering a contract unless Lanza intended to bid Hollywood farewell. Bing would not entertain the idea of employing singers who were also working in what he considered to be commercial, non-artistic ventures. Versatility and the ability to cross over convincingly from opera to Cole Porter were not considered virtues in the 1950s; not only Bing, but most lovers of "serious" music felt this way.

Bing later made his viewpoint abundantly clear when he expressed his disapproval of soprano Helen Traubel's involvement with television and nightclubs, ultimately forcing the great Traubel to resign from the Metropolitan in 1953.[4] Baritone Robert Merrill suffered a similar fate. Possessed of a childlike infatuation with the movie world and openly envious of Lanza's film career, Merrill walked out on the scheduled Metropolitan Opera spring tour and headed for the Paramount studios in Hollywood to make his first film. Bing's instant response was to fire him.[†]

For Lanza, struggling with his predicament of commercial success at the expense of artistic fulfillment, much depended on his perception of how the studio was using him and the type of film he would be making during the next three years.

Regardless of the inexorable path his career was taking, he assumed that following the success of *The Great Caruso*, he would now be making films of a similar caliber. Not necessarily *operatic* movies, but—at the very least—quality films with good stories and scripts.[5]

Accordingly, when Pasternak informed him that his follow-up to *The Great Caruso* was to be the Sigmund Romberg operetta *The Student Prince*, Lanza was overjoyed. He loved everything about the project and confessed to his accompanist, Callinicos, that he was expecting it to be an even bigger success than *The Great Caruso*.[6]

Then suddenly, and much to the singer's dismay, Joe Pasternak

[†]After the dismal failure of his first and last film venture—appropriately titled *Aaron Slick from Pumpkin Creek*—Merrill had to eat humble pie for almost a year before Bing would allow him to return to the Met.

informed him that he had decided to postpone *The Student Prince*. Instead Lanza was to appear in a film about a famous opera singer who is drafted into the Army. Reasoning that he did not want Lanza set in the public consciousness only as an opera star, Pasternak declared that he wanted the tenor to be accepted also as a man.[7]

In reality, it was a question of Pasternak ingratiating himself with Dore Schary by cutting expenditure and capitalizing on Lanza's huge popularity. Mayer was still in charge of the studio but his authority was being constantly undermined by Schary, who had the backing of MGM's powerful parent company, the New York-based Loew's, Inc., headed by Nicholas Schenck.

When it became clear to MGM that *The Great Caruso* was going to be a bigger box office draw than even the greatest optimist at the studio had anticipated, Metro realized that Lanza would be a success no matter what they starred him in.[8]

Pasternak was aware that the new film, scheduled to start production in May 1951 with the working title of *The Big Cast*, could be made on a lower budget than *The Student Prince*. Pasternak's decision had wider implications and came at a bad time for Lanza. Not only was the tenor contending with increasing criticism from operatic circles for not performing as a legitimate opera singer, but he was now expected to make the type of films that would do nothing to enhance his image as a serious singer.

If Pasternak's decision to postpone *The Student Prince* came as a bitter blow to Lanza, he was even more disappointed when he read the script of his forthcoming picture. In what would ultimately be released with the title of *Because You're Mine*, Lanza was to play a famous opera star who is drafted into the Army and falls in love with his sergeant's sister. Lanza considered the story weak and lacking in artistic quality and wasted no time in telling both Pasternak and Dore Schary that he thought the script was "junk."[9]

The studio responded by claiming that success had gone to Lanza's head, and that his behavior would not be tolerated.[10] Schary, who was now in charge of MGM after Mayer's forced resignation two months earlier, was not remotely interested in what Pasternak produced as long as it made a profit for the shareholders. Schary's principal aim was to produce low budget so-called "message" films such as *The Next Voice You Hear.*

Although ambitious projects, these were ultimately box office failures and would help precipitate his ouster from MGM five years later. Unlike the paternal Mayer, any complaint from Lanza would be unwelcome by Schary, who would simply tell the singer to do what he was told—or else. The studio, Schary reminded Lanza on at least one occasion, had managed to survive without Greta Garbo and a score of other stars and would have no problem surviving without him.[11]

Given this sort of ultimatum, Lanza's only choice was to either go ahead and make the film or refuse and be sued by MGM for breach of contract. The studio had the upper hand. Under the terms of his contract Lanza was bound to make whatever films the studio chose. Still, he felt he had proved himself as a big box office attraction and money-maker for Metro, and was entitled to a say in the films he would make.[12] However, no matter how much Lanza protested or expressed dissatisfaction with the project, the studio was adamant: on production matters he had no part in the decision-making.

The film would go ahead as planned. Although Pasternak would complain that after having completed only three films Lanza thought he knew more about making musicals than he did—which may very well have been the case. Lanza surely knew more about music. It was Pasternak, after all, who had once instructed an incredulous Andre Previn to add an orchestra to the first movement of the Schumann String Quintet because he thought that it would sound much better that way.[13]

The disagreements over *Because You're Mine* were the beginning of a series of battles between Lanza and the studio that a year later would culminate with his much publicized walk-out on *The Student Prince.* In the meantime—still hoping that MGM would change its mind—Lanza delayed the start of filming on *Because You're Mine* for as long as he could. As he was prone to do in times of difficulty and stress, Lanza began to eat and drink without restraint in order to compensate for his emotional turmoil. The result was that his weight increased daily at an alarming rate.

Lanza's metabolism was such that he would put on extra

pounds just by consuming what for others constituted a normal meal. With his prodigious appetite he could easily increase as much as 15 pounds (7 kg) in a week. With principal photography finally due to get underway in mid-May, Lanza reported for work weighing 234 pounds (106kg). Filming was sporadic with Lanza frequently absent from the set. The tenor's ploy of gaining weight in the hope that the film would be cancelled failed. Instead the studio issued a further ultimatum: *lose weight or else.*

MGM did however make one concession. They promised that if he got back into shape the script would be rewritten by scenarists Karl Tunberg and Leonard Spigelgass. The pair had initially based it on a story by Ruth Brooks Flippen and Sy Gomberg. Spigelgass, who was not keen on rewriting the script, took his frustration out on Lanza by stating publicly that "His [Lanza's] ability as an actor is less than zero."[14] Not to be outdone, Lanza responded by saying: "Perhaps with a better script my acting might improve!"[15]

Finally accepting that he would have to go ahead with the film, Lanza decided to rent Ginger Rogers' ranch on the Rogue River near Medford, Oregon. Here he would get himself back into shape. Accompanied by Betty, the time spent in Oregon was akin to a second honeymoon for the Lanzas.

Despite having to undergo his usual punishing routine of chopping wood and running along the woodland trails in a heavy rubber suit, the Lanzas still found the time to go fishing, shooting, and horseback riding. The six weeks spent in the beautiful Oregon country amounted to the first peaceful interlude the Lanzas had experienced since settling in Los Angeles. It was also an opportunity for spending some time with Betty, away from the children and the problems associated with MGM.

By the end of September Lanza was back in Hollywood ready to resume work on *Because You're Mine*. He had managed to shed about 30 pounds (13.6 kg), but he still weighed 204 pounds (92kg), much to the displeasure of Pasternak, who wanted him to lose more weight.[16]

Lanza continued to diet but was now increasingly uncomfortable with the thought of losing too much weight. His fear of damaging his voice was a constant one. He was afraid that by opposing nature and reducing too much he would indeed end up damaging his voice. In the end there can be no doubt that his health was destroyed by repeated crash dieting, whatever its effect on his voice. Referring to Lanza's problems at MGM his friend Barry Nelson recalled:

> Slimming him down to look good in the acting part, he feels the voice is slipping away. He has another problem. He's being broken with problems. A man who, if everything went well, would have a lot of problems. He would make the problems. His life could never be tranquil. But on the other hand he couldn't take all of those pressures that a more tranquil person could maybe grapple with.[17]

Nelson went on to illustrate the performer's psyche.

> This isn't a business where you have tranquil people. If they're tranquil they can't act, they can't sing. Your pores are open and that's why actors and singers and so forth get such bad reputations. That they are difficult people. If you are on the set all day having to perform, keeping open, almost like pushing buttons to be able to radiate all of these emotions and thoughts, if someone speaks ill to you, you're going to take it a lot more sensitively than say, a carpenter or a producer. They don't have to keep open. You do. And so you sometimes act unreasonably, flare up—because you're hyped up to it.[18]

In Lanza's case it was even more difficult. He was in many ways like a child, so that it was much harder for him to accept the fact that someone could be antagonistic towards him and not allow him to express his opinions. All his life, Lanza had experienced love and warmth. Lanza was either loved, liked, or admired by those who knew him and he genuinely reciprocated their feelings. It was therefore difficult for him to understand the dictatorial behavior of the snobbish Schary, who continually threatened him with dismissal unless he obeyed orders. As a result he was not in the best frame of mind when pre-recording began for *Because You're Mine*.

Unfairly, he took his misery out on co-star Doretta Morrow, who was making her first film and, as a novice in the film business, needed all the support she could get. Miss Morrow, who was born in New York of Italian parents (real name Marano), was an attractive 26-year-old brunette with a limited, but pleasant, well-trained musical comedy soprano voice. Morrow had sung in a number of musicals including *The Chocolate Soldier, The Great Waltz,* and *The Desert Song* prior to making her Broadway debut in 1948 as one of the singing leads in *Where's Charley?* Pasternak had spotted Morrow, who at the time was rumored to be Richard Rodgers' mistress, while she was playing Tuptin in *The King and I* with Yul Brynner and Gertrude Lawrence on Broadway.

Lanza tried a number of other ploys to avoid making *Because You're Mine.* He told the studio he was opposed to having Morrow as co-star. It was nothing personal. It was just that he wanted to sing with an operatic soprano as opposed to one from musical comedy. He also told Pasternak that he would like to work with Lana Turner, reasoning that she could be dubbed by a soprano in the musical numbers. Pasternak ruled this out as Turner was already committed to *The Merry Widow,* which he was producing simultaneously with *Because You're Mine.* Doretta Morrow had been signed for the film, and his decision was final.[19]

At their first pre-recording session Lanza was openly antagonistic towards the young singer to the point of employing his well-known repertoire of four-letter words, something that he would not usually resort to in the presence of women.[†]

During the recording of the duet of the title song with conductor John Green, and an orchestra consisting of 75 men and women, Lanza stopped abruptly, turned to Morrow and told her she should be sexier by allowing him to feel her genitals against his. Deeply shocked and offended, Morrow stormed out of the recording session and asked MGM for a release from her contract.[20]

Lanza's reaction was immediate. Realizing how badly and unfairly he had behaved he was genuinely contrite. Explaining to Morrow that he had been forced to make a film that he loathed, he begged her forgiveness and promised he would do all he could to help her in her first movie experience.[21]

From then on Lanza could not have been more helpful and

†Lanza made full use of his four-letter word Italian repertoire during the making of *The Great Caruso,* but stopped as soon as he realized that the rather precious Dorothy Kirsten understood Italian.

cooperative with the young singer. He introduced her to his wife, invited her to his home, helped her with her dialogue and generally engulfed her with his warmth.

By the time the film was nearing completion in early 1952, Morrow was completely captivated by Lanza. "Once you get to know him, how can you possibly stay mad at him for long?" she said.[22]

Also in the film was character actor James Whitmore, who did a fine job in a semi-comical part as Lanza's sergeant and Morrow's brother.

Despite the battle raging between Lanza and MGM, Whitmore found Lanza friendly and easy to work with. Although theirs was only a working relationship, and they never became close enough to discuss anything in depth, Whitmore felt that Lanza was not a happy man during the making of *Because You're Mine*.[23]

The reason for the unhappiness, apart from the film and what he felt was unfair treatment from MGM, may well have been a cover story in *Time* magazine that appeared in the August 6, 1951 issue under the heading "Million Dollar Voice."

The story, a malicious piece of journalism that ridiculed the tenor's eating habits, intellect, singing and—for that matter—his entire personal and public life both past and present, deeply hurt Lanza. It would have been upsetting to anyone, but for the super-sensitive tenor, its impact must have been devastating. After reading the seven-page story he turned to his wife in disbelief asking, "What have I done to deserve this?"[24]

The *Time* story became the basis for many future unfounded articles and reports about the tenor that would appear regularly in magazines and newspapers all over the world. Rightly or wrongly, Lanza was convinced that MGM was behind the spiteful article and this certainly did not help to improve his frame of mind or, for that matter, his relationship with the big brass at the studio.

Lanza's misery took a new and disturbing turn during the making of *Because You're Mine*. To his amazement he lost his appetite completely and continued to lose weight. By the time the last scene had been filmed he was down to a mere 156 pounds (71kg). Lanza's appearance and general behavior came as something of a shock to his accompanist. Callinicos had been in New York, and on his return to Los Angeles he found a tenor who "looked thin, wan, and distraught. Even his voice was thin; the old ring of bravado was gone."[25]

The pressures were beginning to leave their mark. At one stage during the making of *Because You're Mine*, Lanza became so tense that he would wake up each morning with the fear of having lost his voice.[26] Since films are not shot in sequence, the end result of Lanza's excessive weight loss in *Because You're Mine* is clearly visible. In the course of the film, his weight changes almost continuously from scene to scene.

Regardless of his weight fluctuation and the fact that *Because You're Mine* was a mediocre effort after the *The Great Caruso*, on the strength of Lanza's popularity the film was successful, just as MGM had predicted. Although it did not achieve the box office take of *The Great Caruso*, the title song went on to become Lanza's third million-seller. Then to the amazement of all concerned, and the consternation and disgust of British film critics, the film was chosen for the 1952 Royal Command Performance inaugurating the reign of Queen Elizabeth II. Comments in the London papers ranged from: "The story frankly is a stinker"[27] to "You cannot say this is a downright bad film, but just so ordinary."[28]

The American reviews were not much better. *Newsweek* described the script as "cute and commercially secure,"[29] *Variety* commented on the slender plot, but added: "Terrific Lanza singing...Lanza plays well the part of a high-priced star willing to accept the fate that makes him a GI."[30]

Bosley Crowther in *The New York Times*, while pointing out the banality of the story, went on to say: "But it's really Mr. Lanza's singing that should and will attract attention to this technicolored film."[31] Unsurprisingly, *Time* magazine called it "an undernourished musical."[32]

In reality the film, directed by the veteran Alexander Hall[†] was no better and no worse than Lanza's first two films. It was a disappointment simply because it happened to follow the more

[†]Hall was best-known for his work on *Here Comes Mr. Jordan*, for which he was nominated for an Oscar.

substantial *The Great Caruso*. For his part Hall, who had once worked with the conceited tenor Jan Kiepura in the disastrous 1936 *Give Us This Night*, and expected a similarly difficult experience with Lanza, was relieved to discover his fears were unfounded.

Lanza had, in fact, come to terms with the fact that there was nothing he could do to avoid making the movie, and had decided to make the most of the experience. Following the Doretta Morrow episode, he saw no reason to take out his resentment towards the studio on his director.

Hall found Lanza friendly and cooperative, punctual on the set and ready to deliver his lines. Lanza, in his typical fashion, surprised the veteran director by giving him a birthday party and presenting him with an expensive pair of cuff links and matching tie-pin.[33]

What had started out rather disastrously ended up a relatively pleasant experience for all concerned. Lanza gave fine renditions of a number of songs and arias. Among them were two versions of the title song sung with Doretta Morrow, "*Addio alla madre*" from *Cavalleria Rusticana*, and the "*Addio, addio*" duet from the first act of *Rigoletto*. In the latter Lanza again shows his vocal range by sailing up to a high D flat in unison with the soprano on the final note.[†]

The soprano in this instance was Peggy Bonini dubbing for actress Paula Corday, who plays Doretta Morrow's rival in the film.

Lanza also sang an excellent version of "The Lord's Prayer" and gave another thrilling rendition of "Granada," again sung in the impossibly high key of F major. A beautifully sung version of "All The Things You Are" by Jerome Kern was cut from the final print, but has subsequently been released on CD.

[†]Lanza is, however. slightly under the note.

18—RAPHAELA

IT WAS WHILE HE WAS MAKING *Because You're Mine* that a little girl came briefly into Lanza's life, touching him with her plight. Ten-year-old Raphaela Fasano, who lived with her family in Newark, New Jersey, was dying from Hodgkin's disease. Her idol, and the man she had secretly given her heart to, was Mario Lanza. Raphaela's greatest wish was to meet her idol, talk to him, and perhaps even hear him sing.[1]

In a desperate attempt to make Raphaela's dream come true, her mother somehow managed to contact Lanza's household in California. Lanza was not at home when the telephone call came through, but when told of the little girl's condition, he looked at his own daughters, Colleen and Ellisa with tears in his eyes and proceeded to call Raphaela in New Jersey.[2]

Tenderly, he spoke to the little girl for several minutes and then asked her what her favorite song was. "Best of all I like 'Tina Lina,'" Raphaela answered. "Would you like me to sing it for you now?" he asked her. "Over the phone?" she asked, scarcely believing that she was speaking to her idol.[3]

Lanza sang for her. Despite the liveliness of the song, tears began to run down his cheeks as he poured his heart out to the little girl.

He then bid goodbye to Raphaela, telling her that he would call again the following week. As he put down the receiver, Lanza turned to his wife and told her that he would like to bring Rapahela to Los Angeles to spend Christmas with them. Betty, who herself had been considerably moved by the fate of the little girl, readily agreed and arrangements were made to have Raphaela, her mother and a nurse, flown to Los Angeles.[4]

Little Raphaela was beside herself with joy at the news. Lanza asked her to be brave and strong so that she could have a Chrismas party together with his two little girls, Colleen and Ellisa. "I can't remember what he said to me," Raphaela said later. "I was too excited. I called him my boyfriend, because that's what he is. He is my only boyfriend. I love him and he loves me."[5]

When Raphaela arrived in Los Angeles, Lanza and his wife met her at the airport. She was bearing a letter from the mayor of Newark addressed to Lanza.

> Dear Mario, I have asked Raphaela to deliver this letter to you with the blessing and sincere gratitude of myself and all the citizens of Newark. We all want you to know that your wonderful understanding, kindness and consideration for this suffering child has given her the ultimate happiness which she can cram into her short span of life. The trip to Hollywood, which your generosity has made possible, will be like a visit to fairyland for her. Mere words cannot express what all of us feel when we think of how much you have done for someone unknown to you and a continent removed from you. May your Christmas holiday with your family and children be made brighter by the true spirit you have shown.
>
> With warm personal regards and God's blessing on you and your loved ones,
>
> Sincerely, Ralph Villani, Mayor.[6]

Lanza did everything possible to make Rapahela's stay with him and his family a memorable one. He arranged for her to visit him on the set of *Because You're Mine*, and escorted her on a tour of the MGM studios. He and Betty also arranged a party for her at their home, to which he invited thirty children, including those of Kathryn Grayson, Jerry Lewis and Ricardo Montalban.[7]

Lanza had Raphaela entertained by a ventriloquist, a magician and a puppeteer, and in his typical fashion, showered her with gifts. He gave her a beautiful RCA portable radio with a leather carrying case inscribed in gold letters, "To Ray Fasano, with love from Mario and Betty," a jewel-studded gold medallion, a toy sewing machine, a paint set, an album filled with movie stars' autographs, hats, dresses and a grey Persian lamb coat. He also gave her a Cinderella wrist watch as a present from Colleen and Ellisa.

For more than a week Raphaela lived her fairy tale with Lanza and his family. Then it was time to go back to Newark with all her gifts and priceless memories. Lanza would have liked her to stay longer but was afraid that all the excitement would be too tiring for her.[8]

Raphaela lived for little more than a year after she left Los Angeles, and during this time Lanza did not forget her. Every Friday at three o'clock in the afternoon she would wait for a special ritual to take place. The phone in the Fasano household would ring, with the voice at the other end announcing: "Hollywood calling." Lanza would take the phone and talk to Raphaela. Then on Friday, 30 January 1953 instead of Raphaela, Lanza heard the voice of a tired, defeated man. It was her father. "Raphaela can't come to the phone," he said. "She died yesterday."[9]

Raphaela was buried wearing a sterling silver medal of the Immaculate Conception around her neck. It had been one of Lanza's final presents to her.

19—THE MARIO LANZA RADIO SHOW

WITH HIS POPULARITY AT ITS PEAK, Lanza was being flooded with a multitude of offers. Prior to the start of filming *Because You're Mine*, he accepted an offer from CBS to perform on a weekly radio program, sponsored by the Coca-Cola company. Lanza reasoned that the workload would be relatively light, with his portion consisting of four numbers while various guests and Ray Sinatra's orchestra would provide the rest of the music necessary to complete the thirty-minute programs. *The Mario Lanza Show* would go on air coast to coast every Sunday night and Lanza would receive the not inconsiderable fee of $5,300 for each program.[1]

Initially, it was intended to be a temporary summer replacement broadcast beginning on June 10, 1951. However, it proved so popular that it became a regular feature until September of the following year when, at the height of *The Student Prince* controversy, MGM obtained a court order preventing Lanza from performing on radio or, indeed, in any other medium. [2]

Whether Lanza's venture into these radio broadcasts was a wise one is debatable. On the one hand, they would provide his recording company, RCA, with a considerable source of unreleased material both before and after his death. On the other hand, many of these recordings represent Lanza at his commercial worst.

Initially, the programs were to be pre-recorded in front of a live studio audience. However, time constraints made this impossible. As it was, he barely had the chance to learn the music before recording the numbers on a trial and error basis.[3]

The variety of material that Lanza covered in the course of the radio programs is extraordinary, and included his film songs, Neapolitan songs, standards, operatic arias, musical comedy songs and new songs by current composers.

Even with sufficient time, however, it would simply have been too much material to learn, rehearse and perform consistently well on a weekly basis. Although there are some notable exceptions, listening to these performances today it is clear that everything was rushed and under-rehearsed. A great deal of the singing is undisciplined and frankly sloppy, while it is evident that Lanza is often not familiar with the material and would have clearly benefited from extra rehearsal time. The orchestral arrangements—particularly in the Italian and Neapolitan songs— are simply abominable, with the tenor, rather than being accompanied, having to compete with continual blasting from the orchestra.[†]

A vast amount of this original radio material is available, for one reason or another, on various RCA records. In fact RCA began releasing songs from this source as far back as 1954, during Lanza's period of total inactivity.

At the time these so-called "new releases" were passed off as new studio recordings with no mention made of the original source. Entire albums of radio material would be released by RCA in order to satisfy the public's demand for new Lanza recordings.

New LPs kept appearing with such titles as *A Kiss And Other Love Songs*, *The Touch Of Your Hand* and *The Magic Mario*. Even the reverse side of the original *Student Prince* album made use of these radio programs.

Since Lanza's death, RCA has marketed a number of albums and CDs containing both previously released and unreleased radio performances, in these instances acknowledging the original source. Among the more than 160 numbers that Lanza recorded for these programs, there are beautiful renditions of songs such as "The World Is Mine Tonight," Noel Coward's "I'll See You Again," "If," by Tolchard Evans, "Without A Song," Cole Porter's "Begin The Beguine" and "Night And Day," "Some Day" from *The Vagabond King*, and "If I Loved You" from *Carousel*. Lanza also gives good renditions of the arias "*Testa adorata*" from the "other" *La Bohème* by Leoncavallo, "*Un tal gioco*" and "*Vesti*

[†]This was conducted in turn by Ray Sinatra in the popular numbers and a few of the operatic arias and Constantine Callinicos in most of the operatic arias and Neapolitan songs.

la giubba" from *Pagliacci*, "*Cielo e mar*" from *La Gioconda* and the "*Improvviso*" and "*Come un bel di' di maggio*" from *Andrea Chénier*.

Unfortunately there are also simply dreadful performances of songs such as "Diane," "Charmaine," "The Desert Song," and "None But The Lonely Heart" among the English numbers, while Lanza recorded superior versions elsewhere of virtually all the Italian and Neapolitan songs, as well as most of the operatic arias. The voice throughout these radio recordings is consistently brilliant, but the style, particularly in the operatic numbers and Neapolitan songs, is simply inappropriate, with the approach often sloppy, mannered and uneven.

With such a vast range of material ranging from outstanding to downright abominable to choose from, one would think that a recording company would apply certain selection criteria when producing a CD. Instead, in compiling a Lanza release, RCA/BMG has seemed determined to use some of the very worst recordings he ever made, and these inevitably include many from his original radio programs.

This predilection for the worst of Lanza—rather than showcasing his best performances—limits sales to the diehard fans who will buy anything their idol has recorded.

Were RCA/BMG to exercise greater selectivity in their releases, they might perhaps also expand their market to include more discerning and critical listeners who, on the basis of what they have heard, often dismiss Lanza as a second-rate singer. It is difficult to blame them, given the type of material available on the majority of Lanza's LPs and CDs.

Apart from the poor choice of material one is inevitably faced with the re-release—ad nauseam—of the same numbers. Frankly, there is more to Lanza than the forever re-issued—though admittedly exciting—version of "Be My Love," or the equally superb renditions from *The Student Prince*. It is difficult to comprehend why his recording company chooses to release a ghastly version of "*Core n'grato*," taken from a radio broadcast, simply because it is new when there is a far superior studio recording available. Other peculiar reissues include the "Arrivederci Roma" from the soundtrack of *Seven Hills of Rome* in Italian over the far superior studio recording in English, which has never been released on CD. Then we have the forever present *"Funiculì funiculà"* from his 1958 stereo album which happens to be the only bad track out of the total of 12 that were recorded. On the 1999 release, *Mario Lanza: Opera Arias and Duets*, the compilation begins with *"Celeste Aida"* and *"Amor ti vieta,"* two radio performances which are greatly inferior to his commercial recordings of these arias.[†]

One can only hope that, eventually, the task of compiling a Lanza CD will be given to someone musically competent and with sufficient insight to realize what splendid material remains dormant in the RCA vaults.

[†]The CD also includes the 1950 *"O Paradiso"* at the expense of the superior 1955 recording, and places the Third Act monologue, *"Dio mi potevi scagliar"* from *Otello* on the same track as the preceding duet, *"Dio ti giocondi."*

20—THE STUDENT PRINCE

WITH THE CONFLICT over *Because You're Mine* finally resolved, the new year augured well for Lanza. At a rare public appearance at the beginning of 1952, the Lanzas joined more than 500 guests in the Embassy Room at the Ambassador Hotel in Los Angeles for the annual Photoplay Magazine Gold Medals.[†]

Lanza had been nominated for his role in *The Great Caruso* and finished as one of the evening's top winners, receiving a gold medal for the Best Male Performance of the Year. Although the award was based as much on popularity as it was on ability, it was nevertheless an unexpected recognition, and Lanza was both pleased and surprised by it.[1]

Looking thin and very handsome, he addressed the guests and fellow performers in the packed Embassy Room who were clamoring for him to sing. In an emotional speech he told them: "Tonight I do not sing, but I speak of those who helped me."[2] He then paid tribute to Hedda Hopper, Frank Sinatra, and Sam Weiler, sparing also a few kind words for producer Joe Pasternak.

Lanza was in decidedly high spirits as he prepared to start work on *The Student Prince*. Principal rehearsals and pre-recordings were due to begin in late June, while actual filming was scheduled for early August.

Having made *Because You're Mine* under protest, he had waited an entire year and was now excited at the thought of finally playing prince Karl Franz in Sigmund Romberg's delightful operetta.[3] Apart from disagreeing with MGM over the inclusion of three additional songs, Lanza loved everything about *The*

[†]These pre-dated even the Academy Awards, which had begun in 1927.

Student Prince.[†] He loved the music, the story (which concerns a prince who falls in love with a barmaid while attending Heidelberg University), and the beautifully written script by William Ludwig and Sonya Levien, the duo responsible for the screenplay of *The Great Caruso*.[4]

He was also delighted to have Ann Blyth, his *Great Caruso* co-star, appearing once more with him.[‡] He admired and respected the young actress and was always careful with his language in her presence. Blyth reciprocated the admiration. She was genuinely fond of Lanza and had enjoyed working with him on *The Great Caruso*.[5]

Blyth was in fact an accomplished singer and actress. As a youngster, prior to going to Broadway and subsequently to Hollywood, she had received some operatic training while singing for three seasons with the touring American-based Fortune Gallo San Carlo Opera Company. On Broadway she had played the daughter in *Watch On The Rhine* and she had been nominated for an Oscar for her role in the 1945 film *Mildred Pierce* with Joan Crawford.

Another good omen for smooth and trouble-free filming on *The Student Prince* set was that Lanza had not put on weight after the completion of his previous film. He and Betty had recently returned from a holiday with their good friends, the Mexican-American singer Andy Russell and his Italian-American wife Della, whom they had known since their arrival in Los Angeles.

Holidaying at a ranch near Lake Mead, Nevada, the two couples had passed the time relaxing, horseriding, cruising and fishing. Lanza returned from his holiday looking fit, weighing only 161 pounds (73kg) and seeming happy and relaxed.

[†]He felt that the original score was good enough not to warrant the inclusion of the new numbers "Summertime in Heidelberg," "Beloved," and "I'll Walk With God," written especially for the film by Nicholas Brodszky with lyrics by Paul Francis Webster.

[‡]Originally, Jane Powell was to have played the part of the barmaid, Kathy, but by the time filming was scheduled to begin she would have been in an advanced state of pregnancy and was therefore replaced by Ann Blyth. MGM had also tried to get Deanna Durbin, and had reputedly offered her a fortune, but nothing could persuade her to come out of retirement.

He immediately began work on the musical score of the operetta with Constantine Callinicos, who—at Lanza's urging—had been engaged by MGM as his personal Musical Director for the film.[6]

It might have been their best collaboration. For the next three weeks Lanza worked like a man inspired, rehearsing with Callinicos every day in preparation for the pre-recording of the soundtrack.

However, Lanza's enthusiasm and newfound peace of mind were destined to be short-lived.

Unlike *Because You're Mine*, MGM had spared no expense on Lanza's new film. Producer Pasternak had assembled a strong supporting cast that together with Ann Blyth included experienced actors such as Louis Calhern, Edmund Gwenn, S.Z. Sakall and John Williams, as well as newcomers John Ericson, Betta St. John and Richard Anderson.

The direction was given to Curtis Bernhardt, who had directed *The Merry Widow* for Pasternak the previous year. Given that Bernhardt was known chiefly as a "woman's picture director" and that *The Merry Widow* had been a failure, it was an odd choice on Pasternak's part and one that would prove disastrous for all concerned. Bernhardt, who had come to Hollywood in 1940, was a pompous German who had the rather unfortunate habit of giving his directorial orders by waving a stick around and poking the actors in the ribs with it. [7]

Although preliminary discussions involving Lanza, Bernhardt, Pasternak, Callinicos, Musical Director George Stoll, scenarists William Ludwig and Sonya Levien and composer Nicholas Brodszky, had proceeded well with the tenor appearing to be in good spirits, problems began to surface at the start of principal rehearsals. The first day of rehearsals, June 24, Lanza arrived punctually at the studio and clashed with Bernhardt right away. Halfway through rehearsing a scene Bernhardt abruptly stopped the tenor and told him he wanted him to be less emotional. Lanza responded by stating, for everyone to hear, that he had no intention of following such ridiculous orders and promptly walked off the set. Determined to settle the matter the tenor headed straight for producer Joe Pasternak's office and in no uncertain terms announced that he was unable to work with Bernhardt.[8]

The satisfaction he expected from Pasternak, however, was not forthcoming. Although Lanza was a big box office draw for Metro, he had made only four films to date and Pasternak made it clear that he had no intention of giving in to what he considered the unwarranted demands of his star.[9] Had Pasternak anticipated what was to follow he might have acted differently. Alas, he told Lanza that there was nothing he could do. He did not want any problems. Bernhardt had a contract to direct the film and he could not replace him with another director. Lanza's reaction to Pasternak's reply was typical: he simply got up, left the producer's office and failed to report for work the next day.[10]

The impasse between Lanza and the studio would drag on for weeks with meetings and endless discussions. With the crisis mounting over the stalled production, Lanza was being urged by his friends, associates, his wife, his parents and the studio executives themselves to return to work. By the end of July a compromise was finally reached and Lanza agreed to return to MGM and start recording the songs required for the soundtrack.

"I'll Walk With God" was the first number selected. Accompanied only by an organ, Lanza performed a moving and powerful rendition of the song, which would later become closely associated with the tenor. "A Mighty Fortress" followed, only a brief portion of which was used in the film. The following day, with Callinicos and the full MGM orchestra assembled on the huge Stage One, Lanza proceeded to record three additional numbers.

The task would be completed during six recording sessions scheduled over the next two weeks. Having familiarized himself with the script and the relevant scenes that would later be filmed, Lanza gave his best to the beautiful songs. Despite the clash with Bernhardt he was still enthusiastic at the thought of making a film that he felt had some artistic value. He expressed satisfaction with the additional songs composed for the film and the beautiful orchestrations by Maurice De Packh.[11]

Lanza's enthusiasm for the project was unmistakable. Such was his assured delivery that to the amazement of everyone, he recorded most of the numbers from the score in single takes.[12] Lanza was in excellent voice, and the entire soundtrack from *The Student Prince* represents the tenor performing at his very best. Callinicos also rose to the occasion, producing a significantly better conducting performance than usual – though it must be said that the demands of conducting operetta are quite different from those of opera.

Then just as it appeared that things had finally calmed down, Lanza was shattered when his manager and mentor Sam Weiler told him that the two million dollars he had earned during his five years in Hollywood had vanished through a series of unfortunate investments that he (Weiler) had made for the company, *Marsam*, which they jointly owned. Weiler further informed the startled singer that he was in debt to the government for more than $250,000 in back taxes.[13]

Lanza had always placed complete trust in Weiler. To discover that all he had left—after four years in Hollywood—was a mere $100,000 came as an unexpected blow. He'd earned over a million dollars in 1951 alone, and had paid the Federal Government $425,000 in taxes for that year. How could he be left with almost nothing?[14]

Weiler denied any wrongdoing and claimed he had enough money to buy and sell Lanza ten times over.[15] Recriminations, accusations and counter-accusations followed, culminating in Lanza's dismissal of Weiler in August 1952, which marked the end of their more than six-year association.

Lanza grew heartsick after the break with Weiler. He had dismissed the man who had sponsored him, who had come to his aid when he needed someone, and who had taken a chance on him. At the same time Lanza could not come to terms with the way his earnings had vanished.[16]

The sad episode would drag on until the following year. On 25 August 1953 Lanza filed suit in Santa Monica Superior Court for $255,836.37 against Weiler, demanding an accounting of the $5,250,000 that constituted his gross earnings over the previous five years. He also asked the court to terminate a contract signed in January 1951 that had given Weiler five percent of Lanza's earnings for the next fifteen years in addition to his five percent managerial fee. An out of court settlement was reached a year later with Weiler agreeing to pay Lanza $58,000 in exchange for five percent of Lanza's gross earnings ad infinitum.[17]

It was following this important setback that Lanza resumed rehearsals on *The Student Prince*.

Curtis Bernhardt was still directing and it soon became clear to all involved in the production that the Lanza-Bernhardt collaboration was doomed.

Disagreement followed disagreement, culminating with Bernhardt branding Lanza's interpretation of the song "Beloved" over-emotional and asking for more restraint on the tenor's part.[18] Lanza would subsequently re-record "Beloved," and listening to the two performances, there is no doubt that in this instance Bernhardt was right. Not only is the re-take better than the original, it is one of Lanza's best recordings.

Coming at a time, however, when Lanza was living on raw nerves, Bernhardt's request hit him like a thunderbolt. Unable to handle any criticism of his acting, and certainly not of his singing, Lanza was both unable and unwilling to accede to the director's request. "He's an unbending German of the old school,"[19] Lanza complained

Referring to Lanza's strong personality his good friend actor Edmond O'Brien stated, "But then who could direct him? If it was someone like Kazan, one of them would have had to genuflect!"[20] It was quite obvious in this instance that Lanza had no intention of genuflecting to Bernhardt. Although he did not go so far as to yawn in his face, as Elizabeth Taylor would later do during the making of *Beau Brummell*,[21] he obviously abhorred the director.

This is Barry Nelson's asssessment of Lanza's predicament: "To say to Mario *you have to* is startling of course. For anybody to say to Mario *you have to do this* is not the way to get him to do something because he's immediately going to bristle."[22]

The break with Weiler and the state of his finances, together with the drastic dieting and battles that had occurred over the filming of *Because You're Mine* had brought the volatile Lanza to the verge of collapse.

For his part, Lanza continued to urge Pasternak to replace Bernhardt with Richard Thorpe, the director he had worked with so effectively on *The Great Caruso*—all to no avail. The best Pasternak could do was to tell his troubled star that he should follow Schary's suggestion and see a psychiatrist.

Lanza, who did not believe in psychiatry, finally agreed to see Dr. Augustus Rose at the UCLA Medical Center in Los Angeles. Rose was not a psychiatrist, but an eminent neurologist, who over the years had had a number of famous stars referred to him. Rose was sympathetic and listened patiently to the tenor. At the end of the meeting Rose informed Lanza that, in his opinion, he was suffering from megalomania. The diagnosis was incorrect. George Stoll recalled the events that took place at the time: "He was not the crazy man that the studio wanted to portray but he was a man out of control. What Dr. Rose failed to recognize was that Mario's problems stemmed not from megalomania but from extreme nervous tension caused by years of frequent excessive dieting." [23]

Schary, along with studio manager Eddie Mannix, was convinced that Lanza was off the rails and called Nicholas Schenck, Loew's president in New York, to get his go-ahead to fire Lanza and sue him for damages. Schenck managed to convince Schary not to be hasty and to hold on. He was coming to Los Angeles and would talk to the tenor himself.

As well as Schenck and Schary, Eddie Mannix was present at the meeting.

On walking into Schary's office Lanza was met by Nicholas Schenck, who tried vainly to reason with him, but Lanza was having none of it. The discussion became more and more heated, with Lanza finally telling Schenck that Schary and Mannix were a couple of stooges, at which point Schary told the tenor ,"We've heard this before, Mario, you can go home." Lanza's reply was that they could all go to hell and on that note walked out.[24] Again, it's Barry Nelson who best illustrates the conflict taking place between his friend and the studio:

> In time you learn to psyche yourself. But Mario was much too inexperienced to do that, so everything was a frightening experience to go through for a fellow as sensitive as he was. He was ill prepared for that. And to be expected to be this and that when he was still very raw and with these gargantuan tastes. You were not just dealing with an ordinary person— you were dealing with an extraordinary person—so that his problems became much more complex, because he wouldn't fit into an easy way of working with MGM, who had a big monetary interest in him and preferred easy people to work with. The more trouble he gives them, the more trouble they give him. Then his problems are compounded.[25]

Needing a friendly ear, Lanza accepted the invitation of his friend, the actor/singer John Carroll, to spend some time with him in his ranch house in the Chatsworth Hills twenty miles north of Hollywood, where Betty joined him the following day.

As he was still under contract to them, MGM repeatedly asked Lanza to report for work. Then, on August 28, 1952, the studio issued an ultimatum to Lanza to report for work the following day. No reply was received from the singer. Finally on September 4, the film was cancelled. [26]

Carroll, who had experienced his own problems with MGM, was sympathetic and understanding during the two weeks that Lanza stayed at the ranch house, and finally managed to convince him to return to work. [27]

A meeting was arranged between Lanza and Schary and on September 14 the tenor returned to the Culver City Studios.

What the emotionally and physically drained singer needed at this stage was reassurance and understanding. As Barry Nelson remarked, "Mario is a man who needs a great deal of love and he knows the love isn't forthcoming and that they are interested in him monetarily. Not forgetting that Mario [and] Judy Garland and people like that were highly sensitive and needed their hands held a lot." In short, what Lanza needed was the sort of paternalistic approach typical of Schary's predecessor, Louis B. Mayer. Unlike the explosive Mayer, Schary both hated and avoided all displays of anger or temperament and was therefore completely at odds with someone like Lanza, who was his total opposite. In what was destined to be their final meeting, Schary told Lanza in no uncertain terms that his behavior was disgraceful and that either he obeyed orders and worked with Bernhardt or else he would be finished. Lanza's reply to Schary was that he could go "fuck" himself[28]—whereupon he walked out of Schary's office and the MGM studios.

MGM immediately sued Lanza for $695,888, which accounted for their production expenses to date, plus an additional $4,500,000 for breach of contract and general damages. Lanza took the news of the lawsuit particularly badly. He had not anticipated that the studio would go that far and, deep down, remained confident that eventually a compromise would be reached and the film would be completed.[29]

Regardless of his behavior, and what MGM considered to be

unreasonable demands, it is extremely doubtful that Lanza would have been dismissed under the regime of L.B.Mayer. Mayer strongly believed that as long as any star was a box office draw they could do no wrong. When Schary took control of the studio, following Mayer's ouster, he made substantial changes. Priority was given to producers, writers and directors. The stars rated a poor fourth.[30] It was in fact the beginning of the end of the famous star system.

When he succeeded Mayer, Schary began by cutting production and related costs to a minimum. Budget expenditure was reduced and producers given strict orders not to squander money on unnecessary footage while expensively staged production numbers were to be avoided whenever possible.[31]

Above all Schary absolutely refused to cater to whims, but Lanza was not someone that could be pushed around. The repeated excessive dieting, along with his disastrous financial situation and the break with Weiler, had only made matters worse. By this stage little was required to make the volatile singer explode.[32]

Unfortunately for Lanza, at this time studios had total control over actors. Actors' health, their feelings and opinions counted for little. Actors had to behave and do what they were told. If they disagreed with a decision made by the studios they were labelled "difficult" and difficult actors cost the studios money. Temperamental outbursts were not tolerated. Huge talents such as Judy Garland and Mario Lanza were sacrificed as a result.

That MGM had undergone substantial changes with the takeover by Schary was made clear in *The New York Times*:

> Whatever the real reasons, Mr. Lanza's hold-out action made him the target of criticism. Interestingly, and indicative of the new awareness of money matters, most of the comment was about the money that the squabble was costing the studio. In the old days of not so long ago, the studio wouldn't get much consideration on that score...disciplining a star was one thing, but it's not nearly as important as keeping him on the screen to make money for the stockholders.[33]

MGM would leave no legal stone unturned. In addition to the huge lawsuit, a court order was issued preventing him from doing any work whatsoever until the MGM contract expired 15 months hence. When told that *The Student Prince* was cancelled, a distraught Ann Blyth, referring to Lanza, simply cried out "That poor, poor boy!" [34] Blyth both liked and admired her co-star. Reminiscing about the time they spent together working on *The Great Caruso* she said: "Playing Dorothy Caruso put me on my mettle. Mario's great talent, his magnificent voice, and the importance of his role could have made him rather formidable for his leading lady, but everything went smoothly and it turned out well for me." [35]

Although the studio had cancelled the film and sued Lanza for damages, he was still effectively an MGM employee and it would take another seven months before the whole unpleasant episode finally came to an end.

In the meantime, with all the current year's upheavals, the Lanzas had at least one thing to look forward to: the birth of their third child. Once again it was due in December. After the birth of Ellisa, Betty had been told it would be better if she did not have any more children, but they both wanted at least one more child and this time they were hoping for a boy.

Although he was now unemployed and prevented from doing any work pending the MGM lawsuit, Lanza was coping reasonably well with the situation. He was optimistic about the eventual outcome of the dispute and to the end remained convinced that the studio would contact him and work out a compromise. [36] He had obviously not fully realized Schary's determination, not only to sever all dealings with the singer, but also to go ahead with the filming of *The Student Prince* without him. In order to do this, MGM first considered a number of absurd possibilities in selecting someone to play the prince. They ranged from the well-known British actor Stewart Granger, who—at age 40—would have been ridiculous playing a young prince attending university, to the younger but, at the time, equally well-known Farley Granger, to the not exactly charismatic Vic Damone. At least Damone was himself a singer and a good one in the tradition of Crosby, Sinatra and Como. However, since he didn't have the voice for a demanding operetta score such as *The Student Prince* one assumes that, like the other candidates, he would have mimed Lanza's pre-recorded tracks.

Even the famous Italian tenor Mario Del Monaco was at one

stage considered for the part. Renowned not only for his trumpeting voice, but also for his gigantic ego, Del Monaco jumped at the opportunity and headed straight for Hollywood. In typical fashion Del Monaco would often quote Hedda Hopper's statement: "Hollywood didn't want to miss the opportunity of acquiring a great operatic tenor who also has a profile like Tyrone Power!" [37]

In his autobiography, Del Monaco stated that the film test at MGM was successful.[38] Producer Joe Pasternak remembered it somewhat differently. "He had a massive voice but nothing else. He was stiff, couldn't act and couldn't speak a word of English, so we decided to let him go."[39] It stretches the imagination somewhat to visualize Del Monaco playing Karl Franz. Apart from his good looks, nothing else was right for the role of the prince, least of all the voice. Del Monaco, who at the time was 38, had a phenomenally powerful voice, dark—almost baritonal—with plenty of ring. It was a true dramatic tenor voice, which could be thrilling if heard in a theater. But he lacked the feeling and poetry required for a score such as *The Student Prince*.

In any case, whether he made *The Student Prince* or not, Del Monaco had a well-established operatic career to fall back on.

Finally, in May 1953, MGM made Lanza a proposition. They would be willing to call off the lawsuit in return for the rights to use the musical soundtrack he had recorded prior to the dispute. Faced with the alternative, Lanza really had no choice. It was now clear that MGM intended to proceed with *The Student Prince* without him in the starring role but, well aware that his name was still big box office, they wanted to retain his singing voice while using another actor to play the prince. [40]

The MGM proposal came as a virtual deathblow for the singer, one from which he would never fully recover. Up to now, deep down, he had still believed that the differences with the studio would be worked out and that in the end he would end up making the film. [41]

Deeply hurt, he accepted the MGM offer. During the last period of his life, when he was living in Italy, Lanza would confess "I now admit the biggest mistake I ever made was to walk out of Metro. I did not wish to leave and they didn't want me to go."[42] There is a certain amount of truth in this statement because although at times driven to the limit by the tenor's behavior, Joe Pasternak felt a genuine affection for Lanza as well as admiration for his great talent. Years later he would reminisce "He (Lanza) was the pride and joy of my life."[43]

Ultimately it was Schary's decision and he remained unmoveable. *The Student Prince* would be filmed without Lanza. Having discarded all previous actors and singers considered as possible replacements for Lanza, Pasternak decided to gamble on a virtually unknown British actor under contract to the studio: the 29-year-old Edmund Purdom.

The highly cultured Purdom, whose father was an author and drama critic, had previously appeared for two seasons at the Shakespeare Memorial Theater in Stratford-on-Avon and in *Romeo and Juliet* in London, followed by a tour of the United States with Laurence Olivier and Vivien Leigh in *Caesar and Cleopatra*.

Spotted while acting on Broadway with the Olivier Company, Purdom was offered a contract by MGM. At Metro Purdom had appeared in the small role of Strato in John Houseman's production of *Julius Caesar* and, on loan to 20th Century Fox, had played a slightly bigger part in *Titanic*. Even though he would be substituting for the original star and would have to mime to Lanza's voice, *The Student Prince* would be Purdom's big opportunity for film stardom.

Very good-looking and possessing a beautiful speaking voice, as well as a considerable knowledge of classical music, Purdom gave the part of the prince everything he had to make it a success. In preparing for his first major screen role he spent a total of three months listening and singing along to the original recordings made by Lanza. It was not merely a question of achieving the correct movement of the lips. The delivery of the songs had to appear authentic. Purdom shut himself in a soundproof room and listened endlessly to Lanza's recordings of the score at full volume. "I sang with Lanza's voice to learn to express with my face, hands, body and mind what Lanza was expressing with his singing,"[44] he recalled.

> [Lanza's] voice was simply a fabulous voice to act to. Because, after all, I wasn't just standing there imitating a singer singing, or even impersonating him. God forbid! I was play-

ing the prince in the story, a very beautifully written story, and bursting into song at the appropriate moment. It was an absolutely tremendous experience. It was enough to make you sweat, just listening to the voice. [45]

Purdom did a superb job. He looked good and acted the part well, but to provide the face to a voice as well-known and distinctive as that of Mario Lanza would have been an impossible task for anyone. The viewing public simply could not accept Lanza's voice emerging from another actor's face. This remains a serious flaw in what is otherwise a very beautiful filming of Romberg's operetta.

Of course lovers of the original stage musical would find a lot to be dissatisfied with in the MGM film. Not only were three additional songs added but only about half of the original score was retained. Furthermore, some of Dorothy Donnelly's lyrics were changed and new dialogue was added. All of these changes and the tampering with the original score notwithstanding, this is indeed an entertaining and, at the same time, moving film.

That the public wanted Lanza, however, was reflected in the relatively moderate success at the box office at the time of the film's release in June 1954. Unlike the film, the RCA album of songs was enormously successful, becoming Lanza's largest selling LP and his first gold album.

The numbers from the soundtrack of *The Student Prince* are among the very best that Lanza ever recorded. He was also ideally suited to Romberg's music. His phrasing is remarkable and it would be difficult to imagine a more romantic-sounding prince.

Even though the numbers, including the beautiful "Serenade" and the newly-written "I'll Walk With God" can effectively be classified as operatic numbers, Lanza avoids an operatic delivery.[†] Instead, he keeps the tone light and lyrical with frequent use of *mezza voce*, particularly in the beautiful duet "Deep In My Heart" with Ann Blyth, which had to be reworked for the album release.[‡]

[†]This was in stark contrast to the operatic approach he employs on his Rome recording of *The Student Prince* seven years later.
[‡]When the LP was released in 1954, RCA was forced, for contractual reasons, to eliminate the voice of Ann Blyth in the duets and substitute it with another soprano. Initially, the task was given to Nelson Eddy's then singing partner, Gale Sherwood, but eventually she was replaced by Elizabeth Doubleday.

The ultimate irony was that the film ended up being directed by Richard Thorpe, the very man whom Lanza had fought for to replace Curtis Bernhardt.[†] Evidently compromises were possible, and directors could be replaced, but only provided the studio hierarchy made the decisions. Schary was determined to rid the studio of Lanza. Three years later, with the studio suffering mounting losses, MGM ousted both Schary and Nicholas Schenck.

Many saw the end of his MGM chapter as a chance for Lanza to concentrate instead on the operatic career that he kept postponing. Unfortunately, the MGM dismissal had the opposite effect. Lanza withdrew more and more into his own private world, with days of deep depression alternating with days when the future seemed less bleak.[46]

The one bright note during the entire saga with the studio had been the birth on December 12, 1952, of their third child, the much longed-for son, whom they named Damon Anthony, after the author Damon Runyon, who was one of Lanza's favorite writers, and after Lanza's father.

[†]Thorpe begged Schary to bring back Lanza – to no avail

21—AFTERMATH

Since the split with MGM, Lanza had become almost a recluse. He was drinking heavily and apart from his parents and his accompanist Callinicos, who remained on a retainer, he was seeing only close friends such as John Carroll and Andy and Della Russell.[1]

In the short span of six weeks Lanza had been fired by MGM, seen his coast to coast weekly radio program cancelled, his earnings vanish, and he was heavily in debt to the government in back taxes. He was now relying entirely on his recording royalties for an income. His records continued to sell extremely well and, for a while, he was able to go on living in the manner to which he had become accustomed. However, it would be only a matter of time before the government made a legal claim on his royalties due to unpaid back taxes.

In the meantime the press was having a field day. Articles purporting to reveal the latest on Lanza were almost daily items in the papers and whatever could not be verified would simply be invented for the sake of providing the readers with the latest gossip. He was accused of being temperamental, big-headed, ungrateful, impossible to work with and so on. This was a foretaste of the adverse press that would continue to harass him for the remainder of his life.

Through all the fuss and turmoil Lanza kept silent, eventually consenting to an interview with his old friend, Hedda Hopper. "My biggest beef with Metro was that the studio wanted to be commercial and I wanted artistic betterment," he told Hopper. "Put them together: they don't mix." [2]

> For a year I screamed about not wanting to do *Because You're Mine* and delayed it as long as possible...it was not the kind

of picture to follow *Caruso* and foisting it on the public wasn't fair. I wanted to follow *Caruso* with another big artistic picture, but the front office didn't dig my angle. I was told, "You were successful the last time out, so just keep on being successful. Just keep making pictures."[3]

Regarding his walk-out on *The Student Prince* he had this to say.

I loved the script, Metro wanted to make a few bucks and I wanted to make a good picture. The worst thing that can happen to a man is that those in control of his destiny fail to believe in him. I say "Take back your money but believe in me." The producers used to listen to my advice, but when I became a big star they said, "We'll take the reins of this so and so."[4]

Lanza informed Hopper of his struggle with the studio to engage Callinicos to conduct the vocal score for *The Student Prince*, and how it had turned out so well with nearly every number being recorded in only one take. He proved it by playing back the acetate recordings of the score. Hopper was surprised to discover that he was completely familiar with every detail of the film. "He explained graphically the scene that led up to each song. The music seemed to transport him into another world," she said.[5]

Lanza had strong opinions about the correct approach to the singing. "I was asked to play the part as a Prussian. Such a character didn't match the voice. You just don't toss a song into a picture. You sing to what's going to appear on the screen, but the studio couldn't see it that way. Call me immodest, but I felt I was being treated cheaply when I was box office Tiffany."[6]

In a more humorous interview with Hollywood columnist Adela Rogers St. Johns, Lanza said:

The end of it all came for me when Mayer left MGM. Mayer knew how to deal with people. When I got mad I'd go into his office and I'd say what I was mad about and I'd call him a Jew son of a bitch and Mayer would burst into tears and say "Mario, I thought you loved me." I'd say I didn't dislike him but that he and the studio were making me unhappy with their demands on my life and he'd say he'd do something about that and what I was talking about. I'd explain it to him and he'd say again that he'd do something about it and I'd leave feeling a little better. Most of the time nothing was done about it but he knew how to handle me. After Mayer left, I'd go in to see Dore Schary and I'd call him a Jew son of a bitch and he'd throw me out of the office. Now you can't work for a man like that.[7]

Walking out of MGM had been a costly mistake as Lanza himself was to acknowledge years later. This is how his friend Barry Nelson, who had known him since their Army days, assessed the Lanza/MGM association.

In a theatrical environment you don't always act with sheer logic. If you do, you are usually a very technical kind of performer and technical kinds of performers are usually quite easy to get along with. They're very logical, but they're not very interesting or exciting. Mario was exciting, but he paid a very high price for that. When you go into a machine as MGM was, for someone like Mario, it became a predictable conflict. A machine able to project him to great heights and at the same time a machine that would confine him terribly. It's very hard to get it both ways.[8]

Having worked at MGM, Nelson knew how the Hollywood Studios operated at the time. He further expanded on the relationship between Lanza and MGM:

Mario couldn't be controlled. Not to anybody's satisfaction. Metro really had to control what they called their stable of stars. You're a horse running for them. So it's funny in retrospect. And I don't mean funny as such. But we think of these things as storybook and yet I'm talking about somebody I knew as a raw kid, who was my dresser, who walked into this. Who I walked home with every night, and [with whom I] had long talks and lots of laughs and lots of adventures and lots of girls. Just fun. I'm talking about this guy who's taking on MGM, the biggest studio of all time at its height.

They [MGM] weren't really that talented psychologically. They only saw it as a protest by a player who's being difficult to them who are trying to give the player stardom. "Look what we've given you in our family! We have brought you up and made you a star with our facilities you ungrateful person! You must be disciplined and sent to bed without dinner." How else did they know how to handle it with their primitive ways?

It takes courage to tackle MGM. You're alone against them. You really don't have anybody on your side....and you're terribly confused because you are gaining fame, you're making money, and in a sense you should be grateful, and in another sense you know you are being exploited and that you are exploiting your own talent. All that is very hard to reconcile.

I found Mario fascinating and I thought, later on, that he really turned away from those of us that knew him well because of circumstances way beyond anything that had to do with us. There were much larger issues at stake that would make him a troubled man who finally would distrust everyone. It's very sad, but you're talking about a giant; you're not talking about your neighborhood postman.[9]

Nelson concluded by saying:

During the years that I knew him I never had a fight with him, there was never once a bad word between us. It seems to me that a person can't be an animal if you have that long a relationship. So whether it's Mario or other performers, they are all terribly vulnerable people—necessarily so. The giants are weak and yet they are giants. To be a great artist you have to have the vulnerability. To have the vulnerability means there are many people who are going to say: "Yes, but there are weaknesses." You can't have it both ways![10]

22—THE WASTED YEARS

IN THE SPACE OF JUST FIVE YEARS, Lanza had gone from dazzling heights in the film and recording business back to nothing. By 1954, having just turned 33, he had to face the fact that his finances were now precarious. He would need to modify his extravagant lifestyle, and the back taxes he owed the IRS were a serious concern. By now the IRS had imposed a lien on his recording royalties to recover unpaid back taxes, which still amounted to $169,153. Fortunately for Lanza, however, he was still RCA's best-selling artist, and would remain so until the advent of Elvis Presley in 1956.

After two years of inactivity and self-imposed exile, Betty felt obliged to sell one of her fur coats to keep them afloat. The Lanzas approached Al Teitelbaum, a wealthy Beverly Hills furrier who supplied furs to many Hollywood stars. Teitelbaum and his wife Sylvia had numerous contacts in the film industry and had known the Lanzas for some time.

Financial difficulties notwithstanding, it would turn out to be another costly mistake to approach a man like Teitelbaum. As subsequent events would prove, Teitelbaum was a dishonest person who wanted to capitalize on the tenor's misfortune.[1] Upon learning of Lanza's financial state, he immediately offered to advance him $60,000 for the chance to become the singer's personal manager.

A shrewder person than Lanza would have stayed well clear of the shady Teitelbaum, but neither the childlike tenor nor his wife, who was usually quite perceptive in assessing people, foresaw the implications of such an association. They gladly accepted the furrier's offer to take over the management of Lanza's career, which had come to a near standstill.

Indeed, Lanza's only activity in the preceding two years had been the re-recording of "Beloved" at MGM in May 1953 and four songs for RCA at Republic Studios in Hollywood the following month. The remainder of the time he had been living as a recluse. With his career at MGM over, what should have been an ideal time to begin an operatic career had turned instead into a long period of deep depression and lethargy, from which little could rouse him.[2]

He would seek refuge in food and alcohol, drinking steadily until he would fall into a deep sleep, gaining temporary relief from his inner torment. Meanwhile Betty was unable to cope with the situation, and tended to try avoid confrontations by retiring to her room. To make matters worse, Lanza's tolerance for alcohol (never great to begin with) had become very low during this period, and he would become intoxicated on two or three glasses of wine. The resulting mood swings would turn him from the immensely likeable person that he usually was into someone who was unreasonable and quarrelsome. Betty only exacerbated this tendency by withdrawing.[3]

Lanza's drinking, which had begun eighteen months after his arrival in Hollywood five years earlier, had now reached the point of near addiction. The tenor would consume vast quantities of beer, champagne, wine or scotch before passing out, often awakening much later covered in perspiration. Callinicos recalled the despair of this period.

> Then in a moment of naked exposure he would sit weeping violently and crashing his fists against his knees. "Why can't I stop drinking?" he would cry. "Why? Why? I hate the stuff. What am I doing to myself?"[4]

His so-called friends—the hangers-on and the sycophants—had all deserted him. Yet there would still be the occasional visitor such as his old friend George London or the heavyweight champion of the world, Rocky Marciano, whom he had recently met through his trainer Terry Robinson. Lanza loved boxing and genuinely admired Marciano, who for his part returned the compliment.[†] But aside from these infrequent visits Lanza saw only

[†]Marciano was in awe of Lanza's voice. After seeing the film *Serenade* in New York in 1956, he sent Lanza a telegram with the message "When you hit they stay hit!"

his wife and children, his parents, his accompanist Constantine Callinicos and his trainer Terry Robinson, who had become a sort of semi-permanent house guest.

Robinson disliked Betty. "She didn't like me and I didn't like her. She kept firing me and Mario kept bringing me back." Robinson also felt that the Lanzas were mismatched. "She was wrong for him. He should have married someone like Della Russell," he said.[5]

Lanza's accompanist, Callinicos, was still being paid to work on a daily basis with the tenor, but much of the time Lanza was too hung-over to rehearse properly. His heavy drinking bouts were now the cause of frequent arguments with his wife. Unable to cope with the situation Betty, who was expecting their fourth child, would simply withdraw to her own world. As much as she loved her husband, Betty was unable to confront Lanza's self-destruction.[6]

His few remaining friends urged him to join Alcoholics Anonymous, but Lanza would hear none of this. His good friend George London went so far as to suggest psychoanalysis, but Lanza rejected the idea instantly.

As London later recalled, "There was no reasoning with him on this point. He had a real fear of psychiatrists. Going to one was to him an admission of being *pazzo* [crazy]."[7] Nor could it be suggested to Betty, who was unwilling even to consider that her husband might need help.

The years of repeated crash dieting, combined with the pressures of his film career, the break with Sam Weiler, the dismissal from MGM and the state of his finances had brought Lanza's nerves to the breaking point. He was no longer the singing sensation he had been only two years before. The studio had fired him; he felt betrayed by his manager, abandoned by those he had thought his friends, and he was without an income.

Terrified, Lanza chose to isolate himself rather than confront the reality of his predicament. There would still be times when he could overcome his apathy and curb his drinking, but they would be few and far between.

There was a glimmer of hope when he expressed a desire to work on some of the lesser-known operatic arias. He had always been interested in neglected operas that, nevertheless, contained wonderful isolated pages of music. When his accompanist, Callinicos, came back from New York with fifteen scores of seldom-heard operas such as *Zazà*, *Chatterton* and *La Bohème* by Leoncavallo, *Gloria* by Cilea, and *Madame Sans-Gêne* by Giordano, he seemed to temporarily abandon his depression and reduce his alcohol intake.[8]

For a time he resumed his daily sessions with Callinicos, working for two hours on the 35 arias that he had selected from the scores. Soon, however, he was forced to confess to his accompanist that he could no longer pay him. Aware of Lanza's financial situation, Callinicos claimed that he offered to work for nothing.[†] "I know he was deeply touched, but he didn't utter a word. Instead he started to cry. I walked out of the music room, leaving him alone with his thoughts," Callinicos recalled.[9]

What Callinicos failed to mention in his biography of the tenor, however, is that he had been asking Lanza for more than two years to record a song that he had written titled "You Are My Love." Callinicos, ever eager to capitalize financially on his strong connection with the tenor, had been paid an advance of $2000 by RCA back in 1951. Lanza eventually agreed to record the song which, together with a superb rendition of "Song of India" and two other numbers, was part of the recording session of June 17, 1953.

Meanwhile, throughout the long period of self-imposed exile Lanza's dream of an operatic career seemed to be as unattainable as ever. Could he really turn his back on fame and fortune and concentrate on an operatic career? This question must have constantly haunted him.

An answer of sorts came when Lanza's newly-appointed personal manager, the furrier Al Teitelbaum, proceeded to negotiate a deal with CBS for the tenor to appear in the premiere of their new television spectacular, *Shower Of Stars*. Probably reasoning that it would be far simpler to perform on a television show than work for months on an operatic role to be sung in an opera house,

---

[†]This may well have been the case. However, when I first approached Callinicos about an interview, he refused unless I was willing to pay him. Upon learning that he was the first interviewee to demand payment, he asked instead that I find him a conducting job in Australia! I told him that I was neither an agent nor an impresario, and finally he consented to an unpaid interview.

Lanza accepted the challenge without objection. To secure him, CBS had agreed to pay Lanza the then-huge sum of $40,000, providing him with two new Chrysler cars as a bonus. The task would be a relatively simple one: Lanza could sing three numbers of his choice, and would appear in a sketch with comedian Fred Clark. Ultimately, however, the Chrysler-sponsored CBS Television Show would turn out to be a comedy of errors.

The television spectacular was scheduled for September 30th, 1954. As the date grew near the thought of appearing on nation-wide television after more than two years of inactivity filled Lanza with renewed anxiety.[10] During his self-imposed exile, rumors had begun to circulate that he had lost his voice. Subsequently, the announcement by CBS that he was making a comeback in the premiere of a nation-wide television show would make world-wide news.

In order to promote the event CBS, in conjunction with the Chrysler Corporation, spared no expense and mounted a massive publicity campaign. They invited 125 members of the press to Los Angeles to view the show, which would be followed by a lavish party to be held on the television sound stage. In a sense Lanza wanted to prove to the public, the press and perhaps even to himself that he could still sing. But the closer he got to performing, the more terrified he became that his voice might let him down, that it would not respond on the night in question.[11]

CBS had told Lanza that he could perform in any way he preferred. He could either sing live on the night of the broadcast or else pre-record his numbers as his co-performer Betty Grable would be doing. The extent of the damage that the MGM experience—in particular the *Student Prince* saga—had inflicted on the fragile Lanza psyche is evident in what followed.

Since he had a choice, he decided that he would pre-record his three numbers along with Betty Grable and her husband, the bandleader and trumpeter, Harry James, who were the other two headliners in the show.

Such was the extent of his anxiety after more than two years of inactivity, however, that Lanza made the extraordinary decision to mime to some of his old recordings.

To add to his problems, he also felt self-conscious about his appearance due to the massive amount of weight he had put on during the months of constant eating and drinking. In order to try and get into shape, at least marginally, for his television debut he had no alternative but to revert back to his crash diet routine.

On this occasion he decided to enter Las Encinas Hospital in Pasadena where, under the supervision of sanatorium head Dr. F.M. Briggs, he returned to his familiar diet of one grapefruit for breakfast, one boiled egg and black coffee for lunch, and a light snack for dinner. Surprisingly, he also managed to stop drinking. By the time he was due to report to the CBS Studios he had succeeded in reducing from 265 lb (120kg) to 225 lb (102kg). Once again, however, his weight loss had been at the expense of his health.

Feeling edgy and exhausted from the crash diet Lanza proceeded with his misguided plan of using his old recordings, two of which, the Neapolitan song "*Marechiare*," and the aria "*Vesti la giubba*" from *Pagliacci*, had been recorded three and four years earlier respectively, and were available commercially. The third number he chose to "sing," the instantly recognizable "Be My Love," was taken from his radio broadcasts and had also been recorded three years earlier.

Having made what would turn out to be a disastrous decision, it was now a question of practicing the lip-synching to his old recordings, a task he worked on for two weeks with the help of Callinicos.

On the day of the television show, aware that his every move and gesture were being scrutinized by a huge television audience—together with a large contingency of press representatives who were viewing the show on a large television monitor on the adjoining stage—Lanza made a concerted effort to mime convincingly to his old recordings. However, without the help of retakes, to which he could resort when filming in Hollywood, the deception soon became obvious. As it was, he might *just* have got away with it had the story not leaked out that he was lip-synching to his old recordings.

Overnight what had started out as his much-publicized comeback turned into a nightmare. The press had a field day. The morning papers were filled with headlines screaming "Hoax" and "Fraud." *Shower of Stars*—the title of the ill-fated show—

was labelled "Shower of Shellac" by *The Hollywood Reporter*, which also wrote: "Lanza was there but he brought along his voice on disks!"[12]

Not surprisingly, the viewing public felt cheated, while the longstanding rumors that Lanza had lost his voice became a reality, according to the press. His pride hurt by such reports, Lanza reacted to the allegations that he had used old recordings by boasting: "Why should I do a thing like that? I can still out-sing anyone in the world!"[13] While his boast was probably true, the tragedy is that he did not believe it.

In the meantime, CBS complicated matters further by at first denying that Lanza had used old recordings. Then, with the evidence mounting, they were forced to issue a statement in which CBS president J. L. Van Volkenburg not only admitted that virtually everyone from the vice-president down had lied, but proceeded to tell a lie of his own.

Van Volkenburg came up with the story that Lanza was feeling unwell and so weak from dieting that his doctor had forbidden him to sing.[14] The sad truth, of course, was simply that Lanza was terrified of singing, live or otherwise, after such a long period of inactivity and had taken the easy way out. Had he anticipated the rage that followed, he most certainly would have chosen to sing regardless of his fears.

With every newspaper saying that he had lost his voice, there was only one choice for Lanza: he had to prove to the entire world that not only could he still sing, but that his voice was as good as ever. The proof, he decided, would be supplied in a special performance at his Beverly Hills home for selected members of the press.

Four days after the television fiasco Lanza, accompanied at the piano by his sometime-coach Giacomo Spadoni, sang for fifteen members of the press that included Bob Thomas, Paul Price, Hollywood gossip columnists Sheilah Graham, Louella Parsons, James Bacon, and his old friend and staunch supporter Hedda Hopper. Most of them had come convinced that they would be hearing only the threads of what had been a magnificent voice.

After extending a cordial welcome to all present in the huge lounge-room of his rented Beverly Hills mansion, a fairly relaxed Lanza proceeded to captivate the press with his renditions of three operatic arias. He sang *"Che gelida manina"* from *La Bohème* in the original key with a stunning high C, together with *"Un tal gioco"* and *"Vesti la giubba"* from *Pagliacci*. In between numbers he explained to his audience the meaning of each aria, bringing to a close the impromptu recital with his signature tune, "Be My Love."

At the end of the unusual concert the journalists, photographers and press agents broke into spontaneous applause. The consensus was that vocally Lanza had nothing to worry about. The incredulous journalists could not understand why he had mimed on the TV show. Pressured for an explanation, Lanza extricated himself from the difficult situation by repeating what CBS had stated publicly and resorting to the time-worn excuse that he had been under doctor's orders not to sing because the dieting had weakened him too much.[15]

The news-making tragicomic saga of Lanza's television debut had a further surprise in store. Ironically, because of the fantastically high ratings that the first show had registered, CBS invited Lanza to appear in a second *Shower of Stars* spectacular and advanced him another $40,000, which he promptly handed over to the Government as part payment for his back taxes.

The second show, which took place on October 28, 1954, less than a month after the first disastrous appearance, was planned so that there would be no question that Lanza was actually singing. It proved to be quite an ordeal.

Aware once again that the huge television audience would be weighing every note that he sang, and that his entire future career depended on this single appearance, Lanza was very nervous.[16] Facing the cameras as he stepped out on the stage, his fear was palpable. Then, having overcome his initial terror, Lanza—with the support of Spadoni conducting the orchestra—proceeded to conquer both audience and critics alike with his splendid singing of the aria *"E lucevan le stelle"* from *Tosca*.

He had won the battle. He had managed to overcome his overwhelming fear and accomplish his first live singing in almost four years. As the applause died down, a slightly more relaxed Lanza introduced his next and final number, the beautiful "Some Day" from *The Vagabond King*, which he ended with a sustained high A.

As nervous and uncomfortable as he obviously was during the entire ordeal, there is no doubt that once he started to sing Lanza was in total control. Viewing the surviving kinescope of the show, there is no evidence of nerves affecting his performance. Lanza's phrasing is brilliant, his tone round and well-projected, and his diction in both English and Italian difficult to surpass. This is not a TV or movie tenor. This is an operatic tenor. Watching this appearance today reinforces the sense of loss, and the queasy certainty that here was a tenor who was wasting his great talent in second-rate films and television shows.

23—THE LAS VEGAS FIASCO

AL TEITELBAUM'S FIRST ASSIGNMENT as Mario Lanza's manager had not exactly been a success. His next move in attempting to handle Lanza's career would prove an even bigger disaster.

After Lanza had shown conclusively that he could still sing, a number of offers began coming in. One in particular interested Lanza. This was an offer from Warner Brothers to film *Serenade*, the steamy novel by James M. Cain, whose other work included *The Postman Always Rings Twice, Double Indemnity*, and *Mildred Pierce*, all of which had been filmed successfully. Lanza had read *Serenade* following the suggestion of his old friend Edmond O'Brien, who thought it would be an ideal role for him, and the tenor had fallen in love with the possibility of making a film out of it.[1]

The announcement that Lanza was to star in *Serenade* was made by Warners in December 1954, but it would take several months and countless script alterations before the actual start of filming. In the meantime there was still the problem of Lanza's debt to the government for the unpaid income tax. As a goodwill gesture Jack Warner, who was aware of the state of Lanza's finances, offered to advance him $1000 a week, beginning January 1, 1955. Ultimately Lanza would be paid $150,000, plus 35% of the domestic gross and 40% of the foreign gross for *Serenade*.

While he waited for the *Serenade* script to be completed, Teitelbaum came up with an offer for a two-week engagement at the New Frontier Hotel in Las Vegas. It was not the first time that Las Vegas had tried to get the tenor to perform there. For more than a year he had been receiving offers from various hotels.[2] Even though Lanza knew that several important artists had performed in Las Vegas, including some of the opera greats such

190

as soprano Helen Traubel, heldentenor Lauritz Melchior, bass Ezio Pinza and baritone Robert Merrill, he had been reluctant to accept. He felt that his voice did not belong in a gambling city nightclub.[3]

The New Frontier management, however, was not easily discouraged. They were determined to secure him for the opening of their newly built two-million-dollar nightclub, the luxurious Venus Room. With all the controversy that had surrounded Lanza in recent years, it would indeed be a coup if The New Frontier succeeded in securing Lanza to open for them.

However, Lanza had his mind set on *Serenade*, and he continually rejected attempts to lure him to Las Vegas until the management of the New Frontier responded with the staggering sum of $100,000 for a two-week engagement, an unheard-of amount at the time. It was in fact far more than anybody had ever been paid for singing in Las Vegas.[†] Lanza, pressed as always for money, finally accepted.

Apart from his desire to repay the IRS debt, Lanza was by this stage hoping to buy a home for his wife and four children. Since coming to Los Angeles six years earlier, they had lived in a succession of rented homes in Beverly Hills and Bel Air. In a couple of instances they had even been sued for damages that the children had caused to the properties. Now, with the addition to the family of their latest child Marc, who was born a few months earlier on May 11, 1954, they felt the need to settle down in a place that they could call their own.[4]

With the money he would receive from the Las Vegas engagement, together with what Warner Bros would pay him for making *Serenade*, Lanza could at last afford to buy a home.

In order to prepare in peace for the Las Vegas engagement and work on the music he would sing in *Serenade*, Lanza, in typical disregard for his limited finances, decided to rent a luxurious house for $3000 a month in the familiar surroundings of Palm Springs.

Here he would spend the next three months rehearsing both the numbers that he would be singing at the New Frontier and

---

[†]That same year, for an engagement at the Sands Hotel, baritone Robert Merrill was paid $10,000 a week.

the operatic arias that he would be recording for *Serenade*. He was joined by his friend Ray Sinatra, who had last worked with him three years earlier on the weekly radio programs, and who would be conducting the orchestra at the New Frontier. Maestro Giacomo Spadoni would also be in Palm Springs in order to continue the work they had been doing for the past two months on the operatic arias for *Serenade*. Unlike other tenors, he would also have to look the part for his Las Vegas engagement. In order to meet expectations, he once again submitted his body to severe dieting and strenuous exercise.

Once in Palm Springs, Lanza began to relax. He not only had ample time in which to prepare for his forthcoming commitments, but he could also spend time with his wife and play with his four children, to whom he was devoted. His weight had again increased—to 260 lb (119kg)—and he needed to lose approximately 50 lb (22.6kg). Ignoring the damage he was doing to his health, Lanza again began a program of stringent dieting and exhausting exercise that would ensure he would meet the deadline by the time he was due to leave for Las Vegas.

On Monday April 4, 1955, four days before the opening, the tenor and his entire entourage of twelve, which consisted of his wife and four children, two nurses, his manager Al Teitelbaum, his press agent Bob Lewin, his MCA agent Arthur Parks and Lanza's coach, Maestro Giacomo Spadoni, arrived at Las Vegas station and descended from the Union Pacific streamliner that they had boarded in San Bernardino.

Looking fit and healthy despite the weeks of gruelling exercise and stringent dieting, Lanza greeted the local reporters, posed for the photographers with his wife and children and appeared to be in excellent spirits. He willingly stayed on to answer a barrage of questions from the press before leaving to settle into the luxurious quarters that the New Frontier's management had put at his disposal.

That day there was a scheduled rehearsal of the numbers he was to sing for the show with Ray Sinatra. When he failed to appear, the hotel management began pressing Sinatra for an explanation. "Mario has a slight cold,"[5] the conductor told the hotel's entertainment director Sam Lewis. Sinatra informed Lewis that since they had rehearsed all the music in Palm Springs it did not matter if Lanza was unable to prepare on this occasion. All he needed to do, Sinatra told Lewis, was to see the stage before the start of the show so that he could get the feel of the room.

If Lewis had been temporarily reassured by Sinatra's explanation, he became increasingly panicky as opening night approached and there was still no sign of Lanza. Lewis had arranged to fly more than 100 reporters to Las Vegas for the highly publicized opening that would mark Lanza's nightclub debut. He had also arranged for an elegant cocktail party to be held on the eve of the opening.

The guests included some famous names from show business such as Robert Young, Ann Miller, Jimmy Durante and Sonja Henie, but the main attraction—the opening night star—was missing. It was left to Lanza's press agent Bob Lewin to come up with an explanation.

Lewin calmly addressed the guests and informed them that Lanza was not present at the cocktail party because he had caught a little cold while standing on the station platform talking to the local reporters on the day he arrived. However, he assured them that Lanza would be fully recovered for the opening of the show on the following night.[6]

Much to the dismay of everyone concerned, Lanza would be far from all right on opening night. Whether his illness was real or imagined, Lanza had stayed in his suite virtually since his arrival and had not been seen by anyone apart from his family, his associates and the occasional servant. In the meantime, as the word spread around Las Vegas that Lanza had a "cold," bookmakers were offering odds of eight to five that the tenor would not appear.[7]

On the morning of the opening, Lanza woke up and insisted that his throat was sore. He mentioned it to his wife, who instead of reassuring him as she had often done in the past, accused him of being up to his old tricks, telling Lanza that there was really nothing wrong with him.[8] Betty's response to the obviously frightened singer only made matters worse. In a state of panic Lanza called his friend, screenwriter Ben Hecht, who had visited him in Palm Springs and had come to Las Vegas especially to see him perform.

The hard-drinking Hecht was staying at the Sands hotel, and

when the agitated singer told him that he feared he might not be able to sing that night, Hecht suggested that he should come over to the Sands Hotel, where they could discuss his problem together over a drink.[9] It was all that Lanza needed. Now instead of facing the reality of the situation—a reality reinforced by Betty's confrontation with her husband—he could escape from his terrifying ordeal by having a drink with a friend that he could confide in.

Over the hours that followed the two men drank champagne together with the only interruptions being provided by the visits to Hecht's room of columnist Louella Parsons and Lanza's manager Al Teitelbaum.[10]

On finding Lanza drunk, a panicky Teitelbaum managed, somehow, to convince him to come back to the New Frontier. There was still time enough for Lanza to sleep and sober up for the opening. Back in his suite at the hotel, Lanza dismissed Teitelbaum and headed for the bedroom where, in a desperate attempt to forget the reality of the moment, he reached for a bottle of his wife's sleeping tablets. He was still in a deep sleep at six in the evening when Teitelbaum came back to Lanza's suite and tried to awaken him. It was then that Teitelbaum, noticing the bottle of Seconal on the bedside table, became alarmed and called for a doctor.[11]

Dr. John McDaniels, head of the Las Vegas Hospital, answered the call from the hotel and instructed Teitelbaum to get Lanza out of bed and force him to walk. He reassured him by telling him that he would be arriving as soon as possible. In the meantime all efforts to awaken Lanza were proving negative, and on his arrival Dr. McDaniels proceeded to give Lanza an injection which caused the singer to vomit the formidable combination of champagne and barbiturates he had ingested. The injection, however, failed to awaken him as by now his system had assimilated the barbiturates.[12]

When Betty, who had taken the children out for the day, came back to the suite, feeling a little guilty about the way she had behaved, she became distraught upon learning what had happened during her absence.[13]

As the hour for the premiere was approaching, the hotel's management was becoming frantic and desperation was in the air. Half an hour before opening time Dr. McDaniels declared that Lanza would be unable to appear. The reason given was acute respiratory infection and laryngitis.[14] Unaware of the drama taking place in Lanza's suite, the opening was proceeding as scheduled in the Venus room. As the orchestra started to play the opening overture and a voice was heard announcing "Presenting a musical review starring Mario Lanza," no one in the audience suspected that the tenor would not be appearing.

Then, as the first production number began, word spread like wildfire. Reporters left their tables and rushed to the nearest phone to call their respective offices. The show proceeded with comedian Larry Storch doing his routine. Then Jimmy Durante, who knew Lanza from the days at MGM, walked slowly onto the stage. In a sad voice he began: "I went up to Mario's room and tried to see him, but he was unconscious and under an oxygen tent. He is a very sick boy."[15] He had hardly finished speaking when bedlam broke loose. The tables emptied and the guests headed in all directions. The show only resumed when singer Mindy Carson and dancer Ray Bolger, who were both in the audience, offered to give their services while Jimmy Durante ad-libbed a few numbers.

In the meantime a furious Sam Lewis was screaming at Dr. McDaniels to sober up Lanza so that he could at least appear for the late show that same night. The doctor tried to explain to Lewis that the problem was not the alcohol, but the barbiturates that the singer had ingested. Lewis, however, was in no mood for explanations and yelled that Lanza had better be on stage for the second show "or else."[16] In the end Lewis had to accept the inevitable. Lanza would not be appearing. For the second show Lewis was able to secure Frankie Laine as a substitute for Lanza.

Aware that it had a frontline story on its hands the press was relentless and pressed Sam Lewis for an answer as to why Lanza had not at least made an attempt to appear for the second show. There was no satisfactory answer. The truth was that throughout the chaos Lanza had continued to sleep soundly, finally awakening the next morning and complaining that he still had a sore throat, but with no idea of what had happened the night before.

A few hours later, during a stormy press conference, Sam Lewis announced that the hotel had cancelled Lanza's 100,000-dollar engagement. Once more the press had a field day with headlines such as "Lanza Ducks Out On Las Vegas Opening"[17] and "Lanza Can't Sing For His $50,000 A Week."[18]

Some of the reporters such as Louella Parsons came to the singer's defense: "What a pitiful disaster to happen to an artist with such a great voice!" she wrote, adding: "He did have a sore throat. I saw him twice and both times he was very hoarse and his throat was sore." Then getting closer to the truth, she added: "However, it could have been psychosomatic. He suffers from an overwhelming clutching terror that he may get up to sing and nothing will come out."[19]

Back in Los Angeles Lanza defended himself as best he could. In reply to the reporters questioning him about his failure to appear, the tenor snapped: "I've never in my life heard so much fuss over laryngitis. You'd think I purposely threw away a hundred thousand dollars just to deprive my wife and children of the money. The hotel got $200,000 worth of publicity while I was losing the $100,000 I needed."[20]

A final semi-comical twist to the entire saga was provided when reports started to emerge stating that Lanza had insured himself for $100,000 with Lloyds of London in the event he would be unable to appear.[21]

The entire affair would not be resolved until the following September when the New Frontier issued a lawsuit against Lanza for $125,000 which included $10,000 that they had advanced him and which the singer had already spent as a down-payment on the home he had purchased in Bel Air. Lanza countersued and the matter was finally settled with the tenor agreeing to pay back the $10,000 he had been advanced plus an extra $3,900 in incidental expenses. [22]

24—BACK TO FILMS

SINCE THE BREAK WITH MGM, a number of films had been mentioned at various times as possible Lanza vehicles. Regardless of the adverse publicity that followed *The Student Prince* episode, or perhaps because of it, Lanza was still a big name and the film studios had not dismissed the possibility of signing the tenor. The bad publicity Lanza had been receiving had made him a controversial figure—an enigma—and as such they believed the public would be curious to see him again on the screen.

The subsequent failure by Lanza to sing on his first television show and Las Vegas opening, however, had caused some of the studios to have second thoughts. Possible projects mentioned prior to the CBS and Las Vegas fiascos had included remakes such as Paramount's *The Vagabond King*, as well as the Grace Moore hit *One Night of Love*, now re-titled *Debut* and *First Night* for Columbia. Other possibilities were *Carousel* for 20ᵗʰ Century Fox, a filmed version of Puccini's opera *La Bohème* and *South Pacific* with Judy Garland. Eventually 20ᵗʰ Century Fox would make *Carousel* with Gordon MacRae while Paramount proceeded to film *The Vagabond King* with the Maltese tenor Oreste Kirkop, whom they had managed to entice from Covent Garden.†

There were no definite projects for Lanza until Warner Brothers announced that they had signed the tenor for the starring role in James M. Cain's *Serenade*. Prior to Warners' announcement, there had been some interest from RKO, which was owned by the eccentric millionaire Howard Hughes. Upon reading the novel Lanza had mentioned his interest in filming the book to his attorney Greg Bautzer, who also happened to represent Howard

†The film turned out to be a box office failure and Kirkop, after a brief return to the operatic stage, ended up retiring at the age of 37.

197

Hughes. An admirer of Lanza's, Hughes responded enthusiastically to the proposal, instructing Bautzer to begin negotiations immediately with Warner Brothers for the purchase of the screen rights.[1]

Warners had owned the rights to the novel since it was first published in 1937, but it had taken almost twenty years and attempts from competing studios MGM and RKO, as well as Warners, before the Breen office[†] would approve the script.

Initially Warners had assigned John Twist to adapt a script with the view to casting John Garfield in the lead role. Then, in 1945, Warners had announced that *Serenade* would be filmed with Ann Sheridan and Dennis Morgan co-starring. The project was shelved in August 1946. A revised script was submitted to the Breen office in 1948 and Michael Curtiz was set to direct with Jane Wyman cast in one of the leading roles. Curtiz experienced difficulty in casting the film and the project was once again shelved until Hughes' expression of interest.

Warners' asking price, however, was a staggering $250,000, a sum that seemed exorbitant even to Hughes, and consequently negotiations dragged on indefinitely until, finally, Warners decided that they would make the film themselves.[2]

The task of adapting a suitable script from John Twist's earlier effort was assigned to scenarists Ivan Goff and Ben Roberts. Given that *Serenade* was still considered a somewhat shocking and steamy novel, with its homosexual and religious implications, their task would prove to be a challenging one.

Under the 1950s production code, homosexuality was still a prohibited subject. Faced with this challenge, Goff and Roberts emerged with a carefully laundered version of the James M. Cain book. They split the original novel's homosexual manager into two characters in the film: an acid-tongued impresario (played superbly by Vincent Price), and a high society "bitch," portrayed equally well by Joan Fontaine. The character of Juana, a Mexican prostitute in the novel, was transformed into the respectable daughter of a famous bullfighter, played in the film by the Spanish actress Sarita Montiel.

[†]Joseph I. Breen headed the Breen office—Hollywood producers' organ of self-censorship, set up to support the production code and prevent Hollywood films from glorifying crime or immorality.

Other changes were equally drastic. Arguably the novel's most famous moment—a torrid act of lovemaking between Juana and the singer behind a church altar—was substituted with a scene of Lanza singing Schubert's "Ave Maria" while kneeling next to Montiel.

After further rewriting the script was finally deemed acceptable by the Breen office in August 1955.

Regardless of the effect of these changes, however, *Serenade* is an underrated film, worthy of more serious consideration than it has received in the past. Lanza makes a concerted effort to act, and is at times decidedly impressive. Yet under Anthony Mann's disappointing direction Lanza often overacts, a fact that contributes to the film's unevenness. Mann's effort is surprisingly routine and flat for a director of his caliber. In fairness to him, however, it must be said that he spent a great deal of time with Lanza, helping the tenor regain the confidence he needed after his prolonged period of inactivity.[3]

The other contributing factor to Mann's uninspired direction may well have been the affair that took place during production between the 49-year-old director and 27-year-old Montiel.[†] Nevertheless, Mann was patient and caring in guiding the tenor during the 12-week production, later commenting that Lanza was "a nice guy with a world of charm."[4]

Apart from feeling uneasy about the prospect of facing the cameras after a four-year absence from the sound stages, Lanza missed his wife and children greatly during the five weeks of shooting in Mexico. He felt lonely and not a little afraid of the outcome of the film in which, for the first time, he was playing a dramatic role.[5]

After the bitter battle with MGM over *The Student Prince*, Lanza needed the pampering and reassurance that he was getting at Warners, not only from Mann, but also from studio head Jack Warner.

Having already advanced the tenor part of his salary, Warner had also reaffirmed his faith in Lanza by releasing a statement to the press, following the Las Vegas fiasco, confirming that Warners would go ahead with the filming of *Serenade*.[6]

[†]The couple would later marry.

Serenade provides considerably more than the usual paper-thin plots of Lanza's films. Musically, it contains some of the finest material that the tenor recorded. Lanza was at his vocal best, displaying a voice that was rounder and darker than it had ever been. Scenarist Ben Roberts called it "The voice of our time," [7] while Co-Scenarist Ivan Goff described its effect on first hearing it: " The voice was pure. The timbre of his voice was such that it became metallic—in a beautiful way—and it would bounce off the walls unless the room was acoustically right. The walls shook."[8]

Furthermore, the choice of music for the film was interesting, and included some of the less familiar operatic arias in the repertoire. When the head of RCA Victor Emmanuel Sachs heard the soundtrack of *Serenade* he remarked, "Throw out everything else and stick to this. The man is a musical phenomenon."[9] Lanza's solid preparation with vocal coach Spadoni and conductor Ray Heindorf, head of Warner's music department, is also evident in the tenor's excellent renditions of the arias *"Di rigori armato"* from *Der Rosenkavalier, "Amor ti vieta"* from *Fedora* and *"O Paradiso"* from *L'Africana*. There is also a good rendering of *"Lamento di Federico"* from *L'Arlesiana*, together with passable versions of *"Nessun dorma"* from *Turandot* and *"Di quella pira"* from *Il Trovatore*. The latter, though sung as a concert version, is incorrectly presented in full costume as if it were part of an operatic performance.

Lanza also gives excellent performances of Schubert's "Ave Maria" and the perennial *"Torna a Surriento."* The remaining numbers consist of a fine *"La danza"* by Rossini and a passable rendition of the love duet from Act 1 of *La Bohème* with soprano Jean Fenn. There are also two songs, "Serenade" and "My Destiny," written especially for the film by Sammy Cahn and Nicholas Brodszky in an uninspired attempt to repeat the success of the two previous million-sellers, "Be My Love" and "Because You're Mine."

The songs were obviously aimed at the Hit Parade charts, with "Serenade" reaching number nine in Britain, despite a substandard rendition by Lanza.[†]

[†]The same year Lanza scored a minor hit in America with "Earthbound," which stayed in the charts for eight weeks during October and November of 1956.

Of the two popular numbers, "My Destiny" is the better song. Lanza recorded two versions of it and the soundtrack rendition is superior to the version released commercially.

Lanza also sings the title song twice in the movie, with the first—and superior—rendition sung almost *mezza voce*, compared to the commercial version, in which the final high C sounds strained and slightly out of control.

The musical highlight of *Serenade*, however, is the third act monologue "*Dio mi potevi scagliar*" from Verdi's *Otello*. Although Lanza recorded the third act duet, "*Dio ti giocondi, o sposo,*" in its entirety with Metropolitan Opera soprano Licia Albanese, only a small segment was used in the film, while the monologue was given complete. At 34 Lanza was comparatively young to be singing *Otello*, and it is unlikely that he would have attempted to sing the role in the opera house at that stage. Yet the voice—darker, more luscious and ringing than ever—sounds exactly right for the part, while at the same time Lanza's concept of *Otello* is ideally realized.

Under Ray Heindorf's capable direction the tenor holds his own in the lengthy duet with Albanese. It is a thrillingly dramatic performance, notwithstanding the fact that Lanza, à la Corelli, holds on to the High C on the phrase "*Quella vil cortigiana,*" which in Verdi's score is a quaver and should only be held for half a beat. Inexplicably, Heindorf did not correct him. Lanza is even more impressive in the Monologue, which he sings with the appropriate deeply felt intensity, but without the vocal exaggerations and sobs typical of many so-called "great tenors." The Monologue from *Otello* ranks alongside his greatest recordings.

Lanza had met Albanese several years earlier after attending one of her concerts in Los Angeles. On that occasion he had gone back stage to congratulate her and exchange a few words. Now that they were to work together, Albanese would have the opportunity to become acquainted with both Lanza the singer and the man during the 25 days she would spend with him on the set of *Serenade*. She would later remark on the experience.

I had heard all sorts of stories about Mario. That his voice was too small for the stage, that he couldn't learn a score, that he couldn't sustain a full opera, in fact that he couldn't even sing a full aria, that his recordings were made by splicing together various portions of an aria. None of it is true! He had the most beautiful lirico spinto voice. It was a gorgeous, beautiful, powerful voice. I should know because I sang with so many tenors. He had everything that one needs. The voice, the temperament, perfect diction. He also had an infallible instinct for what was good for his voice and knew exactly how to move on a stage. He was a good actor. I can state categorically that he absolutely never had any vocal or musical problems either in the *Otello* recording I did with him or the other recordings I heard him do. Vocally he was very secure. All he needed was coaching. Everything was so easy for him. He was fantastic! I rank him next to Caruso. Next comes Di Stefano, then all the others.[10]

Lanza and Albanese became friends. The soprano spent all the time away from the sound stages in the company of Lanza, his wife and children and his parents. Albanese recalled the time spent in Los Angeles with the Lanzas.

> You know they said he used to get drunk. I never saw him drunk during the more than three weeks we worked together. He drank wine with his meals and a few times he ordered scotch, but when I told him not to because he would ruin his beautiful voice he listened to me and didn't drink it! His wife Betty was so lovely. This talk about her taking drugs. I didn't see any of that.[11]

Albanese was not accustomed to Hollywood routines. The long strenuous hours the actors have to work, getting up at 4 a.m. and leaving the studio at 8 p.m., were completely foreign to a soprano used to theater hours where singers often sleep until noon or later. "We worked so hard on the movie," she recalled. "It was insane, pure madness."[12] Albanese often felt exhausted and would plead with Lanza to allow her to sleep.

> At night we'd go to Mario's house and sometimes with Betty and his parents we'd still be there at 2 a.m. and I'd say to Mario: "I have to get some sleep otherwise I'll look a mess tomorrow even with make-up."[13] Albanese recalled Lanza's amusing imitations of other tenors. "He was incredible! He could imitate any tenor! He would do Martinelli,† Caruso, Gigli and Del Monaco, but he wouldn't do Di Stefano. "Di

†A home recording of Lanza imitating Martinelli singing "*M'appari*" from *Marta* has become a minor classic among Lanza aficionados.

Stefano's voice is light and velvety and mine is too dark for that. Gigli is easier [to imitate] than Di Stefano because he had a little more ring," he'd say. He was right because Mario's voice was a darker voice, closer to that of Caruso.[14]

Lanza would bombard Albanese with questions. He was eager to know all she could tell him about her many singing partners in an illustrious career that had spanned twenty-one years, including the last fifteen at the Metropolitan Opera in New York.

From her debut as Butterfly at the Lirico in Milan in 1934, Albanese had sung at most of the important Italian theaters, including La Scala (in 1935), and several of the important international ones such as Covent Garden, San Francisco and Chicago. Her big break had come in 1938 when she recorded Mimi opposite the Rodolfo of Beniamino Gigli in *La Bohème*, a role she repeated the following year at La Scala again with Gigli.

Albanese knew that Lanza was supposed to have sung *Andrea Chénier* in San Francisco in 1950. "He would have been an absolutely marvelous Chénier,"[15] she said, and often questioned the tenor about his absence from the opera stage. At ease in the company of the soprano Lanza opened up to her, confiding that he suffered from stage fright, but that he was trying to overcome it. Albanese told him what he must have known from the start, urging him to abandon Hollywood for a career in opera in Italy.

He went to Italy and we finally lost touch with each other. The letters stopped, but sometimes he would phone me and we would reminisce about the time we spent together working on *Serenade*. Then I remember being in Italy and seeing what turned out to be his last movie, *For the First Time*. I left for America and it was on the ship that I heard the terrible news that he had died. It was such a tragedy. A great loss. To me he was not a complicated man. He had a great voice and a big soul. He was marvellous company, and he was a gentle man. I am sorry we never sang together in the opera house.[16]

Work on *Serenade* began with five weeks location work in Mexico, primarily in the beautiful 16th century town of San Miguel de Allende. Other sequences were filmed on a 200-year-old hacienda owned by the bullfighter Pepe Ortiz and located just outside San Miguel, and the church of San Felipe Neri. The latter is the setting for Schubert's "Ave Maria" in the sequence in which Lanza, thanks to his newfound love for Juana, finds the voice he had lost.

Filming began with Lanza weighing in the vicinity of 260 lb (118 kg). Producer Henry Blanke thought that since Lanza was playing a singer who had lost his voice and was in the depths of despair following a failed love affair, his weight and appearance were appropriate to the role he was playing. Blanke was convinced that an overweight Lanza with overlong hair towering on top of his head—very much the look in the fifties—would be more realistic. [17] Although Lanza would lose 60 lb (23 kg) by the completion of the film, the result is that in *Serenade* he resembles a typical tenor rather than the matinee idol of his MGM days.

The film alternates between some splendid sequences and scenes that are frankly ridiculous. In one example of the latter, Lanza arrives at his first singing lesson and begins by attacking a high C in full voice. The scene is pure Hollywood and is obviously designed to show off Lanza's high C, but the reality is that no respectable singing teacher would have a pupil start a lesson in such a fashion.

Another sequence that highlights the musical shortcomings of Hollywood is one in which Lanza auditions for the part of Don Ottavio in *Don Giovanni,* immediately after he has sung *Otello*. It is certainly stretching credibility to suggest that a singer would sing a dramatic role such as *Otello*—which requires a dramatic or, at the very least, a *lirico spinto* voice—and then approach a light lyric role such as Don Ottavio.

Another great soprano was briefly to become part of Lanza's life during the making of *Serenade*: Renata Tebaldi. The soprano had made her American debut five years earlier as *Aida* in San Francisco and her Metropolitan debut, in January 1955, as Desdemona opposite the *Otello* of Mario Del Monaco. In October of the same year, having already sung in San Francisco and on her way to the Metropolitan via Los Angeles and Chicago, Tebaldi was singing one performance of Aida at the Shrine Auditorium in Los Angeles and while there expressed a desire to meet Lanza. The tenor had finished location work in Mexico for *Serenade* and was now completing filming at Warner's Studios in Burbank, Los Angeles. Lanza greatly admired Tebaldi, and was overjoyed when informed that she wanted to meet him. Arrangements were made for the two singers to meet at Warner's Studios. Knowing that Lanza was born in America, Tebaldi was surprised to find that he was so typically Italian. "He greeted me in a truly exuberant, Latin fashion,"[18] she later said.

Accompanied by Lanza, Musical Director Ray Heindorf and the film's producer Henry Blanke, Tebaldi attended a specially arranged screening of the musical sequences from *Serenade*. "At the end of the showing," Heindorf recalled, "Tebaldi was so overcome by Mario's singing that she was moved to tears, and embraced him fondly."[19]

Lanza immediately extended an invitation to Tebaldi to meet his wife and children, and the two singers spent a memorable evening at Lanza's recently purchased luxurious 32-room home in Bel Air. A number of selected friends, including Maestro Giacomo Spadoni, were invited for the occasion and Lanza's parents were also present. During the evening Tebaldi asked Lanza if he would sing.

With Spadoni at the piano the tenor obliged and once again—as had been the case with Koussevitzky, Toscanini, Tito Schipa, Licia Albanese and so many others—the effect of Lanza's voice on Tebaldi was overwhelming. The soprano sat in total disbelief as the glorious notes came pouring forth from Lanza's throat. Soon Tebaldi was standing next to Lanza and the two of them spent the remainder of the evening singing together. Tebaldi was lavish in her praise. She told Lanza he had the finest natural tenor voice she had ever heard.[20] Then she asked him the inevitable question: "Why on earth aren't you singing in opera?"[21] On her return to Italy Tebaldi extolled the glories of the Lanza voice to Oliviero De Fabritis, urging the noted conductor to help bring the tenor to the operatic stage.[22]

For her part Tebaldi, in addition to possessing a remarkably beautiful voice, was also an attractive woman who had received a number of offers to make films in America. However, she had not even considered them when told the terms and conditions a film contract would entail. "The film contracts stipulated that I would have to lose heaven knows how many kilos in weight," she recalled, "and I could not have undertaken drastic diets without risking damaging my health."[23]

As an established singer at the peak of a brilliant operatic career, it was far easier for Tebaldi to refuse the offers from the film capital. [24]

Back on the soundstages at Warner Studios, Lanza was finding the task of working on his first film in four years a difficult one. The MGM debacle had undermined his confidence and unlike the old Lanza—the extrovert that was always the life of the party—he now tended to keep to himself. During breaks in filming, he would spend much of his time in the six-thousand-dollar dressing room that Jack Warner had assigned to him. He was eating his lunch there now instead of joining the rest of the cast in the studio dining room.[25]

Initially, relations with the other actors were a little strained, particularly those with Joan Fontaine. Prior to the start of production the notoriously difficult actress had expressed terror at the thought of working with someone reputed to be so temperamental. Her fears turned out to be groundless. Notwithstanding the fact that the only time they spent together was while they were filming, and that the shooting schedule was most sporadic, Fontaine did not experience any problems in working with Lanza.[26] He in turn spent more of his time with the other female lead, Sarita Montiel, who was making only her second American film after *Vera Cruz* the year before, in which she had co-starred with Gary Cooper and Burt Lancaster.

The fiery Montiel experienced great difficulty with the English dialogue, becoming so tense in front of the cameras that on one occasion she collapsed from sheer exhaustion. Lanza offered to coach her with her dialogue, working patiently with the actress and reassuring her about her delivery. By the time the film was nearing completion Montiel commented: "I am very sad. I do not want to finish this picture. Mario is a gentleman. I have worked with other men who are not, but I am a lady, and Mario, he treats me always like a lady."[27]

This may well have been the case by the time they had returned to the Warner Studios in Burbank, but certainly not during the early stages of filming in Mexico. At the start of production, unaware that Montiel was already involved in a relationship, Lanza had made it quite clear to the stunning actress that he would like to make love to her.[28]

They soon established a good working rapport and Montiel was quite vocal in telling her friends how much she liked Lanza and what a fantastic voice he had. Had it not been for the fact that by now director Anthony Mann had fallen in love with her, Lanza might have succeeded in his amorous pursuit.[†] With Mann's declaration both Lanza's dream of bedding the actress and Montiel's previous relationship came to an end, even though she remained close to the tenor and continued to work well with him for the duration of filming.

Lanza's rapport with the rest of the cast while working on *Serenade* was good. He got along well with Vincent Price, and with fellow actors Joseph Calleja—who had started his career as an operatic singer and was playing his singing teacher—character actor Harry Bellaver who played his cousin, and Italian-born character actors Frank Puglia and Silvio Minciotti.

A young Italian-American actor named Vincent Edwards (Vincent Zoina) had recently become friendly with Lanza, and was given a small part in the film courtesy of the tenor's intervention with producer Henry Blanke. Edwards, who would attain considerable fame in the 1960s in the long-running television series *Ben Casey*, saw Lanza simply as a little boy who enjoyed having fun and living life to the hilt.[29] Edwards' was certainly a perceptive description of the tenor. In many ways he *was* a little boy, but by now a much-troubled one. [30]

Vincent Price, in common with Joan Fontaine, had read numerous stories about Lanza's terrible temper, but he had this to say: "I've learned by now not to believe such and such about anyone until I meet them. As for Mario, as has been the case so many times in my career, I met a star who wasn't at all what I expected."[31]

> Mario doesn't have a big ego. He is a man who happens to own one of the greatest voices of our time. For him to pretend he is unaware of this would be foolish and unbelievable. There's a big difference between being aware of your talent and being an egotist, believe me! [32]

Price was also generous in his praise of Lanza's acting per-

[†]In a 2005 interview, Montiel confirmed that had she been available at the time, she would have agreed to having an affair with Lanza.

207

formance in *Serenade*: "He has done a thorough job, a sincerely conscientious one. He's so sincere he is almost dedicated, like a New York actor, and what's more he's as great an actor as he is a singer."[33]

While few would agree with Price's assessment of Lanza's acting ability, Price maintained his appreciation of the tenor in an interview with this author more than twenty years later.

> I always thought that Mario was ahead of his time. He was really quite gifted, but all they cared about was how much he weighed. He used to torture himself to take off weight. If *Serenade* were made today it wouldn't matter what he weighed.[34]

Critical response to *Serenade* was reasonable, but although it had a successful run at Radio City Music Hall in New York, where it opened on April 1, 1956 as the Easter attraction, it ultimately failed to show a profit. Exactly why is open to speculation. By 1956 the music scene had altered considerably with rock 'n' roll and calypso replacing the melodious ballads sung by Crosby, Doris Day, Nat King Cole and others.

Due to this change, the Hollywood musical was also in its last days. Although the studios would continue to produce a number of big successes, the majority of these were based on proven Broadway hits such as *Guys and Dolls, Oklahoma, Carousel, The King and I* and *The Pajama Game*. Another likely factor for the relative failure of *Serenade,* however, was the combination of a melodramatic story revolving around a heavy operatic theme.

While audiences in general would probably walk out of a cinema humming such familiar operatic arias as "*La donna è mobile*" or "*Che gelida manina*" they had never heard of "*Di rigori armato,*" "*E la solita storia,*" or "*Dio mi potevi scagliar.*" In other words, this was a film for opera connoisseurs. What the general public probably wanted was more of the simple formula that Joe Pasternak had been providing for years at MGM; namely, a light story with Lanza singing such banal songs as "Boom Biddy Boom Boom" and "Tina Lina."

A further contributing factor to the relatively poor box office of *Serenade* was all the adverse publicity Lanza had been receiving in recent years. Certainly, the venomous and sarcastic critical assessment of the film that appeared in *Time* magazine did not help:

> Mario Lanza had a great fall several years ago when he rolled
> off the top of the heap for no apparent reason but his own
> fat—over 250 lb (113.3kg) of it, with an undue proportion
> apparently located in the head. This picture proves that he is
> still the biggest thing in the cine-music business. At singing
> weight of 240 lb (108.8kg), he looks like a colossal ravioli
> set on toothpicks, and his face, aflame with rich living, has
> much the appearance of a gigantic red pepper.[35]

Despite this crude attempt to demolish Lanza, the unnamed
critic was unable to deny the tenor's obvious gift. Lanza's voice
is "as big as ever," the writer went on to say, at the same time
criticizing the tenor for singing everything "as though it were
'Sorrento'—at the top of his lungs."

Overlooked were Lanza's sensitive renditions of the Schubert
"Ave Maria," the Monologue from *Otello*, and the first version
of the film's title song. As for Lanza's singing of *"Torna a
Surriento,"* his rendition could hardly be better. The tenor sings it
with unforced warmth, with the appropriate light and shade,
beautiful phrasing and tops it with a splendid high B natural.

Rival publication *Newsweek*, after noting that the original
novel had been watered down considerably for the screen, reported that *Serenade* "serves, if nothing else, to show that Lanza
is still in possession of that God-given high C."[36]

Overall, reviews were favorable. A.H. Weiler, writing in *The
New York Times*, noted: "Mr. Lanza, who was never in better
voice, makes this a full and sometimes impressive musical entertainment."[37] Meanwhile, the trade paper *Variety* thought that
"Lanza comes off adequately in taking care of the dramatics of
his role and is superb in his singing."[38] P. L. Mannock, writing for
the English publication *Films and Filming*, went further:

> The first picture for three years of the Italian-American tenor
> Mario Lanza reveals that his tremendous voice is as power-
> ful as ever...the Lanza voice almost redeems the childish tem-
> perament of the character, with its sulks and brooding. Lanza's
> moods range from amused arrogance to operatic squirms and
> shudders and the parallel of the *Othello* plot is once more
> utilized. [39]

However, the most perceptive assessment of the tenor's efforts in *Serenade*, came in a lengthy article in the American arts magazine *Saturday Review*. Under the heading "The Metamorphosis of Mario Lanza," Roger Brown wrote:

> Great tenor voices generally come in rather unpresentable male packages...In Mario Lanza MGM found in natural and apparently permanent combination a fine tenor voice, youthful handsome appearance, and friendly unassuming American manners. The combination produced the greatest film success ever attained by a singer of operatic quality. The combination has always been a puzzle. It violates everyone's expectations. The operagoer does not expect so good a voice to be heard from the screen and juke box. The moviegoer is startled by a leading man who sings high C. There is a tendency to get rid of the anomaly by denying one or the other of Mr. Lanza's qualities. Some will have it that he is just another actor whose voice is made to sound good through tricks of engineering...Others are sure that this pleasant young man would like to sing pleasant popular music but is forced to sing opera by highbrow producers. [40]

Brown's perception of the "new" Mario Lanza was further reinforced with this accurate assessment:

> In the recent film *Serenade* it is demonstrated that Mario Lanza is more operatic tenor than film star. The voice has taken over and is running away with the man and his manners...The singer who played *The Great Caruso* has begun to look and to act like Italian tenors everywhere. The changes accomplished in the Lanza appearance and manner are clearly maladaptive from the point of view of the movie star. They will doom him at the box office.

After pointing out the considerable differences between stage and film singing Brown went on to write:

> While he sings he moulds the melodic line with his hands. He cocks his ear to savor a pianissimo, trembles with the beauty of his own tone...He displays an immodest infatuation with his own voice, [he] overacts, postures and strains. These are characteristics incompatible with movie stardom and Hollywood where underplaying is the style.

Brown went on to prophesy what many others were hoping would eventually take place: "The voice of Mario Lanza yearns towards the operatic stage and I dare predict that it will carry him there."

Even so, the tenor's insecurity—combined with the desire to continue earning astronomical sums of money—was ever present, and Lanza would continue to postpone any opera commitments.[41] However, what Brown had said about him, subconsciously at least, must have played a part in his next decision: to leave America for Italy.

25—TRAVEL PLANS

Although the thought of leaving Hollywood and travelling to Italy had been on his mind for years, it took some time to materialize following the completion of *Serenade*. Numerous projects had been mentioned as possible follow-up films. Warner Brothers held an option for a second Lanza film and were toying with two possibilities: one was a modern drama based on a story by the famous screen writer Philip Yordan, the other was a filmed version of the opera *Faust* with either Ezio Pinza or Jerome Hines as Mephistopheles and Eleanor Steber or Nadine Conner as Marguerite.

Other possibilities were a proposed remake for Columbia of *Golden Boy*, the film that had made William Holden a star, a remake of *Phantom of the Opera* (an ironic title for a Lanza film if ever there was one) for Universal, while 20ᵗʰ Century Fox was considering another remake, *Be Mine Tonight*, an early Jan Kiepura film. In the latter, Gina Lollobrigida, at the peak of her popularity, was mentioned as a possible co-star. Director Leo McCarey was also planning a musical version of *Marco Polo* with Lanza, Orson Welles and Ann Blyth.[1]

The project that most interested Lanza, however, was producer Mike Todd's proposal to film a series of complete operas in his own Todd-AO process, which had been used in the extremely successful Oscar-winning film *Around The World In Eighty Days*. Following the relatively poor box office receipts of *Serenade*, however, none of the above came to fruition and, overall, 1956 did not turn out to be a very eventful year for Lanza.

The year had begun on a sour note with Lanza gaining some unexpected publicity when he was called upon to give evidence before a grand jury hearing in a case involving his recently appointed personal manager. Al Teitelbaum had been accused of theft. During the hearing it emerged that Teitelbaum had staged a fake robbery by hiring two ex-convicts to steal $280,000 worth of furs from his exclusive Beverly Hills salon.

In his testimony before the grand jury, Lanza said that he had arrived at his manager's salon shortly after the alleged robbery had taken place and had found a nervous and shaken Teitelbaum, who advised him that there had been a holdup. [2] After a second hearing one month later, Teitelbaum was found guilty of fraud and sentenced to serve one year in prison.

In mid-May Lanza was back at Warner Bros. studios where the year before, under the capable direction of Ray Heindorf, he had recorded the soundtrack of *Serenade*. The sessions with Heindorf had produced some of the tenor's best recordings, with the 126 musicians in the orchestra applauding Lanza after he had completed his recording of "*E la solita storia*" from *L'Arlesiana* in a single take.[3] The intervening months had been relatively quiet with Lanza in good spirits, spending time with his wife and children in the comfort and luxury of their new home.

Serenade's mixed reception—in particular the scathing *Time* magazine review of the film, coupled with its modest ticket sales—plunged Lanza into another period of depression during which he again found escape in drinking.[4] The result of his excessive alcohol consumption is clearly evident in what would turn out to be his worst album. Recorded over five sessions at Warner Bros. studio under the direction of Irving Aaronson[†] his first concept album, *Lanza on Broadway,* was an unmitigated disaster.

The numbers chosen for the album included some of the most beautiful ever written for the musical stage—songs from *South Pacific, Kismet, Kiss Me Kate, Carousel* and what was then the current smash hit on Broadway, *My Fair Lady*. The material should have been ideal for Lanza. Unfortunately, there is not a single thing that can be said in favor of the album.

Lanza gives the impression that he is recovering from a massive series of hangovers. He constantly mis-pitches, bellows and strains, with the voice sounding coarse and unfocused. On the

[†]He had previously worked with Lanza on some of the selections in *The Great Caruso.*

very worst numbers, his singing resembles a hideous parody of the "Lanza style." Selections such as "This Nearly Was Mine" or "September Song" make one wonder why the whole project was not abandoned, or at least postponed to a later date. In any event, even Lanza in peak form might well have found Aaronson' abominable accompaniments an insurmountable task, for the latter's conducting is essentially akin to that of an amateur band-leader. Surprisingly, one of the producers responsible for this fiasco was none other than the conductor Henri René, who a mere three months later would conduct for Lanza a far better album of Broadway and show tunes.

That something was amiss on *Lanza on Broadway* must have seemed evident even to RCA, who took the trouble of adding not only a chorus, but also a huge amount of echo to the original recordings.

The ammunition that this album continues to provide to Lanza's detractors is incalculable. Even more damaging are the large number of Lanza "admirers" who remain oblivious to the album's ghastliness. *Lanza on Broadway,* in fact, has been one of Lanza's most frequently re-released albums, appearing with monotonous regularity under such misleading titles as *Pure Gold.*

Lanza was back in the recording studios in early August. At Republic Studios, under the direction of Henri René, the tenor was back in top voice and over the next four weeks, in five different sessions, recorded a total of 23 numbers. These consisted of seven Christmas Carols, four ballads, two of which were released as singles, and the twelve numbers that would make up the album *A Cavalcade of Show Tunes.*

Apart from inferior arrangements of "Rose Marie," and "Lover Come Back To Me", the *Cavalcade* numbers were beautifully done. Highlights included "Yours Is My Heart Alone" from *The Land of Smiles,* "The Donkey Serenade" from *The Firefly,* and the exquisite "All The Things You Are" from *Very Warm For May.*

By late 1956, a major lifestyle change was looming. The Roger Brown *Saturday Review* article had given the tenor the opportunity to reflect on the future direction of his career. The answer became obvious. It was time to bid farewell to Hollywood and seek a new life in Italy.

As always the primary obstacle to the plan was finding sufficient money to enable Lanza and his family to live in the style to
which they had become accustomed. Initially, Lanza intended to
live in Italy for at least two years, during which time he would
lock up his recently-purchased Bel Air mansion, rent a home in
Rome, send the children to a private school and pay for a coach
to work with him on operatic roles.

The solution to the money question was soon forthcoming.
He would simply make a film in Italy, and that—in addition to
his substantial recording royalties—would provide him with the
necessary income. Despite his best intentions, then, nothing about
his career was going to change except the locale. Lanza was still
a big name in Europe, and a film deal was swiftly negotiated.

In yet another irony, MGM would be involved in the new
venture. By the end of 1956, independent producer Lester Welch
had successfully completed negotiations for a joint co-production between MGM, who would be financing the project, and
the Italian film company Titanus, who would be responsible for
the actual filming.

On paper, at least, the film looked promising. Its bohemian
atmosphere, vaguely reminiscent of '*An American in Paris,*' ap-
pealed to Lanza and Titanus was equally enthusiastic about the
project. Titanus vice president Franco de Simone Niquesa had
visited the tenor in his Bel Air home to discuss the film and in
March 1957 wrote Lanza a letter in which he expressed his gratitude and admiration for the singer:

> I have thought often and with a feeling of great warmth of
> our conversations in California and I look forward with con-
> siderable pleasure to having you here in my country where I
> can repay your courtesy on my home soil...... We are confi-
> dent we are going to make a wonderful motion picture and
> we are relying on you to turn in a great performance, even
> greater than usual, Mario.[5]

Although initially Lanza's old friend and co-star from *The
Toast of New Orleans*, David Niven, was to have co-starred,
Titanus decided to re-write the part and use instead the popular
comic, actor and song writer Renato Rascel, a relative unknown
outside his native Italy. The talented Rascel had won both critical and public acclaim with his masterful performance in a dra-

matic role in the 1952 film *Il Cappotto* (The Overcoat), based on the classic Gogol novel, which had won him a silver ribbon, the Italian equivalent of an Oscar. Italy's newest sex symbol Marisa Allasio, who was being hailed as another Sophia Loren, and who had caused a sensation the previous year in the box office hit *Poveri Ma Belli* (Poor But Handsome), was cast as the female lead.

26—ITALY

By EARLY 1957 the time had arrived for Lanza to embark on the long-awaited journey to the land of his ancestors, where he hoped to fulfil his dream of an operatic career. Leaving America for an extended period had not been an easy decision. He would be leaving behind his parents, whom he adored, and his beautiful Bel Air home, in which he had lived for less than two years.

As for Terry Robinson, Betty had issued an ultimatum: "If he comes you can forget me and the children, as you'll be travelling on your own."[1] Robinson stayed in Los Angeles.

Regardless of the difficulty he had experienced in making the decision, Lanza felt the time had come to leave the city where he had spent the last nine years.[2] Italy, he felt, was now his only hope for a new start. Had he been willing to scale down his standard of living and rely on his recording royalties alone, he could have secured an engagement with one of a dozen opera companies and started to work on a specific score as soon as he arrived in Italy. But that was not his style. Instead Lanza would end up living in a luxurious fifteen-room villa in Rome's most exclusive residential area, the *Parioli*. As well as housing himself, his wife and four children, the villa would be home to nine servants, two dogs, one cat and several canaries. The new film would provide the means to pay for all of this.

Back in Los Angeles arrangements were made for Lanza and his family to travel by train to Chicago to say goodbye to Betty's family. They would then proceed to New York, where they would stay for two days before boarding the Italian liner, Giulio Cesare, which would take them to Naples.

In New York the Lanzas were met by representatives from RCA and MGM, who escorted them to their hotel—the Waldorf

217

Astoria. Here the tenor hosted a lavish dinner for some of the immediate members of his family, together with several friends and associates. He had already bid an emotional farewell to his parents in Los Angeles. Lanza invited all of his relatives from Philadelphia to the dinner, and the evening proved a most poignant one.[3]

While Grandfather Salvatore and Lanza's Aunt Hilda reminisced about the early days when they had first heard Lanza's voice as a teenager, the head of RCA, Emmanuel Sachs, recalled the revolution Lanza had made in popularizing opera with the general public, and the astronomical figures his record sales had reached. Lanza's wife Betty contributed a few little-known anecdotes about her famous husband, including his passion for collecting watches, his fondness for silk shirts and underwear, his aversion to driving and going shopping with her, and his uncanny memory for faces and facts.[4†]

Betty also recalled an incident when Lanza, who loved to play practical jokes, had bought her a very expensive fur for her birthday, placing it in a cardboard box wrapped in cheap paper and tied with a piece of string. Lanza had then placed a cheap fur that he had borrowed from the MGM wardrobe department in the proper box and had it gift-wrapped. On seeing the expensive box, Betty opened it straightaway and was somewhat taken back when she saw its contents. Meanwhile, Lanza managed to keep a straight face as she proceeded to open the second box. On seeing the beautiful fur she embraced her husband and they both roared with laughter. He stopped laughing, however, when he asked her if she had liked the red roses he had also bought her for her birthday. There, hidden in the middle of the bunch, he had placed a very expensive watch. Betty replied that the roses were beautiful and pointed to the table where she had placed them in a vase of water. "You never saw Mario move so fast. He jumped up and pulled the roses out of the vase. His face looked as though he was in shock. Well, he wanted to surprise me, and surprise me he did—and himself too!"[5]

On the morning of the departure RCA organized a cham-

†Though he also had difficulty at times in remembering names and telephone numbers, including his own.

pagne breakfast for Lanza's immediate family and friends, together with a selected number of people from the music and film
world. It was just after midday on Friday, May 17 that an optimistic Lanza left New York and sailed with his family in his luxury
suite on board the liner bound for Naples. He would not see
America again.

The reception that awaited Lanza when he arrived in Naples
11 days later (May 28, 1957) was beyond his wildest dreams and
made him feel instantly at home.[6] The buildings on the bay were
decorated with bunting and streamers and huge banners: "Welcome Mario," "Welcome the great Mario Lanza," and "Welcome to Italy, Mario Lanza" could be seen everywhere. The newspapers wrote: "Caruso's successor has arrived." While still on
board the Giulio Cesare, Lanza was greeted by Renato Rascel,
the popular actor/comedian who would co-star with him in the
new film to be made in Rome, where they were due to start filming in a matter of weeks.

Through his films and recordings Lanza had achieved great
popularity not only in Italy but also in all of Europe, while the
music-loving Neapolitans truly worshipped him. In the previous
year the box office takings in Naples for *Serenade* had been almost twice what they had been in Milan.

As Lanza disembarked from the Giulio Cesare and made his
way down the gangplank with his wife and children, the crowd
at the quayside went wild with excitement. Everyone was calling
out and welcoming him to Italy. Lanza was overwhelmed and
felt renewed optimism about what lay in store for him here.[7]

As he stepped off the gangplank an elderly lady approached
him. She was a personal friend of the Caruso family and for years
had been placing flowers on the tomb of the great singer on specific anniversaries. In a touching gesture she presented Lanza
with a locket that had been in the Caruso family for over 73
years.

The locket contained a photo of Caruso on one side, while on
the reverse side the lady had placed a portrait of Lanza. It was
not until she heard Lanza sing that she felt that finally she had
found a singer worthy of occupying the reverse side of the locket.
As she handed the locket to the surprised singer she told him
simply, "I admire you as I admired him."[8] A visibly moved Lanza

promptly invited her to join him at the reception, which had been planned in his honor at the Internazionale, a beautiful restaurant on the waterfront. Later he presented his elderly admirer with a beautiful bouquet of flowers.

Surrounded by various city dignitaries, a number of people from the music and film world as well as a storm of reporters, photographers and a huge crowd, Lanza and his family were then escorted to the Internazionale. Here Renato Rascel entertained everyone by singing some of his compositions while accompanying himself on the guitar. These included the beautiful "Arrivederci Roma," which would be the title for the film's Italian release.

Following the reception the Lanzas proceeded by train to Rome. Another huge crowd, television cameras, radio reporters and the press were ready to welcome them in the eternal city. As the train approached the platform at Rome Termini Station late that evening Lanza could be seen leaning out of the window and blowing kisses to the crowd, which included fans from as far away as England. As the train came to a stop, Lanza lifted each of his four children in turn to the window and made room for his wife, who had joined him in waving to the enthusiastic crowd. Stepping off the train Lanza was met by Bob Edwards, head of publicity at Titanus Studios. Immediately a flock of reporters surrounded the tenor, bombarding him with questions that he answered as best as he could in both Italian and English, while at the same time attempting to oblige scores of autograph seekers.[9]

It was not until 11 p.m. that Edwards was able to pry Lanza away from the adoring crowd. At that point Lanza noticed a horse and carriage nearby, one of the many that could be seen in Rome. Impulsively, he climbed into it, stood up and started waving at the delighted crowd that had followed him outside the station and was calling out his name and cheering madly. It was almost midnight when he finally made his way to the car and headed for the hotel to join his wife and children, who had long since arrived there.

Initially, the Lanzas stayed at the luxurious Bernini Bristol Hotel, located in the Piazza Barberini with its beautiful central fountain, the *Tritone* by Gian Lorenzo Bernini. They then moved to the even more impressive Excelsior Hotel close to the American Embassy on the Via Veneto, which at the time was the heart of the Dolce Vita. While it was ideal accommodation for a short stay, with four small children running wild, a home had to be found as soon as possible. Within a fortnight Lanza had found the perfect place.

The Villa Badoglio was a mansion that the Italian dictator Benito Mussolini had built as a gift to Field Marshal Pietro Badoglio in recognition of the latter's victories in Abyssinia. An inscription placed above the rear entrance to the villa reads: *Today the 5ᵗʰ of May at 4 p.m. at the head of the victorious troops I have entered Addis Ababa. 1936. 14ᵗʰ year of Fascism.*

The five-storey villa was located at No. 56 Via Bruxelles. The Badoglio family occupied the upstairs quarters, while Lanza and his family lived in the ground floor section comprising 15 rooms, which he rented for the then not indifferent amount of $1,000 a month. [10]

Built on huge grounds near the center of the city, the white marble villa was surrounded by a high stone wall, and was accessible through gigantic wrought-iron gates that opened onto the drive leading up to the main entrance. The grounds were filled with trees and included tennis courts, a large swimming pool and a spacious garage that housed the three Lanza cars, conveniently located under the villa.

The palatial interior, with its marble floors and ceilings and huge Venetian glass chandeliers, was expensively furnished, with the predominant colors being white, gold and deep purple. The villa had mirrored walls and countless bathrooms, including a large one that adjoined the master bedroom. One room housed Lanza's television set and radiogram, while another room had his beautiful grand piano, endless bookshelves fully stacked with books, music scores and the scripts of Lanza's films—all bound with his name and the title of each film stamped in gold leaf. The villa also had a fully equipped gymnasium and a ballroom. This was indeed grand living and the only way Lanza could pay for it was with his lucrative film work.

Lanza would be paid handsomely for his new film, *Seven Hills of Rome*, receiving a fee of $200,000 plus 30% of the gross. Prior to the start of production on the film Lanza, as usual, was short of money, so he was forced to ask producer Lester Welch to advance him $50,000, a figure that Welch agreed to pay him provided he passed the obligatory medical examination by the insurance company doctors. First, however, he would have to submit to a crash diet: he weighed 243 lb (110.2kg) upon arrival in Italy. He checked into the Salvador Mundi Hospital, where he began to follow a drastic weight loss regimen.

On this occasion he was under the supervision of Dr. Albert Simons, reputedly one of Europe's leading dieticians. Dr. Simons' method for losing weight was to inject the patient with the urine of pregnant women to raise the rate of metabolism and burn extra calories. Lanza's daily intake was limited to 500 calories, supplemented with vitamin injections.[11]

His daily lunch consisted of a handful of boiled shrimps and a single *grissino* (bread stick). For supper he would drink a cup of unsweetened coffee and eat some fat-free cheese. Occasionally he would allow himself a steak and a salad with no dressing. In nine days he lost 30 lb (13.6 kg) and by the completion of filming three months later he was down to 169 lb (76.6 kg).

Family and friends had often cautioned him about repeated drastic dieting, even if undertaken under medical supervision. However, the warnings continued to fall on deaf ears. He was still convinced that his physique would protect him.[12] In fact his health was now seriously deteriorating from both a physical and emotional standpoint, and by the final days of filming in August 1957 Lanza looked tired and drawn, in contrast to the heavier but happier-looking man who had landed in Naples three months earlier.

Preliminary work on *Seven Hills of Rome* had begun almost immediately on his arrival in Rome, again pre-recording the musical soundtrack while he was heavy and feeling vocally more secure. To his dismay, however, he discovered that the script Titanus had given him was nothing like the one that had been outlined by Franco de Simone Niquesa back in Los Angeles. "It's a different story and a lousy one,"[13] he told Roy Rowland, who had been assigned to direct the film. Rowland was experiencing difficulties of his own with the new script, which was overlong.

The original had been written by Art Cohn, producer Mike Todd's biographer, who less than a year later was to die in the same aeroplane crash that claimed the life of Todd.

Titanus scenarist Giorgio Prosperi had rewritten the script, basing his work on the play *Sera di Pioggia* (Rainy Evening) by the writer/director Giuseppe Amato. Filming began with the script still being rewritten and altered almost every day. As a result the actors often had to run through the dialogue just before filming.[14]

To director Roy Rowland, a Hollywood veteran since the mid-1930s,[†] it was a highly unorthodox way of working.[15] Fortunately he could rely on assistant director, Mario Russo, who was used to unconventional Italian methods of filming.

There were also linguistic problems to overcome. Lanza went over the dialogue with costars Renato Rascel and Maria Allasio during breaks in the filming. Allasio in particular needed help with her words, having only a smattering of English. It was a hot Rome summer and sitting around waiting to shoot interior scenes in the Titanus studios was an uncomfortable experience. The temperature under the lights on the set often reached 130 degrees.[16]

If the script was a mess to start with, the film had at least one outstanding contributor: cinematographer Tonino Delli Colli.

The remaining production team, mostly from MGM, consisted of the workmanlike, but immensely likable, Roy Rowland* to direct and editor Gene Ruggiero, who had worked on all previous Lanza MGM films. Irving Aaronson was music coordinator and George Stoll was the music supervisor and conductor.

Regardless of script and production problems Titanus president, the aristocratic 37-year-old Goffredo Lombardo,[‡] was convinced that on the basis of Lanza's great popularity the film would be a big hit.

Three weeks into production he sent the tenor a telegram: "I feel confident *Seven Hills of Rome* will be the greatest Lanza picture yet stop. Titanus is extremely proud to produce it. Buon Lavoro."[17]

The female lead, the voluptuous 21-year-old Marisa Allasio, had already made a number of films culminating with her sev-

[†]His films included the musicals *Two Weeks With Love*, *Hit The Deck*, and *Meet Me In Las Vegas*.

[‡]The Neapolitan Lombardo was the son of the founder of the company Gustavo Lombardo and silent film star Leda Gys.

enth appearance in *Poveri Ma Belli* (Poor But Handsome), in which she achieved national stardom.[†] Tough and determined, Allasio was well on her way to international stardom when, a little over a year later, she gave up her career and married Count Francesco Calvi di Bergolo, a nephew of Umberto II, the last king of Italy.

Lanza enjoyed joking and flirting with the young actress despite the constant scrutiny of Allasio's mother, who was determined not to let her recently acclaimed daughter out of her sight.[18]

Filming was briefly interrupted when Lanza accepted an invitation to go to Naples to receive the Enrico Caruso Award from the late singer's youngest son, Enrico Jr. Unbeknownst to Lanza the Machiavellian organizers of the event wanted to combine the presentation of the award, during which Lanza would also be made an honorary citizen of Naples, with a political rally. Lanza let Caruso's son know that he was uneasy about being a pawn in a political event. Enrico Jr. assured him that he had nothing to do with the rest of the proceedings, and told Lanza how much he admired him.[19‡]

Singing had not been part of the event, but standing on stage after his words of thanks for the award and for the recognition he had received, and listening to the thunderous applause, Lanza could hardly refuse the huge crowd a song. He agreed to do just one number from one of his films. When the performance was over, the Lanzas headed straight back to Rome.

Receiving the Caruso award had left Lanza in a strangely reflective and depressed mood. He had been recognized as a great singer by Caruso's own son but here he was back on a movie set making yet another film. Sam Steinman recalled: "The situation was becoming unbearable. The conflict within Mario had reached gigantic proportions. Again he turned to the bottle and for the next two days filming had to be cancelled."[20]

Although Lanza managed to control his drinking during the almost three-month shooting, he would often fortify himself during the long breaks by sipping wine he had disguised in small

[†]The film won her additional notoriety when Pope Pius XII condemned the posters advertising it as overly exciting.

[‡]A few weeks later Caruso's son sent Lanza a postcard from Anacapri on which he wrote: Best Greetings from your most devoted friend, Enrico Caruso Junior.

Coca Cola bottles.[21]

Meanwhile, the self-centered Rascel, who could be extremely difficult to work with, took an instant liking to Lanza. Rascel saw through the façade, the bravado that the tenor was forever putting on in order to protect himself. At first he was baffled and was unable understand how Lanza could drink wine when they were working in such extreme heat. But then Rascel understood that for Lanza it was a way of giving himself a boost, a little temporary euphoria to get him through the day.[22] In all likelihood, it was also a way of helping him overcome the reality that he was making yet another film and, in all probability, not a very good one.

In general filming proceeded smoothly. Lanza did manage to cause several headaches for producer Lester Welch and Titanus chief of production Silvio Clementelli. Characteristically, Lanza had promised work as extras to a number of people. Word must have spread quickly about his generosity. His reputation for giving exorbitant tips to waiters, taxi drivers, concierges and others was already well established.[23] At the time, Italy was still suffering from the after-effects of a disastrous war; employment opportunities were scarce and the cost of living was high.

Consequently, when the crew was filming on location, people trying to earn money by working as extras on the film were constantly hounding Lanza. The singer's compassion for the underprivileged—he would get tears to his eyes when he walked past a blind person—ultimately resulted in considerably more people appearing in some scenes than were actually required.

Unfortunately his first film after *Serenade* did nothing to enhance Lanza's reputation as a possible opera singer and serious contender as the world's greatest tenor—quite the opposite. Tenors were not exactly scarce in the Italy of those days. If he really intended to make the long-awaited debut in opera, be it in the provinces or in a major theater, Lanza would have to contend with some formidable names. These included well-established idols such as Di Stefano and Del Monaco, together with rapidly emerging tenors such as Bergonzi, Corelli and Raimondi, and a host of others, including Poggi, Penno and Campora and the still-impressive Tagliavini. Among the non-Italians, there were other top talents such as Jussi Björling, Nicolai Gedda, Richard Tucker,

Jon Vickers and Alfredo Kraus.

Lanza was reasonably sure of his voice and feared no one. Of the current tenors he admired Björling, whom he had met years earlier when the Swede paid him a visit in Hollywood, and Di Stefano, whom he had never met. Years later Di Stefano recalled Lanza telephoning him twice, on one occasion saying, "Pippo—when it comes to tenors there's only you and I." [24]

Yet *Seven Hills of Rome* was hardly the vehicle to enhance Lanza's status as a serious artist. Its paper-thin plot concerned an Italian-American nightclub singer who comes to Italy to search for his American fiancee, and is forced to look for a job. At the same time, he is surprised that regardless of his fame in America, no one has heard of him. During his job-hunting an unbilled heartthrob of the 1930s, singer/actor Alberto Rabagliati, tells him: "We don't import tenors, we export them!" Predictably, the film reaches a happy conclusion, and Lanza ends up forgetting his fiancee and falling in love with the Italian girl, played by Allasio.

Musically *Seven Hills of Rome* is Lanza's weakest film and, furthermore, he is not in particularly good voice. With rock 'n' roll and calypso the current rage, and after the relative failure of *Serenade* with its high operatic content, producer Lester Welch was adopting a different approach. Opera was limited to one aria, "*Questa o quella*" and a snatch of "*M'appari,*" while priority was given to songs, including many written by Rascel—among them his big hit "Arrivederci Roma."

Musical director George Stoll, who had worked with Lanza on the *Toast of New Orleans* and *The Student Prince*, was again on hand to conduct and supervise the music together with another of Lanza's past collaborators, Irving Aaronson, who was credited as musical co-ordinator for the film.

Stoll, a former violinist long associated with MGM as one of their musical directors, had won an Oscar in 1945 for his scoring of the Gene Kelly/Frank Sinatra hit *Anchors Aweigh*. His contribution to the new Lanza film, however, was far from being an Oscar winner.

Given the task of composing a new calypso number for the film, Stoll came up with something called "There's Gonna Be A Party Tonight," also known as "Italian Calypso." The inconsequential tune is further marred by Stoll's inane lyrics.

Other numbers were "*Lolita*"; incomplete versions of the Creole song "Ay Ay Ay," "All The Things You Are," and "The Loveliest Night Of The Year"; also "Come Dance With Me," a song of which Lanza had already made a better recording during his last recording session in America.

In the new film Lanza also sang the title song "Seven Hills Of Rome," written just prior to his death by the noted film composer Victor Young, who had won a posthumous Oscar for his scoring of the film *Around The World In Eighty Days*. The song is rather ordinary and is further hampered by the inferior lyrics added by Harold Adamson. The beautiful "Arrivederci Roma," arguably the highlight of the film, which Lanza sings by one of the Bernini fountains in the Piazza Navona, is ruined by the inclusion of screechy ten-year-old Luisa Di Meo, who joins the tenor in the second part of the song.

It had been Lanza's idea to include Di Meo in the scene. During his stay at the Bernini Bristol Hotel Lanza had noticed the little street beggar singing in the piazza below for a few liras and managed to convince both Titanus and Roy Rowland to include her in the film. While in the context of the picture the scene is quite effective, the recording itself—endlessly reissued by RCA—is less than ideal.

Overall, the reviews for the film were better than expected. They are best summed up by A.H. Weiler in *The New York Times*. After noting that "A solid story might have helped considerably," he went on to praise Lanza's impressions of Perry Como, Dean Martin, Frankie Laine and Louis Armstrong.[25]

Although the impersonations did nothing to enhance Lanza's reputation as an opera singer, they revealed another side of Lanza that was hitherto unknown to the general public. He was, in fact, a gifted mimic who loved putting his talent to use, not only impersonating a variety of diverse singers, including the bass Ezio Pinza and Frank Sinatra, but also in practical jokes on a number of unsuspecting colleagues and associates.[26]

One such instance had occurred two years earlier while working on *Serenade* at Warner Brothers Studios, where the flamboyant Liberace was also making his one and only feature film appearance in the dismal *Sincerely Yours*. The producer for both films was the German, Henry Blanke, who is not remembered for his sense of humor. After the day's filming was over, Lanza would delight in telephoning Blanke and, in a perfect imitation of Liberace's voice, would first list a series of complaints, ending for good measure by abusing the startled producer. Back on the set the following day Blanke would confront a baffled Liberace about his presumed complaints. When the truth eventually emerged, Lanza had a good laugh over it but neither Blanke nor Liberace thought it was particularly funny.[27]

Curiously, in contrast to *Serenade*, in which the musical content was equal to the voice, *Seven Hills of Rome* proved a success at the box office in both Europe and the United States, much to the surprise of Lanza, who considered both the film and his performance in it "awful."[28]

In Italy the film turned out to be an even bigger success, not only on the strength of the popularity of the three leads, but also because of the curiosity factor involving the tenor's first cinematic effort in his newly-adopted country. A mostly uncritical public flocked to see Lanza and the film ended up as the fourth biggest moneymaker for the year.

Meanwhile, Lanza was being evasive as ever regarding a possible operatic debut. American TV host Ed Sullivan had flown to Rome to interview him on the set of his latest film, and asked him about La Scala. Viewing this interview today, an obviously uncomfortable, thin and tired-looking Lanza interrupts Sullivan's question, merely responding that he had been invited years before to open the season at La Scala and that "now, this year" he would be able to "fulfill this suppressed desire."[29] The statement rings hollow, however, leaving one with the distinct impression that he is simply giving Sullivan a standard answer and is eager to change the subject. Similarly he told reporter Sheila Graham: "I don't intend to come back to the United States for a long time. Metro wants me for another five pictures to be made in Europe but I also want to sing (opera) in Verona, Milan and Rome."[30]

Just how much conviction lay behind these statements is hard to establish. It is easy to assume that he was merely reiterating his long-held desire to switch to opera while still having no firm plans to do so and continuing to procrastinate.

27—STAGE FRIGHT

IT WAS A SLIMMED-DOWN LANZA who met Donald Zec, show business reporter for *The Daily Mirror*, shortly after the completion of *Seven Hills of Rome*. Lanza's appearance took the reporter somewhat by surprise. "Lanza...wearing a well-cut navy suit over a lavender shirt, wasn't skinny, but he wasn't fat either," wrote Zec.[1] "I expected something enormous," he admitted telling Lanza.

Zec went on to describe the singer's looks: "Lanza has coal black hair towering over a sallow, sensitive face. The eyebrows are tragic. The eyes dark and expressive. The lips, which help to form the most magical sounds in music, are delicately shaped." In response to the inevitable question: "Is it true that you're highly temperamental?" Lanza's reply was typically frank. "Not at all. Impulsive—yes. Devilish if you like. If anybody punches me I punch back. When I'm in a temper I go for broke! But a minute later it's all forgotten."[2]

"I've never been so happy since I left Hollywood," said Lanza, describing his state of mind. "Beverly Hills is like a kid who's suddenly grown too big for his pants. I've had some of the most miserable years of my life there."

Clearly impressed by Lanza, Zec concluded: "[Lanza] is an amiable extrovert protecting a fragile magical talent in the movie "glass houses" where nearly everybody throws stones. He is a fine host, affectionate husband and proud father of four nice kids...To hell with the backbiters of Hollywood. I like Lanza."

Lanza undoubtedly knew how to charm. Zec was an important reporter and Lanza entertained him by wining and dining him in style at the villa. Zec's visit was not without embarrassment for the reporter, however. The maid at the Villa Badoglio

had neglected to supply the guest toilet with sufficient paper, causing Zec some anxious moments. Almost two years later, shortly
before Lanza died, Zec was surprised to receive a full crate of
toilet rolls accompanied by a note in which Lanza quoted the
title of a popular song. The note read:

"Dear Donald, these foolish things remind me of you. Love,
Mario."[3]

The one observation in Zec's article that did not escape those
concerned with the tenor's health was the word *sallow*. Lanza
may have appeared relatively thin and in good spirits, but in reality he was slowly digging his own grave with his repeated massive fluctuations in weight. The bouts of excessive eating and
drinking followed by drastic dieting were by now taking their
toll.

Adding to his problems was a dramatic loss of confidence.
The lack of live singing during the previous six years had increased his stage fright to gigantic proportions. Now the prospect of singing before a live audience, or even live in a studio
setting, filled him with anxiety, as his appearance on *The
Christophers* plainly showed.

Filmed in the Vatican in October 1957, the 30-minute television program was made for a Catholic charity organization based
in New York. Lanza and his wife are seen talking to the founder
of the Christophers, Father Keller, about the singer's early life
and subsequent career. Lanza looks well, and appears reasonably relaxed. He is also extremely articulate in recounting various anecdotes about his life. However, the change is evident when
he is asked to sing. The body language tells the entire story. Suddenly he becomes tense and is obviously conscious of the camera
filming him. Yet he is merely singing three songs in a small room
without an audience, with the exception of Father Keller, the technicians and a newly-acquired accompanist, Paul Baron, who provides the rather poor backing.[†] Watching Lanza and listening to
him sing "*Santa Lucia*," "*Because You're Mine*" and Schubert's
"*Ave Maria*," one wonders why the singer is so tense. Vocally he
is superb, technically he is secure. Why is he so nervous? The
answer is simple. He had spent too many years away from the

[†]Baron would later conduct for Lanza on three albums.

stage and live singing.

A singer needs to perform regularly in front of an audience in order to gain confidence and conquer stage fright. All artists are nervous to various degrees before a performance. As Caruso used to say, "The singer with no nerves is no singer!"[4] The great Sarah Bernhardt expressed it even better. When a young actress, told her that she had never in her life suffered from stage fright, Bernhardt replied, "Don't worry, that will come when you begin to develop talent!"[5] In extreme cases the nervousness can turn into a paralysing fear, as was the case with soprano Lily Pons—who would vomit before each performance, and with Rosa Ponselle, who would sometimes circle the Metropolitan theater for hours before summoning sufficient courage to enter it. One of the worst cases of nerves was that of tenor Franco Corelli, who would experience his own private hell on each occasion that he performed. Frequently, his wife would resort to physically pushing him onto the stage to perform. Corelli described his fear in an amusing interview with *Newsweek* in 1976.

> I have always been afraid. In the beginning I didn't have the high C so I was afraid. Then I did have the B and the C but was afraid I would lose them. Sometimes I get up in the morning and the voice doesn't answer. If I'm on holiday and not singing, I worry if it's still there. I tape every performance. I then spend three hours listening to the tapes. I am exhausted. I need rest but I can't sleep. If the performance was good I can't sleep for joy. If not, I cannot sleep for despair. What is this life? It is the life of a prisoner, in a hotel room, in front of the television or playing solitaire.[6]

Even Caruso—after 24 years of singing—would still suffer from first-night nerves and could be seen backstage banging his forehead with his fist, shouting: "Never again! This is the last time! No man should be asked to go through this!"[7]

In Lanza's case, his fear of singing live was accentuated by the fact that he was not performing regularly in public as he should have been. Had he been singing on the stage, he would have managed to control his nerves as he had done, very successfully, at the beginning of his career. Since his arrival in Hollywood Lanza's live singing had been limited to one concert in 1948, 14 in 1949, three in 1950, 22 in 1951 and a television appearance in

1954. These performances were hardly sufficient to provide him with the confidence he badly needed. Apart from the visit to Naples and the Christopher's program Lanza's Italian appearances consisted of four events and a single recording session. In August, along with Betty, he had attended the premiere of co-star Renato Rascel's film '*La Nonna Sabella*' (Grandmother Sabella) which was given in Rome's first drive-in cinema.

One of his appearances involved a promise that he had made several weeks earlier to visit his father's birthplace. The Mayor of Filignano, Celeste Mancini, had personally extended the invitation to him while he was making *Seven Hills of Rome*. In early September, with filming now completed, Lanza and his wife headed for the little village of Filignano in the Molise Mountains.

He was welcomed like royalty by the citizens, some of whom were relatives who had emigrated to France and were returning for the occasion. A banquet was given in Lanza's honor and a band from the nearby town of Roccasecca was engaged for the festivities, which went on until the early hours of the morning. These simple people were immensely proud and excited at the thought of having such a celebrity as their guest. But Lanza, who loved what he often referred to as "the little people," made them feel at ease by joining in the fun, playing *Bocce* with them and even beating the band's drum in the village square.

At the height of the festivities a plaque commemorating the tenor's visit was uncovered outside where his father had been born. Lanza responded with a speech thanking the citizens and then delighted those present by offering an impromptu recital. Buoyed by the occasion and with nothing to fear from his uncritical audience, Lanza, without the benefit of any accompaniment, sang his heart out to his appreciative listeners.[8]

Back in Rome Lanza was further honored at the presentation of the yearly gold and silver masks for the best achievements in the performing arts, one of Italy's top awards. At a luxurious reception at the Casina Della Rosa, situated in the beautiful Villa Borghese gardens, Lanza was awarded the *Maschera d'Oro* (Golden Mask) in recognition for being the artist who had done the most in introducing Italian music—and opera in particular—to world audiences.

September also saw Lanza in Milan where, in one of his rare

public appearances he and co-star Marisa Allasio were guests of Renato Rascel, who was opening in a new musical revue named *Un Paio d'Ali* (A Pair Of Wings) at the Lirico Theater. At the end of the performance the audience burst into applause when Rascel acknowledged the presence of his two co-stars sitting in the front row.[9]†

†This, however, was not appreciated by the authors of the play, Garinei and Giovannini, who expected to be called on stage by Rascel, in keeping with tradition, to bask in the applause.

28—ROYAL COMMAND PERFORMANCE

SEVEN HILLS OF ROME NOW COMPLETED, Lanza reflected on his unorthodox career in a candid interview.

> Looking back maybe I had it too easy at the beginning. Maybe success came too fast. I didn't have the usual rags to riches struggle. In fact there is no chapter in my life that could be entitled "My Struggle." Mine has been a mixed up back to front career. My heartbreaks, my setbacks, my disappointments all came after I reached the top, not during the climb up. After I had become world famous and earning millions.[1]

With the initial euphoria that accompanied his arrival in Italy slowly dying down, the subject of preparing for an operatic career re-emerged but was again quickly discarded. Availability of offers was certainly not the issue. *Any* theater, not only in Italy, but also throughout Europe, would have jumped at the chance of securing the world-famous Mario Lanza even for a single operatic performance. Yet this was precisely the problem. If he took the plunge, he would undergo the closest scrutiny of any debut singer ever. Or he could forget it all and continue to be paid astronomical sums for his films, records and the occasional concert.

Again Lanza procrastinated and opted for the latter course.

With no specific goal or direction to follow—other than making another film, more recordings and a yet to be finalized concert tour—Lanza fell into a mood of depression, typically seeking refuge in alcohol to escape his fears and anxieties. By drinking constantly for hours, and sometimes for days on end, he could avoid the realities of the moment and temporarily find peace and solace.[2]

Then, in the midst of his depression, he received a temporary lift. It appeared in the unexpected form of an invitation to sing a Command Performance at the London Palladium in the presence of Queen Elizabeth II.

The Palladium was neither La Scala nor Covent Garden, but knowing that throughout the years many famous artists, including Beniamino Gigli, had been honored with an invitation, Lanza felt both elated and terrified at the thought of singing there. In anticipation of the ordeal, he started drinking to the point that he no longer resembled the handsome singer whom Donald Zec had interviewed in September. By the time he arrived in London, Lanza looked not so much overweight as bloated. As a consequence of the binges, his body was now retaining large amounts of fluid.[3]

Lanza was immensely popular in England. Given that this was to be his first appearance in the United Kingdom, Columbia Artists in New York and Leslie Grade in London had arranged for him to sing for the English public in the highly-rated weekly television show *Sunday Night At The London Palladium*. The show, as well as being televised across the country, would also have a live audience.

Four days before the Command Performance, which was scheduled for November 18, 1957, Lanza set out for London together with his wife and his accompanist Constantine Callinicos. Lanza was aware that his films and recordings had been received extremely well in England. *The Toast of New Orleans, Because You're Mine* and *The Great Caruso* had in fact been even bigger box office successes in England than in America. Even *The Student Prince* had been a success in England, while his recordings were in constant demand. Nevertheless, the tumultuous welcome that he received on his arrival at Victoria Station as the Golden Arrow came to a stop was of a magnitude not even he had anticipated.

As he stepped down onto the station's platform more than 200 people, mostly women, surged forward and broke police barriers in an effort to get close to their idol. In the mad rush that followed, Lanza was knocked to the ground. Dazed but smiling, he picked himself up and headed back to the safety of his train compartment. It was more than evident that he had not been forgotten. There were banners everywhere with "Welcome Mario" on them, while the women kept up an incessant chorus of "We love Mario!" It might have been noisy and unruly, but as with any artist this was the kind of reassurance that—at least temporarily—gave him a surge of adrenaline. Leaning against the window of the train compartment Lanza broke into snatches of song to the delight of his fans while extra police had to be called to hold back the crowd, which was growing increasingly restless in an effort to get a glimpse of its idol.[4]

After a short while Lanza emerged once again from the train but was cornered by a reporter who had somehow managed to get close to him. Among other things, she asked him what he would be singing for the Queen. Displaying both charm and diplomacy, Lanza smiled and extricated himself by answering, "Let's leave it as a secret, shall we?" He then headed to the car that was waiting to take him, his wife and his accompanist to the Dorchester Hotel. As he struggled to get to the car he smiled, shouting: "It's just like a football match, with me as the ball!"[5]

Lanza's British agent Leslie Grade had arranged for a press conference to be held the following day in the luxurious Oliver Messel suite that the Lanzas were occupying at the Dorchester. While he waited for the reporters to arrive, Lanza became increasingly tense. He was not looking forward to what he anticipated would be familiar questions about his weight and temperament. In his anxiety he reached for a glass of champagne, quickly drinking it and following it with another and then another.[6]

As the reporters entered the suite, most of them were surprised to see a relatively slim Lanza. "Very good-looking, elegantly attired in a navy blue suit, white shirt and blue tie," was the verdict of one journalist.[7]

Lanza had put on 13 lb (5.9 kg) in the past two months, but at 182 lb (82.5 kg) he looked reasonably well, with only the puffiness around the eyes providing a true indication of his physical condition.

As Lanza had anticipated, the press reception was off to a bad start when one of the reporters asked him to state both his current weight and his top weight in the past. Visibly annoyed by the question, the tenor replied by asking a question of his own.

Why doesn't somebody ask me about singing for a change? For God's sake, isn't there anything else you can ask an artist?...All this stupidity about waistline and overweight.

Did I come here to fight [prize-fighter] Richardson? I'm here to sing for the people so why do you guys keep burning hell out of me about personal things like weight? [8]

Wisely dropping the subject, the reporters then asked him about his latest film, *Seven Hills of Rome*. "I don't think the new one is so good," he replied candidly, adding: "It's my own performance I'm speaking of, but of course the public may go for it. *Serenade*, a failure relatively speaking, had the best singing I ever did. So this one may sell." [9]

He then referred to negotiations that had again resumed with director Leo McCarey and 20th Century Fox for a musical version of *Marco Polo* to be filmed mainly in Venice. The reporters, however, appeared to be more interested in asking him about his temperament, provoking a typical response: "Surely you have the right to say no once in a while, especially if the script they dream up is a bunch of rubbish! I'm not explosive, just truthful." [10]

He proved it the next moment when a reporter murmured, "I'm inclined to agree with you, Mario," over a point of taste. "I don't care whether you agree or not," he responded, adding: "Please, I'm not meaning to be rude with you gentlemen, but I don't care about reporters. Yesterday's news is forgotten by everybody except newspapermen. No, it's the public applause that counts! He's the one you have to satisfy." [11]

With the ordeal of the press conference over, Lanza ordered more champagne, and with neither his wife, Callinicos, nor the Grade Agency Representative, Peter Pritchard able to stop him, or willing to, he continued to drink for the remainder of the day. Eventually he fell into a deep sleep, waking up the following day feeling strangely refreshed, rather than hung over, and ready to attend the afternoon rehearsal at the Palladium. [12]

Initially, Callinicos went through Lanza's three scheduled numbers while the tenor sat listening in the stalls. Then Lanza made his way onto the stage and began his first number. Many of the other artists assembled there were extremely curious to hear his "live" voice, and it became immediately clear that the tenor was in excellent vocal shape. At the same time they were puzzled by the fact that he appeared to be very tense and fearful of forgetting the lyrics. [13]

It was hardly surprising that Lanza was nervous after an almost seven-year absence from the concert stage. His anxiety was such that he had asked Callinicos to mouth some of the lyrics while he was conducting.[14] This was an exceptional request: he had sung countless concerts with Callinicos out of view at the piano, and therefore unable to assist him—with the exception of the occasional cue.

Although the rehearsal had gone very well, the thought of performing in front of a live audience after such a long time terrified Lanza. Back in his suite at the Dorchester, he continued to order champagne, drinking solidly for almost the next 24 hours. The magnums of champagne were being delivered virtually around the clock by a succession of obliging waiters, eager to pocket the huge five-pound tips he was handing them. By the Sunday, which was the eve of the Command Performance, Lanza was still drinking. Meanwhile his agent, Peter Prichard, was beside himself with anxiety, unable to stop the binge.[15]

Then on the Sunday afternoon Lanza suddenly stopped drinking. He soon fell into a deep sleep, only awakening the next morning. Incredibly, there were no apparent signs of the punishment he had inflicted upon himself. On the contrary, his speaking voice sounded clear and—to the surprise of all concerned—he seemed in good spirits, declaring himself eager to perform that evening.[16]

As was usual before a performance, he would speak only in a whisper—or not at all—in order to rest his voice. Then as the time grew nearer, Lanza became increasingly anxious.

His fears were not difficult to fathom. For his first live stage appearance in almost seven years he would be facing a somewhat "stuffy"[17] audience comprising the immediate members of the British Royal Family, together with figures from British high society and the aristocracy. Furthermore, as the headliner for a show that included Judy Garland and British performers Gracie Fields, Vera Lynn, Harry Secombe, David Whitfield, Frankie Vaughan, Dickie Valentine and Tommy Steele most of the attention would be centered on him, the controversial American tenor with a reputation for last-minute cancellations.

At last his name was announced. The moment had come to face the more than 2300 people packing the theater. Lanza gave Callinicos a final reminder to mouth the lyrics for him and then, bravely trying to camouflage his nervousness, proceeded in the direction of the huge Palladium stage. As he stepped out from the wings he was accorded a thrilling reception, but it was clear that he was extraordinarily nervous and uncertain.[18] The applause went on and on until Lanza was forced to wave his hands and signal to the audience that he was ready to begin.

His first number, "Because You're Mine," was received with thunderous applause. He then captivated his audience further with "*E lucevan le stelle*" from *Tosca*. Then after more rapturous applause there was a slight pause; he seemed to have forgotten the title of his next song. Pulling himself together, he concluded with "The Loveliest Night Of The Year."

Cyril Ornadel, who was the musical coordinator for the entire show, recalled the occasion: "He got royal acclaim. Absolute roars, which is most unusual for there."[19] Lanza's agent Leslie Grade added for good measure: "Singing film stars are sometimes disappointing when you hear them off the screen. But not Lanza. At the Royal Performance he was tremendous. Everyone present was amazed at the power and quality of his voice."[20]

At the end of his ordeal Lanza stood transfixed as he absorbed the rapturous reception he was receiving. He then acknowledged the Queen's presence in the royal box before finally walking off the stage. Shortly afterwards—together with the rest of the performers—he was presented to the Queen, as is traditional at Command Performances. After the usual handshake, the Queen exchanged a few words with Lanza. Asked by reporters what the Queen had said to him, Lanza replied simply: "She told me I was wonderful."[21]

Her actual words were: "I never knew that human lungs could produce such volume. I thought your hands were very expressive and I enjoyed your singing immensely." [22] Lanza was further complimented for his performance by Prince Phillip and the Queen Mother, who were also present for the occasion.

The reviewers were unanimous in their praise of Lanza's singing, although several pointed out his excessive nervousness. "There was an uncertain air about him as he made his entry and, of course, it might be that nervousness got the better of him," wrote the *Record Mirror*, at the same time acknowledging that Lanza was "undoubtedly the possessor of a magnificent voice."[23]

The News Chronicle reported that "Mario Lanza's 'live' voice is nothing short of superb."[24] *Melody Maker* concurred: "Mario Lanza proved that he is in better voice than ever. There were no tricks, no striving after effects."[25] The *Sporting and Show Business Review* was equally impressed: "Mario is good and he knows it. His robust top notes almost tore the roof off. I doubt if the Palladium has heard a tenor of such lungpower before. Lanza shows he can also belt out those top notes without the benefit of mechanical amplification."[26]

Six days later Lanza appeared on the same stage, this time in front of a very different audience that included many of his fans, in the popular *Sunday Night at the London Palladium*. On this occasion, which was being relayed live on television all over England, Lanza sang the same three numbers from the Royal Command Performance to equally tumultuous acclaim. Looking at the surviving kinescope of this performance, Lanza appears both shy and nervous. Yet once again, the singing is extraordinary. Vocally Lanza is in total control, with the voice perfectly placed. There is no doubt whatsoever that technically he knows exactly what he is doing. He knows how to turn his voice and cover on the critical *passaggio* notes. The diaphragmatic support, essential for correct voice production, is superb. This is surprising in itself, given that he was not singing regularly.[†]

Lanza's singing at the Palladium is further proof that his absence from the operatic stage had nothing to do with any limitations on his part as a singer. Indeed, Lanza's British debut had been so successful that even before he left London plans were being finalized by Columbia Artists Management for a European Concert tour at the beginning of 1958. In fact negotiations between Lanza and Columbia Artists had begun before the tenor left for Italy but at the time were quite nebulous. Back in May Columbia's Vice President William Judd had written to John Coast, his European representative in London, asking him whether he would be interested in handling a proposed concert tour at the same time adding that "One thing is for sure. If he sings at all it will be for crushingly big fees!" [27] Coast replied: " I

[†]He did, however, keep up his daily vocal and breathing exercises as best he could when he was not drinking.

am very interested indeed to work for Mario Lanza. It is very good of you to offer me this opportunity."[28]

The initial plans for a European concert tour were more than ambitious. The tour was to begin in Italy in late November with two concerts in Genoa, one in Turin, one at the Teatro Nuovo in Milan and finally two in Rome, the first on December 16 at either Teatro Adriano or Teatro New York and the second on December 18 at Teatro New York.

Sandwiched in between these were concerts in Belgrade, and possibly Copenhagen, Oslo and Stockholm. The Italian and Jugoslav bookings were being handled by Mrs. Alberto Erede, wife of the conductor, who was operating her own agency in Milan. It was up to Lanza to approve the dates so that Mrs. Erede could in turn finalize the preliminary arrangements that she had made with the theaters in question but the tenor did not get back to her. Why he didn't is open to speculation but the most likely reason is that he wanted to avoid facing the notoriously critical Italian audiences.

Certainly the Lanza of ten years earlier would not have had any such qualms but now it was a different story. The confidence and assurance of those golden years was gone and it was becoming doubtful that he would ever fully regain it.

One interesting aspect of the London sojourn was Lanza's revelation that he was interested in recording six complete operas. However, there were a number of logistical problems relating to the project that he felt would first need to be resolved. "I think British recording is the best in the world, but the best singers for the necessary chorus are in Italy," he told the *New Musical Express*. "I don't know what will happen."[29]

29—EUROPEAN CONCERT TOUR

BACK IN ROME Lanza spent Christmas and New Year's Eve with his wife and children. He loved his family and would treasure the time he spent with Betty and the four children. However, the years of stress had taken their toll not only on him, but on his wife as well. The constant pressures of living with someone as volatile as Lanza, coupled with his increasing alcohol dependency, had made it difficult for the fragile Betty to cope, and she too was now drinking, and relying more and more on tranquilizers. Their arguments were also more frequent; yet it was obvious to anyone who knew them and saw them together that they still truly adored each other.[1]

They had much in common apart from their four children. Equally quick-tempered, they were both vibrant people with a genuine zest for life. Both were childlike, with a wonderful sense of humor. Lanza would make up marvelous stories that he would relate to their wide-eyed children, while Betty loved organizing Halloween and birthday parties, and Christmas and Easter gatherings. Where they differed was in disciplining the children. It was up to Betty to play the disciplinarian. Lanza, on the other hand, was always the most indulgent and lenient of fathers. Asked for a toy he would buy the entire shop. An entire room at the Villa Badoglio was filled with all manner of toys: pedal cars, tricycles, scooters and dozens of dolls.[2]

When he was not drowning his fears and anxieties in alcohol, Lanza would spend hours playing with his children or singing lullabies to them. At heart a little boy, Lanza adored getting down on his hands and knees while the children would take turns riding on his back. Whenever possible he would take them to concerts or the opera, making sure to explain what was happening on stage. Christmas was a special time with numerous presents for everyone.[3]

The children were allowed to stay up late and the household staff of nine was always made to feel as though they were part of the family and invited to join in festivities. Years later the family janitor, Antonio Fabianelli, recalled the time spent at the villa working for Lanza and his family. "He was truly a worthy human being," he reminisced. "I never felt as if he was my employer. He treated me as his equal, like a brother. He was kind, warm and considerate, and his tragic death was a personal loss to me."[4]

The New Year had hardly started, and it was time for Lanza to set out for England on the first leg of his European concert tour. Such was Lanza's popularity that there had been an unprecedented demand for tickets, with all concerts sold out in record time and extra dates having to be hurriedly arranged. The first Albert Hall concert sold out in three hours, with a second one hastily announced three days later. When that, too, sold out equally fast a third concert was scheduled for mid-February.

The tour started on Saturday January 4, 1958, in Sheffield. At City Hall a capacity audience numbering 2878, gave Lanza a rousing, three-minute welcome. The tenor had again gained weight since his visit to England in November, and the handsome face clearly betrayed the signs of the punishment its owner had inflicted upon himself. While he was in great voice, it was now only a matter of time before the body gave in to the years of constant abuse and strenuous dieting.

As usual Lanza sang a typical concert consisting of classical songs and operatic arias in the first half, and Neapolitan songs, popular songs and some of his film hits in the second half. This was his standard program throughout the tour:

Lamento di Federico	from *L'Arlesiana* by Cilea
Lasciatemi morire	from *Arianna* by Monteverdi
Gia il sole dal Gange	by Scarlatti
Pietà Signore	attributed to Stradella
Tell Me O Blue Blue Sky	by Giannini
Bonjour ma belle	by Behrend
The House On The Hill	by Charles
E lucevan le stelle	from *Tosca* by Puccini

After the interval he sang:

Mamma mia che vo' sape	by Nutile
A vucchella	by Tosti
Marechiare	by Tosti
Softly As In A Morning Sunrise	by Romberg
I'm Falling In Love With Someone	by Herbert
As encores he usually sang:	
Because You're Mine	by Brodszky
Seven Hills Of Rome	by Young
La donna è mobile from *Rigoletto*	by Verdi

The tour continued with concerts in Glasgow, Newcastle, Leicester and the two Albert Hall dates.

On Tuesday, January 14th, Betty flew into London in order to be present at her husband's Albert Hall concert two days later. Coincidentally that same Tuesday night the American tenor Richard Tucker was making his Covent Garden debut as Cavaradossi in *Tosca* and Lanza expressed a desire to see the performance to his British agent John Coast, who also represented Tucker. The latter, a longstanding admirer of Lanza's, was delighted at the request, and arranged for Lanza and Betty to sit with his wife Sara and John Coast in his own private box. Lanza sat well back in the box in order to avoid attracting attention to himself, a gesture much appreciated by Tucker's wife.[5]

Between acts, fearing photographers and autograph seekers, Lanza stayed in the box with Betty and Sara. Eager to learn more about Tucker's career, Lanza used the opportunity to ask Sara a number of questions, which she answered as best she could. Lanza reciprocated the Tuckers' hospitality by inviting them to join him and Betty for a late night supper in his suite at the Dorchester Hotel.

Throughout the evening the two men talked like long-lost friends about their childhood, years of vocal training, first breaks, their religious backgrounds, ethnic roots and family lives. These were topics normally reserved for classmates at a reunion and unusual for two men who had nothing more in common, ostensibly, than their American birthplaces and tenor voices. "It was as if Mario wanted to figure out why Richard's life had gone one direction and his own life another," recalled Sara Tucker. "He

244

was very subdued that night and seemed to hang on every word that Richard spoke. He seemed to want and need a friendly ear and in Richard he found one."[6] Lanza was happiest, Sara observed, when he was talking about his boyhood in Philadelphia, his mother and father, and his children. His career, in contrast, seemed far less fulfilling. "Richard and I both got the impression that for all his wealth and great success Mario wasn't really happy. Something important, something very basic, seemed missing from his life."[7]

As indeed it was. But for the moment, there was still the challenge of performing in one of London's most prestigious venues.

As he stepped onto the stage of the huge Albert Hall, the vastness of the auditorium—with a seating capacity of 8,000-plus—momentarily stunned Lanza. "Is this real?" he exclaimed.[8] Under normal circumstances the size of a theater did not concern him. As Callinicos stated: "Most singers I have known want to scout the hall in which they are to sing. But Mario was hardly ever concerned about this aspect of his art. He would have sung in Ebbets Fields, Carnegie Hall, Madison Square Garden, or the Los Angeles Coliseum. The physical dimensions of the place meant absolutely nothing to him."[9]

Originally, there had been some concern on the part of the London-based Ivan Fielding Agency, which was promoting the tour, regarding the Hall's notoriously bad acoustics and huge seating capacity. They knew that Lanza would refuse to sing with a microphone and felt he should instead sing at the Royal Festival Hall, which enjoyed superior acoustics and a far smaller auditorium. They were promptly reassured by Bill Judd of Columbia Concerts that Lanza would have no problem in being heard at the Albert Hall, regardless of its acoustics or size.[10]

Bill Judd was right. The Albert Hall concert of 16 January, 1958—recorded by RCA and released posthumously in an album titled *A Mario Lanza Program*—offered compelling evidence of Lanza's vocal prowess. The album itself provides a rare glimpse of Lanza on the concert stage and reveals some of the little-known facets of the tenor performing in front of an audience. It also provides evidence of what the 37-year-old tenor must have sounded like throughout the tour. Revealing a voice that has darkened considerably while retaining its thrilling ring at the top, it

245

also lays bare some stylistic lapses absent in his singing during the Bel Canto Trio days eleven years earlier. In fact, after listening to the tapes of the concert Lanza was not at all impressed with his performance and instructed RCA not to proceed with the planned LP. *A Mario Lanza Program* was subsequently released posthumously.

Lanza is at his best in the two operatic arias, notwithstanding the fact that the voice is by now much too heavy for the *Arlesiana* aria. He also sounds impressive in the English songs, particularly "Because You're Mine," with its brilliant B flat ending that brings the house down. His tasteful treatment of the Scarlatti song "*Già il sole dal Gange*" is another highlight, despite Callinicos's inadequate accompaniment.

The lack of regular live performing is evident, however, in the tenor's singing of the Neapolitan songs, particularly "*Marechiare*," in which he makes the unforgivable mistake of singing the first stanza twice, and in one instance breaks the musical line by taking a breath in the middle of the phrase. These are lapses that clearly indicate not only insufficient singing on the stage, but also lack of proper work with a top coach or conductor. Nevertheless the recording gives a hint of what Lanza could have accomplished on the operatic stage, given the right environment and coach. He displays a *lirico spinto* voice bordering on the dramatic that is ideally suited to the tones of Cavaradossi's "*E lucevan le stelle*," rather than the light lyricism of "*Lamento di Federico*."

Regardless of Lanza's stylistic lapses, the famous tenor Nicolai Gedda, who was present at the concert, would later state: "It's the greatest tenor voice I've ever heard."[11] His opinion was echoed by fellow tenor, the Australian Jon Weaving, who was also present that evening.[12]

Critical response throughout the tour was good. The *Leicester Evening Mail* report was particularly accurate:

First-rate operatic singers whose fame has been coupled with commercial success find it hard to impress the highbrow, suspicious of talent mixed with glamour. Hollywood stepped in first and the highbrow critics stepped back. A film star, and a bobbysoxers idol at that, could never be classed with Caruso or Gigli. Yet the 3000 people who packed Leicester

De Montfort Hall last night to see and hear him sing could only ask "Why not?" He sang with purity and power, with conviction and lucidity. His selections were short but enriched by his phrasing. Not a note was neglected or over-emphasized.[13]

The *Leicester Mercury* wrote: "Here was an entertainer with something tangible to offer; the wonder of an exceptional tenor voice...Lanza has none of the piping clarity of Gigli, his is the more masculine tenor of Caruso."[14]

In between the two Albert Hall concerts, Lanza made his second British television appearance in a show entitled *Saturday Spectacular*. With Callinicos providing the piano accompaniment, he sang three songs from his concert program. In fine voice, Lanza sounds exactly as he does on the Albert Hall recording but again, stylistically, there are flaws.

It is evident that he has not worked enough on the musical aspects of the songs. One has the distinct impression that he has simply selected three songs that he knew and proceeded to sing them with little or no rehearsing. The gamble works in only one out of three songs: Herbert's "I'm Falling In Love With Someone," which he sings well. "Softly As In A Morning Sunrise," on the other hand, sounds labored, and in "*Marechiare*" he again sings the same stanza twice. Clearly he must have assumed that a British audience would not notice such a flaw in a language they did not understand. In Italy he would have been seriously criticized, and rightly so, for such a failing.

The second Albert Hall concert took place on Sunday January 19th. The matinee performance should have been cancelled. The previous day Lanza and his wife had gone to see his old favorite Lana Turner at her home outside London. While descending the steps into the garden he had slipped, fallen and badly bruised his rib cage. He was in considerable pain throughout the concert and his singing was below par. Three days later, Betty went back to the children in Rome and Lanza and Callinicos flew to Germany to fulfil dates in Munich, Stuttgart, Hamburg and Baden Baden. By the time he reached Munich Lanza was feeling unwell. He felt unusually tired and complained of pain in his right leg, but he went on and sang impressively. Callinicos recalled the event:

At the end of the Munich concert, the enthusiastic Germans converged on the stage, making it impossible for us to get off. At one time this kind of response from his fans would have delighted Mario. Now it was unnerving, upsetting... something was wrong. [15]

The following day he was given a medical checkup in his hotel. The doctor's diagnosis was not good. Lanza, stated Dr. Frederic Fruhwein, was suffering from high blood pressure and phlebitis in his right leg. The leg was swollen and painful but worst still was the fact that clots were present in the deep tibial vein. To complicate matters Lanza's system had become poisoned as a result of a tooth infection. The immediate concern was that the phlebitis would cause a blood clot to break away and block an artery. The latter, warned the doctor, could result in almost certain death by pulmonary embolism. Dr. Fruhwein told Lanza in no uncertain terms that if he continued with his present lifestyle he might well be dead within a year.[16]

Medical attention and complete rest were the only solution. Yet Lanza insisted on going through with a scheduled Stuttgart concert, and by all accounts sang grandly. By the end of the concert he was utterly exhausted, however, and agreed to cancel his remaining appearances and return to Rome. There he was immediately admitted to the Valle Giulia, a private clinic located approximately ten minutes by car from the Villa Badoglio.

The clinic, one of the most expensive in Rome, was partly owned and supervised by Dr. Guido Moricca. There the singer was placed under total rest while he underwent a course of injections to relieve the swelling and pain the phlebitis was causing him.

Apart from his wife and a number of close friends, there were also working associates who sincerely cared about the tenor now, and were deeply concerned about his health. Both Bill Judd of Columbia Artists Management, whose association with the tenor dated back to the Tanglewood days, and John Coast, Columbia Artists representative in London, who had grown fond of Lanza and greatly admired him, wrote to the singer pleading with him to take better care of himself.[17] Coast's plea is particularly touching:

Mario, my friend, this is a very serious letter to you, written just as much from me as a human being as from a concert agent. First let me say this. From the start I have had the very highest opinion of your voice. But when listening to you in that fantastic concert in Stuttgart the other night, I felt absolutely confident and sure that yours is the greatest living Italian tenor, and also the only truly robusto one. Your voice was not only black and warm and dead on pitch, but it was strong as a pillar from top to bottom—it showed no trace of thinning at the top or in any other register—and purely as a lover of a good voice I said to myself: "This man must *not* be allowed to destroy himself; this man *must* do the many things in his career which he still can do and should do." I tell you— Di Stefano, Del Monaco, even Jussi—they're not in the same league with you at all. And this brings me to my second point, which is your health. Mario, that doctor in Munich is a hell of a good man. I trust him and his opinion because his medical opinion agrees with my common-sense deduction.

He told you last night what he told me a day before—that you might easily kill yourself within a year if you couldn't get your physical and personal problems straightened out. He said that some day you might have some sort of a clot and just pass out. [18]

In fact, Coast was so concerned about Lanza's health that following a telephone conversation with Larry Kanaga, president of General Artists Corporation – an agency that had by now taken over Lanza's representation from MCA – wrote Kanaga a letter expressing his fears for the tenor's future:

First, though, I wish to urge on you the extremely serious and responsible medical opinion given to me by Dr. Fruhwein in Munich, and which I am sure would be supported by other doctors in London or Rome. This boils down to one sentence: If Mario cannot get his domestic affairs settled in such a way that he is a happier man and does not go on the bottle, or if he simply cannot keep off the bottle, within one year he may well kill himself. [19]

Similarly, a few days later, Bill Judd pleaded with the singer to take better care of himself:

Dear Mario,

I have been very much concerned since receiving a copy of John Coast's letter to you dated January 29th 1958..... I am very proud of my association with you as your concert manager but I do not write to you as a manager. I write to you from a position which to me is much more important—your friend of almost 20 years standing and Betty's friend of over 12 years.

I beg you to seek and follow the best medical advice immediately so that your physical condition will be soon improved. Your family and friends count on you and depend on you. So do your worldwide public.

For the medical part you must depend on good doctors and carefully follow their advice. For anything else, please count on me as a friend to help in any way that you would like to have me do.

Remember, Mario, you are the 'greatest,' and we all count on your friendship as well as professionally.[20]

Stubborn and unwilling to listen, Lanza blamed the medication he had been taking for his tooth infection on his current health problems. "I have a condition of phlebitis, which is the result of having too many antibiotics pumped into me,"[21] he rationalized. He was also growing restless in Rome, where he had now been recuperating for over a month, first confined to the Valle Giulia Clinic and then resting at home.

The recent series of concerts had given him back some of his lost confidence. Proving that there was nothing better in conquering stage fright than performing regularly, Lanza—against his doctor's orders—insisted on resuming the interrupted concert tour. With the aid of a cane and with his leg tightly bandaged in a rubber stocking, he flew to London and then proceeded by train to Bristol, where the concert tour was scheduled to resume on March 4.

In order to rest his voice as much as possible in between concerts he reverted to the old routine of keeping completely silent on both the day of the concert and the day prior to it. When necessary he would communicate with his accompanist Callinicos or anyone else, by writing on a paper pad. Callinicos recalled the day when a teenage girl, who was one of a number from his English fan club who followed the singer throughout the tour, managed to get to Lanza's hotel room while he was resting.

"You don't have much hair on your chest," she told him. Without uttering a word Lanza scribbled on his pad "No I don't, but Costa does."[22]

Before starting his silent routine a strangely confident Lanza told his pianist, "The only time I'll make a sound is at our concerts. Then I'll make sounds nobody will forget."[23] The statement stands as further proof that his fear of performing in public did not stem from fears about his voice, in which he believed completely.[24]

Although the leg was still bothering him, it did not appear to affect his singing. Indeed, his first concert after the interruption was a great success, as the *Bristol Evening Post* reported the following day:

"The tremendous power of his voice—he disdains a microphone—filled the hall and the wide range of the program gave scope to this versatile tenor...whatever the song his voice had a delightful clarity...Mario Lanza is a showman whose personality makes an instant appeal."[25]

Critical response was equally good for the remaining concerts. Following his concert in Manchester the *Guardian* reported:

Without ballyhoo American tenor Mario Lanza strolled casually onto the stage at Kings Hall, Belle Vue, Manchester, and captivated a capacity 6000 audience with the glorious power of his voice...The voice that has sold millions of gramophone records did not disappoint.[26]

Toward the end of the recital Lanza's leg was causing him pain and he finished the concert leaning on his walking stick. He managed to sing the habitual three encores and then, with the audience still cheering and asking for more, he left the stage and struggled to get to his dressing room, where he was given a pain-killing injection by a doctor that had been summoned to the theater. [27] In between concerts, Lanza tried to rest as much as possible by keeping his weight off the leg, and continuing with his silent routine.

Meanwhile Betty and the children remained in Rome. The couple's eldest daughter, Colleen, had developed mumps, making it impossible for Betty to join him on the tour. Lanza disliked being away from his family for long periods. At the same time he was concerned about his wife's increasing dependency on tranquilizers. On more than one occasion he would resort to locking up various medications to keep them out of Betty's reach.[28]

She would even resort to swallowing the pills he was taking for his phlebitis condition. Always fearful for his children's safety, Lanza would try to ensure that his family accompanied him whenever possible.[29]

Meanwhile the tour proceeded with appearances in Newcastle, Brighton and Bradford. Prior to the Brighton concert, and again in Bradford, Lanza was given pain-killing injections before each performance, as the phlebitis was causing him considerable distress. With dramatic flourish he told the English reporters who questioned him: "I'm determined to fulfil my commitments even if it means falling down on the stage."[30] After the Bradford concert he flew to Rome to attend the confirmation of daughters Colleen and Ellisa.

He was due back in England on March 21 for a concert in Birmingham but this was cancelled as he was feeling unwell again. A worried Betty urged him to cancel his remaining dates and undergo medical treatment, but Lanza was undeterred. He was adamant that he would finish the tour. With his health in a precarious state, however, some cancellations were inevitable. Together with Birmingham, Croydon was also cancelled but he was able to fulfill two dates in Scotland, in Edinburgh and Dundee on 25 and 27 March respectively. Two days later he sang before an enthusiastic audience numbering close to 10,000 at King's Hall in Belfast, Northern Ireland. Lanza seemed to bearing up reasonably well to the strain of frequent travel and closely programmed dates.

However, by the time he reached Paris in early April, he was feeling exhausted. A somewhat disappointed audience at the Olympia Theater had to content itself with a mere six numbers from the ailing tenor. [31]

From Paris it was on to Belgium and Holland, where Lanza sang in Ostend and Rotterdam respectively. He was feeling better again, and consequently did not disappoint his audiences, giving full concerts in both cities.

The tour was scheduled to conclude with three performances in Germany. Before they left for their first concert in Hanover, Lanza told a worried Callinicos that he had a sore throat and suspected he might be getting a cold.[32] Surprisingly, however, he appeared to be in great voice and sang an excellent concert. The music critic of the *Hanoverische Algemein* reported: "There is no equal to this naturally beautiful tenor voice in the world today...nothing could deprive the evening of the infatuating attraction of the voice."[33]

Despite the sore throat Lanza was in spectacular voice again for his next concert, which took place two nights later in the 7000-seat Ostsee Halle in Kiel. Callinicos recalled the evening, which was destined to be Lanza's very last concert.

> He seemed that night to be at the height of his powers as a singer. His voice, "darker" and richer than I had heard it in years, thrilled me. Its volume and substance rivalled any male voice I had ever heard in my life.[34]

Dr Kurt Klukist, music critic of the *Lubecher Nachricten*, concurred. Freely acknowledging his scepticism about the ability of the famous 37-year-old "film" tenor prior to the concert, he was greatly impressed by what he heard:

> [Lanza] really can sing. The material belonging to this wonderfully melodious tenor is a natural gift...It is difficult to know what to admire the most. The faultless breathing technique, the elastic precision of his wording, the light "piano." The constantly disciplined "forte." The well-synchronized join between registers. When he is not singing, he seems a little nervous...When he sings, he is fully relaxed...[there was] applause and more applause.[35]

Dr. Klukist was merely another of the sceptics who had been won over by Lanza after hearing the tenor sing live. At the same time, it is clear from such reviews that Lanza was gaining more confidence with each concert. Had he been able to abandon films, control his drinking and restore his poor health this period would arguably have been his best opportunity to make the transition to opera.

Instead there would be one more film. In the meantime, further bouts of heavy drinking would contribute to the serious deterioration of his health. After the impressive performances in Hanover and Kiel, the next concert was scheduled for Hamburg on 15 April. Lanza had already cancelled an earlier concert in Hamburg at the onset of his health problems back in January, and consequently there was considerable anticipation for his re-scheduled appearance. A last-moment cancellation would cause a scandal.

After the Kiel concert Lanza and Callinicos travelled by car to Hamburg, followed a little later by John Coast and the German Tour promoter Gustav Fineman. Concerned by Lanza's incipient cold Coast had arranged for a doctor to examine the tenor at the Vier Jahreszeiten Hotel, where they were staying. Coast arrived at the hotel around midnight and on learning that Lanza and Callinicos had not yet checked in became alarmed. Unbeknownst to Coast, Lanza, in one of his rare extramarital escapades, had decided that the best way to cure a cold was to make love to a beautiful girl. Spurred on by the chauffeur, who no doubt wanted to ingratiate himself with the tenor, and consequently earn himself a bigger than usual tip, they headed for a local Dance Hall and picked up an attractive oriental-looking young woman.

Coast together with David Tennant, who had replaced Peter Prichard as tour manager, finally made contact with Lanza. Upon learning that the tenor, with the help of the chauffeur, had contrived to have a prostitute in his bedroom, Coast was furious. Dismissing the chauffeur for his bad influence on Lanza, he reprimanded the obviously embarrassed singer, who jokingly told Coast that the girl was a present for him.[†]

A scandal was narrowly avoided by paying the prostitute's pimp a thousand dollars. [36]

By now it was early morning and despite his bad cold Lanza again refused to see a doctor, claiming that Callinicos had given him some medication and that he was feeling better. That same day, April 14th, the eve of the concert, he was joined in his suite by Alex Revides, a Shakespearean actor he had befriended in Rome and who was now, against Betty's objections, the latest in a long line of sycophants that were sponging off Lanza.[37‡] Betty's assessment turned out to be right on this occasion.

Revides, whom Coast referred to as "this miserable Greek,"[38] wasted no opportunity to ingratiate himself with the tenor. Having gained Lanza's trust, Revides had devised a scheme which, unbeknown to the tenor, would ensure that he would get half of any deal from any party he had been instrumental in introducing to Lanza. [39] Much to Betty's consternation Revides, instead of encouraging Lanza to stop drinking, was doing the exact opposite. [40]

With a sore throat and all the symptoms of a cold, by rights Lanza should have been having an early night on the eve of his Hamburg concert. Instead he and Revides became involved in a

---

[†]Coast's wife was Javanese.
[‡]Unlike her husband, who tended to feel sorry for anyone spinning him a sad tale, Betty could often see through the phonies and the leeches.

heated discussion over *Otello*, Lanza's favorite operatic role and the part he hoped one day to sing on the operatic stage.

Drinking large quantities of beer and singing various arias from *Otello* over and over again till the early hours of the morning, regardless of complaints coming from the other guests in the hotel, Lanza finally fell asleep through sheer exhaustion.

Not surprisingly he awoke around noon the following day with his throat feeling worse than ever. A worried John Coast immediately called Dr. Schaake, an ear, nose and throat specialist, from the Hamburg State Opera. After examining Lanza the doctor sprayed the singer's throat and gave him an injection. Dr. Schaake told Coast that Lanza's vocal cords didn't look right but that, hopefully, the tenor would be able to sing that night. Lanza instantly demanded a second opinion and by 6:30 another doctor, Dr. Worch, was summoned to Lanza's suite. The doctor gave the singer a thorough checkup and offered an alarming diagnosis. He found that Lanza was suffering from an enlarged heart that needed at least two to three month's attention. He added that the liver was badly damaged, his general health poor, and told the tenor that he had to stop drinking immediately. At this point Dr. Schaake came back to the hotel, re-sprayed Lanza's vocal cords and gave him a tonic. Both doctors concurred that Lanza's health was in a precarious state. The tenor decided to cancel the concert.

It was almost the Las Vegas episode all over again, except that on this occasion Lanza's illness was real and far more serious. That evening, with only minutes left before curtain time, the director of the Musik Halle, Kurt Collien, realized that he had no alternative but to cancel the concert.

Bravely facing the 2000 people filling the auditorium Collien made the announcement and nearly risked being lynched in the uproar that followed. The crowd surged forward and headed furiously towards the stage, yelling and cursing Lanza, tearing up programs and screaming abuse at both the helpless Collien and Callinicos, who by now had joined the Musik Halle director on the stage in an effort to placate the unruly mob. [41]

Meanwhile, back at the hotel there were policeman posted everywhere, as there were fears that the wild crowd that had gathered outside might try to get to Lanza. For his part, the tenor was amused. He found it difficult to believe what was happening and was convinced that the Germans had "gone crazy."[42] He had been unable to sing because he had caught a cold, he reasoned. When he recovered he had every intention of resuming the tour and fulfilling the remaining engagements, including the Hamburg one.

Callinicos was furious at what had occurred. He felt that Lanza had been irresponsible by not taking greater care of himself and at least attempting to fulfil the engagement.[43] While the conductor was right to chide Lanza, his motives were not entirely altruistic. Callinicos was concerned for his accompanist fees, not only for the Hamburg concert, but for the remaining seven concerts, which were also cancelled. Back in January Callinicos had made some exorbitant demands—much to the disgust of John Coast, who in a letter to the head of Columbia Artists in New York, William Judd, stated: "He (Callinicos) is actually trying to stick Mario for a salary of $250 per week plus $750 a performance. We are all determined Mario shall not pay this. We have a young British accompanist standing by called Geoffrey Parsons and he would undertake the tour for expenses plus $85 a concert." Coast also told Judd: "Mario says he wants to get rid of Costa as soon as possible."[44] Nevertheless, Callinicos eventually settled for the $550 that he was offered and continued on the tour. This prompted Coast to tell Judd yet again, on the question of retaining Callinicos as accompanist: "Mario is not happy about this at all."[45] There is no doubt that Callinicos was truly in awe of Lanza's voice; yet, ultimately, he was always more concerned with the amount of money his association with the tenor could bring him.[46]

Reservations were made to fly back to Rome on the the morning of April 17th. Lanza, together with a somber Callinicos and Alex Revides, arrived in Rome in the early afternoon. As the tenor descended from the SAS plane he was dragging his right foot a little. He slowly made his way towards the terminal, where Betty and the children were waiting for him. Hugging and kissing his family, he reassured a worried Betty that he was fine.

30—MORE WARNINGS

IMMEDIATELY UPON ARRIVING at the Villa Badoglio, Lanza's personal doctor, Professor Giuseppe Stradone, was summoned. Dr. Stradone had been treating Lanza for his phlebitis and had in fact advised the singer not to go on the concert tour. Contrary to what Lanza had told his wife, the doctor's examination confirmed the German doctor's diagnosis. The singer's health was in a precarious state. As well as an enlarged heart and bad liver he was suffering from bronchitis and the leg inflammation caused by the phlebitis had not improved. His blood pressure was 290.[1]

During the time he had been treating him, Professor Stradone had come to know Lanza and his family, becoming fond of the troubled tenor. His recollections of Lanza were of "An extremely warm and tender man."

> He was a very soft, sensitive person with the typical temperament of an artist. Very emotional, but capable of formidable tenderness, as I often witnessed in his behavior with his wife and children. He was incredibly sensitive, which was in distinct contrast with his big build and manly appearance. In fact, in many respects he was just like a little boy.[2]

As a result of the tenor's poor state of health all his engagements, including an important and lucrative gala appearance at the Brussels' World Fair,[†] were cancelled.

Furthermore he was being sued for breach of contract and non-appearances by various promoters and concert managers and was in debt to the UK tax department to the tune of more than 2000 pounds.

Naturally the Hamburg episode again made world headlines.

[†]He was to have been the headliner, with the appearance being relayed by television throughout Europe.

257

It prompted Hy Gardner, columnist for the *New York Tribune* to telephone Lanza and ask him for a face to face interview, which the tenor gladly agreed to. In typical fashion he told Gardner: "How about coming over to the little castle I call home and I'll cook you a ton of fettuccine and chicken cacciatore and answer all your foolish questions."[3]

A week later Gardner flew to Rome. He began by asking Lanza for the truth about the Hamburg incident, noting that *Time* had already referred to the tenor's penchant for skipping dates. "*Newsweek* reported your failure to show was 'the old theatrical bromide that he was suffering from a cold,'" began Gardner, to which the tenor promptly replied: "*Time* and *Newsweek* should report facts, not fantasy.

> I caught a cold that was so bad I sounded like Andy Devine, and people were paying to hear Lanza. Dr. Shaake, the Hamburg State Opera's own physician examined me before the concert and told the impresario: 'I won't allow him to sing. If he wants to sing with this kind of a throat the last responsibility is up to the artist.'[4]

Gardner continued to prod Lanza about his previous record for not showing up on schedule, to which the tenor replied that it had only happened three times in his career. He cited *The Student Prince*, Las Vegas and Hamburg as the three instances, humorously adding:

> Does *Time* think a kid from South Philadelphia could have grossed more than $5,250,000 in five years and paid Uncle Sam more than $4 million in taxes if he didn't sing? What do they think? That I am a ventriloquist?[5]

The sceptical Gardner was completely won over by Lanza and after the tenor's sudden death paid him tribute by stating that "Mario was one of the nicest, brightest and most spirited persons I ever met, almost the antithesis of the picture painted by the press. His four youngsters have a rare and beautiful heritage, and I hope they never forget that their dad was a fine man."[6]

31—ONE LAST FILM

DESPITE THE BAD PUBLICITY that followed the Hamburg cancellation, extremely lucrative offers for Lanza to perform were coming in from all directions. There were bids from South Africa, and even from such faraway countries as Australia and New Zealand. Guarantees were as high as $10,000 per concert against 65% of receipts plus paid transportation for three.[1] Nor were the expressions of interest confined to concerts. During Lanza's recent concert tour in Britain, Covent Garden, for example, had contacted the tenor's British agent John Coast and told him they were interested in having Lanza perform in a number of operas.[2]

Coast himself was urging Lanza to take time off to study the part of *Otello*.[3] The subject had arisen months earlier when Lanza was in London and had granted an exclusive interview to journalist Godfrey Winn. John Coast and his wife, as well as representatives from Columbia Artists Management in New York, were also present.

Arriving at Lanza's suite at the Dorchester Hotel, Winn was amazed by the liveliness of his host, whom he knew was not a well man at the time. "His name should be 'Mercurial' not Mario," reported Winn, "for I have never met a man with such overflowing energy and such spontaneous vivacity. The man himself is so tremendously alive and real."[4]

The talk had soon turned to music, and while Lanza was involved in conversation with his American representatives, Winn took the opportunity to ask Coast his opinion of Lanza as a singer. Coast's reply encapsulated the conflict and the dilemma that Lanza had been fighting for years. "I would give anything in the world for Mario to study the title role of *Otello* and sing it at Covent Garden,"[5] replied Coast.

I know that they would like to have him appear there in some opera. But how is he to find the time to do all the necessary study? It is so frustrating to hear that superb voice holding an audience in thrall and not see it put to its highest use. The question is how much of the year should be given to films, how much to concerts, how much to television? I long for bigger challenges for him. There is nothing that he couldn't tackle. He has such compelling power in his voice, it is what we call a really big voice, but he possesses such subtlety and sustained softness too. I have watched him at close quarters again and again and I never cease to marvel at what complete control he possesses. He can do anything with his voice.[6]

Coast, who as well as Lanza represented a number of top singers, was quite adamant in telling Winn that in his professional judgment, Lanza possessed the greatest voice of any singer.[7] At this point Coast turned to Lanza, who was resting his bad leg over the side of a chair and holding a glass of champagne, urging the tenor to make his debut at Covent Garden: "Just like Menuhin, who gave up a whole year to re-study, shutting himself away in California, couldn't you do it too, with *Otello*?" pleaded Coast. "If I had your voice..."[8]

The tenor replied in his typically evasive manner: "If you had my voice, my friend, you would realize as I do that it is a gift from God."[9]

Money continued to be at the root of Lanza's dilemma. He was being offered huge amounts for relatively short periods of work. Even for his concerts he was receiving far in excess of any other classical performer. Taking a year off to study a role would have entailed turning his back on income that he needed to sustain his extravagant lifestyle. Ironically, however, the recent European concert tour had helped Lanza to regain some of his confidence.[10] He was again becoming accustomed to performing before live audiences. If it hadn't been for his increasingly poor health this would have been an ideal moment to switch to grand opera, but pressed for money, he accepted an offer to make yet another film.

It is indeed doubtful whether any singer, operatic or otherwise, would have been able to turn down the fantastic sums of money that Lanza was being offered to make films. The latest proposal came from the German producer Alexander Gruter. He offered Lanza $200,000 plus 40 percent of the gross profits to star in a co-production between his own company, Corona Films, and the Italian Astor Films. MGM would again be responsible for supplying the technical staff, as well as distributing the film worldwide.

The Hungarian writer Andrew Solt, who had been active in Hollywood for a number of years, was chosen to write the screenplay. Solt decided to write a story loosely based on Lanza's reputation. It would be about a tenor notorious for his temperament, his unpredictability, and his non-appearances, who finally finds love when he meets a deaf girl who loves him for himself and not for his voice or fame.

Preliminary work on the film, initially titled *Silent Melody*, was due to start in early May, but because of Lanza's ill health and massive weight gain, the starting date had to be postponed. The tenor was in no condition to face the cameras. His weight had shot up to 260 lb (118 kg), his blood pressure was 290 and the phlebitis was still bothering him.[11]

Determined to go ahead with the film Lanza embarked on yet another severe diet. By now, however, he was experiencing considerable difficulty in shedding the excess weight. No matter how much he starved himself, the extra pounds just did not seem to come off. In the meantime, Gruter was becoming increasingly impatient and eventually, with Lanza appearing not to make any progress with his dieting, he considered replacing him with Italy's current operatic idol and heartthrob, Franco Corelli. [12]

Corelli, who at 37 was exactly Lanza's age, had had a late start as a singer, having made his operatic debut at the age of 30. He had since quickly established himself as a tenor to be reckoned with after a number of successful appearances at La Scala, and elsewhere in Italy and Europe. Gruter discussed Lanza's weight problems with Alfredo Panone, who along with conductor Paul Baron was one of the associate producers on the film. Panone contacted Corelli, and when the tenor expressed interest in the project, arranged a meeting with him. Together with the author of the screenplay Andrew Solt, Panone went to Corelli's home. The two men were instantly impressed by the tenor's good looks. "He looked perfect," recalled Solt.

He was very handsome, but during the course of our conversation we became aware of a couple of problems. The first was that he couldn't speak a word of English, but we figured that could be remedied. The second problem, however, was a serious one. We noticed that every time he smiled so much of his gums showed that the look closely resembled that of a horse.[13]

Panone and Solt concluded that this was an insurmountable handicap in a prospective movie star. "We decided," Solt continued, "that while we could teach him to speak his lines in English, or at worst dub him, there was nothing we could do to lower his upper lip when he smiled, and so we had to forget about him and go back to Lanza."[14]

Andrew Solt's recollections of Lanza when they were working on *For the First Time* were that "He was a good husband and good father. He was a lovable person. Highly intelligent, very smart and fast and funny."[15]

In the meantime, Lanza had decided to go ahead with a concert tour of South Africa. But as the date of departure grew closer, it became clear that both physically and psychologically it was unthinkable that he could stand up to the strain of another concert tour. At the very last moment the tour was cancelled, much to the consternation of Callinicos, who again was more concerned about the fees he would be foregoing than about Lanza's well-being.[16] What Lanza desperately needed was rest and a period of sustained therapy in order to wean him off alcohol and hopefully improve his general health.

Still intending to proceed with his film, and concerned about Lanza's health, Gruter suggested to the tenor that he go to Walchensee, a sanatorium for alcoholics and overweight people situated in the Bavarian Alps, a short distance from Munich. At first Lanza would not hear of it,[17] but after a concerted effort Gruter managed to persuade him that Walchensee presented his best option. On May 28, 1958 Lanza entered the sanatorium.

Initially it was planned for Lanza to undergo a two-week "twilight sleep" therapy, during which he would be fed intravenously. As well as being an effective method for losing weight, the sleep therapy meant that after the prolonged period of total rest, the patient would wake up feeling better both physically and mentally.

Although the therapy was at first attempted, Dr. Fruhwein realized immediately that a standard injection of Megaphen, the drug required to put the patient to sleep had no effect whatsoever on Lanza. A stronger dose of the drug, given the singer's bad liver condition, could have proved fatal. Submitting him to the effective, but potentially dangerous, sleep therapy was out of the question.[18]

Dr. Fruhwein confirmed the seriousness of Lanza's ill health. The tenor, as well as the liver condition, was suffering from an enlarged heart, abnormally high blood pressure and phlebitis. Again, Lanza was told quite categorically that, unless he cut out drinking, his life would be in danger.[19] The stern warning from Dr. Fruhwein had little effect on Lanza, who kept insisting that he had a strong constitution and an indestructible body. In order to emphasise the seriousness of his condition Dr. Fruhwein had even showed Lanza the x-rays of his sick liver and placed them next to those of a healthy patient's liver. The difference was startling and the singer had been temporarily taken aback.

By now, however, Lanza's addiction had become a serious one. He would consume large amounts of alcohol that ranged from beer and wine to spirits, including his latest discoveries, Campari and Cognac. Under the circumstances the confinement at Walchensee was extremely difficult at first. Although he was under strict supervision and stuck to a rigid diet, he still managed to bribe a member of the staff to bring him alcohol.[20]

At the sanatorium he felt like a caged animal and was desperately lonely. After two weeks he was unable to bear it any longer and telephoned Betty, arranging for her to bring the family for a visit.[21]

With his family near him, his mood began to improve. He stopped drinking, began to exercise, went swimming in the nearby lake and played with the children. In view of the planned film, various meetings began to take place with those involved such as director Rudolph Maté, scenarist Andrew Solt and George Stoll, who again had been assigned as Musical Director on the film. Also on hand were the film's producer Alexander Gruter, associate producers Alfredo Panone and conductor Paul Baron, and the ever-present Callinicos, who was working with Lanza on the operatic selections for the film, which was now ironically entitled *For the First Time.*

With all the activity taking place around him, Lanza managed to pull himself together, and on August 23—after more than 12 weeks in the sanatorium—having lost 45 pounds (20.4 kg), his health temporarily restored and in better spirits, he left Walchensee and returned to Rome.

The operatic numbers for the film were to be recorded and filmed during the last week of August at the Rome Opera House. Lanza would sing with Callinicos conducting the 150-member Rome Opera Orchestra, together with soloists and chorus.

For years speculation had been rife throughout Italy as to exactly what kind of voice Lanza possessed and what he sounded like in person. Since his arrival Lanza had not sung any concerts in Italy, and consequently his appearance for the recording sessions created considerable interest among the staff and musicians of the Rome Opera. In common with most of their colleagues, not only in Italy but indeed throughout the world, they tended to think that Lanza's voice was largely the product of the sound technicians. The curious, the sceptics and the critical were in for a considerable surprise.

As soon as he had finished recording his first number, the triumphal scene from the second act of *Aida*, there was a spontaneous reaction from the members of the orchestra. Both surprised and excited, they proceeded to congratulate the tenor, asking him if he was going to sing at the Rome Opera.[22] As the recording sessions progressed, with Lanza singing "*Vesti la giubba*" from *Pagliacci*, the Death Scene from *Otello* and the Trio from *Così fan tutte,* one could feel the excitement mounting among those present. They found it difficult to believe that the much maligned "film tenor" was actually the possessor of a remarkable voice.

Riccardo Vitale, Artistic Director of the Rome Opera, complimented Lanza and invited him to open a season. Among the roles mentioned as possibilities were Canio in *Pagliacci* and Cavaradossi in *Tosca.*[23]

Coincidentally, La Scala in Milan, who wanted the tenor for an initial minimum period of two years, also repeatedly offered him the role of Cavaradossi. As usual, Lanza was non-committal and limited himself to telling Vitale that one-day he would be back. [24] Years later Vitale was to say: "Mario Lanza was a tenor of great quality who possessed an exceptional timbre, and was very musical."[25]

For the First Time went before the cameras soon after with interior scenes filmed in Rome and at the CCC Studios in Spandau, Berlin, together with location work in Capri, Salzburg and Vienna. The producers had decided to give the film an international flavor and surrounded Lanza with a mixture of nationalities. Included in the cast were Zsa Zsa Gabor—essentially playing herself and contributing nothing to the film—the experienced Austrian actor Kurt Kasnar, who was amusing as Lanza's long-suffering manager, and a charming and talented young German actress, Johanna von Koczian, in the female lead.

As with *Seven Hills of Rome,* the new film's chief drawback was the script, which contained some inane dialogue. The direction of the Polish/Hungarian cinematographer-turned-director Rudolph Maté was somewhat better. Maté had been scheduled to direct Lanza in *Seven Hills of Rome* the previous year, but had been forced to withdraw due to delays in the start of filming.

Maté had gained considerable renown as a first-class cinematographer working with Carl Theodore Dryer on such classics as *The Passion of Joan of Arc* and *Vampyr,* and later in Hollywood on *Dante's Inferno* with Spencer Tracy. Nominated five times for an Academy Award, he had turned to directing in 1947 with uneven results.[†]

Maté knew his craft and in *For the First Time* made the best of his material. If the story was weak and the script poor, there were the compensations of Lanza's singing, Johanna von Koczian's delightful performance, some beautiful location photography, well-staged operatic sequences, and good acting from the supporting cast, which included veteran German actor Hans Sohnker. Recalling his working relationship with Lanza, Sohnker was highly complimentary.

So much has been said about Lanza's magnificent voice that

[†]His directorial career included some good minor thrillers such as *The Dark Past* and *Union Station,* both with William Holden, *D.O.A.* with Edmond O'Brien and the juvenile costumer, *The Prince Who Was a Thief,* which had made a star out of Tony Curtis.

there's no need for me to mention it again. Some people maintain that he was not a good actor, but I had a different impression. I had the chance to see him during the recording of the scene when he sang the aria from *Pagliacci*. At that time he made an unforgettable impression on me both as a singer and as an actor. In fact he stood on the stage like a wounded deer.[26]

Lanza's appearance in his last film, however, laid bare the sad reality. Although he was in excellent voice, he looked tired, edgy and considerably older than thirty-seven throughout most of the film. Gone was the vitality and exuberance of the tenor who had taken Hollywood by storm just a decade earlier. Instead his last film reveals a tired, worn-out man. The smile is forced. The distinctive sparkle in his eyes is gone.

As was often the case when he was working, Lanza managed to control his drinking throughout the three-month filming schedule. He stuck bravely to a strict diet, which saw his weight drop to 196 lb (88.8kg) by the time the cameras had stopped rolling in early December.

The atmosphere throughout filming was possibly the most congenial since Lanza had worked on *The Great Caruso* eight years earlier. He got on extremely well with all concerned, from director Maté to his co-stars Kurt Kasnar and Hans Sohnker, and most importantly with female lead Johanna von Koczian. The 25-year-old von Koczian was herself a singer. That same year she had sung the part of Polly Peachum in a recording of Kurt Weill's *The Threepenny Opera* with Lotte Lenya as Jenny. Years later, she would sing Eliza in a German production of *My Fair Lady* in Frankfurt. The daughter of an Austrian Army captain, she had come to films via the stage where she had recently appeared in the title role in *The Diary of Anne Frank*. This would be her first English-speaking role and as such she required considerable help, patience and understanding with her dialogue. She found a sympathetic guide in Lanza, who was by now well accustomed to helping his co-stars with their lines.

The young actress worked well with the tenor and became very fond of him. She genuinely admired him as a singer and liked him as a person. Less than a year later she was shattered by the news of his untimely death, saying: "I had never worked with such a charming and lovable colleague. I enjoyed his company very much." [27] While Lanza found the young actress enchanting, he reaffirmed his love for his wife on the set. "My love for Betty is like an atom explosion," he declared when his wife joined him in Berlin.[28] It was true. Despite all the triumphs and despair, they still clung to each other. Theirs was an indestructible love. A month before he died Lanza told Sam Steinman: "You know what Betty said to me this morning? 'Let's have another baby.'" [29]

It was while he was filming in Berlin that news reached him that his friend Tyrone Power had died from a heart attack while filming *Solomon and Sheba* in Spain. Lanza was visibly upset by the news. Power was only 45 and, in a way, his demise reinforced Lanza's own premonition of an early death.[30]

Back in Rome where the last sequences of *For the First Time* were being filmed, Lanza appeared to be the happiest man in the world. He enjoyed making fun of Zsa Zsa Gabor and her reputation as a *femme fatale*. On the first day of filming in Rome, he presented her with a gift basket containing a typical *double entendre* note. It read: "Zsa Zsa, while in Germany you said the sausage was a delight, so while in Italy you must treat it just right!" [31] His agent Sam Steinman recalled their good-humored relationship.

> [Lanza] used to rib her all the time, but she took it pretty well. Mario used to ask her, "Did you get anything last night?" and Gabor, who had a ready answer for everything, would smile and say "No, It's been a pretty bad night for pickings."...Zsa Zsa had this Italian prince who was taking her out and one morning when she came on the set, Mario asked her straight out, "Did he fuck you?" Unperturbed by the direct question, Gabor, with a shrug of the shoulders and a note of disappointment in her voice, replied: "No, he didn't even try!" [32]

If, on the surface, Lanza came across as a happy-go-lucky extrovert, very few were given the opportunity to see behind the façade. However, in those rare moments when he was alone he would sometimes be caught off-guard with his head buried in his hands, a man in the depths of despair. As soon as he became aware of someone's presence he would immediately recompose himself, sit up, smile and act as if nothing was wrong. Occasionally his make-up man, Otello Fava, would ask him if there was anything bothering him, but he always insisted that everything was fine. [33]

If working on a film made it easier for him to control his drinking, the moment the cameras stopped rolling he would revert back to the bottle.

The overall critical reception of *For the First Time* was reasonably good and the general consensus was that Lanza's voice was extraordinarily rich and big. As a rule, a singer's voice gradually becomes darker and rounder as he gets older. It is a natural process, enabling a singer to take on heavier roles. In the past year Lanza's voice had in fact darkened considerably, not so much due to age—he was, after all, only 37—but due to the abuse he was inflicting on his body. From a stylistic point of view, however, he had made considerable progress since his Hollywood days, particularly during the last few months.

This was mainly the result of his work with two gifted musicians, Annibale Bizzelli and Franco Zauli. Bizzelli was a respected coach from the Rome Opera.[34†] Zauli was not only a fine coach, but also an excellent pianist. Under the two men's guidance, Lanza's singing had become more controlled and operatic.

The progress is particularly evident in the more demanding arias in the film, such as "*Vesti la giubba*" from *Pagliacci*. In contrast to his youthful, albeit exciting, performance in *The Great Caruso* eight years earlier, the *For the First Time* version is more operatic and shows that Lanza would have been an ideal Canio on stage. Lanza also gives a straightforward and convincing rendition of the Death Scene from his favorite opera, *Otello*.

If anything this is underplayed by Lanza. Absent here is the sobbing and ranting of some of his famous colleagues, whose mannered performances are often mistaken for dramatic singing.

A surprising inclusion in the film is also the brief trio "*E voi ridete*" from the first act of Mozart's *Così fan tutte*. The lightness

---

†Lanza reportedly drove Bizzelli to distraction with his habit of rehearsing seminaked – a practice that dated back to his MGM days, when he would frequently emerge from his dressing room wearing only an athletic supporter, oblivious to the spectacle of females on the lot fleeing in all directions.

1. *Lanza's maternal grandparents, Ellisena (Ellisa) and Salvatore Lanza.*

2. *Lanza's parents, Antonio and Maria Cocozza (1920).*

3. *Lanza was born in the bedroom with two windows on the third floor of the middle building.*

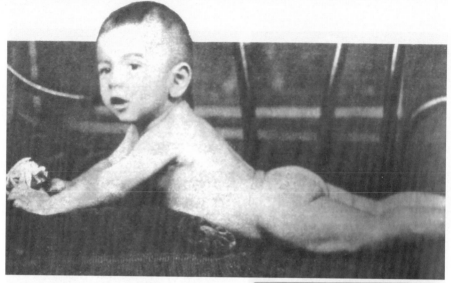

4. *Freddie at six months.*

5. *Freddie at age 1.*

6. *Freddie at 18 months.*

7. *Freddie at age 3.*

8. *Freddie at age 7 on his confirmation day.*

*. At the beach in the early 30s. Freddie is in the back with his father's arm around
im; his mother is sitting in front of him.

10. Freddie (arrow) at 16 with bocce players in 1937. His father is at far right
standing next to the truck.

11. *Lanza in his operatic debut as Fenton in* The Merry Wives of Windsor. *Tanglewood,* 1942.

12. *(left to right) James Pease as Marcello, Laura Castellano as Musetta, Mario Lanza as Rodolfo and Irma Gonzales as Mimi in the 3rd act of* La Bohème. *Tanglewood, 1942.*

13. Lanza with fellow student Giovanni Fiasca. Tanglewood, 1942.

14. Lanza in the chorus of Winged Victory, 44th St. Theater, Broadway. New York, 1943.

15. Betty Hicks at the time she met Mario Lanza.

16. *Mario and Betty Lanza on their wedding day, April 13, 1945.*

17. *RCA Victor's newly signed artists: (from left) Blanche Thebom, Robert Merrill, Ann McNight, Ania Dorfmann and Mario Lanza. New York (October, 1945).*

18. *(from left) Ania Dorfmann, unknown RCA executive, Robert Merrill, Ann McNight, Blanche Thebom, Mario Lanza. RCA studios, New York (October, 1945).*

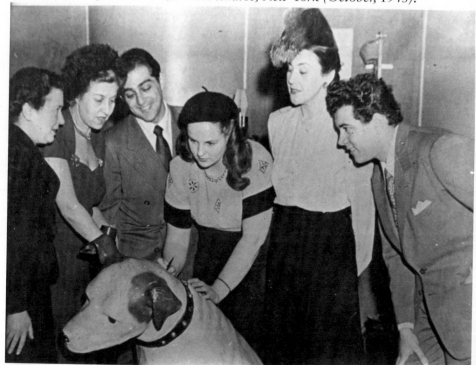

19. With Jean Tennyson on the radio program "Great Moments in Music." New York, 1945.

20. Telegram congratulating Lanza for his debut on "Great Moments in Music." October, 1945.

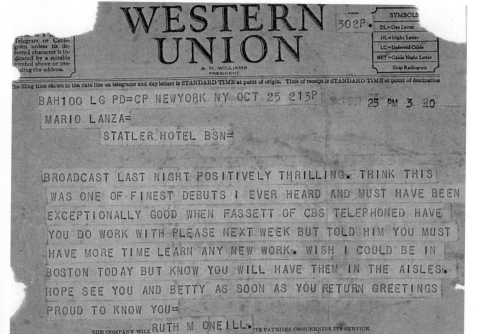

21. *With Betty in New York, 1945.*

22. *In front of Concert Hall in Atlantic City. September, 1945.*

23. Lanza's singing teacher, Enrico Rosati.

24. Postcard to his teacher after first two concerts in Chicago. July, 1946

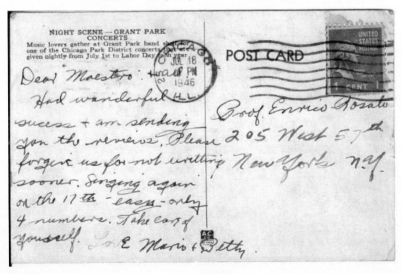

25. Mario and Betty Lanza surrounded by Betty's family and relatives after a concert in Chicago's Grant Park. July, 1946.

26. Lanza standing with Robert Weede, left, and George London, right. NewYork, 1946.

27. *Mario Lanza, Frances Yeend and George London: Bel Canto Trio publicity photo,* 1946.

28. *Lanza rehearsing with Frances Yeend, George London and Josef Blatt at the piano during Bel Canto Trio concert tour, 1947.*

29. *Lanza with Frances Yeend and George London. Los Angeles, 1947.*

30. *Rehearsing with Frances Yeend, George London and Eugene Ormandy for the concert at the Hollywood Bowl, August 1947.*

31. *On the eve of his first Hollywood Bowl concert. August, 1947.*

32. *With Betty on the grounds of the Hollywood Bowl. August, 1947.*

33. Mario Lanza, Frances Yeend and George London during Bel Canto Trio tour (1947)

34. Rehearsing with George London (1947).

BRILLIANT YOUNG AMERICAN TENOR
MARIO LANZA
ELECTRIFIES
AUDIENCE AT HOLLYWOOD BOWL—August 28, 1947

"THE SORT OF TENOR VOICE THAT NEARLY EVERY OPERATIC STAGE IN THE WORLD HAS BEEN YEARNING FOR, LO THESE MANY LEAN YEARS. LANZA'S IS THE WARM, ROUND, TYPICALLY ITALIAN TYPE OF VOICE that caresses every graceful phrase and makes the listener breathe with him as it molds each curve of the melody . . . He is young but it is the sort of youth all the world loves."
— Los Angeles Times

"ELECTRIFIED a large audience that cheered for several minutes . . . He has a truly rare asset in a naturally beautiful voice, which he already handles with intelligence, and a native artistry which, rightly developed, should prove his to be ONE OF THE EXCEPTIONAL VOICES OF THE GENERATION."
— Los Angeles Daily News

"AN ANSWER TO AN OPERA LOVER'S PRAYER AND ANY IMPRESARIO'S DREAM . . . Lanza gave us tenor singing in the BEST ITALIAN STYLE WITH A THRILLING VOICE, resonant and warm throughout its entire range. THIS 24-YEAR-OLD IS FAIRLY BURSTING WITH SONG. His voice has been beautifully trained . . . acquitted himself brilliantly."
— Hollywood Citizen-News

"Tenor Mario Lanza, from his opening notes, demonstrated why RCA Victor signed him to a recording contract. THERE'S A CARUSO-LIKE THROB TO HIS VOICE WHICH IN ITSELF IS BIG."
— Los Angeles Herald-Express

P.S. He got the job... an MGM Contract!!!

CONCERT MANAGEMENT ARTHUR JUDSON, Inc. · Division of COLUMBIA CONCERTS, Inc.
RCA Victor Records   434   PRINTED IN U.S.A.   113 West 57th Street, New York 19, N.Y.

WESTERN UNION

CLASS OF SERVICE		SYMBOLS
This is a full-rate Telegram or Cablegram unless its deferred character is indicated by a suitable symbol above or preceding the address.	JOSEPH L. EGAN PRESIDENT	DL = Day Letter NL = Night Letter LC = Deferred Cable NLT = Cable Night Letter Ship Radiogram

The filing time shown in the date line on telegrams and day letters is STANDARD TIME at point of origin. Time of receipt is STANDARD TIME at point of destination

SA512 PD=TDS BEVERLYHILLS CALIF 28 501P   '47 AUG 28   5

MARIO LANZA=
    BACKSTAGE HOLLYWOOD BOWL HD=

CANNOT TELL YOU HOW MUCH I'M LOOKING FORWARD TO HEARING YOU AGAIN TONIGHT I KNOW EVERYBODY THERE WILL BE IN FOR A GREAT TREAT BEST OF LUCK=

    WALTER PIDGEON.

THE COMPANY WILL APPRECIATE SUGGESTIONS FROM ITS PATRONS CONCERNING ITS SERVICE

35. *(opposite, above) Promotion orchestrating critical response to the Hollywood Bowl concert.*

36. *(opposite, below) Telegram from Walter Pidgeon following Hollywood Bowl concert.*

37. Program cover for Quebec concert with Agnes Davis. October, 1947.

38. With friend Barry Nelson in 1947.

39. Lanza in concert with unidentified soprano, circa 1947.

40. In concert with unidentified soprano, circa 1947.

41. *(above, left) Lanza as Pinkerton in professional operatic debut with New Orleans Opera (April, 1948).*

42. *(above, right) Backstage with conductor, Walter Herbert.*

43. *(below) In dressing room.*

4. (above) Backstage with
~~am~~ Weiler on left,
~~B~~etty and others.

5. Backstage with Betty.

46. *Lanza in second Hollywood Bowl concert (July, 1948).*

47. *(from left) Sister-in-law Jan Hicks, niece Carol Jane, Helen Spadoni, Giacomo Spadoni, Betty and Mario Lanza. Beverly Hills (Dec., 1948).*

48. *Wardrobe test for Lanza's first film,* That Midnight Kiss. *MGM Studios, 1948.*

49. *Rehearsing with Giacomo Spadoni. Los Angeles, 1949.*

50. *With Keenan and Ed Wynn on the set of* That Midnight Kiss *(1949).*

51. With Ethel Barrymore on the set of That Midnight Kiss. *MGM Studios, 1948.*

52. With Kathryn Grayson in publicity still for That Midnight Kiss *(1949).*

53. *With José Iturbi in scene from* That Midnight Kiss *(1949).*

54. Singing "*Celeste Aida*" in That Midnight Kiss (1949).

55. *With Kathryn Grayson in publicity still for* That Midnight Kiss *(1949)*.

56. *With Kathryn Grayson in final sequence of* That Midnight Kiss *(1949)*.

57. Publicity portrait for That Midnight Kiss *(1949).*

58. With baby Colleen and brother-in-law Bert Hicks. Beverly Hills, 1949.

59. *Oklahoma concert program.*
March, 1949.

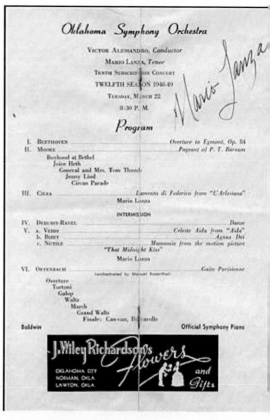

60. *With Constantine Callinicos at*
first RCA recording session.
New York, May 5, 1949.

61. *(above)*, 62. *(below left)*, 63. *(below right) With Betty and Colleen. Beverly Hills, 1949.*

64. *With pet dog "Tenor."*
Beverly Hills, 1949.

65. *(below) With Colleen*
and pet canary "Pretty
Boy." Beverly Hills, 1949.

66. *In scene from* The Toast of New Orleans *(1950).*

67. *With Betty, his mother and Colleen on his 29th birthday. January, 31, 1950.*

68. *On* The Toast of New Orleans *set on his 29th birthday, holding Colleen, with Betty and his mother beside.*

69. *With young musicians on the set of* The Toast of New Orleans *(1950).*

70. *Lanza, Betty and Joe Pasternak having fun on Dorothy Pasternak's birthday. Dorothy is on Betty's right. The woman next to Lanza is not identified.*

71. Listening to an Edison cylinder on the set of The Toast of New Orleans *(1950).*

72. Stage director Armando Agnini showing Lanza and Grayson how to perform the love duet from The Toast of New Orleans *(1950).*

3. *With Kathryn Grayson in the Madama Butterfly scene from* The Toast of New
Orleans *(1950).*

74. *With Kathryn Grayson in scene from* The Toast of New Orleans *(1950).*

75. *With David Niven and Kathryn Grayson on Grayson's birthday. February, 1950.*

76. *Publicity portrait for* The Toast of New Orleans *(1950).*

77. *(from left) Kathryn Grayson, Lanza, Sam Weiler and Norman Taurog on* The Toast of New Orleans *set (1950).*

78. *With Sam Weiler on* The Toast of New Orleans *set (1950).*

79. *(below)With Rita Moreno in scene from* The Toast of New Orleans *(1950).*

80. MGM *publicity portait, 1950.*

81. With Betty in Honolulu (March, 1950).

82. (below) With Betty, Howard Keel and concert manager Fred Matsuo standing behind them. Honolulu (March, 1950).

83. On stage during Honolulu concert.

84. Esther Williams presenting Lanza with a token of appreciation after Honolulu concert.

85. Dorothy Pasternak greeting Lanza on stage after Honolulu concert.

86.Betty with Tyrone Power.

(from left) Peter Herman Adler, Richard Thorpe, Joe Pasternak and Lanza during recording session for The Great Caruso.

With Peter Herman Adler, seated, and Irving Aaronson listening to playback of pre-ording for The Great Caruso *soundtrack (1950).*

89. With Jarmila Novotna on the set of The Great Caruso *(1950).*

90. (above) with Ann Blyth in publicity still for The Great Caruso and 91. (right) with Blyth on the set of The Great Caruso.

92. *With Ludwig Donath in scene from* The Great Caruso *(1950).*

93. *(from left) Carl Milletaire, Lanza, Ann Blyth. In background, Vincent Renno,
Ludwig Donath and Shepard Menken in scene from* The Great Caruso *(1950).*

94. *With Dorothy Kirsten in publicity still for* The Great Caruso.

95. *With Dorothy Kirsten in final scene of* Aida. The Great Caruso, *1950.*

96. *(below) With Marina Koshetz in* Cavalleria rusticana *sequence from* The Great Caruso.

97. *With Jarmila Novotna in publicity still for* The Great Caruso *(1950).*

98. *With Blanche Thebom in* Rigoletto *scene from* The Great Caruso *(1950).*

99. *Singing* Cielo e mar *from* La Gioconda *in scene from* The Great Caruso.

100. Getting into character on the set of The Great Caruso *(1950).*

101. (from left) Lanza, Carl Milletaire, Mario Siletti and unidentified player in scene from The Great Caruso *(1950).*

102. *As Enrico Caruso in publicity still for* The Great Caruso *(1950).*

103. With Betty and Colleen on
The Great Caruso *set (1950).*

104. With his father on The Great Caruso *set.*

105. Singing Vesti la giubba *from* Pagliacci. *Richard Hageman conducting in scene from* The Great Caruso *(1950).*

106. With Jimmy Durante on The Great Caruso *set in 1950.*

107. *(above) With studio boss Louis B. Mayer.*

108. *Publicity still for* The Great Caruso *(1951).*

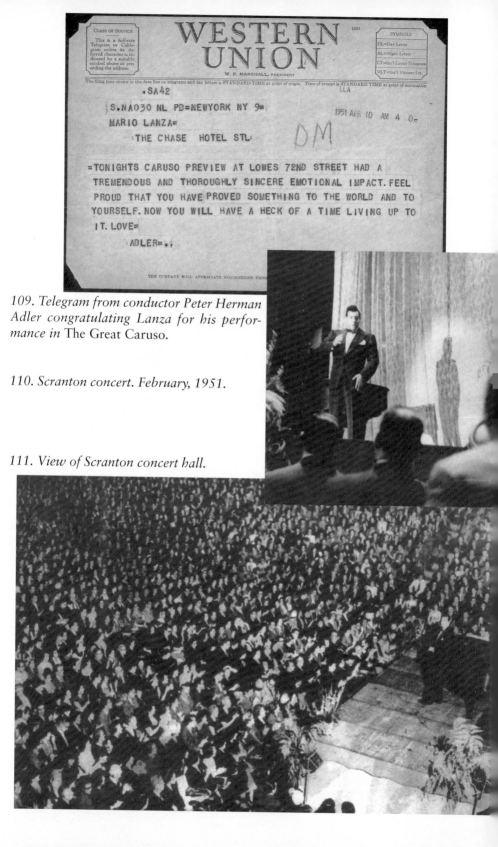

WESTERN
UNION

W. P. MARSHALL, PRESIDENT

1201

The filing time shown in the date line on telegrams and day letters is STANDARD TIME at point of origin. Time of receipt is STANDARD TIME at point of destination

LLA

•SA42

S•NA030 NL PD=NEWYORK NY 9=

MARIO LANZA=

:THE CHASE HOTEL STL:

1951 APR 10 AM 4 0=

DM

=TONIGHTS CARUSO PREVIEW AT LOWES 72ND STREET HAD A
TREMENDOUS AND THOROUGHLY SINCERE EMOTIONAL IMPACT. FEEL
PROUD THAT YOU HAVE PROVED SOMETHING TO THE WORLD AND TO
YOURSELF. NOW YOU WILL HAVE A HECK OF A TIME LIVING UP TO
IT. LOVE=

:ADLER=••

THE COMPANY WILL APPRECIATE SUGGESTIONS FROM

109. *Telegram from conductor Peter Herman Adler congratulating Lanza for his performance in* The Great Caruso.

110. *Scranton concert. February, 1951.*

111. *View of Scranton concert hall.*

112. *With Betty, receiving keys of the city from the mayor of Scranton.*
February, 1951.

113. *With Sam Weiler in Scranton record store. February, 1951.*

114. *Rehearsing for concert with Pittsburgh Symphony Orchestra. March, 1951.*

115. *(left) With Betty prior to concert in his native Philadelphia. March, 1951.*

116. *Cover of Richmond Concert Program.*

117. *With Ellisa on his knees,*
Betty holding Colleen.
Beverly Hills, 1951.

118. *With his parents.*
Beverly Hills, 1951.

119. *(below) With Betty and producer*
Jesse Lasky at the Hollywood premiere
of The Great Caruso. *April, 1951.*

120. Cover story in Time magazine.
August 6, 1951.

121. Relaxing with Betty.
Beverly Hills, 1951.

122. *On weightloss program for* Because You're Mine.

123. *With Betty in Oregon.*

124. With Doretta Morrow in scene from Becasue You're Mine *(1951).*

125. Another scene from Because You're Mine *with Doretta Morrow.*

26. With Doretta Morrow.
Publicity still for Because You're
Mine (1951).

27. (below) Going over script with
Paula Corday and Doreta Morrow
on the set of Because You're Mine
(1951).

128. (above, from left) Lanza,
Coretta Morrow, Mrs. Hall,
Alexander Hall and Betty Lanza
celebrating director Hall's birthday
on the set of Because You're Mine
(1951).

129. Celebrating Alexander Hall's
birthday on the set of Because You're
Mine.

130. *(from left) Lanza, Joe Pasternak, Ray Sinatra and Irving Aaronson at the piano on the set of* Because You're Mine. *December, 1951.*
131. *With his parents, Colleen, Ellisa and Betty on the set of* Because You're Mine. *January 31, 1952 (Lanza's birthday).*

132. *Lanza with (from left) Raphaela Fasano, Colleen and Betty. Beverly Hills (December, 1951).*

133. *(from left) Ellisa, Lanza's mother Maria, Lanza, Lanza's father Antonio, Colleen and Betty celebrating Lanza's 31st birthday on the set of* Because You're Mine. *January 31, 1952.*

134. With Catherine Chapman
in Cavalleria rusticana *scene
from* Because You're Mine
(1952).

135. With Sam Weiler on the set
of Because You're Mine. *January
31, 1952.*

136. *Rehearsing the aria* Questa o quello *for scene in* Because You're Mine, *with Wolfgang Martin at the piano and Irving Aaronson standing beside (1952).*

137. *(from left) Lanza's parents, Antonio and Maria, Dick Wessel, Lanza and Bobby Van in scene from* Because You're Mine *(1952).*

138. *Ricardo Montalban introduces Mexican lightweight world champion boxer Lauro Salas to Lanza on the set of* Because You're Mine *(1952).*

139. *Evidence of drastic weight loss during final days of filming* Because You're Mine *(1952).*

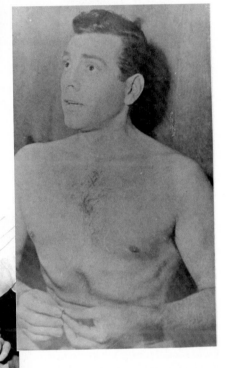

0. *With Alexander Hall on the set of* Because u're Mine *(1952)*

141. *With Paula Corday in scene from* Because You're Mine *(1952).*

142. *Relaxing in between films* *(1952).*

143. *Receiving Photoplay's Gold Medal for his performance in* The Great Caruso *from Editorial Director Fred Sammis (1952).*

144. With Betty in Beverly Hills.

145. Telegram from TCA's Vice President George Mrek (1952).

CLASS OF SERVICE		SYMBOLS	
This is a full-rate Telegram or Cablegram unless its deferred character is indicated by a suitable symbol above or preceding the address.		DL=Day Letter	
		NL=Night Letter	
		T=Int'l Letter Telegram	
		VLT=Int'l Victory Ltr.	

WESTERN UNION : (04)..

W. P. MARSHALL, PRESIDENT

The filing time shown in the date line on telegrams and day letters is STANDARD TIME at point of origin. Time of receipt is STANDARD TIME at point of destination

OA134

O.NB170 PD=NRI NEWYORK NY 8 1128A=   1952 AUG 8 AM 9 16

MARIO LANZA=

236 1/2 SOUTH SPALDING DR BEVERLYHILLS CALIF=.

JUST HEARD YOUR LATEST RECORDINGS CONGRATULATIONS ON WONDERF

PERFORMANCE LOOKING FORWARD TO MORE MILLION SALES FOR YOU=

:GEORGE MAREK RCA VICTOR DIVISION=

THE COMPANY WILL APPRECIATE SUGGESTIONS FROM ITS PATRONS CONCERNING ITS SERVICE

146. *MGM studio portrait.*

147. Recording weekly radio program, 1952.

148. Recording radio program (1952)

149. *With Betty and friends Andy and Della Russell vacationing on a ranch near Las Vegas prior to start of production on The Student Prince. April, 1952.*

150. *(above right) On ranch near Las Vegas. April, 1952.*

151. *Relaxing on ranch near Las Vegas. April, 1952.*

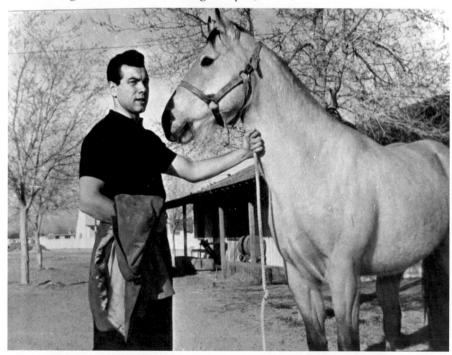

152. *During a pause, while working on the score of* The Student Prince *(1952).*

153. *(below) With Joe Pasternak and Constantine Callinicos at the piano rehearsing songs for* The Student Prince *soundtrack (1952).*

154. *(below) Going over the score of* The Student Prince *with Joe Pasternak (1952).*

155. Telegram advising Lanza that he has been voted best classical male vocalist radio. January, 1953.

CLASS OF SERVICE

This is a full-rate Telegram re Cablegram unless its deferred character is indicated by a suitable symbol above or preceding the address

WESTERN UNION

1201

SYMBOLS

DY—Day Letter

NL—Night Letter

LC—Int'l Letter Telegram

VLT—Int'l Victory Ltr

W. P. MARSHALL, PRESIDENT

The filing time shown in the date line on full-rate telegrams and day letters is STANDARD TIME at point of origin. Time of receipt is STANDARD TIME at point of destination

.0A151

0-C3U218 NL PD-CB NEW YORK NY 4

1953 JAN 4 PM 6 30

MARIO LANZA

=622 TOYOPA DRIVE PACIFIC PALISADES CALIF=

=THIS INFORMATION CONFIDENTIAL UNTIL JANUARY 23RD. WE ARE
HAPPY TO INFORM YOU THAT YOU HAVE BEEN ELECTED THE BEST
CLASSICAL MALE VOCALIST IN RADIO. THIS SELECTION WAS MADE BY
THE RADIO EDITORS OF THE UNITED STATES IN THE SEVENTEENTH
ANNUAL BALLOTING CONDUCTED BY FAME MAGAZINE FOR MOTION PICTURE
DAILY. FURTHER DETAILS AVAILABLE FROM ERIC WARNER AT OUR
HOLLYWOOD OFFICE GRANITE 2145

=RAYMOND LEVY VICE PRESIDENT QUIGLY PUBLISHING CO=

156. (left) With Colleen, who is holding baby Damon, and Ellisa. Bel Air, 1953.

157.(from left) Seated, Colleen, Lanza, Ellisa and Lanza's mother; standing, Lanza's father and Betty holding baby Damon. Bel Air, 1953.

158. *With Betty and his mother after the first* Shower of Stars *TV Show. September 30, 1954.*

159. *Miming to his 1950 recording of* Vesti la giubba *on the* Shower of Stars *show. CBS Studios (September 30, 1954).*

160. *(below)* *With Harry James (2nd from left) and Betty Grable after* Shower of Stars *TV show. September 30, 1954.*

WESTERN UNION

CLASS OF SERVICE

This is a full-rate Telegram or Cablegram unless its deferred character is indicated by a suitable symbol above or preceding the address.

W. P. MARSHALL, PRESIDENT

SYMBOLS

DL=Day Letter

NL=Night Letter

LT=Int'l Letter Telegram

VLT=Int'l Victory Ln.

The filing time shown in the date line on telegrams and day letters is STANDARD TIME at point of origin. Time of receipt is STANDARD TIME at point of destination.

0A629 SSM427

0.BHA494 PD=BEVERLY HILLS CALIF 30 745PMP=

MARIO LANZO=

135 COPLEY DR BEVERLY HILLS CALIF=

TONIGHT YOU ARE BRINGING HAPPINESS NOT ONLY TO US BUT TO MILLIONS OF PEOPLE. IN LIFES PATTERN DARK THREADS APPEAR ONLY TO MAKE THE GOLD SHINE MORE. WE LOVE YOU AND GOD BE WITH YOU=

MOM AND POP=

161. Telegram from his parents.

162. Singing for members of the press at his Beverly Hills home. October 4, 1954.

163. With Sarita Montiel in scene from Serenade *(1955).*

164. On location in San Miguel, Mexico, during filming of Serenade *(1955).*

165. With Frank Puglia and Sarita Montiel in cut scene from Serenade *(1955).*

166. (right) Scene from Serenade. *San Miguel, Mexico (1955).*

167. Telegram from his wife and children on completion of location filming in Mexico. October, 1955.

CONGRATULATIONS

by WESTERN UNION

LAO 48
L WLAO60 RX CGN PD= WESTLOSANGELES CALIF 16 145PMP=
MARIO LANZA=   1955 OCT 16 PM 2 49
    HILTON HOTEL EL PASO TEX=!

DEAR DADDY WELCOME HOME WE LOVE YOU AND CAN'T WAIT TO
SEE YOU. PLEASE BRING HOME THE BACON HUGS AND KISSES=
    COLLEEN ELISA DAMON MARC BETTY AND SUGAR=

168. *With Jean Fenn and Vincent Price in scene from* Serenade *(1955).*

169. *With Joan Fontaine in scene from* Serenade *(1955).*

170. *Anthony Mann showing Lanza how to play a scene in* Serenade *(1955).*

171. *Scene from* Serenade *(1955).*

172. *With Joan Fontaine in cut scene from* Serenade *(1955)*.

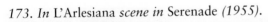

173. *In* L'Arlesiana *scene in* Serenade *(1955)*.

174. As Cavaradossi with Lilian Molieri in cut scene from Serenade *(1955).*

174. As Rodolfo with Norma Zimmer in cut scene from Serenade *(1955).*

176. Holding Marc and Damon on Warner's lot (1955).

177. With Betty, Marc, Damon, Ellisa and Colleen on Waner's lot (1955).

178. *With Licia Albanese during* Otello *recording session. November, 1955.*

179. *Singing monologue from Act 3 of* Otello; *Licia Albanese sitting at far right. Scene from* Serenade *(November, 1955).*

180. (from left) Henry Blanke, Lanza, Renata Tebaldi and Ray Heindorf. Warner Brothers Studios (October, 1955).

181. With Renata Tebaldi (October, 1955).

182. Singing 3rd Act duet from Otello *with Licia Albanese in scene from* Serenade *(1955).*

183. With Licia Albanese in Otello *sequence from* Serenade *(1955).*

184. *In Otello costume in his dressing room.* Serenade, *1955.*

5. With painting of him- *f as* Otello. Serenade, *55.*

186. With Sarita Montiel on the set of Serenade *(1955).*

87.. Final scene from
erenade (1955).

8. Telegram from
thony Mann

SAW ALL THE FILM. THE REPORTS WERE HONEST. THE FILM
IS WONDERFUL. YOU NEVER LOOKED BETTER. YOU NEVER ACTED
BETTER. I WAS THRILLED, SO WILL YOU BE WHEN YOU SEE IT.
MY DEEPEST LOVE=
⎯⎯⎯ ANTHONY MANN=.➤➤

189 With Anthony Mann on the et of Serenade *(1956).*

190. With Betty in suite aboard the Giulio Cesare on the way to Italy. May, 1957.

191. (above right) On board the Giulio Cesare, on arrival in Naples, kissing Ellisa with Colleen on his knees, and with Marc, Betty and Damon. May 28, 1957.

192. Welcomed on arrival in Naples. May 28, 1957.

93. *On train upon arrival at Rome station with Betty, Ellisa and Colleen next to him. May 28, 1957.*

94. *With Marisa Allasio and Renato Rascel on the set of Seven Hills of Rome. June, 1957.*

195. *With Marisa Allasio and Renato Rascel on the set of* Seven Hills of Rome. *June, 19*

196. *With 1930s singing and screen idol Roberto Rabagliati, in scene from* Seven Hills Rome *(1957).*

197. With Marisa Allasio on location filming in St. Peter's Square. Seven Hills of Rome *(June, 1957).*

198. Indian wrestling with Marisa Allasio during location filming on Seven Hills of Rome *(June, 1957).*

199. (above) and 200. (right) With Betty on location filming for Seven Hills of Rome (1957).

201. *Piazza Navona sequence in* Seven Hills of Rome *(1957).*

202 *(above right) Signing autographs. Makeup man Otello Fava is standing behind him. During location filming on* Seven Hills of Rome *(1957).*

203. *(below) Damon, Marc, Betty, Ellisa Lanza, and Colleen, on location filming for* Seven Hills of Rome *(1957).*

204. *Singing* M'appari *in* Seven Hills of Rome *(1957).*

205. *(right) With Betty, 1957.*

206. *(below) Listening to playback (1957).*

207. *Arriving in Naples to receive the Enrico Caruso Award. July, 1957.*

208. *(below left) Arriving in Naples, as above.*

209. *(below) With Betty and mayor of Napels during presentation of the Enrico Caruso Award.*

210. *In Naples, waving from a boat.*

211. *View of the Villa Badoglio. Rome, 1957.*

212. *In the Villa Badoglio. Rome, 1*

213. *At home in the Villa Badoglio (1957).*

214. *With Ed Sullivan. Rome, 1*

215. (left) and 216. (below) Moments during the visit to his father's birthplace, Filignano. September, 1957.

217. Playing bocce in Filignano.

218. *In front of banner welcoming him.*

219. *(below)* With Maria Rosa *cousin of his grandfather Pompili*

220. *(below) Signing a record.*

221. *Singing to the fans in London. November 14, 1957.*

222. *Mobbed by fans on arrival at Victoria Station. London (November 14, 1957).*

223. *(above) and* 224.
(below right) With
Betty at press recep-
tion in the Dorchester
Hotel. London
(November 15, 1957).

225. Signed photo.

226. Meeting Queen Elizabeth II after Royal Command Performance. London Palladium (November 18, 1957).

227. *With Richard Tucker in Tucker's dressing room at Covent Garden. London, January 14, 1958.*

228. *With Richard and Sara Tucker, and Betty, at Covent Garden. London, January 14, 1958.*

PROGRAMME

I

Il lamento di Federico - - - - - - F. Cilea
From the opera L'Arlesiana first produced at Milan in 1897.

II

Lasciatemi morire - - - - - - C. Monteverdi
The only surviving aria from the opera L'Arianna which was first heard in 1608 but of which all the other music has been lost. Ariadne deserted by Theseus wishes to die.

Gia il sole dal Gange - - - - - A. Scarlatti
Pieta Signore - - - - - A. Stradella
O Lord have mercy on me a sinner.
O let my prayer, O let my grief
Avail to help my unbelief . . .

III

Piano Solos played by Constantine Callinicos

Nocturne in C minor (Posthumous) - - - - F. Chopin
Scherzo in B minor - - - - - F. Chopin

IV

Tell me O blue, blue sky - - - - V. Giannini
Bonjour ma belle - - - - - A. Behrend
There were roses in the garden.
There was laughter in the sky . . .
She was French and I was English,
So what was a man to do . . .
The House on the hill - - - - E. Charles
I have a house on the top of a hill
Where the clouds go drifting by,
And I have a lovely garden of dreams
In this house close to the sky . . .

V

E lucevan le stelle - - - - - G. Puccini
From the opera Tosca first produced at Rome in 1900. Cavaradossi, about to be executed,
sings of his love for Tosca. "When the stars were brightly shining, She came to me in the
garden, clasped me in her arms. . . . Now my dream of love is dispelled for ever: I lived
uncaring and now I die despairing. And never was life so dear to me!"

INTERVAL

VI

Piano Solos played by Constantine Callinicos

Nerantzula (from "Two Greek Dances") - - - C. Callinicos
Sonetto del Petrarca, 104 - - - - - F. Liszt
Feux D'artifice - - - - - C. Debussy

VII

Mamma mia, che vo sape? - - - - - E. Nutile
Mother always comes to ask me why
I am weeping, but I can't confess . . .
Ah can't you feel for me, why do you treat me so?
Mother always wants to know,
But I can not calm her fear
With a kiss that is a tear.
A Vucchella - - - - - F. P. Tosti
Marechiare - - - - - F. P. Tosti
When the moon rises over Marchiare
'Tis then that lovers' vows are softly spoken . . .
Ah, melody, sweet memory,
Your song of love is ever in my heart.

VIII

Softly as in a morning sunrise (from the operetta "The New Moon") S. Romberg
Softly as in a morning sunrise
The light of love comes stealing
In to a newborn day
A burning kiss is sealing
The vow that all betray.
I'm falling in love with someone - - - - V. Herbert

229. (above) Program of concert at Royal Albert Hall. London, January 16, 1958.

230. Lanza on stage during concert at Royal Albert Hall. London, January 16, 1958.

231. At Royal Albert Hall concert, January 16, 1958.

232, 233, 234. (right) Scenes from the Royal Albert Hall concert.

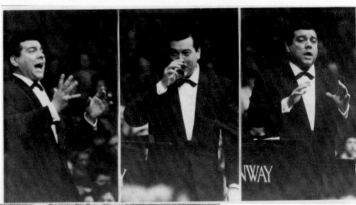

235. During the Royal Albert Hall concert. London, January 16, 1958.

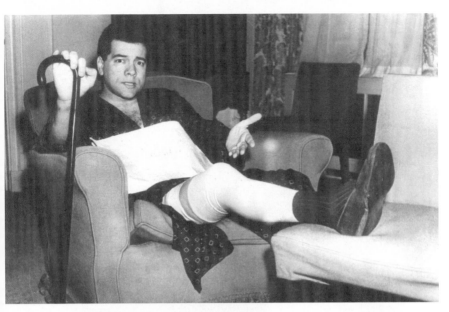

236. *Problems with phlebitis. Dorchester Hotel, London (March, 1958).*

237. *Weith journalist Godfrey Wynn. Dorchester Hotel, London (March, 1958).*

238. (above) During the 1958
European concert tour.

239. With Ellisa, Colleen, Marc and
Damon on boat to Capri during
filming of For The First Time
(1958).

240. With Johanna von Koczian in scene from For The First Time (1958).

241. With Johanna von Koczian during a pause in location filming on Capri for For The First Time (1958).

242. *(above) With Alex Revides on the left, George Stoll with back to camera. In a cafe on the Via Veneto (1958)*

243. *With Johanna von Koczian on the set of* For The First Time. *Berlin (November, 1958).*

244. *With Rudolph Maté and Zsa Zsa Gabor on the set of* For The First Time *(1958).*

245. *With the film crew of* For The First Time. *From left, Director Rudolph Maté, Zsa Zsa Gabor, Scriptwriter Andrew Solt, Cinematographer Aldo Tonti, Lanza, Editor Gene Ruggiero and Musical Director George Stoll sitting next to mascot made by Betty Lanza.*

246. *In* Così fan tutte *scene from* For The First Time *(1958).*

247. *As Otello in* For The First Time *(1958).*

248. With Johanna von Koczian in publicity still for For The First Time *(1958).*

249. Betty with group of children at a Christmas Party in 1958.

250. Betty with Marc, Damon, Ellisa and Colleen. Rome, Christmas 1958.

251. Lanza with Ellisa and Colleen; Betty with Damon and Marc. Rome, Christmas 1958.

252. *With Marc on train on way to vacation in Switzerland. December, 1958.*

253. *With Marc on train to Switzerland.*

254. *With pet dog Fury on the way to Switzerland. December, 1958.*

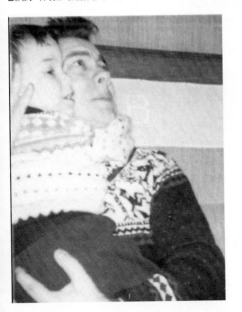

255. Holidaying in St. Moritz, Switzerland. January, 1959.

256. On holiday in St. Moritz.

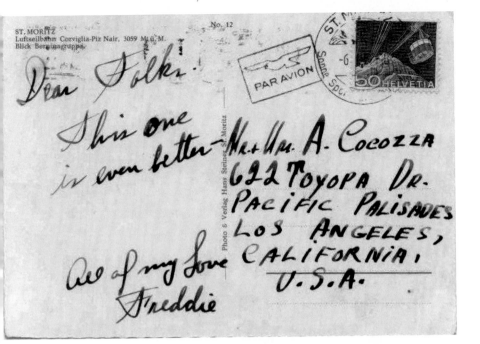

ST. MORITZ
Luftseilbahn Corviglia-Piz Nair, 3059 M ü. M.
Blick Bernagruppe

No. 12

Dear Folks!

This one is even better—

All of my Love

Freddie

Mr. + Mrs. A. Cocozza
622 Toyopa Dr.
Pacific Palisades
Los Angeles,
California,
U.S.A.

257. (above) and 258 (right): Post-cards to his parents from Switzerland. January, 1959.

SWISS HIT

VISTAPHON-Schallbild
Musical Picture · Reflet Sonore

VAL SILVRETTA et le Weisshorn
VAL SILVRETTA ed il Weisshorn

Im SILVRETTATAL mit Weisshorn, 3088 m · Graub.
SILVRETTA VALEY with Weisshorn, 10200 ft. - Grisons

«Im Dörtli» - Schottisch

Kapelle: RIBARY + HAGEN
Musik: Jost Ribary

Colorphoto Schneider, Luzern
Farbdruck: ENGADIN-PRESS, Samedan

Dear Folks —

It's just not true — You look and can't believe it. Wish you were here —

Love

Freddie

Mr. + Mrs. A. Cocozza
622 Toyopa Dr.
Pacific Palisades
Los Angeles,
California,
U.S.A.

LUFTPOST
PAR AVION VIA AEREA

Best.-Nr. / Order with: 14. R 53

Spielt mit 33 U./min.   Use 33 RPM

BIEM   Tous droits du producteur phonographique
et du propriétaire de l'oeuvre enregistrée
réservés.
Duplication, exécution publique, radiodiffusion interdites.

259. Coffin with Lanza's body being carried out of the Villa Badoglio. October 10, 1959.

260. The Immaculate Heart of Mary church in Piazza Euclide, Rome, on the day of the funeral (October 10, 1959).

261. *Outside the Immaculate Heart of Mary church on the day of Lanza's funeral (October 10, 1959).*

262. *(from left) Dr. Frank Silvestri, Betty, Marc, Damon, Ellisa and Colleen. Rome funeral (October 10, 1959).*

263. Mass at the Rome funeral.

264. Aerial view of funeral ceremony.

265. Betty with Dr. Frank Silvestri.

266. *Betty and Ellisa during Requiem Mass.*

267. *Lanza's grandfather and mother during the mass.*

268. Betty at Los Angeles funeral.
October 21, 1959.

269. Lanza's parents during Requiem
Mass in Los Angeles. October 21, 1959.

270. *Lanza as Canio.*

of this music is in marked contrast to the drama of Verdi and Leoncavallo, yet Lanza is just as good in the brief Mozart excerpt, further illustrating his versatility. Lanza also sings an excellent "*O sole mio*," and gives a good performance of the new ballad "Come Prima," which was the title of the film in Italy. There is also Schubert's "*Ave Maria*," complete with heavenly chorus, the Bavarian beer drinking "Hofbrahaus Song" and a snatch of Grieg's "*I love thee.*"

Unfortunately, he also attempts to sing a ghastly rock n'roll number entitled "Pineapple Pickers," written expressly by George Stoll, which, apart from an unnecessary brawl sequence in a bar, is the low point of the film.[†]

For the First Time performed well at the box office. In New York alone, where it opened at the Roxy Theater on August 13, 1959 it took $420,000 in four weeks. Gene Gleason in *The New York Herald Tribune* singled out the beautiful scenery and the technical proficiency of the filmmakers, adding: "Mr. Lanza never sounded better and...Johanna von Koczian has lovely brown eyes."[35]

Kay Proctor of the *Los Angeles Examiner* thought Lanza was no longer believable as a romantic lead but added: "The voice is still the Mario Lanza voice compared by many to the glorious quality of Caruso." [36]

Time's review mixed scepticism and sarcasm as usual:

The pre-recorded songs seem unable to locate Lanza's lips and might even have been scraped off old Lanza's soundtracks...If, like Johanna, moviegoers could keep their ears closed and their eyes open, they might enjoy Salzburg, Rome, Capri and Anacapri in fetching color.[37]

The best review came from Howard Thompson in *The New York Times*: "With the appeal of Mr. Lanza's voice, Miss von Koczian's performance and the splendor of the background the tenor has his most disarming vehicle in years."[38]

[†]The soundtrack album of *For the First Time* was nominated for a *Grammy* at the Awards that were jointly held on November 29th 1959 at the Beverly Hilton Hotel in Los Angeles and the Waldorf Astoria Hotel in New York. It lost out to *Porgy and Bess.*

32—THE FINAL MONTHS

FOR THE FIRST TIME WAS HARDLY COMPLETED when a succession of offers for further films started to pour in. The producer of *For the First Time*, Alexander Gruter, wanted to make another film called *That's My Man*, in which Lanza would co-star with the popular Spanish /Italian singer Caterina Valente. Another German producer, Arthur Brauner, was interested in the tenor for two films: *Granada*, and a musical version of Robin Hood. Al Panone and Irving Pisor, who had formed a company called Thor Films, wanted Lanza for *Laugh Clown Laugh* and *Gerardo the Great*. A further possibility, also for Brauner, was a film based on Johann Strauss, appropriately titled *Tales of the Vienna Woods*.

With the final studio scenes of *For the First Time* completed in Rome in December, Lanza was back in the recording studios for what would turn out to be one of his best albums. It was a collection of Neapolitan songs with some fine arrangements by two of Italy's up-and-coming musicians: Ennio Morricone, who would later gain fame as the composer of the scores of Sergio Leone's "Spaghetti Westerns," and Carlo Savina, who had already worked with Lanza on *For the First Time*.

In charge of the conducting was Franco Ferrara, the well-known and respected conductor from the Academy of Santa Cecilia in Rome. The tenor Ferrara encountered was a much-improved artist in many respects from the man who had recorded many of the same songs during the hectic Coca-Cola radio sessions of 1951/52. The voice was no longer as fresh or sparkling, and is almost baritone-like in parts, but the singing is more even and controlled. Displaying complete immersion in the Neapolitan idiom, Lanza combines superb phrasing and haunting intensity in outstanding performances of songs such as "*Tu ca nun*

270

chiagne," "*Voce 'e notte,*" "*Canta pe'mme,*" "*Na sera 'e maggio*" and "*Passione.*"

Ferrara's memories of Lanza during the recording sessions were of the tenor being "vocally extraordinary with a voice that had both steel and warmth." According to Ferrara it was "a Caruso-type voice" and Lanza "possessed a great musicality."[1] Perhaps surprisingly, given the obvious rapport between tenor and conductor on the album, the two men had only met on two occasions in the singer's home prior to recording the 12 songs. Nevertheless, the beautifully recorded album that emerged – simply entitled *Mario!* – would provide enduring proof of the scale of achievement that Lanza was capable of attaining when working under the right artistic conditions. Indeed, for many aficionados, the *Mario!* album ranks alongside the tenor's soundtrack recording of *The Student Prince* as his best performances of songs.[†]

1958 ended with the family celebrating Christmas and the respective birthdays of their first three children, who were all born during that month. The usual lavish festivities were planned for the joint birthday party to be held on December 20.

The night before the party, at nine in the evening, Lanza had summoned the guests he had been entertaining, including his agent Sam Steinman, to the television room. A gala concert with Maria Callas was being relayed through Eurovision from the Paris Opera and Lanza did not want to miss it.

He had followed Callas's career and her subsequent success closely, and admired her artistry more than the quality of her voice. For her part, Callas had paid Lanza the supreme compliment by describing him as "Caruso's successor." Replying that he was both flattered and frightened by the comparison, Lanza added that there would never be another Caruso.[2]

As Callas sang through excerpts from *Norma, Il Trovatore, Il Barbiere di Siviglia,* and finally the complete second act of *Tosca,* Lanza entertained his guests by serving Moët-Chandon 1947 champagne, delighting them with his explanations of various aspects of the performance.[3]

The children's birthday party on the following day resembled

[†]The album is best heard on the 2006 BMG/Sony Super Audio (SACD) release *Mario! Lanza At His Best.*

a miniature league of nations, with many of those attending the children of diplomats or show business people. There were American, Italian, German, British and Ceylonese children among them, all dressed up in their party dresses. The Lanzas spared no expense, even hiring four of the clowns who were appearing with the Great International Circus in Rome, as well as a magician and other entertainers. The food included chicken, salads, almost every variety of fruit available, ice cream, sweets and especially-prepared American hamburgers, which were a rarity in Rome at the time. Betty brought in a huge four-tier cake and the children sang "Happy Birthday." Then around seven in the evening, just before the party ended, all the children lined up in front of a beautiful oriental screen. Lanza suddenly emerged from behind the screen dressed as Father Christmas, and began handing presents to each of the children as they filed past him. Even though he had a recording session scheduled that evening, he did not want to miss the fun of dressing up and entertaining the children.[4]

What was destined to be their last Christmas together started, as it usually did, with the children getting up very early to see what Father Christmas had brought them. Among the many presents under the huge Christmas tree were all sort of toys, jigsaw puzzles, typewriters for the girls and toy cars for the boys and two presents that stood out from the rest. Each received a Zither, which Lanza had brought back from Austria, and a set of The New World Encyclopaedia.[5]

The following day the family left for a brief holiday and some fun in the snow in the Swiss resort of St. Moritz.

1959 began with Lanza still plagued by ill health. An electrocardiogram taken by heart specialist Professor Loredano Dalla Torre on 14 February 1959 revealed damage to the myocardium and coronary insufficiency. Two months later, on 17 April, Lanza complained of chest pains, and had to be admitted to the Valle Giulia Clinic. He had suffered a minor heart attack.[6] The phlebitis was also bothering him and, due to the weight he had put on since completing his last film, his blood pressure had again risen to 290. Under the supervision of Dr. Stradone, Lanza underwent a number of tests, resulting in medication for the phlebitis and blood pressure, and was placed on a diet and complete rest for two weeks.

Lanza was hardly out of the clinic when he began to rehearse for a number of newly scheduled recordings for RCA. On the planned recordings he was now working with Paul Baron, an American conductor who had been living in Rome for some time and had been his accompanist on the *Christophers* television show two years earlier. In the intervening time Baron, who had been introduced to Lanza by Alex Revides, had managed to ingratiate himself with the tenor—much to the annoyance of his regular conductor, Constantine Callinicos, who saw his privileged position threatened.[7]

Although a competent conductor, Baron's credentials were not exactly glowing. He had, in fact, been dismissed from his post as Musical Director for the CBS Network in America when it emerged that he had pirated the music of the song "Rum and Coca-Cola," for which he had written the lyrics, and passed it off as his own composition.[8] In short, he was just the sort of character whom Lanza seemed perennially to attract. "Mario Lanza was more sinned against than sinner," recalled agent and friend Sam Steinman. "There were an awful lot of people who had an angle, who wanted to get to him in order to make a dollar. Callinicos was sponging on him. Paul Baron was another one. Lanza trusted too many people and, as it turned out, he trusted the wrong ones."[9]

This time, however, the association between singer and conductor was to last a mere two months. Baron had already acted as co-producer on the tenor's last film, but his plan to join the long list of opportunists and spongers failed to materialize when he made the mistake of asking Lanza for 15% percent of his earnings in return for working with him.[10] Although still generous to a fault, Lanza had by now become a little wiser. He told Baron, "I don't even give that to Sam! (Steinman)" and with that statement permanently dismissed Baron.[11] On the positive side, the tenor's association with Baron produced three albums that also benefit from stylish conducting, good orchestrations and some excellent arrangements from Ennio Morricone and Baron himself. On the downside, the abuse that Lanza had inflicted on his body through the years and the resultant physical deterioration is clearly evident in this series of recordings.

The sessions started with a new stereophonic recording of *The Student Prince,* which had been scheduled for recording the previous year with Anna Moffo. The new album retained the three songs composed for the film, but was both more complete and faithful to the original operetta than the earlier soundtrack recording. To anyone used to the 1952 film version, at first hearing the 1959 recording appears to be sung by a different tenor. Lanza's voice is very dark and heavy, and at times there is a certain amount of harshness in it. It is the sound of a tired, sick man. The great voice is still there, but emerging from a body that has been subjected to the most severe punishment by its owner. It is imperative for a singer to be in top condition physically for the voice to be at its best, and clearly this was far from the case with Lanza at this stage. Nevertheless, when it comes to the actual *singing,* Lanza is very good indeed.

Under Paul Baron's capable conducting, Lanza's approach is completely different from the earlier recording. On this occasion, his singing is frankly operatic. Comparing the two recordings, one misses the freshness and poetry of the film soundtrack. "Beloved"- sung in a lower key and with a particularly poor arrangement – is a far cry from the superb 1953 recording, and, similarly, "I'll Walk With God" and "Serenade" suffer from the extreme heaviness of the voice. Lanza's singing, however, in the 1959 version is closer to what one would hear in a stage performance. This record is one of the first examples of RCA's practice of dubbing in other soloists and chorus in New York to the original tracks recorded in Rome with only Lanza and the orchestra. The disappointing results of this shoddy practice are particularly evident in Lanza's last recordings.

The remaining albums with Baron were part of a new five-year recording contract that Lanza had signed the previous year and which guaranteed him an annual income of $200,000. A dismal stereo re-make of his Christmas Carols album[†] came first, followed by a collection of songs that had been closely associated with Caruso.

In the latter album, *Mario Lanza Sings Caruso Favorites,* the tenor again sounds heavy and tired at times, but as a singer, this

[†]Time magazine included it in their list of the year's best LPs.

is a far more poised and musical performer than the overly emphatic one of the radio days. With Baron's sensitive conducting and excellent arrangements by Baron, Morricone and Nadin, Lanza gives good performances of a number of Tosti songs including "*Luna d'estate*," "*L'Alba separa dalla luce l'ombra*," and "*Pour un baiser*." He also sings a restrained and moving "*Ideale*". Other highlights include fine renditions of "*Senza nisciuno*" and "*Vaghissima sembianza*," and the demanding "*Serenata*" by Bracco, for which Caruso himself wrote the lyrics.

After dismissing Baron, Lanza turned again to Callinicos for what were destined to be his final recordings, *The Vagabond King* and *The Desert Song*. In the meantime, the question of an operatic career continued to haunt him. The Rome Opera had not given up on Lanza. Its Artistic Director, Riccardo Vitale, had not forgotten the impression Lanza had made on him the previous year and was hoping to convince the tenor to open the 1960-61 season. Both the Rome Opera and the San Carlo in Naples had given Lanza *carte blanche* to perform in any opera he wanted.

Incredibly, there was a breakthrough. Lanza agreed to appear in *Pagliacci* for the 1960/61 season. He advised Vitale that he would begin preparing for the role of Canio early in the new year after undergoing an operation for the thrombosis that was affecting his right leg.[12]

Sam Steinman recalled: "He wanted to do an opera. That was his prime ambition. The plan was that the Rome Opera would present him in 'Pagliacci.' He was in touch with Vitale and I know that they were discussing it."[13]

Canio was a role he knew. It was part of his repertoire, and had he been in reasonable health he would almost certainly have scored a big success with it.

The burning ambition to be accepted as an opera singer was certainly ever present, as is evident in a discussion with his old friend, conductor Peter Herman Adler, who paid the tenor a visit at the Villa Badoglio a few months before the latter's death.

Back in 1950 Adler had urged Lanza to leave America and the movies and start working on an operatic career in Italy. Nine years later Lanza's health and life had changed dramatically. What hadn't changed, however, was Lanza's respect for Adler and the conductor's sincere admiration for the tenor's talent.

During that last meeting at the villa Lanza asked Adler whether he would be willing to work with him in preparing an operatic career in exchange for a percentage of his future earnings. "I agreed with him, but not for a piece of him like a boxing manager... I promised all possible help if first of all he disciplined himself and reduced his basically impressive and excellent body."[14]

As much as he wanted Lanza to fulfill his operatic dream Adler thought that it was now too late—that all the excesses had taken their toll.

It is tantalizing to contemplate what might have been. Would Lanza have *really* gone through with it? Having already suffered one heart attack, would his physical condition have been able to withstand the gruelling preparation required? Would he have backed out at the last minute? Or would his overwhelming desire to be accepted as an opera singer have *finally* got the better of him? We shall never know, but given his track record and precarious state of health it's highly unlikely he would have been able to fulfil his lifelong dream.

Sadly, I think of Lanza as a modern day Werther. I see a parallel between Goethe's sentimental young poet who commits suicide because of his unhappy love for Charlotte and Lanza, unable to realize his rightful artistic destiny.

By July, Lanza was back in the familiar setting of the Cinecittà Film Studios for the recording of Rudolf Friml's operetta, *The Vagabond King*. His wife and children attended the marathon recording session, which lasted from five in the afternoon until eleven in the evening. Also present were Lanza's grandfather Salvatore, Aunt Hilda and Betty's mother May, who were over on an extended visit from the States.

It was a most unusual practice to record all eight numbers in one session, and what emerged is indeed disappointing. Lanza's voice is that of a sick man. His singing is uninspired and uneven, Callinicos's conducting dull, and the recording quality extremely poor.

Having collected his $75,000 fee,[†] the tenor began rehearsing with Callinicos for his next and what would turn out to be his final project, *The Desert Song*. Once again going through a bout

---

[†]He always insisted on being paid in cash.

of depression he resumed drinking and the planned recording sessions had to be postponed.

Betty, increasingly concerned about her husband's health, was forever hoping that he would stick to his promise and stop drinking and would confront him each time he started one of his binges.[15]

Then late one evening, following a drunken argument with his wife, Lanza fell asleep on the marble walk outside his bedroom after Betty had retired to one of the guestrooms. It rained that night, and it was not until the following morning that the much-alarmed servants discovered the drenched tenor still asleep on the patio.[16] He was immediately rushed to the Valle Giulia clinic, where he was diagnosed as having double pneumonia. Tests and X-rays taken at the clinic further revealed that the phlebitis he was suffering from had caused part of a blood clot to break loose, partially obstructing the pulmonary artery. In other words he had narrowly escaped death. This is precisely what Dr. Fruhwein and his agent John Coast had warned him about the year before.

Callinicos went to visit him at the clinic. "He greeted me with a wan smile. He looked years older than his 38 years,"[17] the conductor recalled. While recuperating at the clinic, Lanza again spoke of singing at the Rome Opera and the San Carlo in Naples. Ironically, at the same time that he was receiving heavy doses of antibiotics to combat the pneumonia in his ailing body, offers and projects from all over the world continued to pour in.

One of the most ambitious was RCA's plan to hire the Comunale Theatre in Bologna for Lanza's first recordings of entire operas, scheduled to take place during the next two years.[18]

Other projects included a "television spectacular" for screening in the United States and, inevitably, at least four other films. Lanza was giving priority to *Laugh Clown Laugh,* an adaptation of *Pagliacci* for Thor Films Productions. Lanza's fee was even greater than for his two previous films, and he would also be receiving 50% of the gross.

Filming was scheduled for the beginning of November. Lanza had high hopes for this venture, telling his old friend from his Army days, Peter Lind Hayes, that "Wonderful things have been written in the script [which] tell me that this might be the successor to *The Great Caruso.*[19]

Discharged from the Valle Giulia clinic in late August, Lanza resumed work on the interrupted recording of *The Desert Song.* As with his previous recording of *The Vagabond King*, he again sounds tired, heavy, and lacking in vitality, while the orchestra is badly conducted by Callinicos and the recording quality poor. There are occasional reminders that the great voice is still there. On the album's highpoint, the demanding "One Flower In Your Garden," Lanza copes admirably with the high tessitura of the song. In spite of everything, the voice was not irreparably damaged. Nor had Lanza lost the ability to move listeners, with the poignant and sensitively rendered "One Alone" – sung in his most burnished and sonorous voice — providing an inescapably touching conclusion to his final album.

In mid-September, in what would turn out to be his final public appearance, together with Betty and the children he went to see a performance of *Aida* at the famous Baths of Caracalla, the setting of the first of the "Three Tenors" concerts in 1990. The spectacular amphitheatre erected by the Roman senate between 215 and 217 AD in honor of the emperor Caracalla and his two sons has long been an ideal setting for open air performances— particularly *Aida*. Although the cast that night did not feature any of the major names it did include some more than competent singers such as Floriana Cavalli in the title part, Pier Miranda Ferraro as Radames and Gian Giacomo Guelfi as Amonasro. Angelo Questa conducted.

In spite of Lanza having taken the precaution of wearing dark glasses in an effort to remain incognito, he was soon recognized. During the intermission after the first act the tenor was surrounded by virtually hundreds of Italians as well as American tourists asking him to autograph their programs. After the second act the word that Lanza was in the audience had spread and an even bigger crowd was keeping the tenor busy signing autographs and acknowledging greetings. He appeared to be terribly tired and left the arena berfore the start of the 3rd act.[20]

Lanza had often expressed a premonition of early death, and during his final years in Italy would often be heard saying, *"La vita è breve, la morte vien."*[21] (Life is brief, death is coming.) Was he merely being melodramatic, or was it indeed a foreboding of

278

the tragedy that was about to unfold? A mere two months earlier, he had asked his parents and his beloved 83-year-old grandfather Salvatore to stay with him for a while. His father did not feel up to facing the journey, but in June his mother visited, together with her sister Hilda, her father Salvatore, and Betty's mother. Mary returned to America at the end of June but the others stayed on. It had been their first reunion in more than two years, and Lanza was overjoyed at having them all at the beautiful Villa Badoglio. He still missed his father, however, and begged Callinicos, who was returning briefly to America, to try to convince him to make the trip to Rome. As Callinicos was about to depart he turned to him and said, "You know Costa, none of us lives forever."[22]

Lanza was again grossly overweight, and in view of all the planned activities would have to undergo another stringent diet to meet the filming deadline for *Laugh Clown Laugh*. He decided that his best option was to enter the Valle Giulia clinic, and allow Dr. Moricca to supervise his treatment. The worst aspect of entering the Valle Giulia clinic was that it entailed another two-week separation from his wife and children.

However, he was not particularly concerned on that Friday, September 25, as he awaited the arrival of Frank Silvestri, a young Italian-American doctor living in Rome, whom he had known for some time. Silvestri had become a friend and had latterly acted as a sort of personal physician. Silvestri had offered to accompany Lanza to the Valle Giulia. As the two men made their way to the car that was waiting inside the grounds of the Villa Badoglio, Lanza hesitated for a moment—almost as if he felt a premonition—then shrugged, kissed his wife, smiled and headed for the car.[23]

At the clinic everything had been made ready for the arrival of their famous patient. As usual, an entire wing located in the most secluded section of the building on the fourth floor had been reserved for him. He would occupy room 404, in which he had stayed on previous confinements, while the remaining rooms would serve as living-room and spare bedrooms for family or servants staying overnight and for nurse Guglielmina Anselma Mangozzi, who was looking after him. Lanza had already been a patient at the clinic six times previously, the most recent occasion being six weeks earlier when he was admitted suffering from double pneumonia and a near heart attack. By now Lanza had become friendly with the staff, who had reacted with surprise on his initial visit when he registered with his real name for fear of publicity.[24]

Although the basis of this latest hospital confinement was to lose weight, it also meant a period of complete rest, both physical and psychological, after which he would emerge feeling relaxed, fitter and in better spirits. His medical file, however, presented a grim picture. Lanza suffered from a serious liver dysfunction caused by frequent heavy drinking; arteriosclerosis, aggravated by high blood pressure; as well as phlebitis and gout. At 253.5 lb (115 kg) he also weighed approximately 80 lb (36.3 kg) more than he should have for his age and height. He was definitely not a patient who could safely undergo the "twilight sleep" therapy considered—but eventually abandoned—by Dr. Frederic Fruhwein the previous year at Walchansee.

In handing over Lanza's medical file to Dr. Guido Moricca, Dr Fruhwein had been quite categorical in telling his Italian colleague, who was in charge of treating Lanza, that under no circumstances should the singer undergo the sleep therapy. He told Moricca that Lanza's serious liver condition and his constant need for alcohol precluded such potentially dangerous therapy. He also informed Moricca of the danger of deep vein thrombosis were Lanza left immobile for prolonged periods. Should a blood clot (embolus) detach from the deep-lying veins in his leg, Dr. Fruhwein added, Lanza was at risk of death by pulmonary embolism.[25]

Dr. Fruhwein could not have been clearer in his assessment, yet Dr. Moricca chose to ignore his German colleague, proceeding with the sleep therapy as planned.[26] Consequently, Lanza received only two visitors during his confinement in the Valle Giulia: his friend Dr. Silvestri and Mrs. Alfredo Panone, whose husband was co-producer for *Laugh Clown Laugh*.

Meanwhile Betty had been ill and confined to bed, unable to look after the children or visit her husband in hospital. Lanza was concerned and eager to return to his family. His discharge from the clinic had been set for Thursday, October 8. The previous Tuesday evening, at the request of nurse Santina, he had consented to sing for the clinic's staff, performing one of his favorite operatic arias, "*E lucevan le stelle*" from *Tosca*.[27] It would turn out to be a prophetic choice. "The moment has fled and I die in despair. And I have never loved life so much," are the words Cavaradossi sings as the aria ends.

The following morning, Wednesday, October 7, Lanza spoke briefly on the telephone to his wife and to his agent Sam Steinman. He'd had more than a business relationship with Steinman—a strong friendship, with the agent frequently a guest at the Lanza's villa. Steinman recalled that during Lanza's initial months in Rome he wanted to find out as much about the ancient city as possible. "'Lets just ride in the car,' he'd say, 'and you talk.' He was just like a litte boy, just picking up things. I would explain things to him and he would repeat 'Is that so. Is that so.'"[28]

There had been the usual ups and downs in the course of the two years that Steinman had worked for the tenor, but any differences were only temporary and soon resolved. During one argument, Lanza had told Steinman that his services were no longer required. Steinman had left determined not to return.

Two days later the maid at Steinman's home had informed him there was a man that wanted to speak to him. Steinman: "I went to the entrance and there he was on his knees saying: "This is your old friend Moshe Lanza. Can't you take a joke?"[29]

On that fateful Wednesday morning the two men had another minor tiff, but one that in view of the subsequent tragedy would haunt Steinman for the rest of his days. He had promised to pay Lanza a visit at the clinic that day, but at 10 a.m. he telephoned the tenor, telling him that he would not be able to keep the appointment, as he wanted to interview Audrey Hepburn and her husband Mel Ferrer, who were coming to Rome. Steinman told Lanza he would visit in the afternoon instead. With a note of resentment in his voice, Lanza asked him: "Who do you make more money from?" [30]

At approximately 11 a.m. Dr. Silvestri came to see Lanza, chatted with his friend for some time before performing a routine checkup. Everything appeared to be in order, and he left the room. At around midday, as Silvestri was coming out of the lift on the ground floor, he heard an emergency call coming from the fourth floor. Feeling a sense of premonition, Silvestri made a frantic rush up the stairs to the fourth floor and Lanza's room. The tenor, wearing a blue jumper on top of his short pyjama pants, was lying unconscious on the divan. The alarm had been raised moments earlier when a nurse entered his room and found him reclining on the divan, motionless, extremely pale and with his head bent to one side.[31]

Immediately summoning help, Silvestri tried desperately to revive his friend by massaging his chest and giving him mouth to mouth resuscitation—to no avail. He also tried administering cardiotonics but these had no effect.[32] The clinic was equipped with an artificial heart machine but it was too late. At 12:15, before the precious machine could be set in motion, Mario Lanza was dead.

Dr. Frederic Fruhwein's warning to his Italian colleague had gone unheeded. Moricca had proceeded with the treatment and submitted Lanza to the twilight sleep therapy, which had indirectly precipitated the fatal pulmonary embolism.

At the age of 38 Mario Lanza had finally found peace. It was the tragic conclusion to the unfulfilled career of a great talent. A shocked public could only react in disbelief at the news. "Lanza was a bigger success than any classical artist I have handled," declared English impresario Victor Hochauser. "Every one of the 21 concerts he did for me was sold out in a matter of hours. I was hoping to bring him back to Britain later this year or early next year."[33]

Meanwhile at the Villa Badoglio, Betty had learned of her husband's death and collapsed. Now under heavy sedation, she was refusing to allow anyone apart from the immediate family and servants to view the body.

Her grief was absolute.[34]

EPILOGUE

"My children are falling in love with Italy, just like me,"[1] Lanza had said shortly before his death. He loved the country, the people, their way of life, and was proud that his children were speaking Italian well. Even Betty had made considerable progress with the language since arriving in Italy.

For their part, the Italians were just as fond of him and had adopted him as one of their own. From the moment he had landed in Naples, more than two years before, they made him feel as if he had always belonged to them. Now, stunned by the news of his sudden death, the entire population gave vent to their feelings in an open display of sincere sorrow.

Three thousand of them attended Lanza's funeral in a true public participation of grief, saying goodbye to the young tenor they had regarded as *simpatico*. Many had doubtless criticized him over the years for not fulfilling his potential, but now was only a time for paying homage to a unique artist. They came on a Saturday, which in 1959 was still a working day in Italy.

At first the Valle Giulia Clinic had issued a statement denying that Lanza had died at the hospital. They said that the singer had been discharged from the clinic the previous day and that he had died at home. In a state of total panic the medical staff had in fact hurriedly transferred Lanza's body from the Valle Giulia Clinic to his home. Just after 6 p.m. on the very day that he died a City Council's mortuary van with the numberplates Rome 320241 had carried the body, which had been placed in a mahogany coffin, from the clinic to the Villa Badoglio. An autopsy had not been performed.

Placed in the open coffin in the center of the living room, the body lay in state for the next two days. By now Betty had relented and friends, colleagues and admirers were allowed to file past the coffin and pay their last respects.[2] Among those that came were sopranos Maria Caniglia and Lidia Nerozzi and actors Franco Fabrizi and Enzo Fiermonte. Countless others signed their names on the death register placed near the entrance of the living room. In the meantime hundreds of telegrams and messages of bereavement including those from Frank Sinatra, Joe Pasternak, Allan Kayes from RCA, Ray Sinatra and Rudolph Maté, poured in from all parts of the world. Betty was urged by Lanza's friends and colleagues to allow her husband to be buried next to Caruso in the Caruso's family chapel in Naples.[3] Apart from the absurdity of burying Lanza in someone else's family chapel, the matter was settled with the arrival of Lanza's mother from America. She arrived in Rome on the morning of the funeral. The singer's father had been unable to travel with her, having taken ill at the news of his son's sudden death. Once in Rome, with Betty unable to function and reduced to the status of a robot, it was Lanza's mother who decided that her son should be buried in Los Angeles, where she and her husband lived, and the place to which Betty and the children would be returning.[4]

The day of the funeral began with people filing past the coffin. Some had been waiting silently outside the gates of the Villa Badoglio since the early hours to bid a final farewell to the singer. Then at 10:45 a.m., under a barrage of photographers' flashes, the coffin carrying Lanza's body emerged from the villa and was carried across to the funeral carriage, drawn by four black horses waiting in the villa's grounds. Pallbearers were actors Rosanno Brazzi, Robert Alda and Sandro Giglio as well as Lanza's friends and associates Sam Steinman, Dr. Frank Silvestri, Alfredo Panone, Lawyer Mario Beltrame, Business Manager Myrt Blum, RCA's Executive Frank Folsom, and Journalist Mike Stern. Also paying his last respects was Lanza's friend Professor Luigi Casciana, first violinist with the Rome Opera Orchestra.

With hundreds of people silently lining both sides of the streets, traffic came to a standstill as the funeral cortege slowly made the 20-minute journey to the church of the Immaculate Heart of Mary in Piazza Euclide, in the center of the Parioli district where Lanza had lived. Hundreds more were waiting as the carriage pulled up outside the church.

In a total daze and wearing dark glasses, Betty approached the steps of the church helped by their friend Dr. Silvestri, with the four children crying beside her. Behind her were Lanza's mother, grandfather Salvatore, Betty's mother and other relatives, friends and associates of the singer.

The Roman Polyphonic Choir, under the direction of Maestro Gastone Dossato, was heard throughout the entire ceremony, which through a twist of fate was conducted by Father Paul Maloney, the same priest who had baptized all four of the Lanza's children in Los Angeles. Lanza's recording of Schubert's "Ave Maria" from his last film was to have been played, but due to recently introduced regulations forbidding reproduction of recorded sound in Catholic churches, the "Ave Maria" was instead sung by the baritone Giuseppe Forgione.[5]

Two other funeral services were to follow. Lanza's body was first flown to his native city of Philadelphia, where on October 16 an estimated 15,000 people filed past it at the Leonetti funeral parlor. At midnight the doors of the funeral parlor were closed with two thousand people still waiting to pay their respects. Distraught, they attempted to force their way past the police. Then, at the request of Lanza's grandfather Salvatore, the doors were again opened. "These people have queued for hours to see Mario, and I'll wait until the last one has filed past if it takes all night," he declared. Salvatore would never get over the loss of his grandson. A little over a year later he would say, "Mario was the dearest friend I ever had. The happiest years of my life were undoubtedly the years I knew him. The world seems such a cold and empty place without him."[6]

The following morning a requiem Mass was celebrated at the church of Saint Mary Magdalen De Pazzi, where Lanza had served as an altar boy and had sung the Bach-Gounod "Ave Maria" nearly twenty years earlier.

The body of the singer was then flown onto its final destination, Los Angeles, where the third and most distressing of the funerals took place. There, at the Blessed Sacrament Catholic Church in Hollywood, and then at the cemetery chapel, the final rites were held. Among the 1500 present at the Requiem Mass were Kathryn Grayson and daughter Patti Kate, Zsa Zsa Gabor,

George Liberace and Betty Lanza's niece Dolores Hart. Pallbearers were Lanza's boyhood friends Fred (West) Callaccio and Louis De Bona, his brothers in law Bert Hicks and John Abbatacola, his stand-in Mickey Golden and trainer Terry Robinson. Honorary pallbearers were producer Joe Pasternak, music director George Stoll, Editors Gene Ruggiero and Peter Zinner, Conductor Irving Aaronson and RCA executive Art Rush. Numb with grief, Betty Lanza sat motionless next to her sister Virginia throughout the church service officiated by the Reverend Harold J. Ring assisted by the Reverend John Hopkins and the Reverend Walter Hancock. During the service the Gregorian Mass was sung by soloist Anne Marie Biggs accompanied by the organist and three male voices. The casket holding her husband's body was now closed and draped with the American flag.

Betty had bid her final goodbye to him the previous night, during the Rosary service.[7] Her eyes had filled with tears as she looked down at the body of her husband, but somehow she had been able to hold her composure while the singer's parents, overcome by grief, had to be led away from the service. Now Betty had nothing left. There were no more tears. Only the immense pain she felt closed inside her. She was oblivious to the people who were trying to comfort her. At one point during the church service she had turned to her grief-stricken in-laws in an effort to comfort them: "Papa, Mama, Please! It'll be all right."[8]

At the burial site the singer's parents were utterly distraught. His mother was able to retain her composure until the last moment, when she burst into tears as she leaned over to kiss her son's casket for the last time.

His father, who had been sobbing intermittently through both services, cried out: "Take me, me! Not my poor boy! Say something to me Freddie, say something to me!"[9] At the conclusion of the burial service at Calvary Mausoleum,† Betty Lanza was presented with the American flag that had covered the casket throughout the services.

Five months later Betty joined her Mario in death. She had been unable to accept the loss of the man she loved. Despite the great love for her four children, she did not possess the strength

---

†The body would later be moved to a chapel in Holy Cross Cemetery.

to go on without him. In the depths of depression she drifted in a daze through the months following her husband's death, drinking and taking tranquillizers to control her overwhelming grief.

At 3:20 on the afternoon of March 11, 1960, she was found dead by her two maids, Liliana and Anna-Maria, who discovered the body in the bedroom of the home she was renting in Beverly Hills. The maids called the police and an emergency squad who attempted to revive her. Found lying face down on her bed, she had died of apparent asphyxiation caused by a respiratory ailment for which she had being receiving medication.[10]

The coroner's office report read: "Blood alcohol content .23. Throat constricted by swelling of tissues. Cause of death: asphyxiation." Dr. Morris Wilburne, who had been treating her for the respiratory ailment, was quite categorical in stating: "Mrs. Lanza's death was definitely not suicide."[11] Her brother Bert would comment: "She never recovered from Mario's loss. She died of a broken heart."[12]

In a unique career that encompassed films, recordings and the concert stage, Lanza was able to bridge successfully the gap between popular and classical music. His multiform interpretative capacity and extensive repertoire formed a wide spectrum that ranged from popular songs to show tunes, musical comedy, art songs and opera. No other singer before or since has achieved this with the same degree of success, and to this day he remains a unique phenomenon. His singing continues to inspire successive generations of singers, all of whom have expressed their admiration and acknowledged the influence Lanza has had on them. From Di Stefano and Corelli to the three tenors Carreras, Domingo and Pavarotti, to more recent opera stars such as tenors Richard Leech, Vincenzo La Scola, Roberto Alagna, Ramon Vargas, Joseph Calleja and Andrea Bocelli, baritones Tom Krause, Dmitri Hvorostovsky, Thomas Allen and Leo Nucci, and sopranos Reneé Fleming Angela Gheorghiu and Olivia Stapp, the list is seemingly endless. Nor is Lanza's influence limited to the operatic world. Elvis Presley once acknowledged Lanza as having had a major influence on his own singing style.

Mario Lanza Societies and Fan Clubs continue to flourish around the world. Foremost among them is The Mario Lanza Institute, founded in 1962 in his native city of Philadelphia, which awards annual scholarships to promising young singers. Columbus House at 712 Montrose Street, Philadelphia is the site of the Mario Lanza Museum, which contains many mementos of the singer's career including photographs, costumes and records.

Fifty years after his death Mario Lanza continues to hold listeners enthralled with the magnificence of his voice. New generations are discovering the legacy of recorded music that he left behind, which in vastness and variety few other singers can equal. This is a legacy that will live on as long as music continues to be heard and appreciated. In paying tribute to Lanza his contemporary, tenor Oreste Kirkop once said: "I sincerely and honestly want to honor a great man with a great heart. Only a great heart can sing the way Lanza sang, and it was that that the man in the street felt when he heard his records and saw his films."[13]

Mario Lanza was once asked to express his musical philosophy. "I sing each word as though it were my last on earth," he replied without hesitation. Lanza would live by that statement throughout his brief but extraordinary career.

After Betty's death custody of the four children was given to Lanza's parents. They grew up with them in the home Lanza had bought for his parents at 622 Toyopa Drive, Pacific Palisades. Lanza's mother, Maria, died on July 7, 1970, following a stroke. She was 68. Lanza's father Antonio died peacefully on May 22, 1975, at the age of 81.

Lanza's first-born child, Colleen, possessed a fine lyric soprano voice and at one stage contemplated a singing career. Instead she married Alberto Caldera, Jr., the nephew of the president of Venezuela. The marriage did not last and eventually she remarried—though again unhappily. On July 19, 1997, she was run over by two cars in succession while crossing a street near her home. She died without having regained consciousness sixteen days later at the age of 48.

Second-born Ellisa Lanza is happily married to businessman Bobby Bregman. They have two sons, Tony and Nick, and reside in Beverly Hills.

Lanza's oldest son, Damon, together with longtime family friend Bob Dolfi, has been active in promoting his father's legacy. He resides in California.

Youngest son Marc shared the Toyopa Drive home with his brother Damon and, sadly, died of a heart attack at the age of 37 in 1991.

POSTSCRIPT

THE CAUSE OF MARIO LANZA'S DEATH has been the subject of much debate and controversy over the years. One absurd hypothesis claims—purely for the purpose of sensationalism—that he was murdered by the Mafia for refusing to appear at a charity concert in Naples. I will not dignify this ridiculous statement by commenting further. The truth of the matter, as I discovered during my research for this book, is that Lanza was seriously ill and that he was improperly treated at the Valle Giulia clinic. After Lanza's death, Dr. Frederic Fruhwein, the German doctor who had treated Lanza in the Walchensee Sanatorium the previous year, stated publicly that he had advised the doctor in charge [Dr. Guido Moricca] not to submit Lanza to a sleeping cure. Dr. Fruhwein further declared that it was during this cure, applied against his advice, that Mario Lanza had died.

Naturally, both Dr. Moricca and the Roman Medical Association denied that there was any evidence of improper treatment, and Dr. Fruhwein was consequently summoned before a tribunal by the Munich Medical Association, and severely reprimanded for having violated the sacred rule of absolute medical secrecy. In other words, the medical profession had closed ranks to protect one of its own—in this case, Dr. Guido Moricca. I tried to speak to Dr. Moricca on two separate occasions but both times I managed to get no further than his wife, Mrs. Aurelia Moricca. On the first occasion she nervously inquired if I was a lawyer acting on behalf of the Lanza family. On the second visit she conveyed her husband's message that "Mario Lanza's death was caused by an embolism." I told her that I already knew this, but wanted to know what had caused the embolism. She said her husband had nothing further to add and made it clear that that was the end of the interview.

I also tried repeatedly to speak to Dr. Frank Silvestri. Initially, through the efforts of Sam Steinman, he agreed to a meeting. When I subsequently phoned him to arrange a time, however, I was told by an obviously embarrassed maid that he was not in Rome and would be away indefinitely. The truth, as I later found out from Steinman, was that Silvestri had changed his mind and instead of telling me this himself had hidden behind the maid. Other attempts to speak to him over the years have met with continuous refusals, not only in my case but also when Lanza's Italian biographer Eddy Lovaglio and tenor Roberto Scandurra attempted to talk to him. Dr. Silvestri simply slammed the phone down the moment the name Mario Lanza was mentioned. What is he so afraid of? Does he have anything to hide?

It has been suggested that regardless of the cause of death, Lanza's state of health—coupled with his repeated dieting, drinking and erratic living—would not have led to a long life. Although this is probable, it can hardly be regarded as an excuse for negligence. Indeed, no amount of medical incompetence can justify the unnecessary shortening of a patient's life – even if that person might have lived only a single additional day.

DISCOGRAPHY (with Filmography and record of Concert, Opera and Radio/TV Appearances)

The relationship between Mario Lanza and RCA was quite remarkable. Consider: Mario was virtually an "unknown quantity" when he was sent the first contract dated February 15, 1945. "Confirming our conversation of this morning," it stated, "the Radio Corporation of America (Victor Division) hereby agrees to pay you $250.00 per month for a period of one year beginning February 15, 1945. The total payments of $3,000 to be in consideration for signing a five (5) year Red Seal contract with RCA which will provide a 10 percent royalty." There would be quite a number of iterations within the next several years, but this was probably the most significant contract for Victor since the one signed with Enrico Caruso early in the century.

This was an interesting period in recording industry. Wartime restrictions had had a profound effect on the record busir ss during the early 1940's, and there was the additional problem of the recording "ban" brought about by James. C. Petrillo, which ended in 1944. By the mid 1940's, however, there was great enthusiasm, and the record companies were clearly positioning themselves for dramatic growth in record sales. But the tenor roster at Victor was "thin" – James Melton, Jan Peerce for opera and the "lighter classics" and Allan Jones for the film and "Broadway" music. (Richard Crooks would soon retire.) A dynamic, new "operatic tenor" would be quite a plus for RCA's prestigious Red Seal division. Note the selection of the "trial records" below to see where the plans for Lanza were targeted. Obviously the company was clearly convinced of the quality of the talent or they would not have offered a five-year contract to the essentially unknown young singer. Who, in 1945, could have realized what a "gold mine" for RCA Victor Mario Lanza would become?

Bill Park

The Private Recordings*

April 1940   Spoken introduction by Lanza, who dedicates the three numbers to his parents on the occasion of their twentieth wedding anniversary.

Pagliacci (Leoncavallo): Vesti la giubba
La Fanciulla del West (Puccini): Ch'ella mi creda
De Curtis: Torna a Surriento

293

April 1940 cont'd

Introduced by Lanza and dedicated to his father on his birthday.

Pennino: Pecché?
Tosca (Puccini): E lucevan le stelle
La Traviata (Verdi): Dei miei bollenti spiriti

December 1942 (Recorded at the home of Robert Weede)

La Bohème (Puccini): O soave fanciulla *with* Lois McMahon
La Bohème (Puccini): Marcello finalmente *with* Lois McMahon and Robert Weede (partial)

May 1944

Recorded as a gift to friend and patron Maria Margelli. Lanza addresses Margelli before the first and third of the arias.

Andrea Chénier (Giordano): Un di all'azzurro spazio
Andrea Chénier (Giordano): Come un bel di di maggio
Part of unknown aria
Tosca (Puccini): E lucevan le stelle
Pagliacci (Leoncavallo): Vesti la giubba
Cavalleria Rusticana (Mascagni): Addio alla madre

*All with piano accompaniment.

RCA test records
June, 1945

Leoncavallo: Mattinata
Tosca (Puccini): E lucevan le stelle

Pagliacci (Leoncavallo): Vesti la giubba
Herbert: I'm Falling In Love With Someone
Carmen (Bizet): La fleur que tu m'avais jetée

later in 1945

MGM test records
Sept. 8, 1947   La Bohème (Puccini): Che gelida manina
                Pagliacci (Leoncavallo): Vesti la giubba

Andre Previn, pianist

Date	Title	Time	Matrix/Take No.	Cat. No.
Studio: Manhattan Center New York				
May 5, 1949	Aida (Verdi) Celeste Aida	4:22	D9-RC 1728	49-0632-B
	La Bohème (Puccini): Che gelida manina	5:01	D9-RC 1729	49-0632-A
	Nutile: Mamma mia che vo' sape	2:35	D9-RC 1730	49-0633-A
	Cardillo: Core 'ngrato	3:22	D9-RC 1731	49-0633-B
RCA Victor Orchestra; Constantine Callinicos, conductor				
Studio: Republic Hollywood				
August 23, 1949	Kern: They Didn't Believe Me	5:10	D9-RC 1257	49-0634-B
	Kaper: I Know, I Know, I Know	4:02	D9-RC 1258	49-0634-A
	Leoncavallo: Mattinata	3:44	D9-RC 1259	49-0902-B
RCA Victor Orchestra; Ray Sinatra, conductor				
October 28, 1949	Di Capua: O sole mio	4:15	D9-RC 1282	49-0902-A
	Buzzi-Peccia: Lolita	3:35	D9-RC 1283	49-1169-B
	Lara: Granada	3:49	D9-RC 1284	49-1169-A
	Granada	3:49	D9-RC 1284-2	Unpublished
RCA Victor Orchestra; Ray Sinatra, conductor				
April 8, 1950	L'Africana (Meyebeer): O Paradiso	3:20	EO-RC 336-1	49-1250-B

Carmen (Bizet): La fleur que tu m'avais jetée 3:35	EO-RC 337-1	49-1249-B
La fleur que tu m'avais jetée 3:28	EO-RC 337-2	GD 60889(3)
Marta (Flotow): M'appari 3:31	EO-RC 338-1	49-1248-B
RCA Victor Orchestra; Constantine Callinicos, conductor		
April 11, 1950		
Madama Butterfly (Puccini): Love Duet Part 1* 3:45	EO-RC 339-1	49-12
Madama Butterfly: Love Duet Part 1* 3:35	EO-RC 339-2	Unpublished
Madama Butterfly: Love Duet Part 2* 4:23	EO-PC 340-1	49-1250-A
Madama Butterfly: Love Duet Part 2* 4:17	EO-PC 340-2	Unpublished
La traviata (Verdi): Brindisi*+ 3:29	EO-RC 341	49-1248-A
La traviata: Brindisi*+ 3:01	EO-RC 341-2	GD 60889 (3)
La traviata: Brindisi*+ 3:29	EO-RC 341-3	Unpublished
RCA Victor Orchestra and Chorus+, Constantine Callinicos, conductor		
*with Elaine Malbin, soprano		
Studio: Republic Hollywood		
May 11, 1950		
Bach-Gounod: Ave Maria 4:25	EO-RC 350	49-3228
RCA Victor Orchestra, Constantine Callinicos, conductor		
Eudice Shapiro, violin solo		
May 15, 1950		
L'Elisir d'Amore (Donizetti): Una furtiva lagrima 4:11	EO-RC 351	49-3203-B
Pagliacci (Leoncavallo): Vesti la giubba 3:29	EO-RC 352-1	49-3201-B
Vesti la giubba 3.30	EO-RC 352-2	GD 60889(3)
Vesti la giubba 3:29	EO-RC 352-3	Unpublished
Rigoletto (Verdi): Questa o quella 1.45	EO-RC 353-1	49-3201-A
Rigoletto: La donna è mobile 2:03	EO-RC 353-1B	49-3202-A
RCA Victor Orchestra, Constantine Callinicos, conductor		
May 18, 1950		
Andrea Chénier (Giordano): Un di all'azzurro spazio 5.02	EO-RC 354	ERA 110A

Date	Title	Time	Matrix/Take No.	Cat. No.
	Andrea Chénier: Come un bel dì di maggio	4:12	EO-RC 355	ERA 110B
	Tosca (Puccini): Recondita armonia	2:39	EO-RB 3645	49-3204-A
	Tosca: E lucevan le stelle	3:02	EO-RB 3646	49-3204-B
RCA Victor Orchestra, Constantine Callinicos, conductor				
May 29, 1950	Adam: O Holy Night+	4:04	EO-RB 357	49-1338-A
	Cavalleria rusticana (Mascagni): Addio alla madre	3:30	EO-RB 358-1	49-3209-A
	Addio alla madre	3:32	EO-RB 358-2	GD 60889(3)
	Reger: The Virgin's Slumber Song+	3:20	EO-RB 359	49-1338-B
	Rigoletto: Parmi veder le lagrime	4:39	EO-RB 360	49-3203-A
	Parmi veder le lagrime		EO-RB 360-2	Unpublished
	La Gioconda (Ponchielli): Cielo e mar	3:57	EO-RB 361	49-3202-B
RCA Victor Orchestra and chorus+, Constantine Callinicos, conductor				
June 6, 1950	*La Forza del Destino* (Verdi): O tu che in seno agli angeli	4:48	EO-RB 363-1	49-3209-B
	Toselli: Serenata	3:27	EO-RB 364	49-3155-A
	Drigo: Serenata	3:01	EO-RB 365	49-3155-B
RCA Victor Orchestra, Constantine Callinicos, conductor				
June 27, 1950	Brodszky: Tina Lina	3:14	EO-RB 3685	49-1352-B
	Brodszky: Be My Love	3:27	EO-RB 3686	49-1353-A
RCA Victor Orchestra and the Jeff Alexander Choi, Ray Sinatra, conductor				
June 29, 1950	Brodszky: Toast Of New Orleans+	3:05	EO-RB 3687	49-1351-A
	Brodszky: Boom Biddy Boom Boom+	2:47	EO-RB 3695	49-1352-A
	Brodszky: Bayou Lullaby+	3:25	EO-RB 3696	49-1351-B
	Brodszky: I'll Never Love You	3:26	EO-RB 3697	49-1353-B
RCA Victor Orchestra and the Jeff Alexander Choir+, Ray Sinatra, conductor				

Date / Performers	Title	Time	Matrix	Catalog
August 26, 1950	Beelby: My Song My Love	3:26	EO-RB 3770	49-3208-A
	d'Hardelot: Because	2:31	EO-RB 3771	Rejected
	Grieg: I Love Thee	2:26	EO-RB 3772	49-3208-B
	Geehl: For You Alone	2:47	EO-RB 3773	Rejected
RCA Victor Orchestra, Ray Sinatra, conductor				

Studio: Manhattan Center New York

Date / Performers	Title	Time	Matrix	Catalog
February 19, 1951	Geehl: For You Alone	2.38	E1-RB 1167	49-3207-B
	d'Hardelot: Because	2.07	E1-RB 1168	49-3207-A
RCA Victor Orchestra, Constantine Callinicos, conductor				
February 23, 1951	Rosas-Aaronson: The Loveliest Night Of The Year	3:36	E1-RB 1166	49-3300-A
	Tosti: A vucchella	2:48	E1-RB 1186	49-3435-B
	Tosti: Marechiare	2:30	E1-RB 1187	49-3435-A
RCA Victor Orchestra, Constantine Callinicos, conductor				

Studio: Republic Hollywood

Date / Performers	Title	Time	Matrix	Catalog
September 28, 1951	Marx: Guardian Angels+*	3:55	E1-RB 777	49-3639-B
	Gruber: Silent Night+	3:20	E1-RB 778	49-3640-B
	Traditional: The First Noel+	3:10	E1-RB 779	49-3640-A
	Traditional: O Come All Ye Faithful+ (Adeste Fidelis)	3:12	E1-RB 780	49-3641-A
	Kirkpatrick: Away In A Manger+	2:51	E1-RB 781	49-3642-A
	Redner: O Little Town Of Bethlehem+	2:43	E1-RB 782	49-3641-B
RCA Victor Orchestra and the Jeff Alexander Choir, Ray Sinatra, conductor				
*Harpo Marx, harp				
Sept. 29, 1951	Hopkins: We Three Kings Of Orient Are	3:00	E1-RB 783	49-3642-B
	Malotte: The Lord's Prayer	3:30	E1-RB 784	49-3639-A

RCA Victor Orchestra and the Jeff Alexander Choir, Ray Sinatra, conductor

Studio: **Republic, Hollywood**

Date	Title	Time	Matrix/Take No.	Cat. No.
July 24, 1952	Brahms-Aaronson: The Song Angels Sing	3:30	E1-RB 0297	49-3914-A
	Brodszky: Because You're Mine	3:30	E1-RB 0298	49-3914-B

RCA Victor Orchestra and the Jeff Alexander Choir, Constantine Callinicos, conductor

| August 1, 1952 | Lehmann: Lee Ah Loo | 2:49 | E2-RB 0299 | 49-3961-B |
| | Porter: You Do Something To Me | 2:21 | E2-RB 0300 | 49-3961-A |

RCA Victor Orchestra, Constantine Callinicos, conductor

Studio: **Republic, Hollywood**

June 17, 1953	Rimsky-Korsakoff: Song Of India	3:53	E3-RC 2414-1	49-4209-A
	Merrill: If You Were Mine	2:56	E3-RC 2415-1	49-4209-B
	If You Were Mine	2:56	E3-RC 2415-2	Unpublished
	Kauderer: Call Me Fool	3:04	E3-RC 3071-1	49-4211-A
	Callinicos: You Are My Love	3:40	E3-RC 3070-1	49-4211-B
	You Are My Love	3:40	E3-RC 3070-2	Unpublished

Orchestra and Chorus, Constantine Callinicos, conductor

Studio: **Warner Brothers, Hollywood**

| December 28, 1953 | Brodszky: Summertime In Heidelberg | 2:43* | E3-RC 2530-1 | Unpublished |
| | Brodszky: I'll Walk With God | 3:21 | E3-RC 2532-1 | Unpublished |

Orchestra, Constantine Callinicos, conductor

*with Gale Sherwood, soprano

299

Studio:

Warner Brothers, Hollywood   Lanza on Broadway

Date	Song	Time	Cat No. LM2070
May 14, 1956	Youmans: More Than You Know	3:40	G2-RB 3295-2
May 14, 1956	Kern: Why Was I Born	3:24	G2-RB 3296-5
May 14/29, 1956	Rodgers: This Nearly Was Mine	4:02	G2-RB 3297-2
May 14/31, 1956	Rodgers: Falling In Love With Love	2:51	G2-RB 3298-4
May 15/29/31, 1956	Porter: So In Love	3:33	G2-RB 3299-5
May 15/31, 1956	Weill: Speak Low	3:25	G2-RB 3300-3
May 15/29, 1956	Rodgers: My Romance	3:32	G2-RD 3113-6
May 15, 1956	Weill: September Song	3:27	G2-RB 3114-6
May 17/29, 1956	Rodgers: Younger Than Springtime	2:33	G2-RB 3115-4
May 17/31, 1956	Wright: And This Is My Beloved	3:20	G2-RB 3116-1
May 17, 1956	Loewe: On The Street Where You Live	3:16	G2-RB 3117-10
May 17/31, 1956	Rodgers: You'll Never Walk Alone	2:51	G2-RB 3118-1

Orchestra - Irving Aaronson, conductor. Jeff Alexander Choir overdubbed separately

Studio:

Republic, Hollywood

Date	Song	Time	Cat No. LM2070	
August 10, 1956	Taylor: This Land	2:20	G2-PB 4779-5	47-6644-A
	Taylor: Earthbound	3:11	G2-PB 4780-6	47-6644-B
	Traditional: Deck The Halls	1:56	G2-PB 4781-4	LM 2029
	Mendelssohn: Hark The Herald Angels Sing	2:32	G2-PB 4782-4	LM 2029
	Traditional: God Rest Ye Merry Gentlemen	2:28	G2-PB 4786-2	LM 2029
	Handel: Joy To The World	2:12	G2-PB 4787-2	LM 2029
August 15, 1956	Traditional: O Christmas Tree	2:00	G2-PB 4788-6	LM2029
	De Paul: Love In A Home	2:22	G2-PB 4789-3	20-6664-A
	Hill: Do You Wonder	2:57	G2-PB 4790-3	20-6664-B
	Traditional: I Saw Three Ships	1:35	G2-PB 4791-1	LM 2029
	Willis: It Came Upon A Midnight Clear	2:50	G2-PB 4792-2	LM 2029

Discography

Date	Title	Time	Matrix/Take No.	Cat. No.
August 27, 1956	Kern: I've Told Every Little Star	3:15	G2-RB 4824-10	LM 2090
	Friml: Only A Rose	3:53	G2-RB 4825-5	LM 2090
	Romberg : Will You Remember	4:00	G2-RB 4826-2	LM 2090
	Lehar: Yours Is My Heart Alone	3:50	G2-RB 4827-1	Unpublished
August 31, 1956	Friml: Rose Marie	3:25	G2-RB 4832-2	LM 2090
	The Donkey Serenade	3:03	G2-RB 4833-3	LM 2090
	Kern: All The Things You Are	3:17	G2-RB 4834-4	LM 2090
	Herbert: Gypsy Love Song	3:21	G2-RB 4835-4	LM 2090
September 6, 1956	Romberg:Lover Come Back To Me	4:06	G2-RB 4828-2	LM 2090
8/10/56 to 9/6/56	Herbert: Tramp Tramp Tramp	2:43	G2-RB 4829-3	LM 2090
	Friml: Giannina mia	2:47	G2-RB 4830-2	LM 2090
	Herbert: Thine Alone	3:04	G2-RD 4831-2	LM 2090
	Lehar: Yours Is My Heart Alone	3:50	G2-RB 4827-3A	LM 2090

All with Orchestra and the Jeff Alexander Choir, Henry René, conductor

Date	Title	Time	Matrix/Take No.	Cat. No.
April 15, 1957	Kalmanoff: A Night To Remember	2:50	H2 PB 0527-6	20-6915-B
	Reed: Behold	2:20+	H2 PB 0528-6	20-6915-A
	Leibert: Come Dance With Me	2:45+	H2 PB 0529-6	20-7119-A

Orchestra and the Jeff Alexander Choir+, Henry René, conductor

Cinecittà Studios, Rome

Date	Title	Time	Matrix/Take No.	Cat. No.
November 7, 1957	Green: Never Till Now	3:06	H2 PB 8042-3	20-7119-B
	Rodgers:Younger Than Springtime	3:25	H2 PB 8043-2	20-7164-B
	Aaronson-Webster: The Loveliest Night Of The Year	2:47	J2 PB 0730	unpublished in USA
	Rascel: Arrivederci Roma	2:52	J2 PB 0731	20-7164-A

Recording of Concert at Royal Albert Hall 16 January, 1958

Title: A Mario Lanza Program   **Cat No.**   LSC 2454

Composer	
Cilea	*L'Arlesiana*: Lamento di Federico
Monteverdi	*Arianna*: Lasciatemi morire
Scarlatti	Già il sole dal Gange
Stradella	Pietà Signore
Giannini	Tell Me, Oh Blue, Blue Sky
Behrend	Bonjour, ma belle
Charles	The House On The Hill
Puccini	*Tosca*: E lucevan le stelle
Nutile	Mamma mia che vo' sape
Tosti	A vucchella
Tosti	Marechiare
Romberg	Softly, As In A Morning Sunrise
Herbert	I'm Falling In Love With Someone
Brodszky	Because You're Mine
Young	Seven Hills Of Rome
Verdi	*Rigoletto*: La donna è mobile

Constantine Callinicos, piano

Date | **Composer** | **Title:** Mario | **Song Title** | **Time** | **Cat. No. LSC-2331**

Cinecittà Studios Rome

Date	Composer	Song Title	Time
December 1958	Denza	Funiculì funiculà	2:31
	Fusco	Dicitencello vuie	3:22
	Di Capua	Maria Mari'	3:17
	De Curtis	Voce e notte	4:06
	De Curtis	Canta pe' me	3:19
	Cannio	O surdato 'namurato	2:28
	Gambardella	Come facette mammeta	1:54

Mario	Santa Lucia luntana	3:28
Anonymous	Fenesta che lucive	3:37
De Curtis	Tu ca nun chiagne	2:34
Cioffi	'Na sera e maggio	3:18
Valente	Passione	4:03

Orchestra: Franco Ferrara, conductor; Chorus: Franco Potenza, conductor

Title: The Student Prince   Cat. No. LSC-2333
Cinecittà Studios Rome

Date	Song Title	RCA-Italy Matrix No.
April 1959	Overture	Kkbw-5699
	Summertime In Heidelberg*+	Kkbw-5700
	Gaudeamus igitur**	Kkbw-5701
	Just We Two *	Kkbw-5702
	Thoughts Will Come Back To Me	Kkbw-5703
	Golden Days	Kkbw-5704
	I'll Walk With God+	Kkbw-5705
	Serenade	Kkbw-5706
	Beloved+	Kkbw-5707
	Drink, Drink, Drink	Kkbw-5708
	Deep In My Heart Dear*	Kkbw-5709
	Student Life (chorus only)	Kkbw-5710

Music by Sigmund Romberg, +Additional songs by Nicholas Brodszky
**Traditional
\Orchestra - Paul Baron, conductor
*With Norma Giusti soprano (N.B. Soprano and chorus overdubbed in New York, 9/24/59)

Title: Lanza sings Christmas Carols   Cat No. LSC 2333
Cinecittà Studios, Rome

Date	Song Title	Time	RCA Italy-Matrix No.

May 1959

Song	Time	Catalog
Hopkins: We Three Kings Of Orient Are	3:04	Kkbw-5823
Traditional: O Come, All Ye Faithful (Adeste Fidelis)	3:38	Kkbw-5824
Redner: O Little Town Of Bethlehem	3:09	Kkbw-5825
Traditional: The First Noel	4:18	Kkbw-5826
Gruber: Silent Night	4:00	Kkbw-5827
Traditional: Away In A Manger	3:20	Kkbw-5995
Marx : Guardian Angels	3:21	Kkbw-5596
Handel: Joy To The World	2:23	Kkbw-6018
Mendelssohn: Hark! The Herald Angels Sing	2:23	Kkbw-6019
Willis: It Came Upon A Midnight Clear	2:48	Kkbw-6020
Traditional: God Rest Ye Merry Gentlemen	4:15	Kkbw-6024
Traditional: O Christmas Tree	1:45	Kkbw-6025
Traditional: Deck The Halls	1:23	Kkbw-6026
Traditional: I Saw Three Ships	1:45	Kkbw-6027

Orchestra, Paul Baron, conductor
Chorus Overdubbed in New York, 16-17 September, 1959

Title: Mario Lanza Sings Caruso Favorites   Cat. No. LSC 2393
Cinecittà Studios, Rome

Date	Composer	Time
June 1959	Anonymous: Vieni sul mar	2:24
	De Curtis: Senza niuscuno	2:44
	Galdaston: Musica proibita	3:13
	Donaudy: Vaghissima sembianza	2:51
	Bracco: Serenata	3:47
	Buzzi-Peccia: Lolita	3:17
	Tosti: Luna d'estate	2:17
	Tosti: L'alba separa dalla luce l'ombra	3:03

Tosti: Pour un baiser	2:13	
Tosti: La mia canzone	3:11	
Tosti: Ideale	3:05	
Anonymous: Santa Lucia	2:37	

Title: The Vagabond King
Cinecittà Studios, Rome   Cat No LSC 2509

Date	Song Title	RCA Italy Matrix No.
July 1959	Love Me Tonight	Kkbw 6085
	Tomorrow*	Kkbw 6088
	Drinking Song	Kkbw 6089
	Nocturne+	Kkbw 6090
	Nocturne reprise (unpublished)	Kkbw 6091
	Song Of The Vagabonds+	Kkbw 6092
	Finale*+	Kkbw 6093
	Only A Rose *	Kkbw 6094
	Someday*	Kkbw 6096

Constantine Callinicos, conductor, +with Chorus
*with Judith Raskin, soprano (Judith Raskin and chorus overdubs recorded in New York, March 1960)

Title: The Desert Song
Cinecittà Studios, Rome   Cat No LSC 2440

Date	Song Title	RCA Italy Matrix No.
August 1959	Then You Will Know*+	Kkbw 6141
	Riff Song+	Kkbw 6142
	The Desert Song*	Kkbw 6143
	My Margo	unpublished
	Let Love Go. One Flower In Your Garden #+	Kkbw 6150
	One Alone	Kkbw 6151
	One Alone (reprise)	unpublished

Azuri's Dance+   Kkbw 6154
I Want a Kiss*+ <   Kkbw 6155
One Good Boy Gone Wrong*+   Kkbw 6157

Constantine Callinicos, conductor
*With Judith Raskin, soprano
< With Raymond Murcell, baritone
With Donald Arthur, bass
+ with chorus
Soloists and chorus overdubs recorded in New York, March 1960

FILM SOUNDTRACK RECORDINGS

MGM Studios Culver City: **That Midnight Kiss**
With the MGM Studio Orchestra except where otherwise noted

Dec. 1, 1948   Nutile: Mamma mia che vo' sape*
               Kaper: I Know I Know I Know
               Kern: They Didn't Believe Me** - Rhino: Mario Lanza at MGM CD R272958

Charles Previn, conductor
*Giacomo Spadoni, piano
**Kathryn Grayson, soprano

Dec. 9, 1948   *Aida* (Verdi): Celeste Aida
               L'Elisir d'Amore (Donizetti): Una furtiva lagrima*

José Iturbi, conductor
*José Iturbi, piano

Dec. 30, 1948   Tchaikovsky: Love Is Music* - Rhino: Mario Lanza at MGM CD R272958

José Iturbi, conductor
*with Kathryn Grayson, soprano
Dec. 31, 1948   Tchaikovsky: One Love Of Mine *+
José Iturbi, conductor
*with Kathryn Grayson, soprano
+Not included in film's theatrical release

MGM Studios - Culver City: The Toast of New Orleans
With the MGM Studio Orchestra except where otherwise noted

Dec. 5, 1949   Puccini: *Madama Butterfly*: Love Duet
                 Madama Butterfly: Love Duet (alternate take) Rhino: Mario Lanza at MGM CD R272958

John Green, conductor
with Kathryn Grayson, soprano

Dec. 6, 1949   *La traviata* (Verdi): Brindisi*+
                 Carmen (Bizet): La fleur que tu m'avais jetée**
                 Marta (Flotow): M'appari (partial)**
                 L'africana (Meyerbeer): O Paradiso (partial)**
                 Brodszky: I'll Never Love You*** - Rhino: Mario Lanza at MGM CD R272958

*John Green, conductor
+with Kathryn Grayson, soprano
**Jacob Gimpel, piano
***George Stoll, conductor

Dec. 15, 1949   Brodszky: Bayou Lullaby
                 Brodszky: Be My Love - Rhino: Mario Lanza at MGM CD R272958
                 Brodszky: Be My Love (alternate version)

George Stoll, conductor
With Kathryn Grayson, soprano

Dec. 27/28, 1949   Brodszky: Tina Lina - Rhino: Mario Lanza at MGM CD R272958
George Stoll, conductor
with Rita Moreno and chorus

Dec. 28, 1949   Brodszky: I'll Never Love You (alternate version)
                 Brodszky: Be My Love (retake)
George Stoll, conductor

Jan. 25, 1950   Brodszky: Tina Lina*(alternate version)
                 Brodszky: The Toast of New Orleans
George Stoll, conductor, *with chorus

Feb. 17, 1950   Brodszky: Boom Biddy Boom Boom
George Stoll, conductor

MGM Studios - Culver City: The Great Caruso
with the MGM Studio Orchestra except where otherwise noted

July 17, 1950   *Pagliacci* (Leoncavallo): Vesti la giubba
                 Pagliacci (Leoncavallo): Vesti la giubba (outtake) - Rhino: Mario Lanza at MGM - CD R272958
Peter Herman Adler, conductor

July 22, 1950   *Tosca* (Puccini): E lucevan le stelle
                 La Bohème (Puccini): Che gelida manina (rejected)
                 La Gioconda (Ponchielli): Cielo e mar (rejected)
Peter Herman Adler, conductor

August 7, 1950   Leoncavallo: Mattinata (a cappella)
                 De Curtis: Torna a Surriento

308

De Curtis: Torna a Surriento (outtake)
Rossini: La danza

Irving Aaronson, piano

August 9, 1950   d'Hardelot: Because
Anonymous: Santa Lucia
Tosti: Marechiare*

Peter Herman Adler, conductor
*Irving Aaronson, piano
August 11, 1950 Bach/Gounod - Ave Maria - Rhino: Mario Lanza at MGM CD R272958
with Jacqueline Allen, soprano
St. Luke's Choristers
Wesley Tourtelotte, organ

August 18, 1950   *Tosca* (Puccini): Voglio avvertirlo
with Giuseppe Valdengo
and Teresa Celli, soprano

    Aida (Verdi): O terra addio

with Dorothy Kirsten, soprano
and Blanche Thebom, mezzo-soprano

    Andrea Chénier (Giordano): Un di all'azzurro spazio (outtake)

Peter Herman Adler, conductor

August 19, 1950   *Trovatore* (Verdi): Sconto col sangue mio
with Lucine Amara, soprano
    Aida (Verdi): Celeste Aida
    Celeste Aida (alternate take) - Rhino: Mario Lanza at MGM CD R272958

Peter Herman Adler, conductor

August 22, 1950   *Rigoletto* (Verdi): Bella figlia dell'amore (partial)
with Giuseppe Valdengo, baritone
Blanche Thebom, mezzo-soprano
and Olive May Beach, soprano

               Marta (Flotow): Finale
with Dorothy Kirsten, soprano
Nicola Moscona, bass
Blanche Thebom, mezzo-soprano

August 23, 1950   *Cavalleria rusticana* (Mascagni): Viva il vino+
           Lucia di Lammermoor (Donizetti): Chi mi frena in tal momento - Rhino: Mario Lanza at MGM CD R272958
with Dorothy Kirsten, soprano
Giuseppe Valdengo, baritone
Blanche Thebom, mezzo-soprano
Nicola Moscona, bass
Gilbert Russell, tenor
Peter Herman Adler, conductor, +with chorus

August 28, 1950   *Rigoletto* (Verdi): E il sol dell'anima (outtake)
                   with Jarmila Novotna, soprano

Peter Herman Adler, conductor

August 29, 1950   *La Bohème* (Puccini): Che gelida manina (retake)
           La Gioconda (Ponchielli): Cielo e mar (retake - partial)
           Rigoletto (Verdi): La donna è mobile
                       La donna è mobile (alternate take) - Rhino: Mario Lanza at MGM CD R272958
           Marta (Flotow): M'appari (partial)

Peter Herman Adler, conductor

Oct. 17, 1950   *Cavalleria Rusticana* (Mascagni):   Bada, Santuzza
with Marina Koshetz, soprano
John Green, conductor

Dec. 18, 1950   *Aida* (Verdi): Consecration Scene
with Bob Ebright, tenor
and Nicola Moscona, bass
                                        Tosti: A vucchella

John Green, conductor

MGM Studios, Culver City: Because You're Mine

With The MGM Studio Orchestra except where otherwise noted

July 12, 1951   Kern: All The Things You Are - Rhino: Mario Lanza at MGM CD R272958
                            Nutile: Mamma mia che vo' sape
                            L'Africana (Meyerbeer): O Paradiso

John Green, conductor

August 2, 1951   Malotte: The Lord's Prayer - Rhino: Mario Lanza at MGM CD R272958
John Green, conductor
Wesley Tourtelotte, organ

Oct. 19, 1951   Lehmann: Lee Ah Loo
                            Kern: All The Things You Are (outtake)
                            Brodszky: Because You're Mine* - Rhino: Mario Lanza at MGM CD R272958

John Green, conductor
*with Doretta Morrow, soprano

Oct. 23, 1951   Brahms-Aaronson: The Song Angels Sing
John Green, conductor

Oct. 30, 1951   Lara: Granada - Rhino: Mario Lanza at MGM CD R272958
John Green, conductor

Nov. 1, 1951   Malotte: The Lord's Prayer (outtake)
John Green, conductor
Wesley Tourtelotte, organ

    Il Trovatore (Verdi): Sconto col sangue mio (a cappella)
    Anonymous: You're In The Army Now* (outtake)

*with chorus

Nov. 10, 1951   *Cavalleria Rusticana* (Mascagni): Addio alla madre*
Nov. 28, 1951   Addio alla madre* (alternate take) - Rhino - Mario Lanza at MGM CD R272958
John Green, conductor
*with Peggy Bonini, soprano, and Catherine Chapman, mezzo-soprano

Nov. 24, 1951   *Rigoletto* (Verdi): Addio, Addio*
John Green, conductor
*with soprano Peggy Bonini, recorded separately on November 28, 1951

Dec. 1, 1951   Brodszky: Because You're Mine (alternate version)* - Rhino: Mario Lanza at MGM CD R272958
John Green, conductor
*with Doretta Morrow, soprano

May 7, 1952   Because You're Mine (partial)
John Green, conductor

ORIGINAL SOUNDTRACK RECORDING ALBUMS

MGM Studios, Culver City: **The Student Prince** Catalogue No. LM-1837

with The MGM Studio Orchestra except where otherwise noted

July 28, 1952 Brodszky: I'll Walk With God*
Luther: A Mighty Fortress (unpublished)
A Mighty Fortress (outtake - unpublished)
with Wesley Tourtelotte, organ

*Orchestra and chorus added later

July 29, 1952 Romberg: Serenade - Rhino: Mario Lanza at MGM CD R272958
Brodszky: Beloved (rejected) - Rhino: Mario Lanza at MGM CD R272958
Brodszky: Summertime in Heidelberg*

Constantine Callinicos, conductor
with Ann Blyth, soprano

July 31, 1952 Romberg: What's To Be (outtake - unpublished)
Romberg: Golden Days

Constantine Callinicos, conductor

August 5, 1952 Romberg: Drink, Drink, Drink*
Constantine Callinicos, conductor
*Chorus recorded separately

August 7, 1952 Eberwein: Ergo bibamus (unpublished)
Constantine Callinicos, piano

313

Traditional : Gaudeamus igitur (outtake)
Gaudeamus igitur (alternate version - outtake)
Chorus conducted by Constantine Callinicos

| August 12, 1952 | Romberg: Deep In My Heart Dear (unpublished)
Deep In My Heart Dear (partial-retake) Rhino: Mario Lanza at MGM CD R272958
Deep In My Heart Dear (reprise with alternate ending - unpublished) |

with Ann Blyth, soprano
Constantine Callinicos, conductor

| May 20, 1953 | Brodszky: Beloved |
Constantine Callinicos, conductor

Warner Bros. Studios, Burbank: Serenade   **Cat No. LM 1996**

| June 28, 1955 | Rossini: La danza |
Dominic Frontière, accordion

| June 30, 1955 | De Curtis: Torna a Surriento |
Jacob Gimpel, piano

| July 5, 1955 | *La Bohème* (Puccini): O soave fanciulla |
with soprano Jean Fenn, recorded separately on July 23, 1955
Jacob Gimpel, piano

| July 7, 1955 | Brodszky: My Destiny (rejected-unpublished)
Brodszky: Serenade (test recording) |
Jacob Gimpel, piano

| July 11, 1955 | *Der Rosenkavalier* (Strauss): Di rigori armato
Brodszky: My Destiny (remake) |

Jacob Gimpel, piano

L'Arlesiana (Cilea): Lamento di Federico (test recording)

July 13,1955

L'Arlesiana (Cilea): Lamento di Federico
Fedora (Giordano): Amor ti vieta+
Tosca (Puccini): Qual occhio al mondo (unpublished)
La Bohème (Puccini): Ci lasceremo alla stagion dei fiori* (unpublished)
Il Trovatore (Verdi): Di quella pira

Ray Heindorf, conductor
+Jacob Gimpel, piano (orchestra overdubbed separately)
*Soprano Jean Fenn recorded on August 23, 1955

July 15, 1955

L'Africana (Meyerbeer): O Paradiso
Brodszky: Serenade (alternate song, different from song used in film - unpublished)
Serenade (alternate take of above - unpublished)

Jacob Gimpel, piano

July 19,1955

Otello (Verdi): Dio ti giocondi* (outtake-rejected)
Dio mi potevi scagliar

Ray Heindorf, conductor
*with Gloria Boh, soprano

July 21, 1955

Otello (Verdi): Dio ti giocondi (partial - rejected)
Turandot (Puccini): Nessun dorma (rejected)
Nessun dorma
Brodszky: My Destiny
Brodszky: Serenade

Ray Heindorf, conductor
August 18, 1955   Schubert: Ave Maria
Jacob Gimpel, piano

Organ accompaniment by Eugene Le Pique recorded and overdubbed separately

August 25, 1955 Brodszky: Serenade (unpublished)
Brodszky: Serenade (alternate version [same as song in film, sung differently] - unpublished)
Serenade (remake - unpublished)

Ray Heindorf, conductor

August 25, 1955   Brodszky: Serenade (unpublished)
Brodszky: Serenade (original version with different accompaniment [not used in film] - unpublished)
Brodszky: Serenade (remake - unpublished)

Ray Heindorf, conductor

Nov. 22, 1955   *Otello* (Verdi): Dio ti giocondi
with Licia Albanese, soprano
Ray Heindorf, conductor

Vatican Auditorium, Rome: Seven Hills Of Rome   Cat No.   RCA LM 2211
June 1957   Rascel: Arrivederci Roma*
                   Young: Seven Hills Of Rome
                   Young: Seven Hills Of Rome (alternate version - unpublished)
                   Leibert: Come Dance With Me
                   Buzzi-Peccia: Lolita
                   Rigoletto (Verdi): Questa o quella (unpublished)
                   Marta (Flotow): M'appari (partial)**
                   Rosas-Aaronson: The Loveliest Night Of The Year (unpublished)
                   Kern: All The Things You Are (partial - unpublished)
                   Perez: Ay Ay Ay (partial - unpublished)

RAI Symphony Orchestra and Chorus
George Stoll, conductor
*With Luisa di Meo

** Irving Aaronson, piano

Via Margutta Studio Rome

Stoll: There's Gonna Be A Party Tonight (Italian Calypso)*
Imitation Sequence:
Brown: Temptation (as Perry Como)
Shanklin: Jezebel (as Frankie Laine)
Dehr: Memories Are Made Of This (as Dean Martin)*
Traditional: When The Saints Go Marching In (asLouis Armstrong)*

George Stoll, conductor
*with chorus

Rome Opera House: For The First Time Cat No RCA LSC 2338
August 1958

	Italian RCA serial No.
Aida (Verdi): Gloria all' Egitto, ad Iside	JKBW 4613-4614
Pagliacci (Leoncavallo): Vesti la giubba	JKBW 4644
Otello (Verdi): Niun mi tema	JKBW 4645
Cosí Fan Tutte (Mozart): E voi ridete	JKBW 4646 unpublished

Rome Opera House orchestra, chorus, uncredited soloists
Constantine Callinicos, conductor

Cinecittà Studios, Rome   Italian RCA Serial No.
September 1958

Schubert: Ave Maria	JKBW 4672
Schubert: Ave Maria (alternate take)	JKBW 4673 unpublished

George Stoll, conductor

Di Capua: O sole mio	JKAW 4677
Panzeri: Come prima	JKAW 4679
Asso: O mon amour	JKAW 4681
Verdi: Rigoletto: La donna è mobile*	published only in UK- RCA RB16158

Carlo Savina, conductor
*with piano accordion accompaniment

Berlin, Germany
November 1958
Hauff: Hofbrauhaus Song
Stoll: Pineapple Pickers

Johannes Rediske and his band

Cinecittà Studios Rome
December 1958
Grieg: I Love Thee   JKAW 5334
Constantine Callinicos, conductor

The Mario Lanza Radio Show
CBS 6/10/51 to 9/30/51
NBC 10/8/51 to 9/5/52
Recorded at Radio Recorder Studios, Hollywood; Ray Sinatra, conductor, unless otherwise noted

Date	Title
June 8, 1951	Granada
	Serenata (Toselli)
	Because
	Be My Love
June 14, 1951	Boom Biddy Boom Boom
	I Love Thee
	The Loveliest Night Of The Year
	O Sole Mio

June 15, 1951	My Song My Love
	Serenata (Drigo)
	I'll Never Love You
	Pagliacci: Vesti la giubba
June 23, 1951	For You Alone
	La Danza
	Naughty Marietta: I'm Falling In Love With Someone
	I'm Falling In Love With Someone (alternate take)
	Torna a Surriento
June 27, 1951	Funiculi Funiculà (sung in English)
	Mamma mia che vo' sape
	The Vagabond King: Someday
	Eileen: Thine Alone
June 29, 1951	Tina Lina
	Lolita
	Rigoletto: La donna è mobile (sung in English)
	If
July 10, 1951	The World Is Mine Tonight
	The Land Of Smiles: Yours Is My Heart Alone
	Oh, Nights Of Splendor
	Oh, Nights Of Splendor (alternate take)
July 13, 1951	*Tosca:* Recondita armonia
	Very Warm For May: All The Things You Are
	Cover Girl: Long Ago And Far Away
	Roberta: The Touch Of Your Hand

	Music In The Air: The Song Is You
July 17, 1951	Così cosà Diane *New Moon*: Softly As In A Morning Sunrise
July 20, 1951	A vucchella *New Moon*: Wanting You Wanting You (alternate take) Ave Maria (Bach-Gounod)
July 24, 1951	I've Got You Under My Skin *A Connecticut Yankee*: My Heart Stood Still Marechiare *L'Africana*: O Paradiso
July 27, 1951	*Naughty Marietta*: Ah Sweet Mystery of Life If You Are But a Dream
Aug. 14, 1951	*Tosca*: E lucevan le stelle The Lord's Prayer* *The Gay Divorcee*: Night And Day *The Girl From Utah*: They Didn't Believe Me Without A Song *The Desert Song*: The Desert Song
Aug. 21, 1951	*Smiles*: Time On My Hands Wonder Why *Spring Is Here*: With A Song In My Heart
Aug. 23, 1951	Mattinata Song Of Songs

	The Rosary
	Song Of Norway: Strange Music
Nov. 8, 1951	*Babes In Arms:* Where Or When
	Guardian Angels
	Sally: Look For The Silver Lining
	Look For The Silver Lining (Alternate Take)
	Through The Years
	None But The Lonely Heart
Nov. 20, 1951	*Good News:* The Best Things In Life Are Free
	Trees
	When Day is Done
	Siboney
	Valencia
Nov. 29, 1951	*Princess Pat:* Neapolitan Love Song
	Roses Of Picardy
	The Donkey Serenade
	Temptation
	The Thrill Is Gone
	Rigoletto: Questa o quella
Dec. 3, 1951	*Jumbo:* My Romance (Rejected)
	One Night Of Love (Rejected)
	The Hills Of Home (Rejected)
	Ay Ay Ay
Dec. 5, 1951	*Jumbo:* My Romance
	My Romance (Alternate Take)

Dec. ? 1951
Somewhere A Voice Is Calling (Rejected)
One Night Of Love (Remake)
One Night Of Love (Alternate Take)
The Hills Of Home (Remake)
The Hills Of Home (Alternate Take)
The Night Is Young (Rejected)

Dec. ? 1951
Your Eyes Have Told Me So
Ciribiribin
Show Boat: Make Believe
Sylvia
Revenge With Music:You And The Night And The Music

O Come All Ye Faithful
O Little Town of Bethlehem
The First Noel
Silent Night

Dec. 16, 1951
Lygia
Jubilee: Begin The Beguine (Rejected)

Jan. 16, 1952
The Night Is Young (Remake)
Jubilee: Begin The Beguine (Remake)
Somewhere A Voice Is Calling (Remake)

Jan. 29, 1952
Wake Up And Dream: What Is This Thing Called Love
Charmaine
Lady Of Spain

Feb. 1, 1952
Bitter Sweet: I'll See You Again
Among My Souvenirs

	Tell Me That You Love Me Tonight
	Romance
	L'Elisir d'Amore: Una furtiva lagrima
Feb. ? 1952	I'll See You in My Dreams
	Memories
	I Never Knew
	My Buddy
Feb. 15, 1952	*Private Lives:* Someday I'll Find You
	Someday I'll Find You (alternate take)
	Carousel: If I Loved You
	Fools Rush In
	Tell Me Tonight
March 4, 1952	*Show Boat:* You Are Love
	You Are Love (alternate take)
	Day In Day Out
	Day In Day Out (alternate take)
	The Trembling Of A Leaf
March 6, 1952	*Carmen:* La fleur que tu m'avais jetée
	Orange Blossoms: A Kiss In The Dark
	Roberta: Yesterdays
March 11, 1952	Santa Lucia
	Danny Boy
	My Wild Irish Rose
March 13, 1952	*Rigoletto:* La donna è mobile

	La Bohème: Che gelida manina *Cavalleria Rusticana:* Addio alla madre
March 20, 1952	A Little Love A Little Kiss The Moon Was Yellow
March 21, 1952	*La Gioconda:* Cielo e Mar Core 'ngrato *Rigoletto:* Parmi veder le lagrime *Aida:* Celeste Aida
Constantine Callinicos, conductor	
March 25, 1952	*Walk a Little Faster:* April In Paris Marcheta
March 28, 1952	*L'Arlesiana:* Lamento di Federico *Andrea Chénier:* Come un bel dì di maggio Dicitencello vuie Fenesta che lucive
Constantine Callinicos, conductor	
March 31, 1952	*Countess Maritza:* Play Gypsies, Dance Gypsies *The Student Prince:* Deep in My Heart Dear Deep In My Heart Dear- alternate take When You're In Love (rejected) And Here You Are
April 3, 1952	Santa Lucia luntana (rejected) Non ti scordar di me Maria Marì'

Na sera e maggio (rejected)
Musica proibita

Constantine Callinicos, conductor

April 7, 1952   When You're In Love (remake)
The Student Prince: Deep In My Heart Dear (new ending)

April 15, 1952   Love Is The Sweetest Thing
Love Is The Sweetest Thing (alternate take)
Flying Colors: Alone Together
The Royal Palm Revue: I'll Be Seeing You
The Student Prince: Serenade (rejected)

April 18, 1952   *Carousel:* You'll Never Walk Alone
You'll Never Walk Alone (alternate take)
Besame mucho

April 24, 1952   Santa Lucia luntana (remake)*
'Na sera e maggio (remake)*
'Na sera e maggio (alternate take)*
The Student Prince: Serenade (rejected)
Beautiful Love

*Constantine Callinicos, conductor

April 29, 1952   *The Desert Song:* One Alone
A Kiss
Canta pe' me*
Andrea Chénier: Un dì all'azzurro spazio*

*Constantine Callinicos, conductor
May 2, 1952   Somebody Bigger Than You and I

The Student Prince: Serenade (rejected)
The Student Prince: Serenade (remake)
Parlami d'amore Mariu'*
La Forza del Destino: O tu che in seno agli angeli*

*Constantine Callinicos, conductor

May 3, 1952   Tu ca nun chiagne
                Senza nisciuno

Constantine Callinicos, conductor

May 9, 1952   La spagnola
                Pagliacci: Un tal gioco
                La Bohème (Leoncavallo): Testa adorata
                Fedora: Amor ti vieta

Constantine Callinicos, conductor

FILMOGRAPHY

Dates refer to the year of production and release respectively
* Academy Award Nomination
That Midnight Kiss 1948/1949

Metro Goldwyn Mayer.
Produced by Joseph Pasternak
Directed by Norman Taurog
Screenplay by Bruce Manning and Tamara Hovey
Director of Photography: Robert Surtees ASC
Musical Direction by Charles Previn
Operatic Numbers Conducted by José Iturbi
Orchestrations by Leo Arnaud and Conrad Salinger
Musical Supervision by José Iturbi

Recording Supervisor: Douglas Shearer
Film Editor: Gene Ruggiero
Technicolor
Running Time: 98 Minutes

Cast: Kathryn Grayson, José Iturbi, Ethel Barrymore, Mario Lanza, Keenan Wynn, J. Carrol Naish, Jules Munshin, Thomas Gomez, Marjorie Reynolds, Arthur Treacher, Mimi Aguglia, Amparo Iturbi

The Toast Of New Orleans 1949/1950

Metro Goldwyn Mayer
Produced by Joseph Pasternak
Directed by Norman Taurog
Screenplay by Sy Gomberg and George Wells
Director of Photography: William Snyder ASC
Musical Direction by George Stoll
Operatic numbers conducted by John Green
Orchestrations by Conrad Salinger and Robert Franklyn
Recording Supervisor: Douglas Shearer
Film Editor: Gene Ruggiero
Technicolor
Running Time: 97 Minutes
Cast: Kathryn Grayson, Mario Lanza, David Niven, J. Carrol Naish, James Mitchell, Richard Hageman, Clinton Sundberg, Sig Arno, Rita Moreno, Romo Vincent
*Song: Be My Love

The Great Caruso 1950/1951

Metro Goldwyn Mayer
Produced by Joseph Pasternak

Associate Producer: Jesse L. Lasky
Directed by Richard Thorpe
Screenplay by William Ludwig and Sonya Levien suggested by Dorothy Caruso's biography Enrico Caruso: His Life And Death.
Director of Photography: Joseph Ruttenberg, ASC
Operatic numbers staged and conducted by Peter Herman Adler
Musical supervision and background score by John Green
Recording Supervisor: Douglas Shearer
Film Editor: Gene Ruggiero
Technicolor
Running Time: 109 minutes

Cast: Mario Lanza, Ann Blyth, Dorothy Kirsten, Jarmila Novotna, Richard Hageman, Carl Benton Reid, Eduard Franz, Ludwig Donath, Alan Napier, Paul Javor, Carl Millitaire, Shepard Menken, Vincent Renno, Nestor Paiva, Peter Edward Price, Mario Siletti, Angela Clarke, Ian Wolfe, Yvette Dugay, Argentina Brunetti
Operatic sequences:
Blanche Thebom, Teresa Celli, Nicola Moscona, Giuseppe Valdengo, Lucine Amara, Marina Koshetz
*Sound recording (won)
*Best scoring of a musical picture
*Costume design - color

Because You're Mine 1951/1952

Metro Goldwyn Mayer
Produced by Joseph Pasternak
Directed by Alexander Hall
Screen play by Karl Tunberg and Leonard Spiegalgass based on a story by Ruth Brooks Flippen and Sy Gomberg
Director of Photography: Joseph Ruttenberg ASC
Musical Direction by John Green
Recording Supervisor: Douglas Shearer
Film Editor: Albert Akst

Operatic Coach: Wolfgang Martin
Technicolor
Running time: 103 Minutes

Cast: Mario Lanza, Doretta Morrow, James Whitmore, Dean Miller, Paula Corday, Jeff Donnell, Spring Byington, Curtis Cooksey, Don Porter, Eduard Franz, Bobby Van, Ralph Reed, Celia Lovsky, Alexander Steinert
*Song - Because You're Mine

The Student Prince 1953/1954

Metro Goldwyn Mayer
Produced by Joseph Pasternak
Directed by Richard Thorpe
Screenplay by William Ludwig and Sonya Levien from the operetta with book and lyrics by Dorothy Donelly
Music by Sigmund Romberg
Director of Photography: Paul C. Vogel ASC
Musical Director: George Stoll
Vocal numbers conducted by Constantine Callinicos
Orchestration: Maurice De Pack
Recording Supervisor: Douglas Shearer
Film Editor: Gene Ruggiero
Ansco Color
Running Time: 107 minutes

Cast: Ann Blyth, Edmund Purdom, John Ericson, Louis Calhern, Edmund Gwenn, S.Z. Sakall, Betta St. John, John Williams, Evelyn Varden, John Hoyt, Richard Anderson, and the singing voice of Mario Lanza as The Student Prince

Serenade 1955/1956

Warner Bros- Produced by Henry Blanke
Directed by Anthony Mann
Screenplay by Ivan Goff Ben Roberts and John Twist based on the novel by James M. Cain
Director of Photography: J. Peverell Marley ASC
Musical Director: Ray Heindorf
Sound by Robert B. Lee
Film Editor: William Ziegler
Operatic Adviser: Walter Ducloux
Operatic Coach: Giacomo Spadoni
Warner Color
Running Time: 121 minutes

Cast: Mario Lanza, Joan Fontaine, Sarita Montiel, Vincent Price, Joseph Calleia, Harry Bellaver, Vince Edwards, Silvio Minciotti, Frank Puglia, Edward Platt, Frank Yaconelli, Mario Siletti, Maria Serrano, Eduardo Noriega, Jean Fenn

Operatic sequences with:
Licia Albanese
Norma Zimmer+
Joseph Vitale +
Victor Romito+
Lillian Molieri +
Laura Mason
Francis Barnes
+Deleted for theatrical release

Seven Hills Of Rome 1957/1958

A Le Cloud-Titanus co-production released by Metro Goldywn Mayer
Produced by Lester Welch

Titanus Chief of Production: Silvio Clementelli
Directed by Roy Rowland
Screenplay by Art Cohn and Giorgio Prosperi based on a story by Giuseppe Amato
Director of Photography: Tonino Delli Colli
Music supervised and conducted by George Stoll
Music Coordinator: Irving Aaronson
Sound: Mario Messina
Film Editor: Gene Ruggiero
Technicolor
Running Time: 104 Minutes

Cast: Mario Lanza, Renato Rascel, Marisa Allasio, Peggie Castle, Clelia Matania, Carlo Rizzo, Rossela Como, Guido Celano, Amos Davoli, Carlo Giuffre, Patrick Crean, Adriana Hart, April Hennessy, Alberto Rabagliati, Luisa Di Meo

For The First Time 1958/1959

A Corona-Astor Co-Production Released by Metro Goldwyn Mayer
Produced by Alexander Gruter
Associate producers: Paul Baronand Alfredo Panone
Directed by Rudolph Maté
Screenplay by Andrew Solt
Director of Photography: Aldo Tonti
Music supervised and conducted by George Stoll
Operatic sequences conducted by Constantine Callinicos
Film Editor: Gene Ruggiero
Technicolor
Running Time: 97 minutes

Cast: Mario Lanza, Johanna von Koczian, Zsa Zsa Gabor, Kurt Kasnar, Hans Sohnker, Annie Rosar, Peter Capel, Renzo Cesana, Sandro Giglio, Walter Rilla, Carlo Rizzo, Gisela Mathews, Michael Cosmo, John Stein, Manfred Schaffer

PRINCIPAL CONCERT AND OPERA APPEARANCES

Mario Lanza sang more than 150 concerts. Listed below are the most significant ones.

Date	Appearance
August 7 and 13, 1942	Tanglewood Music Festival, Massachusetts. *The Merry Wives of Windsor* (as Fenton). Rest of the cast: James Pease (Falstaff), Mack Harrell/Giuseppe Gentile* (Ford), Robert Fischer/John Cassidy (Page), George Tinker/John Toms (Slender), Myron Ryan (Dr. Caius), Adelaide Abbot/Laura Castellano (Mistress Ford), Christine Johnson/Jean Handzlik (Mistress Page), Lois MacMahon/Helen Strassburger (Anne Page). Boris Goldovsky, conductor.

*In 1945 Gentile, using the name Grant Garnell, worked with Lanza on the latter's vocal technique. |
Sept. 3, 1945	Atlantic City New Jersey - concert with the NBC Symphony Orchestra, conducted by Peter Herman Adler
July 2, 1946	Toronto - concert with the Prom Symphony Orchestra, conducted by Tauno Hannikainen Songs with accompaniment by Leo Barkin, pianist
July 6 & 7, 1946 conducted	Chicago- Grant Park Concerts with Frances Yeend soprano - Grant Park Symphony Orchestra by Leo Kopp
November 13, 1946	Ottawa - Concert with the Ottawa Philarmonic Orchestra conducted by Allard de Ridder
January 17 & 18, 1947	St. Louis - Concert with Frances Yeend, Soprano - St. Louis Symphony Orchestra conducted by Vladimir Golschmann
October 10, 1947	Quebec - Montcalm Palace Concert with Agnes Davis, soprano; Josef Blatt, pianist
July 8, 1947 to May 27, 1948	Total of 86 concerts with the Bel Canto Trio on tour throughout the United States Canada and Mexico, including Chicago (2) and the Hollywood Bowl

March 5, 1948	Toronto - Massey Hall - Concert with the Toronto Symphony Orchestra, conducted by Paul Scherman
April 8 & 10, 1948	New Orleans - *Madama Butterfly* - (as Pinkerton). Rest of the cast: Tomiko Kanazawa (Cio Cio San), Jess Walters (Sharpless), Rosalind Nadell (Suzuki), George Tallone (Goro), Frederic White (Prince Yamadori and Bonze), Charlotte Miller (Kate Pinkerton), Henri Feux (Imperial Commisioner). New Orleans Symphony Orchestra conducted by Walter Herbert
July 24, 1948	Los Angeles, concert with Kathryn Grayson, soprano - Hollywood Bowl Orchestra conducted by Miklos Rozsa
March 7 to May 25, 1949	North America Concert Tour - 12 concerts with Constantine Callinicos, pianist - Additional concerts in Oklahoma with the Oklahoma Symphony Orchestra conducted by Victor Alessandro and Chicago - Orchestra Hall - Marshall Field and Company Choral Society - Albert P. Stewart, conductor
August 16, 1949	Los Angeles, Concert with Mary Jane Smith, soprano - Hollywood Bowl Orchestra, conducted by John Green
August 29, 1949	Philadelphia - Bellevue Stratford Hotel Ballroom - Luncheon in honor of US President Harry S. Truman and Perry Brown National Commander of the American Legion. Tenor soloist: Mario Lanza
March 22, 24, 27	Honolulu - Concerts with Constantine Callinicos, pianist
February 16 to April 30, 1951 Pittsburgh Concert with The Pittsburgh Symphony Orchestra conducted by Vladimir Bakaleinikoff Cincinnati Concert with Cincinnati Symphony Orchestra conducted by Constantine Callinicos	North America Concert Tour - 22 concerts - Constantine Callinicos, pianist
November 18, 1957 Palladium Orchestra conducted by Constantine Callinicos	London Palladium Royal Command Performance

November 24, 1957   Sunday Night At The London Palladium (Televised)
Palladium Orchestra conducted by Constantine Callinicos

January 4 to April 13, 1958   Concert tour of England, Scotland, Ireland, France, Belgium, Holland and Germany - total 22 concerts

Constantine Callinicos, pianist

PRINCIPAL RADIO AND TELEVISION APPEARANCES

"Great Moments in Music" ABC

October 24, 1945	*Tosca* selections with Jean Tennyson, soprano, Robert Weede, baritone, Sylvan Levin, conductor
November 7, 1945	*Peace Must Be Won*, Victory Loan Program with Robert Weede, baritone, Vivian Bauer, soprano, Burgess Meredith, narrator
November 14, 1945	*Otello* selections with Jean Tennyson, soprano, Robert Weede, baritone, George Sebastian, conductor
December 26, 1945	"In A Persian Garden" selections with Frances Yeend, soprano, Robert Weede, baritone, George Sebastian, conductor
January 23,1946	"Music of Irving Berlin" with Natalie Bodanya, soprano, Leonard Stokes, baritone, Sylvan Levin, conductor
February 6, 1946	*The Student Prince* selections with Winnie Smith, soprano, Robert Weede, baritone, Sylvan Levin, conductor
December 19, 1945	Red Barber Review (Radio)
February 15, 1948	Edgar Bergen Show, NBC Radio

Discography

September 15, 1948	Salute to MGM (Radio)
September 22, 1948	Salute to MGM (Radio)
November 25, 1948	Elgin Watch Special, NBC Radio
December 19, 1948	Edgar Bergen Show, NBC Radio
November 19, 1950	Hedda Hopper's Hollywood, NBC Radio
April 29, 1951	Hedda Hopper's Hollywood, NBC radio
September 30, 1954	Shower of Stars, Premiere Program, CBS TV
October 24, 1954	Shower of Stars, CBS TV
January 18, 1958	Saturday Night Spectacular, London ATV
with Constantine Callinicos, pianist	
1959	Il Musichiere, RAI TV
October 4, 1959	La Mia Vita Per Il Canto, RAI Radio (pre-recorded)

Reference Notes

Introduction

1 Irvin Kolodin: The Metropolitan Opera - Alfred Knopf, 1966
2 ibid
3 ibid
4 Interview with author, 12 June 1976, Auckland, NZ
5 New York Daily News, 28 November 1950
6 Irving Kolodin, op.cit., 1966

Chapter 1

1 Antonio Cocozza to author, 1972
2 James Francis Cooke, I Learned To Sing By Accident - Etude, December 1949
3 Ida Zeitlin, The Mario Lanza Story - Photoplay, September 1951
4 ibid
5 ibid
6 Etude, December 1949
7 ibid
8 Ida Zeitlin: The Mario Lanza Story - Photoplay Sept. 1951
9 Sam Steinman to author, 1977
10 James Francis Cooke: My First Big Opportunity - Etude, January 1950
11 Antonio Cocozza to author, 1972
12 Roger Cohn: The Lanza Legend Today - The Inquirer Magazine, 27 March 1977
13 Eddie Durso: My Memories of Mario Lanza, 1992
14 Zeitlin, op. cit., 1951
15 ibid
16 ibid
17 ibid
18 ibid
19 ibid

20 Eddie Durso, op. cit., 1992
21 ibid
22 Antonio Cocozza, 1972
23 Roger Cohn: The Lanza Legend - Today, the Inquirer Magazine, 27 March 1977
24 Magic In His Music, 1951 - courtesy Elsie Sword

Chapter 2

1 Sam Weiler to author, 1977
2 ibid
3 Antonio Cocozza, 1972
4 Eddie Durso, op. cit., 1992
5 ibid
6 The Evening Bulletin - Philadelphia, 2 June 1942
7 Magic In His Music, 1951
8 Zeitlin, 1951
9 Magic in his Music, 1951
10 Hedda Hopper: Golden Voiced Mario, Chicago Tribune, 1949
11 Matt Bernard: Mario Lanza - MacFadden Bartell, 1971
12 Callinicos, The Mario Lanza Story - Coward McCann, 1960
13 Zeitlin, 1951
14 John Briggs: Leonard Bernstein: The Man, His Work, and His Music - World Publishing Co., N.Y., 1961
15 The Evening Bulletin, Philadelphia, 13 March 1951
16 Zeitlin, op. cit., 1951
17 John Briggs, op. cit.
18 Etude, January 1950
19 Magic In His Music, 1951
20 Boris Goldovsky: My Road to Opera, Houghton Mifflin Co., Boston, 1979
21 The New York Times, 9 August 1942

22 Opera News, 5 October 1942
23 Dorothy Kirsten to author, 1977
24 Ronald Bessette: Tenor in Exile, Amadeus Press, 1999
25 The New York Times, 9 August 1942
26 Etude, January 1950
27 The New York Times, 9 August 1942
28 The New York Herald Tribune, 8 August 1942
29 Opera News, 5 October 1942
30 Sam Weiler to author, 1977
31 Magazine clipping, courtesy Pauline Franklin
32 Newspaper clipping , courtesy Damon Lanza
33 Antonio Cocozza to author, 1972
34 Michael De Pace letter, courtesy Damon Lanza
35 Letter, courtesy Damon Lanza

Chapter 3

1 Barry Nelson to author, 1977
2 Letter from Lanza to Michael De Pace - courtesy Damon Lanza
3 Letter from Lanza to Maria Margelli - author's collection
4 Callinicos, op. cit., 1960
5 ibid
6 Million Dollar Voice - Time, 6 August 1951
7 ibid
8 Zeitlin, op. cit., 1951
9 The Twelve Loves of My Life, June 1951 - courtesy Elsie Sword
10 ibid
11 Barry Nelson to author, 1977
12 ibid
13 ibid
14 ibid
15 ibid
16 ibid
17 George London to author, 1977
18 Edmond O'Brien to author, 1977

19 ibid
20 ibid
21 ibid
22 Antonio Cocozza to author, 1972
23 Edmond O'Brien to author, 1977
24 Columbia Concerts Press release, 1945
25 North American Newspaper Alliance, 5 October 1944
26 Chicago Tribune, January 1945
27 Chicago Tribune, 20 October 1944
28 Letter from RCA, 19 February 1945 - courtesy Colleen Lanza
29 Zeitlin, op. cit., 1951
30 Jack Warner: My First Hundred Years in Hollywood - Random House, New York, 1965
31 Betty Lanza: Love Story, 1951 - courtesy Elsie Sword
32 ibid
33 Zeitlin, op. cit., 1951
34 Betty Lanza: Love Story, 1951
35 Zeitlin, op. cit., 1951

Chapter 4

1 Zeitlin, op. cit., 1951
2 Betty Lanza: Love Story, 1951
3 Letter from Betty Lanza - courtesy Damon Lanza
4 Barry Nelson to author, 1977
5 Caroline Brooks: Life With Lanza, 1952 - courtesy Elsie Sword
6 Sam Weiler to author, 1977
7 The Man I Married, Betty Lanza, 1953 - courtesy Elsie Sword
8 Sam Weiler to author, 1977
9 Brooks, op. cit.
10 Antonio Cocozza to author, 1972
11 Brooks, op. cit.
12 Sam Weiler to author, 1977
13 ibid
14 Betty Lanza: Love Story, 1951
15 Sam Weiler to author, 1977

16 Betty Lanza: Love Story, 1951
17 Antonio Cocozza to author, 1972

Chapter 5

1   Joseph Steele, Encore, Photoplay, 1951
2   Sam Weiler to author, 1977
3   Magic In His Music, 1951- courtesy Elsie Sword
4   Sam Weiler to author, 1977
5   Encore, 1951
6   Barry Nelson to author, 1977
7   A Legendary Performer, LP notes RCA, 1976
8   Sam Weiler to author, 1977
9   Samuel Chotzinoff - The Triumph of Opera in English - HiFi/Stereo Review, December 1960
10 George London to author, 1977
11 Callinicos - The Mario Lanza Story (Coward-McCann, Inc., New York, 1960)
12 George London to author, 1977
13 ibid
14 Hedda Hopper: Golden Voiced Mario - Chicago Tribune, 1949
15 Great Moments in Music Broadcasts - courtesy Clyde Smith
16 George London to author, 1977
17 Barry Nelson to author, 1977
18 ibid
19 George London to author, 1977
20 Sam Weiler to author, 1977
21 Magic in his Music, 1951
22 Milwaukee Journal, 30 March 1951
23 ibid
24 Sam Weiler to author, 1977
25 ibid
26 Callinicos, op. cit., 1960
27 Sam Weiler to author, 1977
28 Time Magazine, 6 August 1951

Chapter 6

1   Sam Weiler to author, 1977

2   ibid
3   George London to author, 1977
4   Los Angeles Examiner, 27 August 1953
5   George London to author, 1977
6   Etude, January 1950
7   ibid
8   Letter from George London to author, 1977
9   George London to author, 1977
10 Callinicos, op. cit., 1960
11 Toronto Daily Star, 3 July 1946
12 Chicago Tribune, 7 July 1946
13 Postcard from Lanza to Rosati
14 Ottawa Journal, 14 November 1946
15 Ottawa Citizen, 13 November 1946
16 Letter from Coronet Concerts and Artists to Columbia Concerts Inc. - courtesy Colleen Lanza
17 George London to author, 1977
18 Etude, January 1950
19 Callinicos, op. cit., 1960

Chapter 7

1   Artist's Life - Columbia Concerts Publication, January 1947
2   Callinicos, op. cit., 1960
3   ibid
4   ibid
5   ibid
6   ibid
7   ibid
8   ibid
9   Antonio Cocozza, to author, 1972
10 Metropolitan Opera Encyclopedia, Thames and Hudson, 1987
11 St Louis Globe – Democrat, 19 January 1947
12 Callinicos, op.cit., 1960
13 Nora London: Aria for George – Dutton NY, 1987
14 Milwakee Sentinel, 9 July 1947
15 Milwakee Journal, 9 July 1947

16 George London to author, 1977
17 Beaumont, Texas - newspaper clipping
18 Chicago Herald Tribune, 20 July 1947
19 Chicago Herald American, 20 July 1947
20 Callinicos ML story, 1960
21 A legendary performer LP notes, 1976
22 Sam Steinman to author, 1977
23 Barry Nelson to author, 1977
24 Callinicos op.cit., 1960
25 ibid
26 George London to author, 1977

Chapter 8

1   Callinicos, op. cit.,, 1960
2   Zeitlin, op. cit., 1951
3   José Iturbi to author, 1977
4   Los Angeles Examiner, 28 August 1947
5   George London to author, 1977
6   Callinicos, op. cit., 1960
7   Walter Pidgeon telegram - courtesy Colleen Lanza
8   Zeitlin, 1951
9   Los Angeles Times, 28 August 1947
10 Los Angeles Daily News, 28 August 1947
11 Hollywood Citizen News, 28 August 1947
12 Los Angeles Examiner, 28 August 1947
13 José Iturbi to author, 1977
14 Jane Ellen Wayne: The Life of Robert Taylor – Warner Paperback Library Edition, 1973
15 Keenan Wynn to author, 1977
16 Magazine clipping - courtesy Pauline Franklin
17 Joe Pasternak: Easy the Hard Way - WH Allen, London, 1956
18 ibid

19 ibid
20 ibid
21 ibid
22 ibid
23 Keenan Wynn to author, 1977
24 Magic In His Music, 1951
25 Hedda Hopper: Golden Voiced Mario Chicago Tribune, 1949
26 Magic In His Music, 1951
27 Time magazine, 8 March 1948
28 Robert Tuggle: The Golden Age of Opera, Holt – Rinehart and Winston New York, 1983
29 Martin Mayer: The Met – Thames and Hudson, London, 1983
30 George London to author, 1977
31 Time magazine, 6 August 1951
32 George London to author, 1977
33 Edmond O'Brien to author, 1977

Chapter 9

1   The Daily Oklahoman, 27 October 1947
2   Newspaper cutting from Mario Lanza files, courtesy Colleen Lanza
3   Domingo: My Operatic Roles – Little Brown & Company, 2000
4   Newspaper clipping from Lanza's scrapbooks, courtesy Colleen Lanza
5   Robert Merrill: Once More From the Beginning – McMillan, New York, 1965
6   Alan Burns: The Lady Behind Pinkerton – courtesy US Mario Lanza Appreciation Society
7   George London letter to author, 1977
8   Stanley Jackson: Caruso – Stein and Day, New York 1975
9   Giuseppe Di Stefano to author, 1982

10 Charles Osborne: Letters of
Giuseppe Verdi – Gollancz,
London, 1971
11 The Autobiography of Geraldine
Farrar – Da Capo, N Y, 1970
12 George London letter to author,
1977
13 Alan Burns, op.cit.,
14 ibid
15 ibid
16 ibid
17 Times-Picayune, April 9 1948
18 St Louis News, April, 1948
19 Hedda Hopper: Golden Voiced
Mario, Chicago Tribune 1949
20 ibid

Chapter 10

1 Joe Pasternak: Easy The Hard
Way, WH Allen, London, 1956
2 ibid
3 Constantine Callinicos to
author, 1980
4 Joe Pasternak op. cit., 1956
5 That Midnight Kiss Press Book,
1949
6 In Movieland - Radio interview
with Harold E. Swisher, 1948
7 Terry Robinson to author, 1977
8 Kathryn Grayson to author,
1977
9 Callinicos, op. cit., 1960
10 Pasternak, op. cit., 1956
11 Keenan Wynn to author, 1977
12 1952 magazine cutting - courtesy
Elsie Sword
13 Los Angeles Examiner, 26 July
1948
14 Terry Robinson to author, 1977
15 Betty Lanza: Love Story -
courtesy Elsie Sword
16 Sam Steinman to author, 1977
17 ibid
18 Keenan Wynn to author, 1977
19 ibid
20 Joe Pasternak to author, 1977
21 José Iturbi to author, 1977
22 ibid

23 ibid
24 Keenan Wynn to author, 1977
25 Callinicos, op. cit., 1960
26 ibid
27 ibid
29 The New York Times, 23 Sept.
1949
30 Musical America, 29 Oct. 1949
31 Newsweek, 3 October 1949
32 A Legendary Performer, LP notes
RCA, 1976

Chapter 11

1 Callinicos, op. cit., 1960
2 ibid
3 Sam Weiler to author, 1977
4 Callinicos to author, 1980
5 ibid
6 Callinicos, op. cit., 1960
7 Alfred Alexander: Operanatomy,
Crescendo Publishing Boston,
1974
8 David Ewen: Dictators of the
Baton, Ziff Davis Publishing,
Chocago-New York, 1943
9 RAI interview with Nicola
Rescigno, date unknown
10 Stefan Zucker Interview with
Franco Corelli, 30 March 1991
11 A Legendary Performer, LP
notes, RCA, 1976
12 The Mario Lanza Collection, LP
notes, RCA, 1981
13 Callinicos to author, 1980
14 Sammy Cahn: I Should Care:
WH Allen, 1975
15 Ibid
16 Helen Rose Just Make Them
Beautiful, Dennis Landman,
Santa Monica, 1976
17 Antonio Cocozza to author,
1972
18 Mario Lanza Fans Star Library,
London, 1959
19 Gift to Enrico Rosati
20 Sam Weiler to author, 1977

21 1948 Magazine cutting from
    Mario Lanza's Scrapbook,
    courtesy Colleen Lanza
22 New York Post Home News, 11
    September 1949
23 Time magazine, 6 August 1951
24 Louella Parsons Los Angeles
    Times, 8 October 1959
25 Time magazine, 6 August 1951
26 Etude, December 1949
27 Mario Lanza interview with Jinx
    Falkenburg, NBC, New York, 25
    September 1949

Chapter 12

1 Joe Pasternak to author, 1977
2 1949 magazine article - courtesy
   Damon Lanza
2 Helen Rose, op. cit.
4 Sam Weiler to author, 1977
5 Kathryn Grayson to author,
   1977
6 David Niven: The Moon is a
   Balloon, GP Putnam & Sons,
   1972
7 Film Show Annual LTA,
   Robinson, Ltd., London, 1957
8 Henry Toby 'Can Europe Save
   Lanza,' Picturegoer, 7 September
   1957
9 David Niven, op. cit.
10 Domenico Meccoli 'Mario Lanza
   Scopre L'Italia,' Epoca, 9 June
   1957
11 James Miller - Fanfare Nov/Dec
   1989
12 Martin Mayer: The Met -
   Thames and Hudson, Ltd.,
   London, 1983
13 Clive Hirschhorn: The
   Hollywood Musical - Octopus,
   London, 1981
14 The Hollywood Hall of Shame,
   Angus and Robertson, 1984
15 Joe Pasternak: Easy The Hard
   Way, WH Allen, London, 1956
16 Sam Weiler to author, 1977

17 The New York Times, 30 Sept.
    1950
18 Film Daily, 24 August 1950

Chapter 13

1 Callinicos, op. cit.
2 ibid
3 Callinicos to author, 1980
4 Hi-Fi News and Record Review,
   June 1976
5 Sunday News, 18 September
   1949
6 Worcester Daily Telegraph, 13
   September 1949
7 Sam Weiler to author, 1977
8 Pasternak, op. cit.

Chapter 14

1 Jesse Lasky: 'I Blow My Own
   Horn' - Gollancz, London , 1957
2 James Drake: Richard Tucker,
   Dutton NY, 1984
3 Annalisa Björling & Andrew
   Farkas: Jussi – Amadeus,
   Portland, 1996
4 Sam Weiler to author, 1977
5 ibid
6 ibid
7 Zeitlin, Photoplay 1951
8 Dorothy Kirsten: A Time To Sing
   - Doubleday, NY, 1982
9 Ava Gardner: Ava, My Story-
   Bantam Books, NY 1987
10 Barry Nelson to author, 1977
11 Lasky, op. cit., 1957
12 Sam Weiler to author, 1977
13 The 12 Loves Of My Life, June
   1951
14 Caruso, by Mario Lanza:
   undated article- courtesy Elsie
   Sword
15 Joe Pasternak to author, 1977
16 Stewart Granger to author, 1981
17 Callinicos, op. cit., 1960
18 ibid
19 ibid
20 ibid

21 ibid
22 Letter from Oreste Kirkop, courtesy Pauline Franklin
23 John Green to author, 1977
24 Hedda Hopper: The Whole Truth and Nothing But – Doubleday, 1962
25 Time Magazine, 6 August 1951
26 George Marek: Magnificent Mario, LP notes, 1973
27 The Great Caruso Press Book, 1951
28 Enrico Caruso Jr. and Andrew Farkas: Enrico Caruso My Father and My Family- Amadeus, 1990
29 Eugenio Gara: Caruso - Rizzoli, 1947
30 William Ludwig: Caruso on the Movies - Courtesy Vivian Gordon
31 ibid
32 Enrico Caruso, Jr., op. cit.
33 ibid
34 ibid

Chapter 15

1 Notes from RCA LP Arie Da Opere Italiane, RCA LM 20036
2 New York Tribune, 24 Nov.1903
3 New York Sun, 3 Dec. 1903
4 Howard Greenfield: Caruso - Da Capo Press, 1983
5 Richard Aldrich, New York Times, 5 March 1906
6 Time Magazine, 6 Aug 1951
7 The New York Times, 11 May 1951
8 Callinicos op. cit.
9 New York Daily News, 11 May 1951
10 Cue Magazine, 1951
11 Newsweek, 14 May 1951
12 Variety, 18 April 1951
13 Cleveland Ohio News, 11 May 1951
14 Lasky op. cit.

15 Jonny Whiteside: Cry, The Johnnie Ray Story - Barricade Books Inc New York, 1994
16 George London to author, 1977
17 Dorothy Kirsten, op. cit., 1982
18 Callinicos, op. cit., 1960
19 John Green to author, 1977
20 ibid
21 Sam Weiler to author, 1977
22 Tito Gobbi: My Life - Macdonald and Jane's Publishers, 1979
23 John Briggs, The Record Shelf, 1949 - courtesy Colleen Lanza
24 Mario Lanza: My Suppressed Desires, 1952- Great Lanza no. 8 - courtesy Elsie Sword
25 Carla Maria Casanova: Renata Tebaldi – Azzali, 1987
27 Giuseppe Di Stefano to author, 1967
28 John Green to author, 1977
29 Time Magazine, 6 August 1951
30 Callinicos, op. cit., 1960
31 Barry Nelson to author, 1977
32 ibid
33 Callinicos, op. cit., 1960
34 John Green to author, 1977
35 ibid
36 ibid
37 ibid
38 Callinicos, op. cit., 1960
39 Sam Weiler to author, 1977
40 The Book of Golden Discs - Barrie& Jenkins, London, 1978
41 Maurizo Scardovi to the author, 2000
42 Magazine cutting - courtesy Pauline Franklin

Chapter 16

1 Antonio Cocozza to author, 1972
2 George Stoll to author, 1977
3 Callinicos, op. cit., 1960
4 ibid
5 Kathryn Grayson to author, 1977

Notes

6   Mario Lanza: My Suppressed Desires, 1952
7   José Carreras: A Life Story – Iambic Productions/Primetime, 1991
8   Annalisa Bjorling and Andrew Farkas: Jussi – Amadeus, 1996
9   Breslin :The Tenors – McMillan, N.Y. 1974
10 ibid
11 Time magazine, 6 August 1951
12 Callinicos op.cit., 1960
13 Pittsburgh Press, 5 March 1951
14 Time magazine, 19 March 1951
15 Variety, 9 May 1951
16 Rudolf Bing: 5000 Nights at the Opera – Hamish Hamilton, London, 1972
17 Los Angeles Times, 26 August 1953
18 ibid
19 Chicago Sun Times, 8 April,1951
20 Richmond News Leader, 3 March 1951
21 Richmond Time Dispatch, 3 March 1951
22 Sam Steinman to author, 1977
23 Callinicos op.cit.,1960 24 Philadelphia Evening Bulletin, 13 March 1951
25 ibid
26 ibid
27 Magic in his Music, 1951
28 Philadelphia Evening Bulletin, 14 March 1951
29 Michael T.R.B. Turnbull: Mary Garden – Amadeus Press, 1997
30 What Love Did For Me – Radio TV Mirror, November 1952
31 Maurizio Scardovi to author, 2000
32 St Louis Globe Democrat, 10 November 1951
33 The Mario Lanza Story, BBC Radio, 1974
34 George London letter to author, 1977

Chapter 17

1   George London to author, 1977
2   ibid
3   Look Magazine, 3 July 1951
4   David Hamilton: The Metropolitan Opera Encyclopedia - Thames & Hudson, 1987
5   Antonio Cocozza to author, 1972
6   Callinicos, op. cit., 1960
7   Pasternak, op. cit., 1956
8   Stewart Granger to author, 1981
9   Arthur L. Charles: Return Engagement - Modern Screen - March 1953
10 Joe Pasternak to author, 1977
11 Dore Schary: Heyday - Little Brown, Boston, 1979
12 Hedda Hopper: Mario Lanza Answers Back – Photoplay, November 1953
13 Andre Previn: No Minor Chords - Doubleday, London 1991
14 John Green to author, 1977
15 ibid
16 ibid
17 Barry Nelson to author, 1977
18 ibid
19 Joe Pasternak to author, 1977
20 Dore Schary, op. cit., 1979
21 Sam Weiler to author, 1977
22 ibid
23 Lindsay Perigo's interview with James Whitmore, 1977
24 Antonio Cocozza to author, 1972
25 Callinicos, op. cit., 1960
26 Domenico Meccoli Epoca, 9 June 1957
27 Hollywood Citizen News, 28 October 1952
28 ibid
29 Newsweek, 13 October 1952

30 Variety, 3 September 1952
31 The New York Times, 26
    September 1952
32 Time, 1952
33 Because You're Mine Press
    Book, 1952

Chapter 18

1 Story For Sinners - courtesy Elsie
   Sword
2 ibid
3 ibid
4 ibid
5 Mario Lanza Institute
   Newsletter, vol 2 No 1, Jan-Apr
   1971
6 Marion Benasutti: The Mario
   Lanza Story, Italian-American
   Herald, 10 August 1961
7 Mario Gives a Party - Movie
   Stars Parade, March 1952
8 Magazine clipping in Mario
   Lanza's files, courtesy Colleen
   Lanza
9 Story For Sinners

Chapter 19

1 Sam Weiler to author, 1977
2 Callinicos, op. cit., 1960
3 Callinicos to author, 1980

Chapter 20

1 Sam Weiler to author, 1977
2 Photoplay, 1952
3 Callinicos, op. cit., 1960
4 Callinicos to author, 1980
5 Joe Pasternak to author, 1977
6 Callinicos to author, 1980
7 Stewart Granger to author, 1981
8 Joe Pasternak to author, 1977
9 ibid
10 Callinicos, op. cit., 1960
11 Callinicos to author, 1980
12 ibid
13 The New Lanza – Newsweek, 9
    April 1956

14 Return Engagement, March
    1953
15 Sam Weiler to author, 1977
16 George Stoll to author, 1977
17 Matt Bernard: Mario Lanza -
    Mac Fadden Bartell, 1971
18 Callinicos to author, 1980
19 Matt Bernard, op. cit.
20 Edmond O'Brien to author,
    1977
21 Stewart Granger: Sparks Fly
    Upward - Granada, London
    1981
22 Barry Nelson to author, 1977
23 George Stoll to author, 1977
24 Dore Schary, op. cit., 1979
25 Barry Nelson to author, 1977
26 Callinicos, op. cit., 1960
27 George Stoll to author, 1977
28 ibid
29 Callinicos to author, 1980
30 George Stoll to author, 1977
31 ibid
32 ibid
33 The New York Times, 20
    September 1952
34 George Armstrong:The Truth
    Behind the Mario Lanza Blow-
    up - Australian Photoplay, May
    1953
35 Ann Blyth: I Don't Forget - Film
    Show Annual, 1954
36 Callinicos to author, 1980
37 Oggi, 12 September 1957
38 Mario Del Monaco: La Mia Vita
    E I Miei Successi - Rusconi,
    Milano, 1982
39 Joe Pasternak to author, 1977
40 George Stoll to author, 1977
41 Callinicos to author, 1980
42 Henry Tody: Can Europe Save
    Mario Lanza? - Picturegoer, 7
    September 1957
43 Joe Pasternak to author, 1977
44 BBC Broadcast, 1974
45 ibid
46 Callinicos to author, 1980

Notes

Chapter 21

1 Antonio Cocozza to author, 1972
2 Hedda Hopper: Mario Lanza Answers Back – Photoplay, November 1953
3 ibid
4 ibid
5 ibid
6 ibid
7 Norman Zierold - The Hollywood Tycoons - Hamish Hamilton, London 1969
8 Barry Nelson to author, 1977
9 ibid
10 ibid

Chapter 22

1 Ann Myers to author, 1977
2 Callinicos to author, 1980
3 ibid
4 Callinicos, op. cit., 1960
5 Terry Robinson to author, 1977
6 Callinicos to author, 1980
7 George London's letter to author, 1977
8 Callinicos to author, 1980
9 Callinicos op. cit., 1960
10 Callinicos to author, 1980
11 ibid
12 Variety, 1 October 1954
13 Los Angeles Daily News, 5 October 1954
16 Matt Bernard, op. cit.

Chapter 23

1 Edmond O'Brien to author, 1977
2 Ray Sinatra to author, 1977
3 ibid
4 Antonio Cocozza to author, 1972
5 Ray Sinatra to author, 1977
6 ibid
7 Russ Newton: His Own Worst Enemy - Motion Picture, 1955

8 Ray Sinatra to author, 1977
9 ibid
10 ibid
11 Matt Bernard, op. cit.
12 ibid
13 ibid
14 Los Angeles Mirror News, 5 April 1955
15 Callinicos, op. cit., 1960
16 Matt Bernard, op. cit.
17 Los Angeles Mirror News, 5 April 1955
18 Melbourne Sun, April 1955
19 Callinicos, op. cit., 1960
20 Los Angeles Mirror News, 5 April 1955
21 Ray Sinatra to author, 1977
22 Newspaper clipping - courtesy Damon Lanza

Chapter 24

I Matt Bernard, op. cit.
2 ibid
3 Vincent Price to author, 1977
4 Helen Gould: Is Lanza A Changed Man? Movieland, April 1956
5 Vincent Price to author, 1977
6 Los Angeles Examiner, 7 April 1955
7 Ben Roberts to author, 1977
8 Ivan Goff to author, 1977
9 Helen Gould, op. cit.
10 Licia Albanese to author, 1980
11 ibid
12 ibid
13 ibid
14 ibid
15 Robert T. Jones notes for Mario Lanza in Opera album: RCA LSC 3101(e)
16 Licia Albanese to author, 1980, and Robert T. Jones notes
17 Henry Blanke to author, 1977
18 Oggi, 1957
19 Ray Heindorf to author, 1977
20 Ivan Goff to author, 1977
21 Ray Heindorf to author, 1977

22 Maurizio Scardovi to author, 2000
23 Oggi, 1957
24 Ray Heindorf to author, 1977
25 Vincent Price to author,1977
26 Domenico Meccoli: Mario Lanza Scopre L'Italia – Epoca, 9 June 1957
27 Helen Gould, op. cit.
28 Ben Roberts to author, 1977
29 Vincent Edwards to author, 1977
30 ibid
31 Vincent Price to author, 1977
32 Hollywood EMS Dispatch, 24 March 1956
33 Sheila Graham interview with Vincent Price, 1955
34 Vincent Price to author, 1977
35 Time, 9 April 1956
36 Newsweek, 9 April 1956
37 The New York Times, 23 March 1956
38 Variety, 14 March 1956
39 Films and Filming, 1956
40 Saturday Review, 29 September 1956
41 George London to author, 1977

Chapter 25

1 The Los Angeles Times, 8 March 1956
2 Ray Heindorf to author, 1977
4 Callinicos to author, 1980
5 Letter from Franco De Simone Niquesa - courtesy Damon Lanza

Chapter 26

1 Antonio Cocozza to author, 1972
2 ibid
3 Matt Bernard, op. cit.
4 ibid
5 ibid
6 Domenico Meccoli, op. cit.
7 Renato Rascel to author, 1977

8 ibid
9 Roman Holiday, 1957 - courtesy Elsie Sword
10 Callinicos op. cit., 1960
11 Henry Thody: Lanza's New Look - The American Weekly, 1 December 1957
12 Sam Steinman to author, 1977
13 Roy Rowland to author, 1984
14 ibid
15 ibid
16 Renato Rascel to author, 1977
17 Goffredo Lombardo's telegram - courtesy Damon Lanza
18 Renato Rascel to author, 1977
19 Sam Steinman to author, 1977
20 ibid
21 Renato Rascel to author, 1977
22 ibid
23 Sam Steinman, to author
24 Giuseppe Di Stefano, to author, 1982
25 The New York Times, 28 January 1958
26 Sam Weiler to author, 1977
27 Liberace, WH Allen, London, 1973
28 Picturegoer, 1957
29 Ed Sullivan interview, 1957
30 Sheilah Graham article, 1957 - courtesy Elsie Sword

Chapter 27

1 Donald Zec: Lanza With The Lid Off, Daily Mirror, 1957
2 ibid
3 Donald Zec: Some Enchanted Egos – St Martin's Press, New York, 1973
4 Afro Poli to author, 1984
5 Ivor Newton: At the Piano – Hamish Hamilton, 1966
6 Newsweek magazine, 15 March 1976
7 Nigel Douglas: Legendary Voices – Andre Deutsch, London, 1992
8 Italian magazine clipping, 1957

Notes

9 Renato Rascel to author, 1977

Chapter 28

1 Henry Thody: Can Europe Save Lanza? - Picturegoer, 7 September 1957
2 Sam Steinman to author, 1977
3 Callinicos to author, 1980
4 Daily Mail, 15 November 1957
5 Daily Mirror, 15 November 1957
6 Callinicos, op. cit., 1960
7 Newspaper clipping
8 Max Jones: Lanza Hits Out at the Press - Melody Maker, November 1957
9 ibid
10 ibid
11 ibid
12 Peter Prichard: My Life As Special Agent To The Stars - TV Times, 18-24 March 1976
13 Cyril Ornadel: The Mario Lanza Story, BBC Radio 1974
14 ibid
15 Callinicos, op. cit., 1960
16 ibid
17 Cyril Ornadel, op. cit.
18 Record Mirror, 23 November 1957
19 Cyril Ornadel, op. cit.
20 Melody Maker, October 1959
21 Robert Mc Donald - Daily Mirror, November 1957
22 Daily Express, 19 November 1957
23 Record Mirror, 23 November 1957
24 News Chronicle, 19 November 1957
25 Melody Maker, November 1957
26 Sporting and Show Business Review, 22 November 1957
27 William Judd's letter to John Coast - courtesy Damon Lanza
28 John Coast letter to William Judd - courtesy Damon Lanza

29 New Musical Express, November 1957

Chapter 29

1 Dr. Giuseppe Stradone to author, 1977
2 Sam Steinman to author, 1977
3 ibid
4 Antonio Fabianelli to author, 1972
5 James A. Drake - Richard Tucker - Dutton - New York, 1984
6 ibid
7 ibid
8 RCA Victor Recording of Albert Hall concert, 16 January 1958
9 Callinicos, op. cit., 1960
10 Letter from William Judd to Maurice Silverstein - courtesy Damon Lanza
11 Maurizio Scardovi to author, 2000
12 Jon Weaving to author, 1987
13 Leicester Evening Mail, 13 January 1958
14 Leicester Mercury, 13 January 1958
15 Callinicos, op. cit., 1960
16 Letter from John Coast to Mario Lanza, courtesy Damon Lanza
17 ibid
18 ibid
19 Letter from John Coast to Larry Kanaga, courtesy Damon Lanza
20 Letter from William Judd to Mario Lanza, courtesy Damon Lanza
21 Melbourne Sun, March 1958
22 Callinicos op.cit., 1960
23 ibid
24 Sam Steinman to author, 1977
25 Bristol Evening Post, 5 March 1958
26 Manchester Guardian, 7 March 1958

27 Newspaper clipping, March 1958
28 Sam Steinman to author, 1977
29 ibid
30 Callinicos, op.cit., 1960
31 ibid
32 ibid
33 Hanoverische Algemein, 12 April 1958
34 Callinicos, op.cit., 1960
35 Lubecher Nachriten, 14 April 1958
36 Letter from John Coast to Ercole Graziadei, courtesy Damon Lanza
37 Sam Steinman to author, 1977
38 Letter from John Coast to William Judd, courtesy Damon Lanza
39 Sam Steinman to author, 1977
40 ibid
41 Callinicos to author, 1980
42 ibid
43 ibid
44 Letter from John Coast to William Judd, courtesy Damon Lanza
45 ibid
46 Sam Steinman to author, 1977

Chapter 30

1 Medical Records - courtesy Damon Lanza
2 Dr. Giuseppe Stradone to author, 1977
3 Hy Gardner Interview with Mario Lanza, May 1958
4 ibid
5 ibid
6 ibid

Chapter 31

1 Telegram from John Coast to Lanza - courtesy Damon Lanza
2 Mario Lanza Tells Godfrey Winn "My Voice is a Gift from God," TV Mirror, 3 May 1958

3 ibid
4 ibid
5 ibid
6 ibid
7 ibid
8 ibid
9 ibid
10 Callinicos to author, 1980
11 Medical Records - courtesy Damon Lanza
12 Andrew Solt to author, 1977
13 ibid
14 ibid
15 ibid
16 Sam Steinman to author, 1977
17 ibid
18 ibid
19 Medical records - courtesy Damon Lanza
20 Callinicos, op. cit., 1960
21 ibid
22 Angelo Carlucci, Chief of Staff, Rome Opera, to author, 1971
23 Riccardo Vitale to author, 1977
24 Callinicos op. cit., 1960
25 Riccardo Vitale to author, 1977
26 Hans Sohnker Life Story: Frau im Spiegel, 1971 - courtesy Elsie Sword
27 German 'Film Revue,' 27 October 1959
28 The Great Lanza No.8 - courtesy Elsie Sword
29 Sam Steinman to author, 1977
30 ibid
31 For the First Time production still
32 Sam Steinman to author, 1977
33 Otello Fava to author , 1977
34 Sam Steinman to author, 1977
35 The New York Herald Tribune, 15 August 1959
36 Los Angeles Examiner, 1 October 1959
37 Time, 31 August 1959
38 The New York Times, 15 August 1959

Notes

Chapter 32

1 Franco Ferrara to author, 1977
2 Gazzetta di Parma, 8 October 1959 - courtesy Eddy Lovaglio
3 The Birthday Party, article courtesy Elsie Sword
4 ibid
5 ibid
6 Medical Records, courtesy Damon Lanza
7 Sam Steinman to author, 1977
8 ibid
9 ibid
10 ibid
11 ibid
12 ibid
13 ibid
14 Derek Mannering: Mario Lanza Singing to the Gods – Robert Hale, London, 2001
15 Sam Steinman to author, 1977
16 Callinicos op.cit., 1960
17 ibid
18 Variety, 14 October 1959
19 Peter Lind Hayes interview with Lanza, September 1959
20 Harry Golden: The Price of Fame – Great Lanza no.7, courtesy Elsie Sword
21 Callinicos op.cit., 1960
22 ibid
23 Giorgio Salvioni: L'inquetitudine ha ucciso il nuovo Caruso, Epoca, 18 October 1959
24 ibid
25 Pour Tours, 17 November, 1959
26 ibid
27 Anita Pensotti : La Breve Avventura Del "Piccolo Caruso", Oggi, October 1959
28 Sam Steinman to author, 1977
29 ibid
30 ibid
31 Il Giornale D'Italia, 9 October 1959
32 ibid
33 Melody Maker, October 1959
34 Sam Steinman to author, 1977

Epilogue

1 Tino Roberto: Proprio a Roma Doveva Succedere? - Italian magazine article, October 1959
2 Sam Steinman to author, 1977
3 Il Messaggero, 9 October 1959
4 Sam Steinman to author, 1977
5 Il Giornale D'Italia, 11 October 1959
6 Marion Benasutti: The Mario Lanza Story - Italian American Herald, 22 June 1961
7 Los Angeles Examiner, 22 October 1959
8 Damon Lanza, Bob Dolfi, Mark Muller: Be My Love; A Celebration of Mario Lanza - Bonus Books, Chicago, 1999
9 Los Angeles Examiner, 22 October 1959
10 Los Angeles Examiner, 12 March 1960
11 Mario Lanza Files - Academy of Motion Picture Arts and Sciences Library, Hollywood , California
12 Los Angeles Examiner, 12 March 1960
13 Letter from Oreste Kirkop to Pauline Franklin

Notes

INDEX
OF NAMES APPEARING IN TEXT

351

Index

357